EVERYBODY'S GUIDE TO THE LAW

Melvin M. Belli, Sr.
& Allen P. Wilkinson

PERENNIAL LIBRARY

Harper & Row, Publishers, New York
Cambridge, Philadelphia, San Francisco, Washington
London, Mexico City, São Paulo, Singapore, Sydney

This book is designed to educate you about the law so that you can deal more effectively with the legal situations that concern you. It is sold with the understanding that the publisher is not engaged in rendering legal services. Federal and state laws are constantly changing, and no single book can address all the legal situations you may encounter.

A hardcover edition of this book was originally published in 1986 by Harcourt Brace Jovanovich, Inc. It is here reprinted by arrangement with Harcourt Brace Jovanovich, Inc.

EVERYBODY'S GUIDE TO THE LAW. Updated materials copyright © 1987 by Melvin M. Belli, Sr. and Allen P. Wilkinson. Copyright © 1986 by Melvin M. Belli, Sr. and Allen P. Wilkinson. All rights reserved. Printed in the United States of America. No part of this book may be used or reproduced in any manner whatsoever without written permission except in the case of brief quotations embodied in critical articles and reviews. For information address Harper & Row, Publishers, Inc., 10 East 53rd Street, New York, N.Y. 10022. Published simultaneously in Canada by Fitzhenry & Whiteside Limited, Toronto.

LIBRARY OF CONGRESS CATALOG CARD NUMBER: 87-45254

ISBN: 0-06-272502-5

94 95 MPC 10 9 8 7

CONTENTS

8 CIVIL WRONGS: TORTS 275

9 MEDICINE, MALPRACTICE, AND YOU 306

10 PRODUCTS LIABILITY 324

11 EMPLOYEES 339

20 Laws, the Courts, and You   *602*

ACKNOWLEDGMENTS

FIRST AND FOREMOST, thanks to our editor, John Radziewicz, for his superb editing, especially his vigilance in ensuring that all "legalese" was translated into plain English. Thanks also to the following persons who lent their time and expertise to critique various portions of the manuscript: Jeffrey Johnston, Thomas Hanrahan, William Ferraro, Craig Smith, Robert O'Connell, Tania Radziewicz, June H. Brown, Maria Marroquin, Kathleen Bursley, and Rosemarie Cappabianca.

INTRODUCTION

IN THE MORE than fifty years that I have been practicing law, I have discovered that much of the law is not "technicalities" but plain, old-fashioned *common sense*. During the last half century, I have studied many other countries' legal systems and have reached the conclusion that ours is indeed the best legal system in the world. All in all, I see a fundamental morality in American law and justice, and an underlying golden rule. "Doing unto others" rings as true today as it has throughout the centuries.

Few of us realize how pervasive the law is in our lives—until we get into a dispute with someone else. Then we are amazed to discover what a tangled web of law there is, and how complex and endless the rules seem. This book will unravel many of the mysteries surrounding the law and give you background in the areas of law that you're most likely to encounter during your life—wills, divorces, traffic tickets, problems with your landlord, being injured in an automobile accident, buying and selling a car or a house, getting hurt on the job, finding yourself the victim of a doctor's malpractice, to name a few. It will help you recognize your legal rights in a given situation and help you determine whether you have a leg to stand on.

When you reach for this book, the chances are that you've got a specific question. You want an answer, and you want it now. With this in mind, we have designed each chapter to be as self-contained as possible, with appropriate cross-references where useful. If you're interested in only one subject—automobiles, for instance—you can turn to that specific chapter and learn what you need to know about buying and selling a car, insurance, fighting traffic tickets, drunk driving, accidents, and other topics.

We recommend that you read the entire chapter pertaining to your inquiry, because it may point you in the right direction concerning other questions or problems you haven't considered but that may be lurking in the background. You should also consult the index at the back of the book, which will guide you to related subjects that may affect your situation.

You'll notice that we have omitted the glossary of legal terms usually found at the back of a law book written for the layperson. This is not due to any oversight on our part, but because experience tells us the reader refers only infrequently to such glossaries. More importantly, we feel that glossaries rarely provide adequate, understandable definitions and examples of legal terms and concepts. We have opted instead to reduce the amount of "legalese" throughout this book in favor of plain English. And when we do use a legal word or concept, we define it then and there, so you don't need to look it up in a glossary.

Can You Do without a Lawyer?

The threshold question in a situation involving the law is whether you can "do it yourself" or whether you need a lawyer to advise you on your rights or to handle the matter for you completely.

With the help of this book, you may be able to take care of many relatively minor problems yourself by reading the appropriate chapter or chapters, then negotiating with the other person or filing your own lawsuit in small claims court (chapter 15). But if you find that it's more than you can handle, or if your case involves a large amount of money, possible imprisonment, or serious injury or death, then a lawyer is certainly required. (In chapter 19, you'll find practical advice on finding the right lawyer for your situation.)

Having this book in your home library is much like having a guide to medicine. Even with the medical guide, you wouldn't consider treating yourself for potentially serious problems. For some minor illnesses you may be able to treat yourself with over-the-counter drugs, rest, and the like. But there's always the danger that your illness is more serious than you think or that it may worsen. In that case you need a doctor to diagnose your condition and prescribe appropriate treatment.

The same applies to law. Only a lawyer can assess your complete "legal health"—by investigating the facts, researching the latest developments in the law, applying his or her legal train-ing and experience, and then advising you of your alternatives. A good lawyer can spot the jagged rocks that may lie below the waters of a seemingly simple dispute and can help you plan a course of action to avoid them.

Just as you have a family doctor whom you visit not only when you have a medical condition that needs attention but also for routine checkups to prevent medical problems, you should have a family lawyer to consult both therapeutically and preven-tively. You'd be surprised how inexpensive many legal "vaccines" are, especially compared to the costs of a legal problem that goes untreated too long.

This book can't take the place of a lawyer. One reason is that the law differs from state to state—often significantly—and your rights vary accordingly. For example, in one state you may have six years to file a lawsuit after you've been hurt, in another you may have three years, while in yet another you may have only one year. (And if the government is at fault, you may have to file a claim with the appropriate agency within as few as sixty days of the incident.) Even adjoining states may have fundamental differences in their laws concerning divorces, wills, real estate law, and small claims court procedures. There simply isn't enough space in this book to provide a state-by-state rundown of every law discussed in the following pages.

Remember, too, that the law is in a continuous state of change. Every day judges are making new decisions and legislatures are passing new laws that affect your life. The advice a lawyer gives a client today may not be the same as the advice he or she might give a month or a year from now. A lawyer must always research the latest developments in the law to make sure the advice he or she gives today is sound and correct. And each case is different from every other case. To you, the layperson, a certain fact may seem unimportant. To a lawyer, however, that particular fact may make or break the whole case.

If you do find the need for legal counsel, read over the applicable material in this book before seeing the lawyer. This will make you more aware of the nature of the problem and your rights, enabling you to ask the lawyer the right questions and to better understand your alternatives. In short, a review of your rights will make you an "informed consumer" in selecting the right lawyer and getting your money's worth for any legal services rendered.

Where Our Laws Come From

The starting point for all laws in the United States is the Constitution. (I have long marveled that a Constitution written so long ago continues as our supreme governing instrument with so few amendments, from the sailing age to the age of nuclear power and space travel, and still works with all its pristine vigor.) No law can be contrary to what the Constitution mandates. Such a law would be unconstitutional and of no force or effect. But the Constitution isn't self-executing. It won't be much help to you unless you know how to use it correctly. A lawyer's job is to free the Constitution from its glass case in the National Archives and put it to work for you.

Each state has its own constitution. A state's constitution is the source of fundamental rights within that state. (One limitation on a state's constitutuion is that no provision can be contrary to the federal Constitution.)

A second type of law are "statutes" enacted by the legislative branch of the United States or a particular state. Cities and counties pass "ordinances" and "codes," which are similar to statutes. Governmental agencies often have the power to make rules and regulations in accordance with the authority given them by the legislative bodies that created the agencies.

Another important type of law is "common law," the law of English customs that the colonists brought with them to America. Common law has its origin early in English history, when the parties to a dispute would go to court to have a judge decide the disagreement. In those days there weren't many precedents the judge could rely on for guidance. IIe therefore based the resolution of the case on what was customary in the community, and if there was no custom, the judge would decide the case on the basis of common sense and fairness.

Finally there is "case law," which essentially is common law being made by the judges here in America rather than being rooted in English law.

The Courts and Precedents

The United States Supreme Court is the highest court in the land. A ruling from it is authoritative; all other courts in the nation must follow that ruling until the U.S. Supreme Court declares otherwise or an amendment to the Constitution is passed. (In some cases, the U.S. Congress can pass a law that modifies the Supreme Court's ruling.) This is due to the legal doctrine of *stare decisis*, which generally means that a judge must follow the decisions laid down in earlier similar cases.

Each state has a high court that is the state's equivalent of the U.S. Supreme Court. These courts are usually called the supreme courts, although there are some exceptions, such as New York's Court of Appeals. A decision of a state's highest court is binding only within that state. Other states (and the U.S. Supreme Court) are not bound by the ruling of another state's supreme court, although they may take into consideration such rulings and their logic when faced with similar questions.

When you consult a lawyer about a legal problem, the lawyer will do research to determine if a case similar to yours has already been decided and in whose favor. The lawyer will go to the state codes (a compilation of all the statutes passed by the state legislature) and then to the "reports" of the decisions of your state courts (the "big books" that line the lawyer's shelves). If the lawyer finds a case "on all fours"—one that is identical in all material aspects—generally that's the law that applies to your case, unless the times have changed so much that the courts may consider changing the law.

If the lawyer can't find a case similar to yours, then he or she will present the court with a "novel" question of law. The lawyer will refer to statutes and rulings from other states and textbooks by legal scholars that support your position. Once a court decides a novel point of view, the decision becomes authoritative for the next similar case and is the precedent that must be followed in the name of *stare decisis*. (This is an example of how case law is made.)

Should the courts act as a quasi-legislature and make new law rather than merely interpret the federal and state constitutions, statutes, and other existing laws? In appropriate situations, yes. With new inventions, computers, medical advances, and so forth, legal problems arise before the legislature has gotten around to dealing with them. (Indeed, it often seems to be the province of the legislature to act only after problems have arisen and not before.) The court is then faced with the option of waiting for the legislature to take action or doing something about it itself. When it is clear that someone has been wronged, justice demands that the court provide that person with legal recourse, even in the absence of any legislative pronouncement.

I must say a word here about military law, formally the Uniform Code of Military Justice. Military law and courts-martial have been grossly maligned by some people. I have seen military law in action, having tried military cases not only in the United States but also in Japan, Okinawa, Vietnam, Italy, and Germany. Military law and the court-martial have taken the best from our civil and criminal laws and our trial procedures to create perhaps the fairest system of justice in the world.

The Threat to Trial by Jury

Above all else in American law is the right to have many disputes decided by an impartial jury. The American system of justice ultimately consists of putting twelve ordinary citizens in the jury box. It's really as simple as that.

One of the most valid criticisms of the legal system today is that it takes too long for a case to wend its way through the courts and that the delay in getting to trial is extremely discouraging to potential litigants (although it's not quite as bad as the scene described in Dickens's *Bleak House*). You've undoubtedly heard much about "the law's delays." You've also heard that justice delayed is justice denied.

In some areas of the United States, five to seven years' delay from the filing of a lawsuit until the trial begins is common. To that add a few more years for the time it takes to appeal the case to higher courts and you can see why many cases take eight to ten years to be resolved through the legal system. A few cases are not terminated for twenty or more years!

To alleviate the delays, some people would like to limit or even abolish the right to a jury trial in America. (Interestingly enough, England, which created the jury system, has drastically limited it.) Others would like to standardize the amount of damages a person can recover, particularly in personal injury cases. They would place a value of x dollars on the loss of an arm, for example, without taking into account the individual's situation.

But each person's loss is personal to him or her alone, and this must be considered in determining the amount of damages he or she deserves.

Some have blamed the whole problem on a new-found spirit of litigiousness in America, with people filing more lawsuits than ever, many of which are criticized as unnecessary. Yet recent studies show that in comparison to the past we are not filing more lawsuits. The overall number of lawsuits filed each year has increased in proportion to the growth of the population, but no more than that. The only way to reduce the backlog of cases and at the same time ensure that every citizen has access to the judicial system is to build more courthouses and hire more judges and courtroom personnel. This solution will cost money—a tremendous amount of money—which probably won't be forthcoming for a long time.

Sometimes it may seem that we bring lawsuits for trivial or frivolous reasons. But the law is individual; it protects each of us from damage that may vex one of us though not our neighbors. A lawsuit has the added bonus of potentially preventing what happened to us from happening to others. One example of this is when someone is injured by a defective product. A lawsuit against a particular manufacturer can serve as an incentive for all manufacturers to warn consumers of the danger, to recall dangerous products, and to modify the product to prevent further injuries. This can hardly be termed a triviality or an abuse of the judicial system.

Printed on one of our colonial flags was a rattlesnake, ready to strike, with the motto, "Don't Tread on Me." Many years later we Americans still heed that motto, although now we do so by filing a lawsuit when we feel trod upon and having a jury decide the controversy. This procedure protects our many rights, including the right to be free from harassment and bodily harm and the right to privacy, free speech, freedom of religion, and due process. Denying or limiting our right to a fair and independent judicial system, complete with a jury trial, could well be the deathblow for justice as we now know it.

If there is to be any general overhauling of our legal system, I would prefer that it be initiated by a combination of judges, professors of law, and lawyers on both sides of the legal fence, rather than insurance companies and other special interest groups that are concerned more with their own profit margins than with the rights of the injured person.

A Final Note

As hard and as long as scholars have tried to define it, justice continues to elude simple explanation. One reason for this is that justice is relative and often subjective. Both sides to a legal dispute usually feel they are right. So regardless of who wins the case, the loser believes he or she is the victim of a miscarriage of justice. Daniel Defoe, the author of *Robinson Crusoe*, noted this paradox when he wrote, "Justice is always violent to the party offending, for every man is innocent in his own eyes."

That reminds me of the story of a certain inexperienced young lawyer. At the end of his first trial, this lawyer was asked by his client to wire him the jury's eventual verdict. The jury, as it happened, returned with a verdict in favor of the young lawyer's client.

The unsophisticated young lawyer gleefully wired his client: "Justice triumphed!"

Came the client's immediate reply: "Appeal. We'll win the next time!"

MELVIN M. BELLI, SR.
San Francisco and Los Angeles
July 1986

1

MARRIAGE, DIVORCE, AND THE FAMILY

FAMILY LAW—sometimes called the law of domestic relations—deals with all aspects of your legal rights and obligations as they apply to the family unit. It covers a vast field: marriages, annulments, divorces, separations, premarital agreements, child support and custody, visitation rights (including the rights of grandparents), property division and alimony, adoption, name changes, child discipline, establishing paternity, living together, responsibility for damages done by other members of the family, and more. Just by reading this list you begin to see how broad and complex this area really is.

Family disputes involve strong emotions—emotions that can get in the way of rational thinking and reasonable settlements. When feelings of anger or revenge take over, we lose sight of reality, so it is important to keep our emotions in check as much as possible. If you find your emotions getting out of control, particularly where a divorce or children are concerned, do yourself a favor and see a family counselor or other professional. The advice of a good lawyer is also recommended for many domestic problems.

Getting Married

Age Limits

All states have limitations on how old you must be before you can marry. In most states, both the man and the woman must be at least 18 years old to marry without parental consent or court approval. The exceptions: in Arkansas, the man must be at least 17 and the woman at least 16; in Delaware and Louisiana, the man must be at least 18 and the woman at least 16; in Georgia and Hawaii, each must be at least 16; in Mississippi, the man must be at least 17 and the woman at least 15; in Nebraska, each must be at least 17; in Rhode Island, the man must be at least 18 and the woman at least 16; and in Wyoming each must be at least 16. In some states, a couple who are between the ages of 16 and 18 can marry without parental consent or court approval if the woman is pregnant or has given birth.

There is no upper age limitation on marriages. Persons over 100 years old have entered into legally binding marriages. Specific information concerning age and other requirements for a valid marriage, as discussed below, can usually be obtained simply by calling your local county clerk's office.

Whom You Can't Marry

You can't marry just anybody. First of all, your spouse-to-be must be a member of the opposite sex. "Marriages" involving persons of the same sex are not legally valid, even if performed by a religious authority.

You can't marry certain close relatives. All states prohibit marriages between a parent and child, grandparent and grandchild, great-grandparent and great-grandchild, brother and sister (including half-brothers and half-sisters), uncle and niece, and aunt and nephew. Many states also ban marriages between first cousins, and some bar marriages between a stepparent and stepchild, a father-in-law and daughter-in-law, and a mother-in-law and son-in-law.

Suppose that first cousins want to tie the knot, but the state they live in won't let them get married. So they go to a state that allows marriages between first cousins, get married there, then come back to their home state. Will their home state recognize the marriage? Maybe not. Ordinarily, if a marriage is valid in the state in which it is made, all other states must recognize its legality. Some states, however, refuse to recognize a marriage if the couple's only reason for going to the other state was to get around the law. If you are thinking about going to another state to marry a first cousin (or other prohibited relative) and coming back to your home state, first consult a lawyer in your home state.

At one time many states had miscegenation laws prohibiting marriages between persons of different races. The United States Supreme Court has ruled those laws unconstitutional, and marriages between persons of different races cannot be banned.

Formal Procedures before Marrying

Before you can marry, you usually must comply with certain procedures. You must complete an application to marry (available at the county clerk's office) and pay a fee. Some states require a premarital medical examination or a blood test showing that the person is free from venereal disease (usually only syphilis) or that the woman does not have rubella. Many states have a waiting period of two to seven days between the time the marriage license is applied for and issued. In most states, you can marry immediately after receiving your marriage license. The license is good in many states only for a prescribed period of time, such as thirty days or six months. A marriage that takes place after the license expires is not legally valid.

The person who performs the ceremony must be authorized by law to do so—either a recognized religious authority, such as a minister, priest, or rabbi, or an authorized civil servant, usually a judge or a justice of the peace. (Contrary to popular belief, the captain of a ship can't perform marriages.) The marriage ceremony normally must be witnessed by a set number of people (such as two). After the ceremony, the person who conducted it will fill in and sign the marriage license, then have the bride, groom, and witnesses also sign. The newlywed couple is given the license. The person who performed the ceremony is usually responsible for reporting the marriage to the county clerk's office.

A few states have a procedure available to qualified couples that does away with many of the formal requirements, such as the blood test and license. This usually applies to couples who have lived together and who have presented themselves to others as married. The couple can apply to the county clerk or clerk of the court for an "authorization for the performance of a marriage." After this is issued, the couple can be married by a person authorized to perform a marriage.

Common Law Marriages

Thirteen states—Alabama, Colorado, Georgia, Idaho, Iowa, Kansas, Montana, Ohio, Oklahoma, Pennsylvania, Rhode Island, South Carolina, and Texas—and the District of Columbia permit a common law marriage, which does away with many formalities, such as the blood test or license. (Another thirteen states recognize common law marriages only if they were entered into before a certain date. For example, Florida recognizes common law marriages made before 1968, while Michigan recognizes such marriages if made before 1957. Common law marriages attempted after the specified date are not valid.)

How is a common law marriage made? A man and woman who live together must agree to be married and thereafter present themselves to the community as husband and wife. The fact that a couple has lived together for a long time does not by itself mean that they have a common law marriage. They must intend to be married, and they must conduct themselves in public as being married. Referring to the other as "my husband" or "my wife," using a common last name, and sharing each other's earnings are all evidence of a common law marriage.

Suppose that a couple enters into a valid common law marriage in Georgia, then later moves to Kentucky, which requires a formal marriage ceremony with a license and such. Will Kentucky recognize the validity of the couple's marriage? Yes. So long as the marriage was valid in the state in which it was made, the other state must recognize its legality, even though it does not permit that type of marriage to be made within its borders.

On the other hand, suppose that a man and woman attempt to enter into a common law marriage in Oregon, which doesn't recognize such a marriage, then move to Colorado, which does. Does the fact of moving to Colorado make the invalid marriage valid? No. The validity of the marriage hinges on the date and the place it was attempted or made. Since it was attempted in Oregon, which doesn't permit common law marriages, it is invalid from the start. However, although the move to Colorado does not validate the purported common law marriage, the couple can enter into a common law marriage in Colorado. Generally, though, the marriage is valid only from the date when it was made in Colorado and is not retroactive to when the couple lived in Oregon.

Bigamy

You can have only one spouse at a time. If you remarry before divorcing your current spouse or obtaining an annulment of the earlier marriage, you are guilty of bigamy. The second marriage is void from the beginning and is not made legal if you later legally terminate the first marriage.

Can you defend a criminal bigamy charge on the ground that your religious beliefs permit multiple spouses? No. Although the First Amendment to the United States Constitution guarantees freedom of religion (see chapter 16), the courts have consistently held that while this gives you the absolute right to *believe* in any religious doctrines, the right to *practice* those beliefs can be restricted when there is an overriding social concern. For example, a person cannot defend a murder charge on the ground that his or her religion requires human sacrifice. The government cannot prevent a religion from teaching that you have a right to have as many spouses as you want. In the interests of society, however, the government can prevent you from practicing that aspect of the religion. Accordingly, the law ordains the rule of one man, one wife, and one woman, one husband, at one time.

Premarital Agreements

A premarital agreement, also called an "antenuptial" agreement, is a contract a man and a woman enter into before marriage, a contract that governs their rights and obligations in the event of divorce or death. At one time, courts enforced only premarital agreements that covered the rights of the couple if one of them died. Premarital contracts that purported to set the couple's rights if they got divorced had no legal force or effect because of the belief that such agreements promoted marital disharmony and divorce. Today most states will uphold a premarital agreement in either situation if it meets some fairly rigorous guidelines.

Not everyone has to be concerned about a premarital agreement, and some people need to be more concerned about it than others. For example, a young couple with no children from prior relationships, no assets to speak of, and no business interests would rarely need a premarital agreement. But a middle-aged person with several children from a previous marriage and his or her own house and other assets should consider a premarital agreement. A person with an established business should also think seriously about a premarital contract.

What can be covered by a premarital contract? Anything you want. It can be as exhaustive or as short as you like. The typical premarital contract, however, does not cover such things as who takes out the trash and who does the dishes. Rather, it usually speaks to the end of the marriage, when the time comes to divide the property and determine alimony payments. Sometimes there is a paragraph relating to the custody and support of any children that are born of the marriage. Any provisions regarding children are not binding upon the court; the best interests and the needs and welfare of the child (discussed later in this chapter) are the deciding factors.

A court will enforce a premarital contract only if, before the agreement was made, both parties made a *full and fair* disclosure of all their assets and other relevant information. If one party misrepresented the nature or extent of his or her property, the court will most likely refuse to recognize the agreement. Also, a court generally will not enforce an agreement that is patently unfair to one party—for instance, one that gives the wife a token cash settlement and little else.

The agreement should by all means be in writing. State law usually requires this, and it also is the only way of ensuring that there can be no dispute as to the terms of the agreement. The premarital agreement should be written in as simple English as possible, to prevent either spouse from coming back at a later date and saying that he or she didn't really understand the agreement and signed it only because everyone was pressuring him or her to do so.

To reduce the chances that a court will refuse to enforce a premarital agreement, each party should be represented by his or her own lawyer. When only one person has a lawyer, there is a greater chance that a court will invalidate or ignore an unfair premarital agreement if the other person later objects to it. When neither person has a lawyer, the courts likewise will frequently invalidate an inequitable agreement, particularly if the person who wrote the agreement has more experience or is better educated than the other person.

Annulments

An annulment is a legal declaration that a marriage never existed, that it was null and void from the beginning, that something at the start prevented the marriage from being valid. The difference between a divorce and an annulment is this: in a divorce, a valid marriage is legally ended, while an annulment means that the "marriage" never existed in the first place.

At one time, courts could not make an award of alimony if an annulment was granted. Today many states permit the courts to award alimony and divide the property much the same as if a divorce were involved. A person has never been allowed to use an annulment to avoid his or her responsibilities toward a child born of the "marriage."

Grounds for an Annulment

We have already discussed three things that are grounds for annulment in most states: an underage party, an incestuous marriage, and bigamy. There are also some general physical and mental conditions that can prevent a marriage from being valid. A person who is insane at the time of the ceremony is legally incapable of entering into a state of matrimony. The fact that a person is somewhat mentally retarded, however, does not necessarily mean that he or she cannot marry. Sexual impotency or physical inability to have sexual intercourse is reason for an annulment in many states, at least if the other person was not aware of it before the marriage. Some states permit an annulment if one party was a drug addict, a habitual criminal, or a prostitute. An annulment is available in some states if the woman was pregnant with another man's child at the time of the marriage. Failure to comply with all of the formalities of marriage (such as getting a blood test or license) or remarrying before the prescribed waiting period, if any, after a final decree of divorce is issued can also be a ground for annulment.

Fraud is sometimes a sufficient ground for an annulment. Suppose a woman falsely tells her boyfriend that he has gotten her pregnant, when she knows that she is not pregnant, and he marries her primarily out of a feeling of duty toward the "child." A court can annul the marriage because of the woman's deception. (If she honestly, but mistakenly, believes she is pregnant, a court usually won't grant an annulment when the truth becomes evident.) An example of deception that isn't enough to annul a marriage: A woman tells a man that she is incredibly rich, has a villa in Spain, a place on the Riviera, and so on. He later learns she is an assistant French fry cook at a local fast food restaurant and has no money. In the eyes of the law, he married the woman for the love of her, not for the love of her money, so it shouldn't make any difference how rich or poor she is.

In some cases, coercion or duress can be a basis for a court to grant an annulment. For example, if the bride's father threatens to physically harm the groom if he doesn't marry his daughter (a "shotgun" wedding), this is probably enough to nullify the marriage.

Void and Voidable Marriages

Some marriages are void from the start; others are merely voidable. The distinction can be critical. A void marriage can never be recognized as legal. A voidable marriage, on the other hand, can be annulled within the time limit set by state law, but if not so annulled, it becomes valid.

A marriage between close relatives, such as a parent and child, is void and can never be made legal. Similarly, if a person is married at one time to two people (bigamy), the second marriage is void.

Marriages based on fraud or coercion are voidable. If you fail to take steps to annul the marriage within the prescribed time after learning that you were deceived or after the coercion ends, the marriage is recognized as valid. If you wait too long, the only way you can then get out of the marriage is through a divorce.

The period of time in which you must file to annul a voidable marriage varies from state to state—anywhere from ninety days to four years after you learn of the ground for annulment. If you think you have grounds for an annulment and want out of your marriage, you should contact an attorney immediately.

A marriage involving an underaged person is voidable. The underage party must file for annulment within the set period— before reaching the age of consent to four years after coming of age, depending upon the state's law—or this ground for annulment is lost. Likewise, a person who was mentally incompetent at the time the marriage took place has to file for an annulment within the time set by law.

If the marriage was valid in the first place, time is generally not a factor in determining whether or not it can be annulled. For example, a week after the marriage, you decide you made a big mistake. Can you get the marriage annulled? No, not if the marriage was legal to begin with. The mere fact that you were married a short time usually is not a ground for annulment. To get out of the marriage, you will have to file for a divorce. If the marriage was not consummated (if, in other words, there were no sexual relations after the marital vows), some states let you get an annulment. Many states, however, do not recognize lack of consummation as a ground for an annulment.

Who Can File for an Annulment?

Usually only a party to the marriage can file for an annulment. Sometimes just one party can ask that the marriage be annulled. For example, if the marriage is between an uncle and niece, either could seek an annulment. But if an underaged person gets married, only he or she can assert lack of age as a ground for annulment. (If both were underage, then either can file.) If fraud or duress was the basis for the marriage, only the person deceived or coerced can ask for an annulment. If one person was impotent or physically unable to have sex at the time of the marriage, only the other person can get the annulment. The one exception to this last example is the rare instance when the person did not know of the problem before marriage; either party can file for an annulment in such a case.

Occasionally someone not a party to the marriage can ask that it be annulled. For instance, the parents of an underaged person can ask the court to annul the marriage. If a mentally incompetent person got married, his or her legal guardian or closest relative can file for an annulment.

Separation

You may want to separate from your spouse for several reasons. Maybe you can't go on living with him or her, yet aren't emotionally ready to get a divorce. Or you may want to use a separation as a "trial divorce" to see whether you really do want a divorce.

To many people, "separation" means simply that a married couple are no longer living together. To a lawyer, it means something more than mere physical distance. Like a divorce, it means a change in the legal rights and obligations of the parties toward each other. It is unlike a divorce, however, in that neither party is free to remarry during the period of separation. To do so would constitute bigamy. If you want to marry someone else, you'll have to get a divorce first.

You can (but generally don't need to) obtain a court order granting a separation. A court can usually grant a separation only for the same grounds as those upon which a divorce is granted (discussed below). You can, however, separate from your spouse by mutual agreement for any reason, or no reason at all. A written agreement regarding any alimony, child support, custody, and visitation rights is always advisable and may even be required by state law to make the separation a "legal" one.

Divorce

A divorce is a legal declaration that a valid marriage is now terminated. Except for the obligations ordered by the court—such as the payment of alimony or child support—the parties are no longer obligated to each other in any way. Once a divorce is final, a person is free to marry again without being guilty of bigamy.

Originally divorces were allowed only if there was sufficient "fault" by one spouse—he or she did something so wrong that it essentially destroyed the marriage. Many states today permit divorces that are based not on any particular fault of the parties but rather on general incompatibility—the parties simply can't go on living together. These are called no-fault divorces. Roughly one-third of the states allow only divorces based on fault. A dozen or so states have abolished the fault concept entirely and provide only for no-fault divorces. The rest of the states allow both no-fault and fault divorces.

Some states with no-fault system of divorce no longer call a divorce a divorce but rather refer to it as a "dissolution" of marriage. (Those states also have some other changes in terminology: alimony, for example, is "spousal support.") The effect of a dissolution is the same as that of a divorce: it ends the marriage, divides the property, orders financial support for the ex-spouse and any children, and provides for child custody and visiting rights.

Divorces Based on Fault

The types of faults most commonly recognized as grounds for divorce are adultery, mental or physical cruelty, desertion or abandonment (usually for at least one year), nonsupport, gross neglect, alcoholism or drug addiction, impotence, insanity, and conviction of a felony (a prison sentence of one to three years may be required). One important ground rule: To obtain a divorce based on fault, the innocent spouse must be the one who initiates the legal proceedings; a person cannot go out and commit adultery, then file for divorce on the ground that he or she has committed adultery. In some states, a divorce is available if the parties have been separated under a court order or written agreement for a specified length of time, ordinarily six months to two years, depending on the state.

Before no-fault divorces, adultery and extreme mental cruelty were the two most common types of faults alleged in divorce actions. The adultery was often staged or committed with the other spouse's approval. The "guilty" spouse would usually be caught in the act by the "innocent" spouse's private investigator, who always had just enough time to take several pictures for evidence.

Divorces based on mental cruelty frequently included testimony from friends, neighbors, and relatives, stating that they heard one spouse verbally abuse or humiliate the other incessantly. The children were also called to testify about general living conditions—the house was unsanitary, a parent was drunk every night—or about constant and heated arguments they overheard between their parents. Not infrequently, much of the testimony was exaggerated, even completely fabricated, to ensure that the divorce would be granted.

No-Fault Divorces

In a no-fault divorce, you don't have to prove that your spouse has committed some sin or physically abused you. You only need to show that such disharmony has developed that the two of you are no longer able to live together, and the marriage is beyond repair. The buzz words usually found in no-fault divorces are that "irreconcilable differences leading to the irremediable breakdown of the marriage" have developed. (Some states refer to it as an " irretrievable breakdown" of the marriage.)

The concept of no-fault divorce evolved for two primary reasons. The first was the realization that the courts should not force two people to live together if they can no longer get along.

The second was the recognition of the emotional effect that fault divorces have on children. Children would, for example, be subjected to the trauma of being put on the stand to testify that they saw Mommy in the company of several men while Daddy was at work. A no-fault divorce is difficult enough for children to go through.

Does the development of no-fault divorce mean that fault is completely obsolete in states where no-fault laws are in effect? Not at all. Fault can still play an important part in determining the rights and obligations of the parties after the divorce. If, for example, the breakup resulted from one spouse's frequent adulterous relationships, some judges consider this in dividing the property or determining whether alimony has to be paid, how much, and for how long. A spouse's misconduct is also important in deciding who gets custody of the children.

Defenses to Divorce

Suppose your spouse sues you for divorce, but you don't want one. Is there anything you can legally do to "defend," or prevent, the divorce? Defenses to divorce actions aren't nearly as important today as they were 30 or more years ago, when divorces were much harder to obtain. Defenses are only relevant in divorces based on fault. No-fault divorces are essentially undefendable: if one spouse wants a divorce, there isn't much the other can do to stop it.

In a fault divorce proceeding, if an innocent spouse forgives the adulterous spouse, the defense of "condonation" stops the divorce. Another defense is the assertion that the other spouse provoked the conduct complained of. The provocation must be sufficient to justify the wrongful act, however. For instance, a husband cannot justify an adulterous relationship because his wife refused to have intercourse with him one night.

At one time, a frequent defense was recrimination: the spouse who filed for the divorce was accused of being equally guilty of immoral or other wrongful conduct. If the wife asked for a divorce on the ground that, say, her husband committed adultery, the husband could defend the divorce on the basis that the wife herself had also committed adultery. In this situation, some courts would not give the couple a divorce, since they were equally culpable. Holy wedlock became unholy deadlock. This made absolutely no sense, as the two people obviously no longer wanted to be married, and the marriage was beyond salvage. Today most courts will simply grant the divorce, end the couple's suffering, and let them get on with their separate lives.

When divorces were permitted only because of one spouse's fault, a couple who could no longer live together would occasionally agree that one of them should commit adultery so they could get the divorce. Unfortunately, if the judge found out about it, he or she often would deny the divorce because of the parties' "collusion."

Residency Requirements and "Quickie" Divorces

Before you can file an action for divorce, most states require that you live in the state for a certain amount of time, usually six months or one year. This type of law is designed to prevent a state from becoming a "divorce mill," a term applied to states that routinely grant divorces even though the person has been there for only a few weeks.

As long as it was properly obtained and issued, a divorce obtained in one state is valid in all other states. But if you get a divorce on an overnight trip to Mexico or some faraway island, don't expect it to hold up, particularly if your spouse wishes to contest it. Before you go to another state or another country to obtain a divorce, talk to two attorneys—one in your home state, another in the other state or foreign country—to see whether the divorce will in fact be recognized as valid when you return home. If you think this is too expensive, rest assured that it will pale in comparison to the costs if your home state doesn't recognize your divorce.

The Divorce Proceedings

The first step in obtaining a divorce is the filing of a complaint (or petition) for divorce in the proper court, usually called the family court or domestic court. When the complaint is filed, the clerk of the court issues a summons for your spouse to appear. The summons is an official court document informing your spouse that a complaint has been filed against him or her and that some legal action must be taken within a certain time (such as 30 days), or the court may decide against him or her. Your spouse must be served with the summons and complaint, which lawyers call "process" or "papers." Depending on the state, service of the summons and complaint generally may be made by a marshall, a registered process server, an employee of the attorney's firm, or anyone 18 and over who is not a party to the lawsuit. If your spouse cannot be found after a diligent search, you can ask the court to permit service by publishing the summons in a newspaper.

Between the time when you first file the complaint for divorce and the time when the divorce becomes final (the procedure for which is explained later), a number of things may require temporary or interim orders. For example, if children are involved, there should be a provisional order not only stating who gets custody of the children and how much child support is to be paid and by whom, but also laying out exactly what rights the other spouse has to visit the children. An interim order should also be obtained regarding how much money one spouse is to pay the other for support. All of these provisions should be part of the interlocutory (temporary) decree of divorce that determines the rights of each party until the judge grants the final decree of divorce.

If your spouse is bothering or threatening you, you should obtain a court order prohibiting harassment. This prohibits your spouse from calling you on the telephone, coming to your house, or otherwise speaking with or annoying you. It can also prevent friends of your spouse from harassing you.

If your spouse threatens to take all of the money out of your

joint bank accounts or give all of the property away, a court order
can and should be obtained to prevent this.

Most divorces are uncontested. Usually your spouse will not
file an answer or objection to the complaint because you will have
already worked out a complete settlement concerning the division
of property, alimony, and child support, custody, and visitation
rights. You will need to show only that your spouse was properly
served with the summons and complaint and that there are "irreconcilable differences" that have led to the "irremediable
breakdown" of the marriage. In a fault state, you may be required
to briefly present the testimony of one or two witnesses to corroborate your claims of your spouse's fault.

If the divorce is contested, your spouse must file an answer
denying the charges of the complaint and stating reasons why the
divorce should not be granted. Sometimes your spouse really
wants to try to work things out; other times he or she is just trying
to make things as difficult as possible for you. The answer generally must be filed within the time limit specified in the summons
(usually 30 days), or a default can be entered against the spouse.
A trial will eventually be held, and each of you will present testimony to support your contentions. Such cases are usually heard
by a judge, sitting without a jury. At the end of the trial, the
judge will either grant or deny the divorce. If the divorce is granted,
the judge will divide the property, decide who gets custody of
the children, and rule on the payment of alimony and child
support.

Many states impose a waiting period between the time the
complaint for divorce is filed and the time the divorce decree
becomes final. This generally varies from twenty days to four
months, although Massachusetts has an eighteen-month waiting
period for no-fault divorces. A handful of states have a waiting
period between the time when the interlocutory decree is issued
and the final decree is granted, and a dozen or so states have
restrictions on how soon a person can remarry after the final
decree of divorce. (Remember that in any state, you cannot remarry until your divorce is final.)

Should You Be Your Own Lawyer?

Because of the emotions involved, a lawyer is more important in divorces than in most other areas of law. Usually you are better off hiring an attorney to handle your divorce rather than trying to do it yourself. One thing many people often overlook is that a lawyer will always first try to save the marriage if that is a real possibility. If the divorce is inevitable, however, and involves children, substantial assets, or disputes as to who gets what, you should by all means have an attorney on your side. (Your spouse should hire an attorney, too.)

What about the low prices you see some lawyers advertising for divorce? Those prices are generally good only if you don't have any children or many assets and your spouse isn't going to contest anything. If your divorce involves more than just filling out and filing the forms, be prepared to pay more. Before you hire a lawyer—any lawyer—get a written estimate of the expected fees based on your individual situation.

Many people today are doing their own divorces, with the help of a do-it-yourself kit or a divorce assistance group. The problem with most prepared kits is that they speak only in generalities and may not adequately address your particular circumstances. Divorce assistance groups can type out the forms and file them for you, but they usually can't tell you what to put in the blanks, since that constitutes legal advice. Many of these companies have an attorney available to assist you, but your cost will most likely go up if you use his or her services. If you do decide to go with a divorce assistance company, make sure you get an estimate in writing that includes an hour or two of attorney's advice. This will give you a more realistic appraisal of your ultimate cost.

One danger of a do-it-yourself divorce is that one party may come back to court a year or two later, asking that the settlement agreement be modified or declared void because he or she didn't understand the agreement, and it is unfair. Courts are more likely to accept this argument if the parties did not have separate at-

torneys advising them when the settlement agreement was made.

Tax considerations are another important reason to stay away from do-it-yourself divorces when more than a nominal amount of property is involved. As an example, let's say the value of your house has increased $30,000 since you bought it. If the settlement agreement is not structured correctly, that amount could be subject to taxes when the divorce is final. All tax questions should be resolved by competent professionals before the settlement is made final.

If your spouse agrees to an "amicable" divorce, and you plan on doing it yourself, try to sit down with your spouse before you file for the divorce and work out your settlement agreement—every bit of it—put it in writing, and have your spouse sign it. If you can't do this now, forget about doing it yourself and hire a good attorney. Never do your own divorce if your spouse is going to contest anything—the amount of alimony, the division of the property, custody of the children, or visitation rights.

Sometimes, to save money, a couple will agree to have just one lawyer represent them. This too should be done only if there are no children, no substantial assets, and no disputes as to the division of property or payment of alimony. If you have decided to use one attorney, that attorney will probably tell you that he or she can really be the attorney for only one of you. A divorce is an adversarial situation, and an attorney can look out for the best interests of only one party. Before signing the settlement agreement, the other spouse should have an independent attorney review it.

Dividing the Property

There are two parts to every divorce. The first part is the termination of the marital relation itself by court decree. The second part consists of dividing the house, cars, furniture, bank accounts, and other assets; providing for the payment of spousal support; and settling issues of child support, custody, and visitation rights. The division of marital assets is referred to as the property settlement. The divorce and property settlement do not have to take place at the same time. When the division of the property is disputed, the divorce is often obtained first, particularly if one spouse wishes to remarry.

If the parties can't agree on how to divide the property, then a judge will do it for them. The manner in which the assets acquired during a marriage are distributed differs greatly from one state to another. Forty-one states and the District of Columbia are so-called separate property states, while the other nine states are "community property" states.

Separate Property States

At one time, when a married couple divorced, who got what depended on where the money to buy each asset came from. Everything a spouse earned or received (such as gifts and inheritances) during marriage was his or her separate property, and anything bought with those earnings was that spouse's separate property. It was that simple. If the family home was purchased with the husband's earnings, for example, it was his and his alone, and the wife had no claim to it.

Strict separate property laws frequently led to unfair results, so a new rule—"equitable distribution"—was developed to remedy this imbalance. Under the equitable distribution rule, the judge looks at the assets of the couple, the length of the marriage, and the contributions each party made during the marriage, and then divides the property in a fair manner.

If the divorce is granted because one spouse was at fault, the judge may adjust the division of the marital assets. For example, if one spouse was guilty of repeated extramarital affairs, the other spouse may get as much as 75 percent of the property and a hefty sum of alimony to boot.

Community Property Laws

Nine states—Arizona, California, Idaho, Louisiana, New Mexico, Nevada, Texas, Washington, and Wisconsin—have community property laws. Community property is split right down the middle, with each spouse receiving an equal share. Community property generally consists of everything earned or acquired by a couple during marriage. For example, the wages earned by a spouse during marriage are community property. If a house is bought with those wages, the house is also community property, and both spouses have equal ownership of that house, even if only one spouse worked during marriage. Under community property laws, anything you own before you get married is your separate property. Gifts you receive during your marriage are also your own separate property, as are any inheritances you receive.

The judge can divide only the community property; separate property remains the property of the spouse who owns it. In dividing the community property and awarding alimony and child support, the court can, however, consider the amount of separate property either of you has.

Problems often arise when separate property is mixed with community property. In some cases, it is necessary for the parties' lawyers to employ accountants to track the history of an asset. For example, a racehorse that one spouse claims to be a community asset may have been purchased by the other spouse with the rental monies from a house he or she inherited from a parent. By going through the financial records of the parties, an accountant may be able to discover just where the money came from.

Alimony

Alimony (or spousal support) is money one spouse pays to the other to help support him or her after the divorce. If you don't agree with your spouse on whether alimony has to be paid, how much should be paid, and for how long, a judge will decide for you. At one time, it was invariably the husband who wound up paying alimony. Today, however, men sometimes collect alimony payments, although this is still relatively rare.

We normally think of alimony in terms of monthly payments. But any other means of payment that the parties agree to or the court orders—such as quarterly or annual payments—is possible. Sometimes a spouse will accept a single, lump-sum payment of alimony and the bulk of the community property in place of monthly alimony payments. When this happens, the other spouse should make sure that he or she is not giving away too much too fast in order to get out of an unpleasant situation.

There is no set formula for determining how much alimony, if any, must be paid in a particular case. The alimony may range from nothing to half of what a spouse makes. The judge will look at all of the circumstances of each case before making a decision. Some of the factors the judge considers are how long the parties were married, how much money each earns, the number of children and their ages, the health of the parties, and how self-supporting each party is. Obviously, a 45-year-old woman who never graduated from high school and who has stayed home taking care of the kids for the last 20 years is not as readily employable and self-supporting as a 25-year-old woman who has a master's degree in computer science. A higher amount of alimony is often awarded for the time a spouse is being trained for the current job market.

Another factor taken into consideration is the overall standard of living the couple enjoyed during the marriage. While most people have heard that the wife is entitled to be supported "in the manner to which she has become accustomed," it is rarely possible for either party to continue living in the same style after a divorce. Earnings that previously supported only one household must now be stretched to two. To allow either spouse to continue in his or her "accustomed manner" could mean that 70 percent or more of the other's paycheck might have to be turned over. Except in the cases of the very rich, a divorce usually will reduce both parties' standard of living for a while.

The judge may also consider the fault of the parties in determining alimony payments. In some states, when a divorce is granted because of one spouse's adultery, that spouse cannot receive any alimony. And if an unfaithful spouse is required to pay alimony to the innocent spouse, the judge may take that misconduct into consideration and order larger payments.

The amount of the alimony payments can be changed by the court upon the request of either party, but only if he or she can demonstrate sufficiently changed circumstances. (Only court-ordered alimony payments can be changed. If a settlement agreement spells out the terms of alimony, the court generally cannot modify it.) The spouse who is paying alimony will frequently ask for a reduction if he or she is out of work for a time, is demoted to a job that pays less, or retires. A reduction in the amount of alimony is often requested if the spouse receiving it begins earning substantially more money than before. The spouse receiving the alimony usually has a harder time getting the payments increased. That the ex-spouse who is paying the alimony received a raise or suddenly came into a great deal of money ordinarily is no reason for the court to increase alimony. The spouse receiving the alimony must show that his or her own situation has changed sufficiently to justify an increase in alimony.

How long must alimony be paid? For as long as the court orders (unless modified) or the parties have agreed that it should as part of the property settlement. Alimony usually stops when the spouse receiving it dies or remarries. If the new marriage is later annulled, however, alimony can be reinstated in some cases. This usually happens only if the marriage was void, not merely voidable, as discussed above.

Say, for example, that Tom and Jane get divorced, and Tom is ordered to pay Jane $500 alimony a month for five years. Two years later, Jane moves in with her boyfriend (but does not marry him). Does this affect Tom's obligation to pay alimony? Sometimes it does. Alimony payments end in some states if the ex-spouse has been living together with a person of the opposite sex for a certain period of time, such as 30 days. Other states apply the rule that if a man and woman present themselves to others as husband and wife, the ex-spouse's obligation to pay alimony ends. Some courts have ruled that signing a hotel register as "Mr. and Mrs." is enough to show that the couple presented themselves as married, and have cut off alimony. In any event, if Jane is receiving financial assistance from her live-in companion, Tom's attorney may be able to persuade a judge to reduce the alimony payments in light of this new support.

Suppose that your spouse has been ordered to pay you $750 a month as alimony for ten years. What happens to the remaining payments if your spouse dies after only five years? In many states, the obligation to pay alimony ends with the death of the person paying it. In some states, however, the obligation to pay alimony can be enforced against his or her estate. But if the person doesn't have much of an estate, a judgment against the estate is worth only the paper it's written on. If you will be receiving alimony, you should insist that the settlement agreement require your spouse to maintain a life insurance policy insuring his or her life, with the proceeds payable to you. If your spouse does die before fulfilling the entire obligation, you are protected. (This type of protection is usually available only if you and your spouse agree to it. A judge generally does not have the power to order a spouse to insure his or her life to guarantee alimony payments.) But this protection is worthless, of course, if your spouse lets the policy lapse. An experienced divorce lawyer can prepare an agreement to prevent this from happening to you.

If your ex-spouse falls behind in alimony payments, your lawyer can obtain a court order requiring that the payments be made current. If the person has moved out of state, it is still relatively easy to enforce the delinquent support obligations through the Uniform Reciprocal Enforcement of Support Act. At a court hearing, the person will be given an opportunity to explain his or her failure to pay. If the court orders the payments brought up to date, and the person fails to do so, he or she can then be found in contempt of court and jailed. Although it is said that there is no "debtors' prison" in America, the fact is that many ex-husbands (and a few ex-wives) are currently spending time in jail for failing to make alimony payments. The law relies on the technicality that the person is in jail not for failing to pay the debt, but rather for failing to comply with a court order. It's really just a matter of semantics, made necessary by the fact that it is unconstitutional to incarcerate a person for failing to pay a monetary debt.

Alimony paid to an ex-spouse (or support payments made as part of a written separation agreement) can be deducted from the payor's federal income taxes if certain requirements are met, and the spouse who receives the alimony generally must include the payments in his or her taxable income in the year received. (Alimony payments may also be deductible or includable on state income tax returns.) The rules regarding the tax treatment of alimony payments are too extensive to go into in any detail here. If you are paying or receiving alimony, get a copy of I.R.S. Publication 504, "Tax Information for Divorced or Separated Individuals," from the Internal Revenue Service or a library for the latest rules regarding alimony and other tax questions involving divorce.

Child Custody, Visitation, and Support

Before we discuss legal questions involving children and divorce, a few observations are in order. Too often, children become the pawns in a divorce, with one parent using them to hurt the other parent. One parent may try to convince a child that the other parent does not love the child or that the other parent is evil and wants nothing to do with the child.

The question of who gets custody of the children can turn into the fiercest battle during the divorce, even if one parent doesn't really want custody; that parent may just want to make sure the other doesn't get custody. Sometimes the parent who receives custody refuses to let the other parent visit the child, even though a judge has ordered visitation rights. All these tactics have a devastating emotional effect on the child.

It is vital to the welfare of the children that the parents put aside any hostile feelings toward one another and cooperate with each other as far as the children are concerned. Parents who find themselves using their children as weapons should obtain family counseling or other professional help.

Who Gets Custody of the Children?

Child custody is an issue only if both parents want custody of the children. If the parents can agree on who gets custody, the judge will almost always accept their decision without second-guessing it. Any understanding regarding child custody should be incorporated into the written settlement agreement. (But any provisions concerning children are generally subject to court modification.)

Custody of the children used to be routinely awarded to the mother. The law presumed that the mother was in a better position to take care of the children. The father could get custody only if he could prove serious charges of immorality, child abuse, or neglect against the mother. Today the judge focuses on the welfare of the child: is it in the best interests of the child to award custody to the mother or to the father?

A stable home environment is at the top of the judge's list in deciding what is in the child's best interests. A divorce is a major disruption in the child's life, and the judge will do everything possible to minimize that disruption. The parent who keeps the family house invariably gets custody of the children, especially if the children have lived there for several years and attend school in the area. If no house is involved, or the house will be sold, the judge will take into consideration how far from the area either parent plans on moving.

If more than one child is involved, the judge usually will want to keep the children together and therefore will award custody of all children to one parent. But if one child is considerably older, the judge may give each parent custody of one child. If there is a boy fifteen years old and a girl only three, for example, the judge may well award custody of the boy to the father and the girl to the mother.

Will the parent be home enough to take care of the child? If the parent works long hours or at night, who will be home looking after the child? Will a young child be left alone for much of the day? Does a parent frequently come home drunk? The answers to these and other questions tell the judge which parent has the time and interest to properly care for the child.

The judge will also consider what types of people the child will be around. If the parent's friends are drug addicts or known criminals, the judge will think twice before awarding custody to that parent. Sexual preference of the parent is considered by the judge but often is not the deciding factor by itself. Judges have awarded custody to, for example, a homosexual father rather than a heterosexual mother where other factors dictated against giving the mother custody.

Depending on the age and maturity of the child, the judge may ask the child which parent he or she wants to live with. The child's preference, however, is only one factor the judge considers; it alone is not controlling. The judge gives more weight to an older (14 and above) child's decision than to a younger one's choice.

If one parent left home one day, abandoning the other parent and the children, the judge will rarely award that parent custody, even if he or she admits to having made a "mistake." Seldom is there sufficient assurance that that parent will not abruptly walk away from the children again.

When one spouse entered the marriage with children from a previous relationship, the stepparent does not have any claim to custody of those children. If, however, the stepparent has adopted the child, then the judge could award the stepparent custody of that child.

Sometimes neither parent is fit to take care of the child. This situation may arise because the parents are minors in high school or both are totally irresponsible. In such a case, the judge may award custody to grandparents or to an aunt and uncle who are willing to provide the child with a loving home. If no suitable relative can be found to take care of the child, and the parents are declared unfit, the child becomes a ward of the state and is placed in a public institution or a foster home.

Once the judge has awarded custody to one parent, the other parent can return to court at a later date and present new evidence showing that the parent having custody is no longer fit to care for the children. Testimony of neighbors may establish, for instance, that young children are left alone for long periods of time, the children are frequently unwashed, and the house is unlivable. The judge can then take custody away from one parent and award it to the other.

Custody orders frequently prevent the parent from moving out of the county or state unless the court's permission is obtained first. A parent who violates such a court order is in contempt of court, subject to a possible fine or jail sentence, and even loss of custody.

Sometimes after a judge awards custody of the children to one spouse, the other spouse will "steal" the children and move to another state and try to convince a judge there to award him or her custody of the children. But even if the parent is successful in getting a change of custody, he or she cannot return to the state from which the children were abducted without risking possible arrest and punishment for contempt of court. Until recently, questions of child stealing by a parent were usually handled in the family law courts along with all other domestic disputes. Lately, however, there has been a push to treat this as a serious crime, much the same as when a stranger kidnaps a child.

Some judges try to solve the custody battle by awarding both parents "joint legal custody." Joint legal custody generally relates to decisions involving the child, such as those affecting schooling and medical treatment. In joint legal custody, each parent has an equal say in these matters. Even so, one parent will have physical custody of the child most of the time. True joint *physical* custody, where each parent has physical custody of the child for six months a year, is rare indeed.

Visitation Rights

If you don't get custody of your children, the judge will usually give you reasonable visitation rights. Again, a judge makes the decision only if you and your spouse can't decide for yourselves about visitation. Visitation rights may consist of one or two weekends a month, alternate major holidays (one parent gets the kids for Thanksgiving one year, say, and for Christmas the next), and several weeks or a month during the summer.

If your spouse refuses to let you visit your children, have your lawyer call him or her. If that doesn't do anything, you'll have to return to court to enforce the visitation order. This can be a costly procedure, emotionally as well as financially. To punish a parent for refusing to allow the other parent to visit the children, the judge might suspend child support payments until visitation is permitted. And if the parent with custody continues to refuse the other parent his or her visitation rights, the judge could well give custody of the children to the other parent.

If you feel that there is a good reason to refuse your ex-spouse his or her visitation rights—you fear your ex-spouse will abduct the child, for example—talk to your lawyer immediately. If your fears are justified, your lawyer can go back to court and ask the judge to terminate your ex-spouse's visitation rights or permit visits only if he or she is accompanied by a marshal or other law enforcement officer.

Grandparents' Rights

To many people, being a grandparent is an even greater joy than being a parent. Do grandparents have any rights to a continued relationship with their grandchildren after a divorce intervenes? You bet they do.

Most states recognize the right of grandparents to visit their grandchildren, even though the children's parents are divorced. Visiting grandchildren ordinarily is not a problem for the parents of the parent having custody of the child. If the mother has been awarded custody, for example, she usually will not deny her parents (the child's maternal grandparents) access to the children. The husband's parents (the paternal grandparents), however, sometimes find it almost impossible to visit the children, especially when their son can't or doesn't want to maintain a close relationship with his children. In determining the visitation rights of the grandparents, the judge looks at the relationship the grandparents and grandchildren had when the marriage was still going strong. If the grandparents were frequent visitors, the judge will grant more liberal visitation rights. If, however, the grandparents were essentially strangers to the grandchildren, and their new interest seems really to be a disguised effort to harass their ex-son-in-law or ex-daughter-in-law, the judge will severely restrict their rights to visit the children.

We noted earlier that if both parents are unfit to care for the children, the grandparents can be awarded custody. In this event, grandparents living in the area are usually the preferred ones to care for the children, assuming they want the children and are physically and financially able to provide for the children's needs. In determining whether grandparents are fit to have custody, the judge will evaluate their age and general health. A judge won't deny custody to the grandparents just because they are in their sixties, particularly if their health is good, and both the grandparents and grandchildren alike agree to the arrangement.

Child Support

The amount of monthly child support the parent not having custody of the children must pay is usually agreed to by the parties as part of the settlement agreement. The settlement agreement should also spell out who pays for such things as medical and dental expenses, college, and automobile or health insurance for the children.

If the parents can't agree on how much should be paid for child support, the judge will order that a certain amount be paid for each child. Two factors determine the amount of child support: the needs of the children and the parent's ability to pay. The "needs" of the children are defined as the necessities of life—food, clothing, and shelter. The amount of child support, whether agreed to by the parties or ordered by a judge, can be modified as the children's needs or parent's ability to pay change.

Unlike alimony, which stops when the spouse receiving it remarries, the duty to support one's children usually isn't affected by either parent's remarriage. The obligation to support a child ends only when the child reaches the age of majority—18 in most states, 19 in a few—or becomes emancipated (gets married or moves out on his or her own and becomes self-supporting). Another difference between alimony payments and child support payments is how they are treated for tax purposes. As we have seen, alimony payments frequently can be deducted from taxable income by the spouse paying it and must be included as taxable income by the spouse receiving it. Child support payments, however, cannot be deducted by the paying spouse, nor does the spouse who receives them on the child's behalf have to include them on his or her return.

Legitimacy and Paternity

Legitimate and Illegitimate Children

A child born to a married couple is legitimate. One born out of wedlock or from a void marriage (such as an incestuous one) is illegitimate.

For years, the law cast a stigma on illegitimate children by treating them as second- or third-class citizens who had fewer rights than "legitimate" children enjoyed. Fortunately, in recent years, the courts and legislatures have realized that an illegitimate child is generally entitled to the same treatment as a legitimate child (although a few vestiges of the distinction still remain). For example, an illegitimate child now has a right to financial support from his or her biological father. If the father dies because of another person's negligence, the illegitimate child can bring a civil lawsuit against that person for causing the death of the father, something illegitimate children could not have done before. If worker's compensation benefits are given for the father's death, an illegitimate child gets to share in them. An illegitimate child generally shares in his or her father's estate when the father dies, provided the child can prove the fact of paternity.

An illegitimate child becomes legitimate when the child's parents marry. A child also becomes legitimate if the biological father acknowledges in writing the child as his and accepts the child into his family. Once legitimized, the child has the same rights as other legitimate children.

Because of the stigma society casts on illegitimate children, the law presumes that a child is legitimate if the parents were married at or near the time of conception or birth. For example, if the parties are married and living together up to ten months before the child was born, the law usually presumes that the child is born of that marital relationship and is therefore legitimate. This is true even if at the time of the child's birth, the parents are divorced or the father is dead. In a few states, the presumption that a child born of a husband and wife who live together is legitimate is a conclusive presumption—one that cannot be rebutted by any evidence. The husband is the legal father of the child, even if the child's appearance clearly indicates otherwise. Some states let the husband prove that he could not possibly be the child's father by, for example, presenting evidence of blood tests.

Proving Paternity

Why is the question of who is the child's father important? Primarily because the mother and child can compel the father to assist in the child's financial support. If the father openly admits that the child is his, then establishing paternity is not an issue. If you are the mother, you should have the father sign a statement saying that he is in fact the child's father, so if you ever need to go to court to get child support payments, the hardest task—that of proving paternity—will already be taken care of.

If the man disputes paternity, then a lawsuit must be filed to prove that he is the child's father. Sometimes the child's mother files the paternity suit of her own accord. In other cases, when the mother applies for public assistance, such as Aid to Families with Dependent Children (AFDC), the agency will usually initiate the paternity suit in an effort to get reimbursed by the father for money advanced to support the child.

How is paternity proved in court? Until the recent development of new techniques, paternity was usually established through circumstantial evidence, such as proof that the couple had engaged in sexual intercourse—even if only once—near the time conception occurred. The child (or photographs) would be brought to court so the jury could compare the physical appearance of the child and the suspected father. Blood grouping tests would also be performed, but such tests could only rule out a certain class of blood types, such as men having type A blood.

Other evidence that was considered: Did the man ever acknowledge that he was the child's father? Witnesses might have testified that they heard the suspected father refer to the child as "my son" or "my daughter." Letters from the father to the child would be used as evidence, particularly if the letter was signed "Dad." The father may also have tacitly acknowledged the child as his by letting the child live with his family and treating him or her as a legitimate child.

Today in many states, the most important tool in establishing paternity is the Human Leucocyte Anitigen (HLA) test, which matches not only blood type but also tissue type and other genetic factors. Unlike the older blood grouping tests, which only excluded a person as being the child's father, the HLA test is used to prove the suspect *is* the father. Experts in this field claim that this test is at least 98 percent accurate. A man whom the HLA test results point to as the father will succeed in his defense only if he can prove beyond any doubt that he was out of the state or was impotent or sterile at the time the child was conceived.

If the blood tests are inconclusive, the suspected father can try to defend the paternity action by proving that the mother had sexual intercourse with other men around the same time, and the father could just as well be one of them. Since it is generally up to the mother to establish which particular man is the father, the judge will usually dismiss the case if she cannot prove which of the men is indeed the father. A judge once made the unusual ruling that it was up to each man in this situation to prove that he could not possibly be the father, and if he couldn't, he had to pay a proportionate share of the child's support. So if there were three suspected fathers, and none could adequately establish that he was not the father, each "father" would have to pay a third of the child support payments.

Custody and Visitation Rights of an Unwed Parent

Unwed mothers are generally entitled to sole custody of their children. This is true even if the unwed mother is a minor living at home with her parents. Unless the father wants custody of the child, the mother usually doesn't need to get a court order awarding her custody. If there is a custody battle, the unwed mother will usually get custody. But if she is physically or emotionally unable to care for the child, the court ordinarily must award custody to the biological father, unless doing so would be detrimental to the child's welfare.

If the mother refuses to let him see the child, the biological father can get a court order granting him reasonable visiting rights. A judge might deny visitation rights if the father's interests in seeing the child are not sincere—if, for example, the purpose of the visits is to harass the mother rather than spend any time with the child—or if the visits are particularly disruptive and emotionally trying for the child.

Abortion

In the 1973 decision of *Roe v. Wade*, the United States Supreme Court made one of its most controversial rulings: that a woman has the right to an abortion. In its decision, the Supreme Court broke the nine-month pregnancy term into separate periods of three months each. During the first three months (the first "trimester") of pregnancy, the government—federal, state, or local—has no say in whether the woman can have an abortion. That decision is left entirely up to the woman, and the procedure left to the judgment of her physician and her. A state can, however, pass laws regulating the medical procedures under which an abortion must be performed during months three to six. A state may be able to prohibit an abortion during this period, but the circumstances under which it can do so are far from resolved. During the final three months, a state can prohibit abortions in most situations. The Supreme Court found that at this point, the fetus is "viable"—capable of surviving on its own outside of the womb—and the government therefore has a recognizable interest in protecting its potential life. But if the pregnancy threatens the woman's life, a state cannot stop her from getting an abortion even at this stage.

Roe v. Wade involved a number of complex issues—legal, medical, and moral—but the Supreme Court focused on whether a fetus is a "person" within the meaning of the Constitution. The Supreme Court concluded that the Constitution applies only to persons who have been born. (This conclusion is in accord with longstanding common law principles that distinguish between an unborn fetus and a child that is born alive.)

Can the woman's husband or boyfriend sue to prevent the abortion? Generally not—at least not during the first three months of the pregnancy. The choice to terminate the pregnancy during the first trimester is the woman's, and hers alone. Even laws that required a married woman to notify her husband before having an abortion have been held unconstitutional. The extent of the father's right in the decision to abort the fetus after the first three months has not yet been clearly decided.

Laws that require a woman to wait a set amount of time— say, two hours or two days—between making the decision to have the abortion and actually having it performed have been struck down as unconstitutional restrictions on the right to an abortion.

Does a minor (someone under 18 in most states, under 19 in a few) need the permission of her parents to get an abortion? In *Roe v. Wade*, the Supreme Court ruled that parental consent is not needed if the girl is old enough to understand the consequences of the abortion and can weigh the issues reasonably well. But if the girl is too immature, parental consent or court approval may be required. Many states have laws that require a minor to obtain either parental consent or court approval before she can have an abortion. If the parents refuse to consent to the abortion, the girl can ask a judge to permit it. (Alternatively, the girl can bypass her parents completely and directly ask a judge for a ruling.)

The initial determination the judge must make is whether the girl is mature enough to make the decision herself. If she is, then the judge must approve her request for an abortion, any objections of her parents notwithstanding. If the judge finds that the girl is too immature to make the decision, the judge will decide what is in the girl's best interests.

In many states, laws require a physician to notify a minor's parents before performing an abortion. The United States Supreme Court has not made any definitive rulings on the extent of the minor's right to get an abortion free from parental involvement. Many lower courts have, however, ruled for the main part that these laws are constitutional.

Artificial Insemination

When a husband is sterile or otherwise incapable of fathering a child, a couple may opt for the medical procedure of artificial insemination, in which a woman is impregnated with the semen of a donor. Usually this donor is an anonymous stranger, although occasionally a relative, such as the husband's brother, agrees to provide the semen for artificial insemination. Who is considered the legal father of the child: the woman's husband, or the semen donor? If the husband consented to the procedure in writing prior to the artificial insemination, he is treated as if he were the child's biological father.

Regardless of whether or not the woman is married, the donor of the semen generally is *not* considered to be the legal father of the child. The donor cannot be compelled to provide any financial or emotional support for the child, nor does the child have a right to any of the donor's estate when the donor dies. On the other hand, the donor usually has no right to visit the child, nor can he gain custody of the child. Indeed, most of the time, the mother does not know the identity of the semen donor, nor does the donor know if a child was ever conceived from his semen. This information is confidential and is released only in exceptional cases.

When the wife is unable to bear children, a couple may decide to have another woman impregnated with the husband's semen through artificial insemination. Often the couple consults an attorney who is experienced in this area to help arrange everything and prepare a contract spelling out the agreement between the couple and the surrogate mother: most importantly, that when the child is born, the surrogate mother must turn it over to the couple. Suppose, however, that after the baby is born, the surrogate mother decides that she wants to keep the child. Can the couple go to court and sue to force her to give up the baby? In this situation, courts do not apply the strict rules governing contract law. This is because although the agreement to bear the child and give it up when it is born is a contract, the subject matter of the contract—a child—obviously involves more weighty considerations than, say, a car or refrigerator. The judge will look at all factors, including what is in the best interests of the child, before making a decision. If the judge does award custody to the surrogate mother, the married couple may be awarded some rights to visit the child. The judge may also order the surrogate mother to reimburse the couple for all medical expenses they paid in connection with the pregnancy and birth.

Recently, in the first case of its kind, a judge ordered a surrogate mother who was impregnated with the sperm and egg of a married couple to turn the baby over to the couple when it was born, as their agreement provided. The judge ruled that the couple were the child's biological parents; it was "their" embryo that was implanted in the surrogate mother.

The development of medical techniques that allow a woman to be impregnated through artificial insemination raises many other legal questions. What happens if the surrogate mother fails to disclose a history of birth defects in her family, and the baby is born physically deformed? Or suppose the woman lies about her age, claiming she is only 32 years old, when in fact she is 39 and at greater risk of bearing a child with Down's syndrome? Can she be sued for misrepresentation for failing to disclose known medical conditions or for lying about her age? Can the couple be forced against their will to take the child? And what becomes of the child if neither the surrogate mother nor the married couple want it? Can a woman who gives birth to a deformed or retarded child after being artificially inseminated sue the donor or depository (sperm bank) for providing defective semen? These are some of the questions that courts will soon be called upon to answer. No set rules have yet been laid down, and every case is evaluated on its individual merits. Anyone thinking about artificial insemination or surrogate parenting should first seek the advice and counsel of a lawyer who is qualified in this particular area.

Adoptions

Adoption creates the legal relationship of parent-child where a person is not a child's biological parent. Three separate parties are usually involved in the adoption: the child, the adoptive parents, and the child's biological parents or a public agency such as the department of social services. A lawyer may also be involved in many adoptions. Single people as well as married couples can adopt children. Someone who marries a person who already has a child may want to legally adopt that child. (If not, he or she becomes the child's stepparent for the duration of the marriage, with considerably different legal obligations from those of an adoptive parent. In some states, for instance, a stepparent is not required to provide any type of support for a stepchild.)

When a child is legally adopted, the adoptive parents take on the same obligations toward the child as if they were the biological parents. They are now responsible not only for the financial support of the child—for food, clothing, education, and so forth—but also for the emotional rearing of the child; providing a safe and happy household and warm and loving support. If an adopted child is injured, the adoptive parents are responsible for seeing that the child receives proper medical care, and they are financially responsible for that care.

When they give up a child for adoption, the biological parents forfeit all rights concerning the child, including the right to visit the child. Conversely, the child generally loses all rights involving the biological parents, including the right to compel them to support him or her and the right to inherit from a biological parent who dies without a will. (A few states still let an adopted child inherit from the biological parents.) Instead, the child acquires rights in and to the estate of the adoptive parents upon their deaths. Of course, the biological parents could still provide for the child in their wills, just as the adoptive parents could expressly disinherit the adopted child in their wills.

How Adoptions Are Arranged

Traditionally, adoptions are arranged through an adoption agency operating under the auspices of the state. The state (if the parents are both dead or have been declared unfit) or the biological parents of the child place the child with the agency, which then takes over. The agency reviews its list of prospective parents, interviews likely candidates, and otherwise conducts an inquiry to determine who is most suitable for the child.

Some states permit a lawyer to arrange for an adoption directly between the biological parents and the adoptive parents, without the intervention of an adoption agency. The lawyer will make an investigation similar to the one an adoption agency would make to ensure that the prospective adoptive parents are well suited to care for the child. The biological parents sometimes want to meet with the prospective adoptive parents before approving the adoption.

In many states, licensed private adoption agencies can also arrange adoptions. Before using a private agency, always know what you are dealing with. Check out the agency with your county social services agency and the Better Business Bureau to make sure it is aboveboard. There are a few disreputable agencies (and lawyers) that arrange adoptions for outrageous fees or make promises and then don't deliver, sometimes absconding with your deposit. A private adoption agency can charge only those fees allowed by state law. If you suspect an agency or a lawyer is charging too much or is engaging in questionable practices, contact the district attorney's office immediately.

The Adoption Procedure

Once a match-up is made (and this can be a lengthy process), the parents who wish to adopt the child must file a petition with the court. The court that has jurisdiction over adoptions differs from state to state: in some it's the probate court; in others, the surrogate court; in a few, the juvenile court; and in others, the superior or district court. The court will set a hearing on the petition at which the judge will approve or deny the adoption. The child's biological parents or legal guardian must be given notice of this hearing so they can oppose the adoption if they want. If a parent is unknown or can't be found, notice of the adoption will usually be published in a local newspaper.

At the hearing, the judge will question the prospective parents and other witnesses to determine their fitness and suitability to take on the responsibilities of parents. In deciding whether a couple is fit to adopt a particular child, the judge takes into account their ages and health and ability to provide the child with a stable environment. The adoptive parents do not have to be rich. They need only be able to provide the child with a loving and secure home, even if that home is a rented apartment. Race and religious beliefs are also considered, but differences between the couple's race or religion and the child's will not prevent an adoption if it is otherwise in the child's best interests to allow it. If the child is over a specified age (ten to fourteen, depending on the state), he or she must also agree to the adoption.

After the judge approves the adoption, in most states the child then lives with the new parents for a probationary period, usually from six months to a year. At the end of this time, if no problems or objections arise, the adoption is permanent, and a new birth certificate for the child is issued.

If a Biological Parent Opposes the Adoption

What happens if a biological parent puts his or her child up for adoption, then has a change of mind? If the change of mind happens within a specified time (for example, 30 days), generally the biological parent can get the child back. But if the biological parents don't act quickly after being notified of a pending adoption, and the adoption is approved, they probably won't be able to do anything about it.

An adoption generally cannot take place over the timely objections of either biological parent, even if the parents are unmarried. About the only way to proceed with an adoption in such a case is to bring a court action to have the biological parent declared totally unfit as a parent, so that any rights he or she has as a parent are legally terminated. For example, if the child's mother marries a man who wants to adopt the child, but the biological father objects, the adoption cannot go through unless and until the biological father's rights are taken away by a judge after a court hearing. A judge will usually terminate a biological father's rights only if he has demonstrated absolutely no interest in the child and is objecting to the adoption in order to harass the child's mother and her new husband; if the biological father frequently abuses the child; or if the child was the product of a casual relationship, and the biological father never had custody of the child. The mere fact that the man who wants to adopt the child will make a better father than the biological father is not an adequate reason for taking away a biological father's rights concerning his child.

Finding Out the Names of the Biological Parents

The courts, adoption agency, lawyers, and others involved in the adoption must treat the names of the biological parents with the highest confidentiality, and all documents, including the child's original birth certificate and all court records concerning the adoption, are kept private ("sealed"). Even the adopted child is frequently thwarted in a search to find out who his or her "real" parents are. A court order must be obtained to open the file, and this will be granted only if there is a good reason, such as a medical emergency requiring a bone marrow transplant from a biological relative. State legislatures are currently being lobbied to pass laws giving adult adoptees access to their adoption records upon request.

Several groups exist to help adopted children in their search and sometimes have success where the child alone has failed. Some reunions are happy, others extremely unpleasant. An adopted child should seriously consider possible consequences before beginning a search for his or her biological parents. One group that provides information on how to search (but does not conduct searches itself) is the Adoptees' Liberty Movement Association, P.O. Box 154, Washington Bridge Station, New York, NY 10033.

Lawsuits Involving Family Members

Does a Parent Have to Pay for Damage Caused by a Minor Child?

Must a parent pay for the personal injuries or property damage caused by his or her minor child? That depends on the circumstances surrounding the incident. Generally speaking, the extent of a parent's financial responsibility for damages or injuries resulting from a child's conduct is largely regulated by state law. Most states hold a parent liable only for harm resulting from the child's willful misconduct; a parent is not liable for a child's mere carelessness or negligence. Some states require the parent to pay for either personal injuries or property damage caused by the minor, but most states restrict the parent's liability to property damage only. Even when the parent is liable, there is usually a ceiling on the amount he or she must pay, generally ranging from $500 to $5,000, depending on the state. In most states, the parent's responsibility is $2,000 or less.

Suppose a teenage driver is driving the family car and causes an accident. Are the parents/owners of the car liable for the damages? In states that have a "permissive use" statute, the parents ordinarily are liable for all injuries resulting from the child's use of the family car (see chapter 2). But in other states, the parents are liable for the minor's careless driving only if the child was doing an errand for a family purpose, such as going to the store at the request of a parent. In those states, the parents would not be liable if, say, the child got into an accident while on a date.

The discussion above relates only to the parents' liability when they themselves have done nothing wrong, when the injury was completely the fault of the child. Sometimes when a child hurts someone else, that child's parents can be held liable for the damages if they were not supervising the child adequately. In this situation, the parents' fault is separate and distinct from the child's act. Let's say that Debby takes her son Peter to a playground, where Peter picks up a branch and starts swinging it as Debby looks on silently. Eventually the branch pokes another child in the eye, blinding that child in one eye. Debby can be held liable for the medical and other costs incurred in treating the injured child, since she should have realized what could happen and therefore taken the branch away from Peter.

Can a Minor Child Sue a Parent?

At one time, a minor could not sue his or her parents for injuries the parent inflicted upon the child, even if the parent had acted with a deliberate intent to harm (for example, by throwing boiling water over the child). Today in most states, a minor can sue a parent for injuries resulting from the parent's intentional wrongful acts. Many states also permit the child to sue if he or she is harmed by the parent's negligence (such as a failure to pay attention while driving, which results in a traffic accident). Adult children are generally permitted to sue their parents without any restrictions.

Why would anyone worry about whether a minor child can sue his or her own parents? Mainly because the cost of medical and other treatment is extremely expensive. The question of a minor's right to sue the parents is important because it determines who has to pay for these and other damages. If a minor child has no right to sue the parents, the parents must pay the bills resulting from the negligence—which can run into thousands of dollars—out of their own pocket. But if the law allows the minor to sue the parents, the parents' automobile liability insurance or homeowner's insurance usually covers the injuries. If the insurance company refuses to pay the damages (by claiming that the injury wasn't the parent's fault, for example), the parent can be placed in the unusual situation of encouraging the child to sue him or her for purely economic reasons.

For a minor to file a lawsuit, a guardian ad litem must be appointed by the court to bring the action on behalf of the child.

Guardian ad litem means guardian "for the suit." Usually a parent (but not the one whom the child is suing) or the legal guardian of the child is the guardian ad litem.

Can a minor sue a parent for not supervising him or her adequately—in effect, for not protecting the child from himself or herself? Usually not. For example, suppose that Hal lets his five-year-old daughter Vera play unsupervised on the front lawn. Vera wanders into the middle of a busy street and is struck by a passing car. Vera cannot sue her father for failing to supervise her.

Now suppose that Jerry and his brother Jeff are playing "cowboys and Indians." Using a bow and arrow his mother, Alice, bought him, Jerry shoots Jeff with an arrow, hitting him in the eye. Jeff *can* sue his mother for failing to supervise Jerry. Had a neighbor's child been injured rather than her own, Alice would have been liable, so the law usually makes no distinction between her own child and a neighbor's child in this situation. But if Jerry had shot himself with the arrow, many states would not permit him to sue his mother for failing to supervise him.

If a parent punishes a child and in so doing injures the child, can the child sue the parent? That depends on whether the punishment was reasonable. Parents have the right to discipline their children reasonably. Spanking a child or sending him or her to bed without dinner one night is considered reasonable punishment. But hitting a child so hard that an arm is broken, or depriving a child of food and water for several days is unreasonable. Dipping a child's hand in scalding water is obviously child abuse. When a parent exceeds the bounds of reasonable punishment, not only can the child sue him or her, but the offending parent may be criminally charged as well.

Suits between a Husband and Wife

Not too long ago in the development of our law, you could not sue your spouse for injuries he or she inflicted on you, even if he or she acted intentionally to hurt you. For example, if a wife intentionally shot her husband and injured him, the husband could not bring a civil suit against her. (But it was different if the wife shot and *killed* her husband: besides being criminally responsible for murder and manslaughter, the wife could forfeit all rights to inherit her husband's estate. This remains the law today.)

A majority of states have abolished the old doctrine of "interspousal tort immunity" and now hold that you can sue your spouse both for intentional acts and for ordinary negligence, such as carelessness in the operation of an automobile. A number of states, however, let you sue your spouse for intentional wrongful acts but not for injuries resulting from his or her negligence. As with suits by children against their parents, the question of whether one spouse can sue the other frequently determines who has to foot the bills for hospital and other expenses—you or your insurance company.

Suing a Third Person for Injuries to a Family Member

If a third party (someone who is not a member of the immediate family) injures a family member, the injured person can sue that person to recover damages. If a minor is injured, the parents can recover damages for medical and other expenses they paid to treat the child. If a member of the family is killed by a third person's negligent conduct, the surviving family members can sue that third person for the death. (In some states, the lawsuit must be brought by the *estate* of the deceased person.) The types of damages recoverable in a wrongful death action are governed by state law and usually include such things as lost wages, medical and hospital costs, funeral expenses, and loss of companionship.

If a third person injures your spouse, your spouse can sue for his or her own injuries, and if you witnessed the incident, you can usually sue for your own emotional or psychological injuries, as discussed below. In many cases, you can sue the third party for loss of consortium, which includes such things as comfort, companionship, affection, solace, and sexual relations. When a child is seriously injured, some states permit the parents to bring an action for loss of "filial" consortium, but damages are usually limited to lost wages the child would have earned and other monetary losses. For example, if a boy worked on his parents' farm, and they had to hire someone else to do the boy's job after he was injured or killed by the carelessness of a third person, the parents could recover this expense.

Only a few states permit a child to bring an action for loss of consortium when a parent is severely injured. But if the parent dies, many states allow damages for loss of consortium as part of a lawsuit for the parent's death. For example, suppose that Victor is drunk and runs into Henrietta's car. Henrietta suffers extensive brain damage and becomes a "vegetable." In all but a handful of states, Henrietta's children cannot sue Victor for loss of consortium even though Victor's conduct has effectively deprived them of their mother. Had Victor's conduct resulted in Henrietta's death, many states would have permitted the children to recover damages for loss of consortium as an element of their wrongful death action.

Witnessing Injuries to or Death of a Parent or Spouse

A mother is watching her child play on the front lawn, when a car suddenly jumps the curb and runs over and kills the child. Although she herself was in no danger of being hit by the car, the mother suffers severe emotional shock from witnessing the accident. Without question, a suit can be brought against the driver of the car for the child's wrongful death. But can the mother bring a lawsuit against the driver for her *own* injuries resulting from the emotional trauma?

Many states allow the mother to recover damages from the driver under the doctrine of "bystander recovery." But (1) there must be a close familial relationship (usually limited to husband-wife, parent-child, and siblings) between the victim and the person who witnessed the accident; (2) the person who witnessed the event must have been located near the scene; and (3) the person must have witnessed the actual accident, not merely seen the results or learned about the accident sometime after it happened.

This last requirement has presented the greatest problems for persons seeking to recover damages for their emotional injuries when a loved one is hurt. Minutes, even seconds, become critical in deciding many of these cases. Clearly the mother who sees her child being struck by an automobile is a witness to the accident. But in one case, the parents and their daughter were leaving church services, and the daughter decided to ride home with a friend and the friend's parents. Her parents followed closely behind. As they rounded a curve, the car with their daughter went out of sight for a brief moment. Seconds later the parents found the car off the road, crashed into a tree. Although the parents arrived at the scene "before the dust had settled," they could not recover damages because they had witnessed only the result of the accident, not the accident itself.

Witnessing an accident does not mean you have to *see* it. Hearing an accident or otherwise perceiving what is happening can be sufficient. In one case, a husband who was sitting in the car while his wife was taking groceries out of the trunk was allowed to recover damages for the emotional injuries he sustained when another car ran into the back of his. Although he did not actually see the accident, he knew where his wife was in relation to the other car and realized what was happening to her.

Injuries to or Death of an Unborn Fetus

A fetus injured in the womb by a third party's wrongful act can bring a lawsuit against the wrongdoer for those injuries, but only if the fetus is born alive. For example, Mary is seven months pregnant when she is involved in an automobile accident caused by Tom's carelessness. When the baby is born two months later, it is discovered that the child suffered head injuries and brain damage in the accident. The baby can sue Tom for these injuries.

But suppose that the accident causes Mary to miscarry, and

the fetus is stillborn. Can Mary (and her husband) sue Tom for the wrongful death of the fetus? Not in all states. Some states hold that a fetus, even a *viable* one—one capable of surviving outside the womb (usually starting around the seventh month of pregnancy)—is not yet a "person" under the state's wrongful death statute. If the child is born alive and lives only a few seconds, however, the child is a "person," and the parents can now sue the third person for the child's death.

Birth of a Defective Child

A 38-year-old woman becomes pregnant. Her physician does not inform her of the baby's risk of being born with Down's syndrome, nor does he suggest any diagnostic tests, such as amniocentesis, to see whether the fetus is normal and healthy. The child is born afflicted with Down's syndrome, and the mother claims that if she had been informed of the defective fetus, she would have had it aborted. Or, a Jewish couple of eastern European descent consult a physician to see whether they are carriers of Tay-Sachs disease. The physician erroneously tells them they are not, and the couple decide to have a baby. The baby is born with Tay-Sachs disease, and the couple claim they would never have conceived a baby if they had known they were carriers. In each case, tremendous hospital costs and doctor fees are incurred in treating the child, and other large expenses are paid for care throughout the child's lifetime.

Do the parents have any recourse against the physician? What recourse does the *child* have? These are difficult legal—and moral—questions, as they ask a judge or jury ultimately to weigh the difference in value between being born in a defective condition and not being born at all. Until recently, the courts would not permit a lawsuit against a doctor, hospital, or laboratory in this situation; the reasoning was that the child suffered no damage, since life, even in a seriously defective condition, is better than no life at all.

Lately, however, some courts have permitted the parents

and the child to recover some damages. Only the extraordinary medical expenses and other costs incurred in caring for the child throughout his or her lifetime are usually recoverable. "Extraordinary" expenses are those over and above the costs of raising a normal, healthy baby. Some courts also permit the parents to recover damages for their own emotional distress resulting from the birth of the defective child.

Unsuccessful Sterilization Resulting in the Birth of a Healthy Baby

Jane has given birth to three children already and decides that is enough. After the birth of the third child, she has her tubes tied. Eight months later, however, she discovers she is again pregnant and later gives birth to a healthy baby boy. Can Jane sue the doctor for negligence in performing the sterilization procedure, even though the baby was born healthy and normal?

A number of states permit the parents to bring a suit in such a situation. But the damages the parents can get are usually limited to the costs of the unsuccessful sterilization operation, the mother's pain and suffering during the pregnancy and birth, any medical complications she suffered, and the mother's lost wages. The costs and expenses of raising the child usually are not allowed. In the few states that do allow the costs of rearing the child, the damages are offset by any benefits the parents receive from the child's aid, companionship, and comfort. In those states which allow this type of action, a lawsuit can be filed on behalf of the child to recover extraordinary medical expenses. Care is taken to ensure that both the child and the parents do not each receive compensation for the same expenses.

Unlike a child who is born in a defective or impaired condition, a child who is born healthy generally cannot bring a suit against the physician based on negligence in the performance of a sterilization procedure.

Living Together

Millions of couples are choosing to live together without benefit of marriage. Before the famous *Marvin* case, the law generally took a hands-off approach to those who "lived in sin." A woman could live with a man for 25 years, bear him two children, raise them and keep house during that entire time, but if one day he told her to leave, there wasn't a thing she could do about it if she knew they had never been married. If title to the house, the car, and other assets was in the man's name, the woman generally would have no claim to any part of it.

Things were better if the woman had an honest belief they were legally married but for some reason the marriage wasn't valid. For instance, the woman may not have known that the man was already married to someone else. Or the person who performed the marriage ceremony may not have had the legal authority to do so. In such situations, the law has always protected the innocent "wife."

The Marvin Case

In 1976, a new era in the treatment of unmarried couples was ushered in with the decision in the case of *Marvin v. Marvin*. In that case, Michelle Triola Marvin claimed that she had given up her career as an entertainer and singer to live with actor Lee Marvin for some seven years. Michelle asserted that in return for this, Lee orally promised that they would combine their efforts and earnings, and they would share equally all property they accumulated. Michelle also claimed that Lee had agreed to provide for all of her financial support and needs for the rest of her life if she gave up her promising career to devote herself to him full time as companion and homemaker.

In the *Marvin* case, the Supreme Court of California ruled that an express contract—one in writing and signed by both parties—between unmarried couples is enforceable, except to the extent that it is based on the performance of sexual services. (To allow a person to collect on a contract essentially for the performance of sexual acts would be tantamount to endorsing prostitution.) In the absence of an express contract, an oral agreement or tacit understanding regarding the property can be demonstrated by the parties' conduct. Even if no such understanding can be shown, one partner can still sue the other for the reasonable value of household services he or she rendered—less the value of any support received—if he or she performed those services in expectation of monetary reward.

Following the *Marvin* decision, a rash of so-called "palimony" suits have been filed, some by the famous and wealthy, more by the not-so-famous and not-as-wealthy. These cases, mind you, are not being tried under traditional family law principles of marriage and divorce but rather upon contract theories. Sometimes there is an express contract that sets forth the rights and obligations of each partner. More frequently, however, one partner alleges that the other partner stated that all property and money acquired during the relationship would belong equally to both partners, or that one would take care of the other for life. Some of these cases based on an implied contract have been successful. More have been unsuccessful because of the difficulty of proving the agreement. And not all states have agreed with the *Marvin* decision.

Get It in Writing

If you are planning on getting into (or staying in) a relationship based upon your partner's assurances that he or she will "take care of you" or will split everything he or she makes with you, get it in writing and signed by your partner. Proving an oral contract of this sort is difficult, to say the least. The courts are aware of the potential for fraudulent claims and want some hard proof that there was in fact an agreement. Without a written document, the chances that you will win your case diminish greatly.

What should you do if your partner refuses to put the agreement in writing, perhaps telling you that there's nothing to worry about, that he or she won't go back on what was agreed? Think seriously about getting out of the relationship now. Putting a signature on a piece of paper is not an arduous task. If your partner refuses to do it, consider yourself on notice that, should disharmony develop and the two of you split, he or she will likely assert that no agreement to share money or property was ever made.

The agreement should be prepared by an attorney experienced in family law, one who can anticipate the types of problems likely to arise and who can protect you accordingly in the agreement. As with premarital contracts, you and your partner should be represented by separate attorneys. This will reduce the chances that either person will succeed later in claiming that the other took an unfair advantage or that he or she did not really understand what the agreement said.

Buying a House Together

An unmarried couple (or even friends) who are living together may decide to buy a house together for tax or investment purposes. Before you buy the house, both of you should sign a written agreement that spells out what percentage each of you is to pay toward the down payment, monthly mortgage payments, property taxes, and insurance, and how the proceeds will be divided when the house is sold. (It's not a bad idea to have a lawyer prepare the agreement.) If you plan to live in the house, the agreement should also specify what rights each of you has if the other moves out. What happens, for example, if you are transferred out of state or find it impossible to continue living with the other person? Some provision should be made to give one person the right to buy out the other at the fair market value or to sell or rent his or her share of the property.

If you are buying a house with someone, it is important to consider how you should hold title to the property. Title to real estate is discussed in detail in chapter 5; however, briefly—if title is in only one person's name, that person can usually sell it whenever he or she pleases. If that person dies, the house goes to the person designated in his or her will, and if there is no will, to the next of kin (see chapter 3). If the property is in the names of both of you as joint tenants, the house automatically goes to whichever of you is the survivor. A provision in a will has no effect on property held in joint tenancy. If title is taken as tenants in common, then upon the death of either owner, only his or her interest in the house is distributed according to the provisions of his or her will or, if there is none, to his or her next of kin. Holding title as tenants in common is usually recommended in this situation.

Injuries, Death, and Unmarried Couples

When one partner in a nonmarital relationship is injured or killed by a third person, the surviving partner generally does not have the right to sue the third person. If a partner dies without a will, the survivor ordinarily has no claim to any part of the estate. If one partner injures a third person, the other partner usually isn't liable for those injuries, unless the property (such as a car) that injured the person was owned by the other partner, or one partner was an employee or business partner of the other, and the injury arose in the course of their business.

Gay Relationships

We noted earlier that a marriage can exist only between members of the opposite sex. If members of the same sex get "married," their marriage is void from the outset and need not be terminated by divorce, since a marriage never existed. If a partner to a gay "marriage" later decides to marry a member of the opposite sex, it is usually not necessary to obtain a "divorce," and he or she can marry without fear of being guilty of bigamy.

Since gays do not acquire any rights under traditional family law concepts of marriage, the rights and obligations when a gay relationship ends must be based on a contract theory of the type found in the *Marvin v. Marvin* situations discussed above. But a court might refuse to enforce the agreement because of some abstract "public policy" argument that the law should not interfere with gay relationships. There is no legal reason why a court should permit a *Marvin* action between unmarried persons of opposite sexes but not allow such an action between partners of the same sex. In neither relationship can the contract be based upon the performance of sexual services. Rather, it is giving up certain rights, such as the right to pursue one's own career to its fullest, and performing household work and other chores that serve as the legitimate legal "consideration" to make the contract binding and enforceable. Still, gays must realize that not all states agree with the *Marvin* decision, and even some courts that allow a *Marvin*-type action for unmarried cohabitants of the opposite sex may not allow such an action between gay couples.

Gays who are living together or buying a house or other property together should have a written agreement (preferably drawn up by a lawyer) fully setting forth the rights and responsibilities of each partner. If one partner in the relationship had substantial assets before the relationship began, the agreement should identify such assets in detail to prevent the other partner from claiming at a later date that the property was acquired with earnings of both partners after they began living together.

As with unmarried heterosexual partners, a gay person usually is not liable for injuries his or her partner inflicts on a third person. If, however, a gay causes an accident while driving a car owned by his or her partner, the partner may be held liable under the "permissive use" statute (see chapter 2) relating to the operation of a motor vehicle. Liability could also be imposed if the wrongdoer was acting at the request of or working as an employee of the partner. If one partner in a gay relationship is injured or killed by another person's wrongful act, the other partner generally does not have any right to bring a lawsuit against the third person. And if one gay partner dies without a will, the other partner usually cannot make a claim against the estate as a spouse, heir, or next of kin.

Changing Your Name

Some people change their names because they have been the butt of tasteless jokes or ridicule. Others change their names because of divorce or fallings-out with family. Many immigrants change their names because of the difficulty Americans have pronouncing or spelling foreign names. At one point in our history, immigration officials arbitrarily changed the names of many immigrants upon their arrival. Applications for United States citizenship still provide space for a name change if the applicant wishes it.

You are free to use any name you want, as long as you don't use the name for a fraudulent purpose, to confuse, or to invade someone's privacy. When one man applied to change his name to "Peter Lorre," the judge found that he only intended to cash in on the reputation of the famous movie star and therefore denied the application. Another man tried for several years to have his name changed to "God" but was repeatedly turned down because of the confusion the name might cause. He was eventually successful when he applied to change his name to "Ubiquitous Perpetuity God."

Although a person's name usually consists of a given name and a surname or family name, in some states, there is no steadfast legal requirement that you have at least a first and a last name. A number of people have legally changed to just one name.

A "name" is legally defined as "the distinctive characterization in *words* by which a person is known and distinguished from others." Several courts have refused to approve a change to a name consisting solely of numbers. For example, in 1976, the Supreme Court of North Dakota rejected Michael Herbert Dengler's petition to change his name to the arabic numerals "1069." Mr. Dengler then applied to a Minnesota court to so change his name, but in 1979, the Supreme Court of Minnesota also denied his request, on the basis that the number was not a "name." A similar result was reached in California in the case of Thomas Boyd Ritchie, III, who wished to change his name to the Roman numeral "III," pronounced "three." If Mr. Ritchie had decided to change his name to "Three," the judge quite possibly would have granted his petition.

How to Change Your Name

Most people believe that a legal proceeding is necessary to change your name, but this is not true. The law has long recognized the right to change your name without legal proceedings. For example, Marsha Bonnet can change her name to Alice Jackson simply by referring to herself by that name and changing her driver's license, credit cards, Social Security identification card, and other documents. As a practical matter, though, many financial institutions and other agencies will not recognize the new name unless it is approved by a judge.

To have a judge change your name, you need to file a petition with the court. The petition must state your current name, age, and address, the name you want to change to, and the reason for the change. Ordinarily you must publish your request for a name change in the newspaper (the court clerk can instruct you how to go about this). There will be a court hearing at which the judge will ask whether anyone has any objections to your name change. If there are none (and there usually aren't), the judge routinely grants the name change. About the only time a judge will refuse a name change when there is no objection is if the new name is obscene or utterly absurd. But a somewhat bizarre or humorous choice of name will not ordinarily prevent a judge from approving the change.

Changing Your Name after Marriage or Divorce

When a woman marries, her last name does not immediately and automatically become that of her husband. Rather, the woman voluntarily chooses to assume the last name of her husband, and continued usage of that name brings about the change. She changes her driver's license, Social Security number, and other identification to reflect the new name. Of course, it is generally not necessary for her to assume her husband's last name. Many women decide to retain their maiden name for a variety of reasons. Others combine the two last names by using a hyphen. For example, after Cindy Jones marries Joe Smith, she calls herself Cindy Jones-Smith. This is perfectly legal and doesn't require court approval.

Many married women wish to go back to their maiden name after they are divorced. This can be accomplished in several ways. One is simply to insert a provision in the divorce decree restoring the wife's maiden name. Another way is to go through a formal name change application. Or a woman can change back to her maiden name simply by using it again (just as she took her husband's last name merely by using it) and changing her driver's license, credit cards, and so on back to her old name.

Changing the Names of Children

By custom, children born of a marriage take their father's last name. On the other hand, children born out of wedlock have customarily assumed the surname of their mother. The mother may, however, choose to use the biological father's last name as the child's surname.

Upon divorce, the children keep the last name of the father (if they have been using that name until then), even if the mother has legal custody. The mother cannot change the last name of the children without court approval, which is usually granted only if the father has essentially abandoned the children or otherwise demonstrated absolutely no interest in maintaining contact with the children.

Other reasons may compel a child's name change. For example, if the father is convicted of murder in a highly publicized trial, a judge will approve a name change to protect the children from the stigma their last name may carry. Names of children can be changed only if the father is notified of the requested change so he can appear at the court hearing if he wants to challenge it. If the father is nowhere to be found, the judge will permit the mother to notify him by publishing the hearing date and all pertinent information in a local newspaper.

AUTOMOBILES

NO SINGLE PRODUCT has had more impact on the law than the automobile. Hundreds of thousands of automobiles are purchased each year and driven billions of miles. Thousands of Americans are killed or injured each year in automobile accidents, and many more are charged with various traffic offenses ranging from illegal parking to drunk driving to vehicular manslaughter. These and other topics are the subject of this chapter.

Some of the advice in this chapter may not appear on the surface to be what you might technically call legal advice—tips about getting the best price on a new or used car, for instance, or on avoiding being ripped off by a repair shop. On a deeper level, though, this same material contains the best type of counsel: preventive legal advice. By following the suggestions in this chapter, you'll have a much better chance of later avoiding a messy—and costly—legal dispute.

Buying a New Car

Next to buying a house, purchasing an automobile is the largest expense in the lives of most Americans. Several things besides the price should be considered in the purchase of every automobile. Probably the single most important factor is safety. The safer the construction of the car, the better your chances of surviving an accident, and with fewer serious injuries. Before buying a particular make and model of car, find out how safe it is by consulting car magazines or publications of consumer interest groups, which can be found in your local library. Your insurance agent can also give you valuable information about which cars generally are safer than others.

Many safety defects have been found in popular makes of cars. Because of the gas tank placement and design of some cars, for example, the fuel tank may explode when the vehicle is rear-ended by another car. Some cars and trucks have automatic transmissions that may slip from park into reverse, resulting in death or injury to a person passing behind or working under the car. Other vehicles have a higher center of gravity, which makes them more likely to roll over, and some lack the strength to protect the occupants if the car lands upside down.

Besides the safety factors of the car, you will also want to find out the costs of operating and maintaining it. The insurance rates for cars can vary drastically for vehicles costing about the same price. A two-seat, convertible sports car, for instance, will have a higher insurance rate than a four-door family sedan. The gas mileage you can expect from the car also affects operating costs. Don't rely too heavily on the EPA test results, as these invariably are considerably higher than the mileage your car will actually get. Also consider routine maintenance in figuring your ultimate costs.

Getting the Best Price

Federal law requires the dealer to place on each new vehicle offered for sale a schedule showing the make and model of the vehicle, the manufacturer's suggested retail price for the base model, every item of optional equipment, and the dealer's charge for transportation. Many dealers will add an additional amount on top of the manufacturer's suggested price, especially if the model of car is popular. Keep in mind that the sticker price on the car is ordinarily the starting point for negotiations. It is up to you to take it from there and get the lowest price you can.

Advice about getting the lowest price from a car dealer abounds, but the most important point to remember is always to shop around first. Some say the best time to buy is when business is slow, such as on a rainy day, during Christmas time, or at the end of the month, when the sales force is trying to meet quotas. Others suggest that you take care of the financing *before* you buy the car. Although car manufacturers may offer interest rates that are lower than those offered by banks, you'll usually make up the difference by paying a little more for the car. Many banks will preapprove a loan up to a certain amount, so you can negotiate for the best cash price from the dealer. Especially attractive financing rates offered by dealers often require a larger down payment and a shorter time for repayment—with a corresponding increase in the amount of the monthly payment—than a bank loan. Compare bank and dealer loans to see which one your budget can handle better.

Does this sound familiar: A salesperson entices you by quoting a good price for the car you want. You are then taken to the office of the sales manager, who tells you that the salesperson had no authority to make such an offer. (Car dealers generally do not give their salespeople the legal authority to enter into any contracts on behalf of the dealership; usually only the sales manager can commit the dealer to selling a certain car at a certain price.) The sales manager then raises the price hundreds of dollars over what the salesperson quoted. Sales managers prey on people who have fallen in love with a particular car, people who let their emotions take charge and already see themselves driving home in their dream car. If this happens to you, offer to pay the price the salesperson quoted you earlier. Tell the sales manager to "take it or leave it." If your offer is refused, show them that you can live without the car—leave the office. You will be surprised at how quickly the sales manager and salesperson will follow you out and come down in price. If they let you go, they'll probably give you a call a day or two later, offering to split the difference. If they don't, don't worry about it. Don't fall for the old "You'll never find another one like it" ploy. Chances are you will find a car that is just as good for a better price somewhere else.

Beware of Illegal Practices

Here are some illegal practices to watch out for: A dealer cannot advertise a car for sale if he or she doesn't have it, unless it is a new car, and the ad states that delivery of the advertised vehicle has been promised by the manufacturer on or before a certain date. An automobile dealer cannot advertise one car, then substitute another. This is the old "bait and switch" game; you are lured to the lot with an extraordinarily good buy, but when you get there, the dealer switches to an older vehicle or one with fewer options than advertised (for the same price, of course) or substitutes another car at a higher price. The dealer must also tell you if a new car has been damaged, repaired, or repainted before you buy it. If you suspect a dealer of any illegal or fraudulent practices, contact the fraud division of the police or district attorney, your state's consumer affairs department, and the Better Business Bureau. You may also want to contact a lawyer to take action on your behalf against the car dealer.

The Purchase Contract

An agreement to purchase an automobile is a contract and must meet certain requirements to be enforceable. There must be an offer to purchase the vehicle, an acceptance of that offer, and something of value ("consideration") given by each side—usually money in exchange for a car. See chapter 13 for a full discussion of making a contract.

Thoroughly inspect and test-drive the car before you sign on the dotted line and give the dealer your money. If there are any problems with the car, have them fixed before you sign the contract. Unless the defect is minor, don't be talked into paying now and bringing the car back later. You have a lot more leverage before you hand over your check, so use it to the utmost advantage.

You usually make an offer to buy the car when you sign a purchase order or similar document. Sometimes the purchase contract is disguised and given a seemingly innocuous title. Read all papers carefully, and don't sign anything that refers to you as the purchaser or says "My offer is $ _____ " unless you are prepared to buy the car. If you're not ready to buy the car, the best advice is not to sign anything. If the salesperson tells you that the paper you are supposed to sign isn't a binding contract, respond that if it's not binding, then there's no need to sign it.

The purchase order normally contains words to the effect that your offer is not accepted and a binding contract not made until it is signed by the dealer or the dealer's authorized representative (usually the sales manager). The Statute of Frauds requires that if the price for the car is over $500 (less in some states), the agreement must be in writing to be enforceable. This means that if the dealer orally agrees to sell you a car for a certain price, you might not be able to force him or her to sell you the car at the stated price if you don't get the agreement in writing.

The purchase order should specify the make, model, and year of the car, as well as the engine type and the vehicle identification number. All options should be listed: air conditioning, power windows, tinted glass, AM-FM stereo radio with cassette player, special wheels or tires, and so forth. A complete description of the car and optional equipment is necessary to prevent the dealer from getting away with a fraudulent or deceptive practice, such as telling you that certain optional equipment has been added when in fact it hasn't, that a used car is a new car or an older model is a newer model, or that a certain engine is in the car when a different engine is actually there.

If the dealer has made any oral representations, such as stating that he or she will install a certain accessory after the sale without charging you for it, this too should be included in the purchase order. Do not sign the purchase order until you are completely sure that everything—repeat, *everything*—has been put in writing and is included in the purchase order. If the dealer refuses to put something in writing or tells you not to worry, that is precisely the time to start worrying.

The purchase order should, of course, state the price of the vehicle, the names of the parties involved in the transaction, and whether the car is to be financed by the dealer or manufacturer. If the dealer or manufacturer will be financing the car, then the purchase order must comply with federal Truth in Lending laws concerning disclosure of the amount financed, annual percentage rate, length of the loan, and total amount of interest to be paid. (Truth in Lending laws and financing in general are discussed in more detail in chapter 14.)

Ordering a New Car

Sometimes you find that the cars on the dealer's lot are not exactly what you had in mind. You like the car as equipped, but you want it in another color. Or you want it with air conditioning or without cruise control. If you can't find the car with just the right equipment and in the right color, you may wish to order a "custom-built" car from the factory through the dealer. (Factory orders are usually available only for American-made cars.) As with buying a new car off the lot, the order form should specify the make, model, and year of the vehicle, engine type, complete list of options, price, delivery date, and other pertinent information. (The vehicle identification number cannot be included since the number isn't assigned until the car is built.)

The dealer usually reserves the right to adjust the price you have agreed upon to cover any additional costs in manufacturing or transporting the car. You should insist upon a reciprocal right to cancel the contract if there is an increase in the price. You don't want to pay $8,000 for the same car you thought was only going to cost $6,500 when you ordered it. If the dealer raises the price because of alleged increases in his or her cost, ask for cold, hard proof of exactly what those increases were. The dealer should merely be passing on additional costs, not making a higher profit off you. You might also include a provision stating that if the dealer's cost for the car goes down (because of, say, a new rebate program or other factory incentive), this savings should be passed on to you.

If you are planning to trade in your old car, have the dealer appraise it and include in the order the amount he or she is willing to give you for it at that time. The dealer will ordinarily reserve the right to reappraise your trade-in when you take delivery of the new car. Your car could be damaged between the time you order your new car and the time you pick it up, and you, not the dealer, assume this risk. If you have driven your car only a few more miles, and no damage has occurred or mechanical problems have arisen, the dealer should give you the same amount quoted earlier. If there is no appreciable difference in the condition of the car since the dealer first appraised it, but he or she tries to reduce the price, the dealer may be guilty of a deceptive or fraudulent practice. You may wish to discuss the matter with an attorney or report your suspicions to the police or district attorney fraud division, the state consumer affairs board, or the Better Business Bureau.

When you order a car, expect to pay a certain percentage of the purchase price as a down payment if you're not trading in your old car. When the car is delivered, you are required to pay the remainder of the purchase price in cash or by cashier's check, unless you have informed the dealer that you will be financing the purchase through the dealer's lender (such as General Motors Automobile Credit). If the dealer agrees, you can use a regular check to pay off the balance. The purchase is contingent upon the bank honoring the check, however. If the bank refuses to honor the check (for example, you are overdrawn), and you are unable to make good on it or obtain financing quickly, the dealer can repossess the car and recover from you damages for the decreased value of the car, as well as other costs, including the costs of repossessing the car and reasonable attorney's fees incurred by the dealer.

When you are ordering a car, the purchase order should include the approximate delivery date. If the car is not delivered within a reasonable time after it is due, you may have the right to cancel the order and recover any damages from the dealer. If the dealer can't give you any estimate as to when the car will be ready, have him or her call the factory and find out. If the dealer knowingly misrepresents the amount of time it will take to deliver the car (telling you it will be two weeks when he or she knows it will take at least four months, or vice versa), not only will you be able to cancel the deal; you may also be able to sue the dealer for fraud.

If the dealer doesn't deliver the car on the agreed date or within a reasonable time after that, he or she is in breach of the contract. Most form contracts used by dealers contain an escape clause that excuses the dealer if the manufacturer fails to build or ship the car as ordered. If the order form contains such a clause, you are usually limited to the recovery of your down payment. In determining what your rights are, carefully study the contract or consult an attorney.

Suppose that the car you ordered arrives on time, but it is not quite what you wanted or there is a defect. Are you obligated to accept it? No. If the car does not comply exactly with the specifications contained in the order form or is defective in any way, you can reject it. But you ordinarily must reject the car at the time it is delivered (that is, when you go to pick it up). If, for example, the car is light brown instead of medium blue, you can reject it on the spot. But if you take it home, you have waived the discrepancy and accepted the car, since the difference in color was obvious.

If the radio, air conditioning, or another feature doesn't work, you are free to reject the car. The dealer, however, usually has a corresponding right to cure the defect (in other words, repair it) within a reasonable time—say, 30 days. If the defect is minor and promptly repaired by the dealer, and the car is sound in all other respects, then you must take the car.

New Car Warranties

When you buy a new car, you get a standard manufacturer's warranty of some kind. Examples of a manufacturer's warranty are a one-year or 12,000-mile guarantee against defects in products or workmanship for most items, a two-year or 20,000-mile power train warranty, and a five-year or 50,000-mile rust protection guarantee. This type of guarantee is called an express warranty and is usually found in the purchase contract or the owner's manual. Except for warranties imposed by law (discussed below), the manufacturer's and dealer's obligations are limited by the wording of this warranty.

There are other ways express warranties are created. For instance, the manufacturer or dealer may tell you that a certain engine is in the car, such as a V-8. If it turns out the engine is only a V-6, the manufacturer or dealer has breached the express warranty. Another common way an express warranty is created is through the manufacturer's or dealer's advertising. For instance, an ad may boast that the car can go from 0 to 60 miles per hour in 8.5 seconds or is capable of pulling a heavy boat. What are your rights when you discover that it takes the car 12 seconds to get to 60, or the only way the car can pull your boat is by going downhill? If you saw the ad before you bought the vehicle, and the ad's depiction of what the car could do was an important factor in your decision to buy it, you've got a good chance of getting your money back. But note well: just as soon as you discover the car isn't as advertised, contact the dealer and manufacturer, inform them of the problem, and demand your money back. Always send a letter to both the manufacturer and the dealer describing the warranty made, by whom and when it was made, and how the car differs from the warranty. If you don't get immediate satisfaction, seriously consider hiring an attorney to assist you. If you fail to notify the dealer and manufacturer promptly and continue using the car, you may lose your right to enforce this warranty.

If the dealer makes a specific warranty about the vehicle, its equipment, its condition, or its performance, get it in writing and see that it is incorporated into the purchase contract before you buy. If the dealer is unwilling to put this in writing, think twice about buying the car. Failure to include the warranty in the purchase contract could result in the loss of the warranty.

In addition to the manufacturer's express warranty, the law imposes certain warranties in the sale of a new car, even if the purchase contract or manufacturer's warranty doesn't mention them. All states except Louisiana imply a warranty that a new car is of "good and average quality" and that it can be operated on the streets and highways in its intended manner with reasonable safety. This is called the implied warranty of merchantability. "Lemon" laws (discussed below) are another type of warranty imposed by law. Frequently the manufacturer's express warranty states that it supersedes all other warranties, including those implied by law. Many states limit the manufacturer's right to restrict or disclaim warranties that are implied by law. Lemon laws in particular usually cannot be disclaimed or limited by the manufacturer, nor can the consumer waive them.

If Your Dream Car Turns Out to Be a "Lemon"

Not too long ago, if you bought a new car that turned out to be a "lemon," your rights against the automobile dealer were quite limited. The dealer was given an almost infinite number of chances to repair the car. Your only recourse was to retain a lawyer and file a lawsuit against the dealer. This was costly and frequently lengthy procedure, and your chances for success were not very good. And even if you did win, you usually could not recover your attorney's fees from the dealer unless the purchase contract permitted it. Many people were discouraged from pursuing their legal rights against the dealer for fear that it would cost more to hire the lawyer than it did to buy the car.

Today, about two-thirds of the states and the District of Columbia have passed so-called lemon laws, and many of the remaining states are studying such laws. Also important, especially in those states that don't have lemon laws, is the federal Magnuson-Moss Act, which lets you sue in state court for the breach of an express or implied warranty involving a consumer product. Although at first consumers weren't winning many cases under lemon laws, that trend is changing. Today more and more consumers are succeeding with their lawsuits against manufacturers and dealers.

Under a typical lemon law, the manufacturer is required either to replace the car (or light truck) or refund your money if a major defect in the car has not been repaired after four tries or if the car has spent a cumulative total of 30 days in the shop being repaired for the same defect during the first year or for the first 12,000 miles you own the car (whichever comes earlier). (In a few states, the lemon law covers the earlier of two years or 18,000 miles.) Some states have slightly different requirements concerning the number of days the car must be in the shop or the number of tries the dealer has at repairing it. For example, in Florida, the manufacturer must replace the car or refund your money if the car has not been repaired in three attempts or has spent a cumulative total of 15 days in the shop. Some states use business days to determine how long your car was in the shop, while others base it on calendar days.

In addition to the price you paid for the car, you can generally also seek reimbursement for other expenses, such as the costs of registering the car, sales tax, license fees, and dealer preparation. Several states also let you recover additional expenses, such as towing the lemon and renting another car while the lemon is being repaired. On the other hand, the manufacturer can usually deduct from the refund a reasonable charge for your use of the car—for example, so many cents a mile. If, for instance, you drove the car 8,500 miles, and the dealer is allowed to deduct ten cents a mile, your refund would be reduced by $850.

If the defect occurs during the warranty period, and you give the manufacturer written notice before the time limit expires, the manufacturer must repair or replace the defective part, even if, for any reason, the repair itself is made after the warranty expires.

For example, if something goes wrong during the last week of the warranty period, and you immediately notify the manufacturer in writing, the manufacturer must make the repair even though the car is not brought in until several days after the warranty has expired.

Your chances of winning your case improve significantly with the amount of documentation that you have to back up your claims of what the problem was, your efforts to resolve it with the dealer or manufacturer, and the number of times and the dates the car was in the shop. Each time you take the car in, get a copy of the work order showing the date the vehicle was brought in and the problem complained of. When you pick up the car, get another copy of the work order showing the work done and the date you got the car back. All conversations with the manager or employees of the manufacturer or dealer should be summarized in letters to the manufacturer or dealer.

Before the warranty period is over, send a letter to both the manufacturer and dealer detailing the problem and the attempts to fix it. This letter should contain such basic information as the make, model, and year of the car, vehicle identification number, and date purchased, as well as a description of the defect, the number of times and days (including the specific dates) the car has been in the shop, and copies of any repair invoices, along with a statement that the defect has not been corrected. Send the letter by certified mail, return receipt requested.

Most states require you to arbitrate the dispute before you can sue the manufacturer. Section 703 of the Magnuson-Moss Act requires the arbitrator to make a decision within 40 days after you file for arbitration. Two American automobile manufacturers—Ford and Chrysler—have set up arbitration boards of their own. General Motors and American Motors, as well as Honda, Volkswagen, Nissan, Porsche, and several other foreign car makers, contract their arbitration out to the local Better Business Bureau. Other foreign car makers avail themselves of Autocap, a program of the National Automobile Dealers Association. In several states, you have the option of using a state-run arbitration program. Information on arbitration requirements can be obtained from the Better Business Bureau, the state department of consumer affairs, or the car manufacturer or dealer.

When it becomes evident that your car probably will never be fixed properly, you should hire a lawyer experienced in lemon law disputes to represent you. You can find a lawyer who specializes in such cases by calling your local trial lawyers association or by checking the yellow pages. Some lawyers require you to pay by the hour as the case goes along. Others will agree to a smaller up-front retainer, then prosecute the case and try to collect attorney's fees from the manufacturer if and when the case is won. Some state lemon laws permit the judge to award attorney's fees if you win, and the federal Magnuson-Moss Act also gives the judge this discretion.

Buying and Selling Used Cars

Buying or selling a used car generally involves a whole different set of rules from those involved in buying or selling a new car. As far as used vehicles go, the law is still pretty much caveat emptor—buyer beware.

While a rose is a rose is a rose, the same is not true of a used car. What is considered a used car in one state can be a new car in another. Some states define a used car as one that has been driven farther than is reasonably necessary to road test or deliver a new car to the buyer. Cars used for demonstration, rental, or the transportation of automobile manufacturers, dealers, and their employees are considered used cars under this standard. Other states define a new car as one whose title has never been transferred to the ultimate purchaser. By this definition, a dealer's demonstrator would be a new car, despite considerable mileage. Still other states define a used car as one that "has beeen so used as to have become what is commonly known as 'secondhand' within the ordinary meaning thereof." The difference between a new and a used car becomes significant in determining what warranties apply. For instance, a consumer in one state who buys a demonstrator car is protected by the more stringent new-car warranties, while a consumer in another state who buys a demonstrator is protected only by used-car warranties.

Used-Car Warranties

As with a new car, the seller of a used car can make an express warranty as to the condition of the car or the optional equipment included with the vehicle. This express warranty can be either oral or written, but it is always best to get it in writing. An oral warranty is always harder to prove than a written one, so don't take any chances.

When a dealer sells a used car, most states impose the implied warranty that the car is merchantable—that it is reasonably safe for ordinary driving. For example, the steering wheel must turn the tires, and the brakes must stop the car. No such warranty is imposed upon a private party who sells his or her car. When a private party sells a used car, the buyer generally takes the car in its present condition and has no recourse against the seller if the car falls apart a block down the road.

This brings up the question of how a "dealer" in used cars is defined. A dealer is one who is regularly engaged in the business of selling used cars. Obvious examples of used-car dealers are the dealership that sells new and used cars and "Honest Bob's Used-Car Lot." In some states, used-car dealers include banks or insurance companies that sell repossessed or damaged cars, rental agencies that sell their used cars, and auctioneers. Some states define a dealer as one who has an established place of business and sells a certain number of cars each year.

Federal law requires used-car dealers to place a window sticker on every used car indicating whether any warranties are given with the car. If the car is sold "as is"—without a warranty—that fact must be clearly shown on the sticker. If a warranty is given, the dealer must state whether it is a full or limited warranty, the systems covered, the length of the warranty, and what percent of the costs for labor and parts the dealer will pay. Before buying a used car with a limited warranty, carefully read all of the warranty information on the window sticker to see just how limited the warranty is. Some warranties are so limited, they really don't cover a thing.

In many states, the dealer can disclaim the implied warranty of merchantability with appropriate language that is conspicuous—that is, it clearly stands out from the rest of the terms (through boldface or larger type, for example). A few states, including Kansas, Maryland, Massachusetts, Mississippi, and West Virginia, do not allow a seller of used cars to disclaim this implied warranty.

New York has a used-car "lemon law" that applies to dealers and that the dealer cannot disclaim or the consumer waive. This warranty covers certain parts—among them, the engine, radiator, drive axle, transmission, steering, and brakes—for 60 days or 3,000 miles if the car has 36,000 miles or less on it, or for 30 days or 1,000 miles if the vehicle has more than 36,000 miles. If a covered part fails during the warranty period, the used-car dealer must repair or replace it at the dealer's expense, refund the consumer's money, or take other action at no extra charge to the consumer. The warranty applies only to vehicles selling for at least $1,500 and does not cover certain types of vehicles, including motorcycles, motor homes, classic cars, and off-road vehicles.

Many dealers offer an optional used-car warranty. Before buying such a warranty, read it carefully to see what it covers and for how long. You may find that only a few things are covered— the things least likely to fail. Some dealers charge an exorbitant amount of money for an extremely limited warranty. Before buying the car and the warranty, you should go to another dealership that handles used cars and ask to see the warranties it offers and find out what they cost. Also consider whether the place you're buying the car will be in business next week or next year. An extended warranty is worthless if no one's going to be there to honor it when you have a problem.

Protecting Yourself When Buying a Used Car

Before buying a used car, first find out whether the car is being offered at a reasonable price. One way of doing this is simply to look through the classified ads in your local paper to see what comparably equipped vehicles for the same year and in a similar condition are going for. Another way is to find out the *Kelley Blue Book* price for the car. The *Blue Book* is the price schedule the automobile industry uses to set guidelines for wholesale and retail prices. You can get the *Blue Book* price by calling either your insurance agent or, particularly if you plan on financing the car, the bank. Alternatively, if you plan to buy the car from a dealer, you can simply ask the dealer to show you the *Blue Book* price. Many libraries have the *National Automobile Dealers Association's Official Used Car Guide*, which many dealers use to set prices. These publications are updated monthly, so make sure that you consult the latest edition. In comparing the guide's price to the price of the car you are considering buying, take into account the overall condition of the car, the mileage, and the optional equipment. Such factors can add or subtract hundreds of dollars from the average selling price.

In addition to satisfying yourself that the price is fair, have the car thoroughly checked out by a competent mechanic not affiliated with the dealer who is selling the car. Remember that the burden is on you to check out the car thoroughly before purchasing it. The person selling the car usually doesn't have to disclose any defects that he or she knows about. Ask your mechanic if there are any known problems with this particular make, model, and year of car, such as a propensity for the engine or transmission to fall apart after so many miles. Check with another dealer or in consumer publications to find out whether the model of car in question has ever been recalled for the repair of any defects. If there has been a recall, find out if the car you are interested in was repaired.

If the seller tells you that certain repairs have been made to the car, such as the installation of a new clutch or new transmission, ask to see the receipts, and get copies of them. In reviewing the receipts, make sure that they apply to the car in question and not some other car. Get the receipts before you have your mechanic check the car out, so that the mechanic can see if the repairs were in fact done. (Perhaps the seller was ripped off by an unscrupulous repair shop!) If the seller doesn't have any receipts or work orders to show, ask that the information be included in the written purchase contract.

When buying a used car, keep an eye open for the possibility that the odometer has been turned back or was disconnected for a while. Another twist: the seller may state that the car has only 50,000 miles on it, when in fact it has 150,000 miles; in both cases, of course, the odometer will show only 50,000. (Some foreign cars do have the extra digit on the odometer and would show 150,000 miles.) Always check the car out to see if the wear and tear on the car is consistent with the mileage reading on the odometer, and have your mechanic do the same. If there is any doubt, you should assume the worst—that the car has extremely high mileage.

If the seller misrepresents the mileage on the car, the damages the buyer can recover are the costs of any repairs made because of the higher mileage, or the difference in value between the car as represented—say, as having only 25,000 miles—and the value of the car as it really is—say, 75,000 miles. Under federal law, any person who alters or disconnects the odometer with intent to defraud is liable for $1,500 or triple the buyer's damages (whichever is greater) and reasonable attorney's fees incurred by the buyer. A person who deliberately tampers with an odometer may also be guilty of a federal or state crime.

When looking for a used car in the classified ads, you will probably see some ads seeking someone to "assume monthly payments." If the seller of the car is a bank or leasing company, the car was probably repossessed, and there's no problem with assuming the payments. But if the seller is a private party, there are a few things to think about. Does the bank know about the intended transfer, and if so, does it agree to have you assume payments? Usually banks will not permit car loans to be assumed. Rather, they will refinance the whole thing, and only if you meet their usual credit requirements. A lease normally cannot be assumed until the leasing company checks out your credit history and driving record and approves the transfer.

If the seller doesn't want the bank to know about the transfer, look out. You're headed for trouble if you're supposed to pay the seller directly, who in turn must make the monthly payments to the bank. If the title remains in the seller's name, and the seller doesn't make the payments, the bank will repossess the car. Your only recourse then is to try to get your money back from the seller.

Protecting Yourself When Selling a Used Car

If you are a private party selling your car, you usually don't have to disclose defects you know about if the buyer doesn't ask. But if the buyer does ask specific questions, you must either answer truthfully and completely, or tell the buyer you are not going to say anything about the car's condition. If you give the buyer only half an answer, the buyer can sue you when the whole truth is discovered.

Never knowingly make any misrepresentations concerning the condition, equipment, or mileage of your car. If you don't know enough to answer the buyer's question, tell him or her so. Offer to let the buyer have the vehicle checked out by a mechanic if he or she has any doubts.

Before letting a potential buyer test-drive your car, check that his or her driver's license is up to date and not suspended. If the buyer refuses to show you the license or tells you it's at home, do not let him or her drive the car. Instead offer to let the buyer test-drive the car when he or she comes back with a license. A buyer's failure to show a license could mean that he or she intends to steal the car, to simply drive away and not come back. Or the buyer could be a careless driver whose license has been revoked because of too many accidents. Remember, you can be liable for any injuries caused by a person who is driving your car with your consent. (For this reason, you should maintain insurance on your car until you transfer the title to the buyer.)

One way of protecting yourself from having your car stolen is to accompany the buyer on the test drive. If you don't want to go with the buyer, have the buyer leave the keys and registration to his or her own car as security. First check the registration to make sure it is in fact the buyer's car. If there is any discrepancy, exercise common sense in deciding whether to allow the buyer to test-drive your car alone.

Paying the Money and Transferring Ownership

If you are buying a used car from a reputable dealer, then there usually isn't much to worry about in paying your money and getting the title. But transactions between private parties should be carefully structured to protect both sides from getting ripped off.

If you are selling your car, always insist that the buyer pay the full price in cash, or better yet, by cashier's check. If you agree to accept a personal check, don't give the buyer the car until the check clears. If you let the buyer take the car and the check bounces, you might have to go through a lot of trouble and expense to get the car back. Don't agree to finance the purchase price unless you're prepared for the headaches that go along with it; if the buyer defaults, you will have to go through the time, expense, and trouble of repossessing the car.

If you are the buyer, before giving your hard-earned cash to the seller, ask to see the owner's certificate of title to make sure the seller owns the car. If the title is in someone else's name, ask for written proof authorizing the person to sell the car on behalf of the owner. (To be on the safe side, it's a good idea to get the license plate number and the vehicle identification number from the certificate of title and check with the police or department of motor vehicles to make sure the car isn't stolen.)

If the legal title is held by a bank, arrange a meeting at the bank between yourself, the seller, and the bank's representative.

At this meeting, pay the outstanding balance of the loan directly to the bank, which will release the certificate of title to the seller. Then give the seller the rest of the purchase price, and have him or her sign the title over to you. In no event should you give the seller your money upon the seller's assurance that he or she will pay the bank off and get the title to you in the near future. What happens if the seller doesn't pay off the bank? The bank may repossess the car, the seller may spend all of your money, and you could be left holding the bag—an empty bag at that.

After the sale of the car is consummated, both the seller and the buyer must promptly notify the department of motor vehicles. The buyer needs to record the new ownership and change the title and registration accordingly. Most states require the seller to send in a form giving certain information, such as the date of the sale, the seller's name and address, the buyer's name and address, a description of the car, the vehicle identification number, the license plate number, the odometer reading, and the purchase price. In many states, the seller remains liable for parking tickets and even personal injuries caused by the new owner until the proper governmental agency is notified of the sale.

In some states, before the ownership of a car can be transferred, it must be tested to see whether it complies with applicable emission regulations. Unless there is an agreement to the contrary, it is the buyer's responsibility to bring the car up to standard if it doesn't pass the inspection. Before completing the transaction, a prudent buyer will have the car checked out at an authorized station, to see whether any work has to be done. If some work is necessary, the buyer should ask for a corresponding reduction in the purchase price.

Title to the Car

When a car is sold by either a dealer or a private party— even on an "as is" basis— the law implies that the seller has title to the car (legal ownership, usually in the form of a certificate issued by the department of motor vehicles) and the legal authority to transfer it. The law also implies that, unless otherwise expressly stated, the title to the car is free from all security interests, liens, or other encumbrances, such as a bank's lien if the car is collateral for a loan. If the seller attempts to disclaim these "warranties of title" or "against encumbrances," this is your cue that something is amiss.

Once in a while, a person who has bought a used car discovers that another person claims that the car was stolen from him or her. If the car was indeed stolen, the person who owned it at the time it was stolen is legally entitled to the car—a thief does not acquire title to the stolen car. If the car you bought turns out to be stolen, you have a right to recover the full price you paid from the person who sold you the car, even if that person didn't know the car was stolen. That person in turn has a right to recover his or her purchase price from the person from whom the car was bought. Of course, the person who unknowingly purchased the car from the thief usually will be left out in the cold.

When more than one person owns the car, how title is held in both names is worth considering. For example, if the title states "John Doe *and* Mary Doe" (or "John and Mary Doe"), this means that both John and Mary must sign the certificate of ownership to transfer title of the car. However, if the title reads "John Doe *or* Mary Doe" or "John and/or Mary Doe," either John or Mary may transfer the vehicle without the other's signature. If the title to the car is held as "John *and* Mary Doe" and one of them dies, the survivor may have to get a court order approving the transfer prior to a sale. In some states, the surviving co-owner only needs to show the Department of Motor Vehicles the death certificate (or other acceptable evidence) of the co-owner's death in order to sell the car.

If you have obtained a loan to purchase the car, the bank's security interest in the car will be noted on the certificate of title. This prevents you from transferring title without disclosing the bank's security interest. As another means to prevent an unauthorized transfer, the bank will keep the owner's certificate of title until it receives the last loan payment. Meanwhile, you have the use of the car and are the registered owner. You cannot sell the car without the bank's permission, which it usually will give only after the loan balance is paid off.

Automobile Repairs

As the owner of an automobile, you are ultimately responsible for keeping it in good repair. If the car is not kept in proper working condition, with all lights operable; brakes, tires, and steering in good shape; and so forth, you can be cited for a traffic offense. Should the car be involved in an accident, your failure to maintain the vehicle in good shape can make you liable for the injuries sustained by the other person.

Consider this example: Donald knows that the brake lights and turn signals on his car do not work and has been planning to have them repaired for some time. So far, he has avoided getting a ticket, although one police officer did stop him and let him off with a warning to get the lights fixed. While driving down a busy street one day, Donald suddenly decides to make a left turn to go into the parking lot of a department store. He hits his brakes, but since the lights don't work, the driver behind Donald has no idea that Donald is stopping. Donald has not bothered to signal the turn with his arm, even though he knows his turn signal is out. The other driver doesn't realize until too late that Donald is making a turn, and runs into him. In this case, Donald is liable for the injuries sustained by the other driver and the damage to the other car, as the cause of the accident was Donald's failure to have the brake lights and turn signal in proper working order. Since the driver of the car behind Donald had no warning that Donald was stopping to make a turn, the driver is not liable for the accident unless he or she was following too closely or speeding.

Maintaining your car in a safe operating condition is what the law calls a "nondelegable duty." You and you alone are responsible for seeing that the car doesn't pose an unreasonable risk of harm to other people on the road. This is true even if you don't know the first thing about car repair or maintenance and have entrusted your vehicle to the best mechanic in town. The mechanic, however, has a duty to perform the repairs in a skillful, or "workmanlike," manner and is liable for any damages resulting from faulty work.

Suppose that you have just had your brakes relined at Joe's Tire and Brake Service Company, a reputable repair shop. You pull out of Joe's driveway and drive down the street about 200 yards. As you come to a red light at a crowded intersection, you hit the brakes. Unfortunately, nothing happens and you crash into the car in front of you. The occupants of that car sue you for not having your brakes in working condition. It is no defense that Joe's Tire and Brake didn't do a good job. But you can turn around and sue Joe's for the cost of your lawyer and the amount of the judgment you must pay because of Joe's faulty work.

How to Avoid Getting Ripped Off

The fraudulent practices of a relatively small percentage of automobile repair companies have given the whole car repair industry a tarnished reputation. Some repair companies have been accused of charging for work not done; using used or reconditioned parts but charging for new parts; doing repairs the customer did not authorize and threatening not to release the car until all charges are paid; stating certain repairs are necessary when in fact they are not; overstating the extent of necessary repairs; and failing to return old parts or to make them available for inspection (which can mean that the customer was charged for a part that wasn't replaced or didn't need replacing and was billed for labor as well).

Despite all the problems and complaints, very few states have comprehensive laws for licensing repair shops, certifying mechanics, and regulating estimates and repair work. California has the best act in the nation, with the Bureau of Automotive Repair as a watchdog agency to investigate consumer complaints. In California, the repair shop is required to give the customer a written estimate and get the customer's express authorization before any work is done. Should the repair shop fail to give the customer a written estimate, the customer may not have to pay for the repairs.

Here are some things you can do to ensure that you don't get ripped off when your car needs repairs:

1. Investigate the repair shop. Contact the Better Business Bureau and ask whether any complaints have been lodged against the shop. Even if the shop isn't a member, the BBB may still have a file of complaints on it. Ask your friends and neighbors if they are familiar with the repair shop and would recommend it. The local chapter of the American Automobile Association may be able to give you information about the reputation of repair shops in the area.

2. Get an estimate in writing. Tell the repair shop that you want only an estimate at this time and that you are not authorizing the shop to do any work. Most repair shops will give a free estimate. About the only time a shop won't do this is when it has to disassemble part of the car to see what the problem is.

If your car is under warranty, you should check the warranty and contact the authorized dealer to determine whether the warranty covers both diagnosis and repair of the problem. Don't let the dealer try to charge you for opening the hood to see what the problem is if the warranty includes the cost of diagnosis, which it often does. If necessary, pull out the warranty information that came with your car, and show the dealer everything that the warranty covers.

3. Request that the estimate itemize the parts needed, their individual costs, and the labor charge for each. Ask whether the parts to be installed will be new, used, or reconditioned. If all parts will be new, that fact should be stated on the estimate sheet.

If some parts will be used or reconditioned, these too should be so specified.

4. Make sure that the shop is competent to handle the work on your particular type of car. If you have an imported car, for instance, you usually would not want to take it to a shop that deals exclusively in domestic cars.

5. *Get at least two estimates*, and get them in writing. This cannot be overemphasized. The first repair shop may be trying to charge you for work that doesn't need to be done or may be grossly overestimating the amount of time that the job will take. If the repair work to be done is extensive and expensive, get three or four estimates. In addition to price and quality of work, you should also find out how long it is going to take. It may not be worth saving $100 if your car is going to be tied up in the shop an extra two or three weeks.

6. Find out whether the repair shop will guarantee its work for any period of time. If the shop doesn't give some kind of warranty, forget the place. If it doesn't have enough confidence in its work to give any kind of guarantee, that only spells trouble—including possible legal trouble—in the long run.

7. Once you have decided on a particular repair shop, and once the work order contains the notations made on the estimate sheet (itemization of parts and labor, whether new or used parts will be installed, and so forth), be sure to have the following provisions added to the work order: (1) If the price exceeds the estimate by a stated amount (say, $25 or $50), the repair shop is to call you before proceeding further; (2) All old parts must be returned to you or at least retained for your inspection, so you can determine that the part needed replacing and was in fact replaced.

If the Shop Refuses to Return Your Car Until You Pay

Most states give the repair shop a "lien" on your car when it does work on the vehicle, to ensure that it will be paid. If you unjustifiably refuse to pay for the repairs, the repair shop can hold your car for a reasonable time and charge you a reasonable storage fee. Should you not pay within a certain period, say two weeks or a month, the repair shop may be entitled to sell the car to pay the bill. If, after the car is sold and the bill is paid off, there is any money left over, this must be given to the owner of the car. Before selling the car, the repair shop ordinarily must notify both the owner and any lienholder (such as the bank) that it intends to sell the car on a certain date and at a specified place.

All too often, people find that they are being charged for work they did not order or the charges are considerably more than they agreed to in advance. They complain to the shop's manager, who tells them that if they don't pay the bill in full, the shop will enforce the lien on their car and sell it. The manager also tells them that if they do not pick the car up by the next day, they will be charged a daily storage fee of $5 or $10. What can a person do in this situation?

In most cases, the easiest thing to do is simply to pay the bill in full, get the car, then file a small claims action (see chapter 15) to recover the charges you believe were unwarranted. If you present your case well and show the judge just what the repair shop did wrong, there's a good chance that the judge will agree with you. Before filing the small claims action, send a letter to the repair shop stating exactly why you believe the charges were excessive or detailing the exact work that was done without your authorization. Your letter should also include a demand that the repair shop refund you the disputed amount. Make it clear that if it doesn't, you will seek reimbursement through the legal system. Often the repair shop will refund all or part of the difference prior to the hearing. You may also want to report your complaint to the Better Business Bureau or American Automobile Association. If you suspect fraud or similar illegal conduct, you should contact your local district attorney. But you generally can't threaten the shop that you will go to the police or district attorney if it refuses to give you back your money. The law does not permit you to threaten criminal prosecution to coerce a settlement in a civil matter.

Some people will write out a check for the full amount, give it to the repair shop, take their car home, and then immediately call the bank to put a "stop payment" on the check. We advise against doing this, since writing a check with the intent to stop payment on it may subject you to criminal penalties. (A number of repair shops have had this happen to them too many times and require payment by cash only.)

If the repair shop lets you make payment with a bank card, such as a Visa or MasterCard, consider paying the bill with the bank card, get your car, then inform the Visa or MasterCard people of a dispute. They may help you resolve the dispute. Before using this alternative, check with the Visa or MasterCard people to see what the current procedure is regarding disputed services.

What to Do If Your Car Wasn't Repaired Properly

Say that you take your car to the repair shop, leave it there for several days, then get it back, only to discover that the problem has not been corrected or returns in a week or so. When this happens, the first thing you should do is take the car back to the repair shop as soon as possible. If, for some reason, you can't get the car back to the shop for, say, a few weeks (because you are going out of town on business, for example), call the repair shop, inform the owner or manager that the problem has not been corrected, and say that you will bring the car in as soon as you can. You should follow up this telephone call with a letter to the repair shop.

Do not drive the car, unless it is safe to do so and will not aggravate the defective condition. For instance, if the problem is with your radio, you can drive the car but just not play the radio.

But if the problem is with something as vital as the brakes, the car should only be driven back to the repair shop, and only if that is safe. (If the car needs to be towed back to the repair shop because a repair wasn't done right the first time, make the repair shop tow the car in or reimburse you for the cost.) If you do any other driving, the repair shop may claim that your continued driving of the car made the problem worse, which relieves the shop of any responsibility for correcting the condition.

All this points up the importance of discussing the guarantee with the repair shop before any work is authorized. Should the shop now claim that no guarantee of any kind was made, you may be up a creek if you don't have a written warranty to back you up. Even if the repair shop insists that there is no warranty, don't take it lying down. The law generally imposes the warranty that all repairs be made in a skillful manner. If the repair wasn't done correctly, then the repair shop must either do it right or refund your money.

After giving the repair shop a second chance, you have several options if you're still not satisfied. You can give the shop a third chance at correcting the problem (at no expense to you, of course). Since it hasn't been able to get it right in two tries, however, a third attempt might not be worth your time. If you are fed up with the repair shop, speak to the shop's owner or manager and demand a refund. If they refuse to give you a full refund, inform them that you are going to have another repair shop fix the problem and that you will seek reimbursement from them for this cost. You should back this statement up with a letter to the shop's owner or manager. Remember to always keep a copy of any letter you send so you can show it to the judge in small claims court if necessary.

Then take your car to another repair shop for an estimate. If you think this new repair shop can do the job, let it do the work, then pay the bill and send a copy to the original repair shop, reiterating your demand that it reimburse you for this cost. If the shop management refuses to do so, you should file a small claims action or have a lawyer call the repair shop on your behalf.

The mechanic at the second shop will frequently be willing to testify that the first shop did not repair the condition correctly. This is usually enough to convince the judge that justice is on your side.

Automobile Insurance

Most states require that you maintain certain minimum liability insurance coverage if your vehicle is driven on a public street or highway. (Technically speaking, these are "financial responsibility laws" that permit the owner of the car, in lieu of purchasing insurance, to deposit an equivalent amount of money in cash or bond with the department of motor vehicles.)

If you don't have insurance as required by your state's law and get into an accident, you face loss of your license for a year or more, plus a fine. A number of states are moving to cut down on the number of uninsured drivers by requiring you to show proof of insurance coverage when stopped for a traffic violation or when renewing the car's registration each year.

Apart from the consequences to your driver's license, getting into an accident without insurance can be very expensive. If you do not have insurance and cause an accident, you will be required to pay out of your own pocket all the property damage, medical costs, lost wages, and other damages suffered by the injured party. If you believe you didn't cause the accident and decide to contest liability, you will have to pay for your own lawyer. An insurance company takes care of all these costs (up to the applicable limits) for insured drivers.

Who and What Is Covered

An insurance policy is a contract between the insurance company and the person who is insured. The terms of the policy specify who is covered, the extent of the coverage, and any limitations. If your claim falls within the provisions of the insurance policy, the insurance company must pay that claim, up to the maximum amount of the policy. On the other hand, if the particular claim isn't covered by the policy, the insurance company does not have to pay you anything. If the policy is vague or a dispute arises about whether a claim is covered, either party—you or the insurance company—can file a lawsuit to have the controversy decided in court.

Suppose you lend your car to someone and that person causes an accident. Or you're driving a friend's car and *you* cause an accident. Does your personal automobile insurance policy cover the damages in those situations? Perhaps. The typical personal automobile insurance policy will pay for all of the injuries and property damages—to the limits of the policy—someone else causes while driving the insured's (your) car, if that person is driving with your permission and for pleasure and does not regularly drive your car. (Your personal automobile insurance policy normally doesn't cover any damages if someone is driving your car for business or if you are driving someone else's car for business.) Similarly, your friend's insurance, if he or she has any, ordinarily covers you while you are driving his or her car with permission and for pleasure.

Your own policy also covers any injuries and property damages you cause others while driving another person's car for pleasure. This is especially important if the car you borrow isn't insured, or if it *is* insured, but for a minimal amount of coverage. Your policy probably doesn't cover the damage to the car you're driving (the borrowed car) unless you have additional coverage. If the owner of the car you borrowed doesn't have collision insurance (see discussion below), the cost of repairing or replacing the borrowed car may have to come out of your own pocket. If he or she does have collision insurance on the car, his or her insurance company will pay for the damage to it; you are responsible for reimbursing the car's owner for any deductible he or she is required to pay, however. To determine the extent of your coverage while you are driving someone else's car or while another person is driving your car, read your policy carefully or check with your insurance agent.

If members of your family (such as your spouse or children) drive your car, you will want your insurance policy to cover each family member who will be driving the car. Having a teenage driver in the house may mean that your insurance premium will be several hundred dollars more each year. If you're thinking of saving some money by not telling your insurance company that your teenager drives the car, think twice. If the teenager gets into an accident while driving your car, the insurance company may refuse to pay because this driver wasn't covered.

How Your Insurance Rates Are Determined

Automobile insurance rates are based on such factors as your age and marital status; the ages of other people who will be driving the car; the make, model, and year of your car, plus any equipment on the vehicle; the driving records of the persons who will be insured; whether the car is used for business; and where you live (your "zone"). Two people with everything else identical may find that their insurance costs with the same company are hundreds of dollars different, just because they live in different zones. The zones are usually determined by the insurance company on the basis of the number of claims made by and the amounts paid to people living in that zone. Frequently it seems unfair that a person living across the street or two blocks away should be paying less for insurance, but insurance companies base their rates on statistical risks, not necessarily fairness.

The cost of a policy is not uniform throughout the insurance industry. By shopping around, you may be able to save as much as several hundred dollars a year. But when comparing the price of policies offered by competing insurance companies, make sure you are comparing the same amount of coverage in terms of monetary limits, coverages, and exclusions. Also consider the reputation of the company for paying claims. It might not be worth a savings of $50 or $100 a year if you'll have to fight tooth and nail to get fair and fast action on your claim.

Personal Injury and Property Damage Insurance

States with financial responsibility laws require that you have certain minimum limits of coverage to pay for the personal injuries or property damage your carelessness causes. Most minimum limits were set years ago, when the costs of medical care and other expenses were much less than they are today. A typical minimum requirement is that you have insurance coverage (or other means) to pay $15,000 maximum for each person injured in an accident, to a total of $30,000 for each accident, and to pay up to $5,000 for property damage. (This is the standard "15/30/5" insurance policy.) Once the insurance company pays its limits under the policy, its obligation stops, and you are personally liable for the remaining amount. Because hospital costs and the prices of cars have risen so much, we recommend that your personal automobile insurance policy provide at least $100,000 coverage per person, $300,000 per accident, and $25,000 property damage. You can also purchase an "umbrella" policy for a relatively small sum, which protects you up to a certain amount, say, $1 million, over your policy limits. Businesses should, of course, have considerably higher limits than this and should discuss their needs with their insurance agents.

Medical Payments Insurance

Medical payments insurance pays medical expenses and funeral costs if you, a member of your immediate family who lives with you, or a nonpaying guest is injured or killed while riding in the car or getting in or out of it. You are also covered if you're walking on the sidewalk and are struck by a car, motorcycle, or other vehicle or if you're injured while riding as a passenger in someone else's car. Medical payments insurance coverage doesn't cost much, and we suggest that you have coverage of at least $5,000 per person.

Collision and Comprehensive Coverage

Collision insurance covers damage to your car caused when the car runs into something (such as a telephone pole), is run into by another vehicle, or flips over. Damage to car windows, whether in a collision or not, is usually covered by comprehensive insurance.

Comprehensive insurance protects you against damage to the car caused by something other than a collision. For example, if your car is stolen, damaged by someone trying to break in, or hit by a falling object, comprehensive covers it. Comprehensive insurance also covers damage to your car caused by fire or natural disaster—for instance, flood, earthquake, tornado, or hurricane.

Collision and comprehensive coverage usually is not required by the law, but is generally a good thing to have, unless your car isn't worth much. Your insurance agent will probably offer collision and comprehensive insurance with different amounts that are designated "deductible," such as $250 or $500. The deductible is the amount that comes out of your own pocket; your insurance company pays the rest. The higher the amount of the deductible, the lower the premium will be. But if your car is damaged, you'll have to pay more money out of your own pocket to fix it if you took the policy with the higher deductible.

The deductible applies to each claim you make. Say that your car is hit by a falling branch that does $500 worth of damage. The next day, your car is struck by a hit-and-run driver who does an additional $500 worth of damage. You will wind up paying a total of $500 (the $250 deductible for the tree damage and $250 deductible for the hit-and-run damage), and the insurance company will pay the rest.

Radio Equipment and Personal Property

Electronic equipment, such as radios, cassette players, and C.B. radios, that was installed by the factory is usually covered in your automobile insurance policy, but generally only up to a certain amount, such as $200. If your equipment is more expensive or if it was installed after you bought the car (so-called aftermarket equipment), talk to your insurance agent about getting it covered.

The typical personal automobile liability insurance policy does not cover loss of or damage to personal property of any value. For example, if you have some jewelry stolen from the car, or if a painting is injured in a car fire, your automobile policy usually won't cover this. You should, however, be able to collect under your homeowner's or renter's policy if you have one.

Uninsured and Underinsured Coverage

Uninsured motorist coverage is designed to protect you in the event that a person who causes an accident and injures you is not insured or you are injured by a hit-and-run driver. Underinsured motorist coverage begins where the other driver's insurance ends. In some states, uninsured motorist coverage is mandatory. Uninsured motorist coverage and underinsured motorist coverage are both good investments and are readily available at low cost.

No-Fault Insurance

About half the states have enacted some type of no-fault insurance system. No-fault insurance is designed to cut down the amount of time and the administrative costs involved in processing relatively minor claims. Some groups, particularly the insurance industry, greatly favor no-fault insurance, as it avoids litigation and cuts down on the time it takes for claims to be processed. Other groups, notably the trial lawyers who represent the victims of automobile accidents, feel that too frequently the damages awarded are inadequate for the injuries suffered, that the system sacrifices justice and fair compensation for expediency.

Under a typical no-fault plan, a driver who is injured in an automobile accident is entitled to collect up to a certain amount (for example, $1,000) from his or her own insurance company. The liability—that is, fault—of the parties is not at issue. Even if one driver is negligent and causes the accident, he or she can still collect up to the maximum amount from his or her own insurance company.

Under a no-fault insurance system, the non-negligent driver usually must first seek compensation from his or her own insurance company. After doing so, the injured person can usually sue the negligent driver for the remaining damages. Thus, if the innocent driver sustained damages of $10,000 in the accident and under the no-fault policy was paid $2,500 by his or her own insurance company, he or she can sue the other driver for the remaining $7,500. If the injuries you suffer are not covered under the no-fault plan, many states let you sue the other driver for those injuries. For instance, a typical no-fault plan does not pay you damages for pain and suffering. In many states, you can sue the other driver for these damages. In some states, however, you can sue the other driver for pain and suffering only if your other medical expenses (hospital and doctor's fees and related costs) exceed a specified amount.

Insurance When You Are Financing the Car

If you are financing the purchase of your car, the bank will require that certain minimum insurance be kept on the car at all times. If you fail to maintain the required insurance, the bank may either repossess your car or purchase the insurance itself and charge it to your account. But keep in mind that this insurance usually relates only to damage to the car itself. The bank just wants to be assured that the security for the loan—in other words, the car—is properly insured against any damage. The bank generally will not get liability insurance for you, even if your liability insurance lapses or is canceled. You should also be aware that the insurance obtained by the bank for damage to the vehicle is generally considerably more expensive than what you could obtain through an insurance agent.

Filing Your Claim

If you are involved in an accident or if your car has been damaged, promptly notify your insurance agent of the claim, regardless of whose fault the accident was. If you fail to let the insurance company know of the accident within a reasonable time, you may unwittingly be letting it off the hook to defend you or pay any judgment against you. Your insurance agent can advise you on the necessary forms to file with the insurance company so it can start processing your claim.

Your insurance company has a duty to deal with you fairly and in good faith. This means that if you submit a legitimate claim to your insurance company and the claim is covered by the policy, the insurance company must pay it. If your insurance company refuses to pay on a valid claim, you can sue it for any damages you suffer, including punitive damages to punish the insurance company for not paying.

Suppose that you cause an accident because you weren't paying attention, and the passenger in the other car is seriously injured. Your automobile insurance policy covers you to the extent of $100,000. The other driver offers to settle the case with your insurance company for $100,000, but your insurance company refuses. A trial follows, and a jury awards the other driver $500,000. You don't have $400,000 to pay the excess over the insurance policy limits, and paying what you can will lead to your financial ruin. Do you have any rights against your insurance company in this situation? Yes. If an insurance company receives an offer to settle a case for the limits of the insurance policy, and there is good reason to believe that a jury will probably award more than the policy limits, the insurance company must settle the case. If it doesn't, the insurance company must pay any sums awarded over the limits. You might also be able to sue the insurance company for other damages, including punitive damages, if the insurance company acted improperly in refusing to settle the case for the policy limits.

If a lawsuit is filed against you, you have a duty to cooperate with your insurance company and assist in the legal defense of your case. If you don't, your insurance company may not have to defend you or pay off on the policy.

Automobile Accidents

Your Liability If Someone Else Uses Your Car

If you let another person drive your car, and that person causes an accident, are you liable for the damage? Some states have a "permissive use" statute, which makes you liable for injuries caused by the carelessness of anyone driving the car with your permission. In other states, you aren't liable unless you yourself did something wrong, such as failing to maintain the car in a safe condition. In all states, you can be held liable for the injuries if you loan your car to someone you know is an unsafe driver. An example: Mary lets her friend Tom drive her car, even though she knows Tom has been the cause of several accidents and has accumulated a number of traffic citations for speeding and other offenses. Tom gets into an accident with Mary's car, caused by his speeding. Is Mary liable to the other driver for the damages? Yes. In this case, Mary negligently entrusted her car to the poor driver, Tom, and is therefore liable for having exercised bad judgment. Before letting someone else drive your car, you should be sure that your insurance policy covers you in case that person gets in an accident. (As discussed earlier, the typical personal automobile insurance policy does cover damages caused by someone else while driving your car in most situations.)

Is a parent liable if a child causes an accident while driving the family car? A number of states have a rule called the family purpose doctrine, which makes the owner of a car liable for injuries caused by a spouse or child while driving the car on a family errand. If, for example, a daughter is on her way to the store at her mother's request and gets into an accident, her parents are liable for the damages caused by the accident (assuming both parents own the car). In states with permissive use statutes, the owner is liable regardless of why the child was using the car, since the child was using the car with the owner's permission. As a practical matter, if you have children who will be driving the family car, notify your insurance company so the children can be included on the policy.

Suppose a thief steals your car and gets into an accident. Can you be held liable for the damages? That depends on the circumstances. If you locked your car and the thief broke in and hot-wired it, you're not liable. But if you parked the car outside a store, with the door open, the keys in, and the engine running, you'll probably be held liable if the thief injures someone while stealing the car. By leaving the car unattended with the keys in the ignition and the engine running, you are "inviting" a thief to steal the car. The law recognizes that a car is a dangerous instrument that can easily inflict death or serious bodily harm, and a driver has a so-called affirmative duty not to leave the keys in an unlocked and unattended vehicle.

The Driver's Liability to Passengers

In a majority of states, if your careless driving results in an injury to a passenger in your car, you are liable for that person's injuries. In some states, however, whether you are liable to that passenger depends on who the passenger is and the extent of your fault. Some states, for example, prohibit a married person from suing a spouse for negligence, and some prohibit a child from suing a parent for negligence.

In some states, a nonpaying passenger (in law, a "social guest") cannot sue the driver of the car for injuries resulting from the driver's negligence. Suppose that Tom and his friend Joe are on their way to see a movie; Tom runs into the car in front of him because he didn't see that the light had turned red, and Joe is injured. In a state having a so-called guest statute, Joe cannot sue Tom because Joe is merely a social guest who did not pay for the ride.

If a state prohibits certain types of passengers from suing the driver, the prohibition usually applies only to injuries resulting from the driver's "ordinary negligence." Ordinary negligence can be defined simply as carelessness: making an unsafe turn or lane change, speeding (but not excessively), or not paying attention to the traffic in front of you. But if the driver deliberately tries to harm the passenger or is grossly negligent (such as speeding excessively or going around a railroad crossing barrier when a train is rapidly approaching), the passenger will usually be able to sue.

Most states permit a passenger (even one who is a social guest) to sue the driver if the driver was intoxicated, since this is considered at least gross negligence. But if you are injured while riding with a drunk driver, a few courts will not let you sue the drunk driver; they hold that by accepting a ride with a person you know to be intoxicated, you have "assumed the risk" that an accident will probably result. As a matter of common sense, always think twice about accepting a ride from someone who has been drinking.

What to Do If You Get in an Accident

If you are involved in an accident, there are certain things you should do.

The first thing to do is stop. If you hit another car (or a pedestrian) and take off, you may be guilty of "hit and run," which has very serious consequences. If you were drunk at the time and leave the scene of the accident, you can be charged with a felony. It is best to remain on the scene and take it from there, rather than complicate your predicament by fleeing.

If you hit an unattended parked car, you must leave a note

with your name, address, telephone number, and license plate number on the windshield of the damaged car. Include a brief description of the damage you caused. Some people will place a note only when they think someone is watching them. Others will place a blank note on the windshield. However, if you get caught doing this (a bystander may have taken your license plate number down), you may be in serious trouble.

After an accident, if possible, move your car to a safe spot at the side of the road. If your car cannot be moved, at least get yourself to a position of safety. Warning signals such as flares or traffic cones should be placed to let approaching traffic know of the danger.

If you have been injured, try to assess the seriousness of your injuries. Unless you absolutely have to, don't move if your back or head has been injured. If you aren't seriously hurt, check to see whether the occupants of your car or the other car are injured. The paramedics should be called immediately if anyone has been seriously hurt. First aid should be administered by qualified personnel. If the impact was strong or you hit your head, you should be taken to the emergency room of the closest hospital even if you feel fine, so you can be checked out for possible fractures, concussion, or internal bleeding.

Anytime someone is injured or killed or a car is damaged beyond a scratch or small dent, call the police. If they don't arrive on the scene, go down to the police station and make a report. If you fail to report an accident in which someone has been injured or killed or that has led to property damage in excess of an amount specified by state law, you face a criminal penalty, even if you didn't cause the accident. If your car was substantially damaged or if you suffered any personal injuries, do not let the other driver talk you into not reporting the accident. Many times one driver will say, "Don't worry about it; I'll take care of everything. I just don't want my insurance company to know about it." The truth of the matter may be that the driver doesn't have an insurance company to worry about. Your legal obligation is to report the accident.

Write down the license number and a description of the other car or cars involved in the accident. Ask to see the other driver's license, car registration, and insurance information. Get the name, address, and telephone number of the other driver. If there were any passengers in the other car, get their names, addresses, and telephone numbers as well.

Get the names, addresses, and telephone numbers of all witnesses. Do not wait for the police to arrive, since some of the witnesses may leave first. Ask each witness if he or she noticed any other person who saw the accident but who left the scene before you could speak to that person. As soon as you can, get a written statement from each witness describing in detail what he or she saw, and have the witness date and sign it.

If someone has a camera, take pictures of the accident scene—as many pictures as you can, from every angle you can think of. If you can, get to the roof of a nearby building and take some "aerial" photographs of the accident scene. When the police arrive on the scene, ask them to take pictures and measurements. The length of skid marks should be measured and the positions of the vehicles after impact recorded. This information can be used to estimate the speed of the vehicles at the time of the collision and help determine who caused the accident.

Avoid taking responsibility for the accident, as this can come back to haunt you. Liability is a legal question to be settled only after *all* the facts have been gathered and studied. Many times a person will think that he or she caused the accident, when in fact the other driver was solely or partially to blame for the accident. And even if you were partially at fault, in many states you can still recover some of your damages.

As soon after the accident as possible, write a thorough account of the facts and events leading up to the accident. Note such things as time of day, weather conditions, road conditions, whether traffic was heavy or light, and how fast you were going. Draw diagrams indicating your movement and speed prior to the accident and the movement and speed of the other car. One diagram should show the final positions of the cars after the accident.

Notify your automobile insurance agent of the accident as soon as possible. He or she will be able to get a copy of the police report and start processing your claim immediately. If you are solely or partially responsible for the accident, your insurance company should provide you with an attorney to defend you in case of a civil lawsuit based on the accident. (If the insurance company refuses to provide a lawyer, consult your family lawyer immediately to see what your rights are.)

If the other driver was at fault, his or her insurance company may pay you for the damages to your car before settling your claims of personal injuries. You should have a mechanic check your car out thoroughly to see that there is no hidden damage from the accident. You can't, though, expect the other party's insurance company to pay for damage to your car that existed before the accident.

Always be careful not to sign any papers sent you from the other driver's insurance company until you have read them over carefully. Discuss them with a lawyer if you have any questions or don't understand how the document will affect your rights. Never sign a release form relating to your personal injuries until you have been thoroughly examined by a physician. Many injuries do not show up until weeks or months after the accident. Since you usually have at least one year to bring suit against the other driver, don't feel pressured by the other driver's insurance company to settle immediately. Particularly if you suffered any injuries to your head, neck, back, or knees, you should be evaluated several times over the course of six months or more to determine whether there will be any permanent injuries.

If you suffered more than minor injuries in the accident, contact an experienced personal injury lawyer as soon as possible. (See chapter 19 for information about finding a competent attorney and the fee structure involved.) Depending on the state, you have from one year to six years to bring a lawsuit for your injuries. However, if you were hit by a government-owned vehicle (such as a police car, department of transportation truck, or city bus), you usually have to file a written claim with the appropriate government agency within a much shorter period of time, such as not more than 60 days after the accident. Your failure to do so may cause you to lose your right to sue the government.

If the other driver was cited for violating a traffic regulation, you may be asked to testify at any criminal proceedings. You may want to have your attorney present with you, as what you say at the criminal trial might have a bearing on a later civil trial. If you were cited, you'll probably want to be represented by your own lawyer at the hearing, certainly if it's a serious charge, such as drunk driving. (Your insurance company usually does not have to provide you with a lawyer in a criminal case against you, only in a civil action based on a claim covered by your policy.)

Preventing Accidents

Lawyers are in a special position to see not only the results, but also the causes of automobile-related accidents. Many accidents could be prevented if every driver realized that driving is a full-time job, one that requires considerable care, skill, and patience. Here are a few things every driver should do to minimize the risk of getting into an automobile accident and to minimize the risk of injury in case of an accident. Most of them are required by law, as well as by common sense.

First, keep your car in good working condition. Tires should be regularly checked for signs of wear and to ensure that they are properly inflated. Headlights, brake lights, and turn signals should all be checked periodically to see that they are working.

Anytime you go driving, whether to the neighborhood supermarket or on a cross-country trip, wear your seat belt. Seat belts with shoulder harnesses are better than lap belts, but even a lap belt is better than no seat belt at all. Children as well as adults should be strapped into their seats. Younger children should be secured in safety seats, which in turn are held in place by seat belts. A number of states have passed laws making it mandatory to wear your seat belt and to have young children fastened in a safety seat.

If you ride a motorcycle, wear a helmet at all times. A number of states have laws that make it mandatory for motorcyclists and their passengers to wear helmets. In some states, a motorcyclist who is not wearing a helmet at the time of an accident cannot recover damages from a negligent driver for injuries a helmet would have prevented.

Never combine drinking and driving or drugs and driving. Alcohol intoxication or drug-induced impairment plays a part in many serious automobile accidents.

Always practice defensive driving. If you can anticipate the accident possibilities of various situations, your chances of having an accident- and injury-free driving record will increase.

Responsibilities of Pay
Parking Lot Operators

If your car is stolen from or damaged in a pay parking lot, your ability to recover damages from the operator of the lot depends on exactly what the parking lot operator provides. If the operator merely gives you a space to park the car, and you are responsible for parking it, locking it up, and taking the keys with you, generally you assume the risk that the car may be broken into. If, however, there is a history of frequent break-ins into cars parked in the lot, the operator can be held liable if a sign informing you of that risk has not been posted in a conspicuous place. And if you can prove that it was the operator or an employee who broke into your car, you can recover damages from the operator, no matter what any sign says.

If there is no attendant or if each driver is responsible for parking his or her own car, the parking lot operator usually is not liable for damage to your car caused by another driver trying to park his or her own car. Liability might be imposed, however, if the parking spaces are small and not marked "Compact Cars Only" or the like, or if there is not enough room to maneuver a car into or out of a space without hitting another vehicle parked in a marked space. Likewise, if the driver who hits your car was following the instructions or directions of the attendant, the parking lot operator is liable. For example, if the attendant tells a driver to keep backing up, that there is plenty of room, and that driver hits your car, the parking lot operator is then liable for the damages, and the driver of the car that hit you is probably liable as well.

When a parking lot attendant damages your car while trying to park it or another car, the operator generally is liable for the damages. If the employee fails to lock your car after parking it, the operator is also usually liable for any items that are stolen from the car. If it is likely that even locked cars in the lot may be broken into, the employee has a duty to maintain a reasonable lookout to prevent break-ins.

Suppose that your car is stolen from an attended parking lot. Does the parking lot operator have to pay for it? If the attendant locked the car and there had never been any previous thefts on the lot and the lot is not in a high-crime area, then the operator probably isn't liable. But if the employee left the keys in the unlocked car or the car was locked but the keys were left unguarded, then the operator is liable.

When you park in a pay parking lot, invariably there will be a "disclaimer of liability" or "waiver of damages." If you receive a ticket stub, the disclaimer will ordinarily be printed on the back. If ticket stubs are not issued, the parking lot operator will usually post one or two signs disclaiming responsibility for damage to the vehicle or for theft of the car or its contents. The courts do not recognize these disclaimers if the parking lot operator or an employee is in any way responsible for the damages.

Driving under the Influence

The criminal offense of driving in an impaired condition is known in various parts of the country as driving under the influence (DUI), driving while intoxicated (DWI), or simply drunk driving. Driving under the influence includes not only driving while intoxicated, but also driving while under the effects of drugs—both illegal drugs, such as marijuana, PCP, or cocaine, and prescription drugs that severely limit a person's ability to operate a motor vehicle. When alcohol is combined with many prescription drugs—or even many nonprescription drugs, such as those taken for colds or hay fever—the impairment may be much worse.

At one time, drunk driving was virtually a "socially acceptable" crime, since it seemed that almost everyone did it at one time or another. That time is long since past. Largely through the efforts of Mothers Against Drunk Driving (MADD), a national group originally formed by mothers of children killed by drunk drivers, the penalties for driving while intoxicated have become much more severe. Previously a person charged with a first drunk driving offense often avoided any time in jail by pleading guilty to a charge of reckless driving in exchange for a dismissal of the drunk driving charge. (This is an example of a plea bargain.) A number of states now have laws severely restricting—even prohibiting—a first-time offender's plea to a lesser offense and mandating that a convicted drunk driver spend at least 48 hours in jail for the first offense.

The new laws have also been made tougher by lowering the blood alcohol content level at which a person is legally deemed too impaired to drive. This means that under the new laws it takes less alcohol for you to be considered drunk. For example, under the old laws in some states, you were guilty of drunk driving if your blood alcohol content level was .15 percent or more. Under some new laws, you are guilty of drunk driving if your blood alcohol content is .10 percent. Only a few drinks within an hour or two can significantly impair your driving ability, especially if you are tired, haven't eaten much that day, or are taking medication (including many over-the-counter drugs, such as antihistamines).

Stopping and Testing the Suspected Drunk Driver

A police officer may detect a drunk driver by his or her erratic driving—weaving from side to side, being unable to stay in one lane, speeding up and slowing down without reason, or making unsafe lane changes, for example. Or the police officer may stop a driver for a routine traffic violation and then smell alcohol when questioning him or her. Some areas of the country have taken to setting up roadblocks on Friday and Saturday nights and holidays to catch drunk drivers.

If a police officer suspects that you may be driving under the influence of alcohol (or drugs), you will normally be put through a variety of field sobriety tests. These tests are designed to assess your awareness and coordination. The police officer may ask you to walk a straight line by putting the heel of one foot in front of the toe of the other foot, proceed forward several yards, then turn around and return. You may also be requested to close your eyes, tilt your head back, and spread your arms. If you can't maintain your balance and start to fall back, the police officer will suspect intoxication.

You may also be asked to touch the tip of your nose with the first finger of your left hand, then with the first finger of your right hand. If you are unable to touch your nose, the police officer will suspect that you are intoxicated. The officer may ask you to stand on one leg for a bit, then the other to see if you can maintain your balance. You may also be requested to recite the alphabet or perform simple additions or subtractions. Or the police officer may have you repeat a tongue twister, such as "Peter Piper picked a peck of pickled peppers." The officer may point a flashlight in your eyes to see how quickly your pupils contract.

If you ever find yourself being asked to perform field sobriety tests, make sure that all conditions are as much to your advantage as possible. For example, at night, ask that the tests be performed in a well-lighted area. The ground should be firm and level, preferably clean concrete. Tell the officer of any physical disabilities that may affect your performance on the tests. Ask the officer to repeat the directions if you don't understand them. If they are still unclear, have the officer demonstrate what he or she wants you to do. When possible, it may be a good idea to have a third person watch the field tests to ensure that the officer conducts them properly.

If you fail the field sobriety test, the police officer will take you back to the station, where a breath test, a blood test, or a urine test will be administered to measure the amount of alcohol in your blood. You are usually allowed to choose which test you will be given. In fact, where the police have the equipment and personnel to perform two or three different tests, some states hold that it violates the suspect's rights to force the suspect to take one test when he or she wants to take a different test.

One advantage to the breath test is that the results usually are known immediately, unlike the blood or urine tests, which must be sent to a laboratory for analysis. If your blood alcohol is within legal limits, the police may let you go on the spot. In addition, many lawyers who defend drunk drivers say that it is generally easier to challenge the reliability and accuracy of breath test results than those of the other tests, although challenging the breath test is still difficult. The blood test is the most reliable and therefore usually the hardest to challenge.

If you refuse to submit to any of these tests for your blood alcohol level you usually face an immediate suspension of your license. As a condition of receiving your driver's license, you are deemed to "impliedly consent" to suspension of your license should you refuse any testing for drunk driving. However, the police officer must normally advise you that your license will be automatically suspended for the time prescribed by law (such as six months or one year) if you refuse to submit to testing. You can still be prosecuted for driving under the influence if you do refuse the test, although it may be harder for the district attorney to prove the case against you.

If the breath test reveals that you are over the limit, or if you choose the blood or urine test, you will be booked. Many jails and police stations do not fingerprint or photograph people arrested for drunk driving because of the sheer volume of drunk-driving suspects. You will be given the chance to call your spouse, a lawyer, a friend, or anyone else to come down and get you. The police will usually release you to anyone who has a valid driver's license and who is not intoxicated.

The police forward all evidence, including the results of the blood alcohol content test, to the district attorney's office, where a decision about whether to prosecute will be made. If the district attorney decides to prosecute you for drunk driving, be advised that because of the stricter laws and more severe penalties nowadays, you should obtain a good lawyer with considerable experience in this particular field. Ask the lawyer how many trials he or she has defended drunk drivers in, and with what rate of success. Since many states now require that even first-time offenders spend two days in jail, many defendants find they have nothing to lose by going to trial. You certainly don't want a lawyer who simply tells you to plead guilty and take the consequences. You could do that by yourself, and it wouldn't cost you a nickel!

Liability for Injuries Caused by a Drunk Driver

When a drunk driver gets behind the wheel of a car and causes an accident, the drunk driver must pay for the injuries suffered by any other person. But can the injured person sue a bar, restaurant, liquor store, or other business that sold or served the alcohol to the driver? Some states allow the injured person to recover damages if the commercial establishment knew that the patron was already intoxicated but nonetheless dispensed additional liquor to him or her. Many states also impose liability if a liquor store, bar, or other business sells alcoholic beverages to a sober minor who then goes somewhere, drinks the alcohol, and causes an accident because of his or her impaired condition.

Suppose you give a party at home one night. One of your friends gets drunk and causes an accident while driving home. Are you liable to the person injured by your friend? A number of states hold that a private citizen who has a party at home and furnishes alcohol is liable for serving alcohol to an intoxicated guest if he or she knows that the guest will be driving. To avoid liability and the possibility of an accident caused by an intoxicated guest, you should do several things. First, limit the amount of alcohol consumed by guests. Second, if a guest does become intoxicated, do not let him or her leave before sobering up. If necessary, let the guest stay overnight. Alternatively, you or someone else who is sober should drive the intoxicated guest home or call for a taxicab to take him or her home.

Employers who give office parties should likewise exercise caution and common sense to keep an intoxicated employee off the road. In some cases, an employer can be held liable if an employee gets drunk at an office party, then drives home and injures someone on the way.

Fighting Traffic Tickets

Before making a decision to fight a traffic ticket, first consider the evidence you have to support your version of the facts. If it's simply a case of your word against the word of the police officer, you can be sure that the judge will believe the officer 99.99 percent of the time. For example, if you received a citation for failing to stop because the police officer claims you only came to a "rolling stop," the judge will believe the officer's version over your word that you came to a complete stop. You will need some solid evidence to back up your testimony.

The testimony of a witness can swing the scales of justice in your favor; however, the judge will consider the reliability of the witness's testimony based on who the witness is. If the witness is your best friend or spouse, the judge probably won't put much faith in his or her story. But if the witness is a stranger to you, his or her testimony is more likely to persuade the judge that your story has merit.

Another thing to consider before fighting a ticket is whether you have a valid legal defense or merely some excuse the law doesn't recognize as sufficient. For instance, a handicapped parking space is for use by persons who have applied for a special permit to park in such areas. You can't park there because your leg is sore that day. Likewise, trying to defend a speeding ticket on the basis that you were late for work is no defense at all. If, however, an emergency situation exists—you needed to take a seriously ill person to the hospital—this may act as a valid defense. Towing a car with a rope instead of a tow bar cannot be justified on the basis you were only towing it to the repair shop; on the other hand, using a rope to tow a disabled car from the middle of a busy intersection to the side of the road could be justified if the car posed a clear danger to passing motorists.

In some cases, you might get out of the ticket by using a photograph. For example, suppose that you are given a ticket for speeding on an unfamiliar road. You were traveling 45 miles per hour, but the posted speed limit was 35 miles per hour. If the sign was hidden by a tree, go back and take a picture of it to support your contention. Should the city maintenance crew trim the tree before you get a picture of it, obtain records from the appropriate city department showing that landscaping work was done in the area after you received your ticket.

Here is another example of how a picture may be helpful: Suppose you were cited for parking in a handicapped zone— something you did unknowingly because the space was not properly marked. You should take a picture of the space when no car is parked there to show the lack of adequate warning. For example, some states require that a handicapped zone be clearly marked by a blue sign and blue painting on the ground. If there was no sign and the painting was faded, you should beat the ticket.

Sometimes it is worth fighting a ticket simply in the sheer hope that the police officer will not appear. (This is more apt to occur if you've received a parking ticket rather than a moving violation.) If the officer doesn't show up, oppose any request for a continuance that the prosecution may make, and ask the judge for an immediate dismissal of all the charges.

The Trial

Trials for traffic tickets are usually informal hearings presided over by a traffic commissioner who acts as judge. You can have a lawyer represent you at the hearing, but this is usually unnecessary because the cost of the lawyer ordinarily will exceed the maximum fine. If, however, you are facing more serious ramifications than a $20 or $50 fine—such as the suspension of your license or greatly increased insurance rates—you may want to have a lawyer represent you.

Before the trial begins, the judge will ask you if you wish to plead guilty or not guilty to the charges. If you plead guilty, the judge will impose the sentence, usually a fine. You may be offered the chance to plead guilty with an explanation. This has the same legal effect as pleading guilty, but the judge may reduce or suspend your fine if he or she sympathizes with your explanation.

Before proceeding with the trial on your violation, you may be given the option of going to traffic school. Traffic school is usually offered only if the offense was routine and not serious, and you have not had a moving violation within a certain period, such as the last year or two. Traffic school generally consists of a six- to eight-hour classroom refresher course on traffic rules and safety. Upon your successful completion of traffic school, the ticket is expunged from your record. This usually means that your insurance company doesn't hear about the ticket, so it won't be used against you in determining your insurance rates.

If you plead not guilty to the charges, the trial then proceeds. A representative from the district attorney's office will prosecute the case against you. He or she will question the police officer and attempt to establish that you violated the traffic code. When the prosecutor is finished questioning the officer, you can cross-examine the police officer. After your cross-examination, the prosecution will usually rest its case, unless there was another officer present at the time the ticket was given. Once the prosecution rests, you present your version of the facts. When you are done, the prosecution has the right to cross-examine you. If you have any other witnesses to present, this is the time to do it.

If you received a traffic citation in connection with a traffic accident, the driver of the other car and any bystanders who saw the accident happen will be called to testify against you. A police officer cannot usually testify to the cause of the accident unless he or she saw it happen. The officer can, however, testify as to evidence he or she observed after the accident, such as the length of skid marks or final positions of the vehicles.

After you have presented your testimony and rested your case, the prosecution may recall the police officer to rebut your testimony. When that is done, you get a chance to make any closing remarks. The commissioner then renders a verdict. Usually this decision is made on the spot, but occasionally the commissioner will take a case under advisement and mail the decision to you in a day or two.

The Winning Edge

Two things will greatly improve your chances for success in traffic court: your appearance and your presentation. Going in neatly groomed and nicely dressed will make a better impression on the judge than arriving uncombed or unshaven and wearing sloppy or overly casual clothes. Practicing a few times beforehand what you plan to say will not only help make your testimony flow better, but also give you more confidence at the hearing. You may want to prepare a few notes the night before to make sure you cover everything, but the judge will not let you read a prepared statement.

Be calm, cool, and methodical during the presentation of your case. Know where you're going, and then thoughtfully and thoroughly plan how you're going to get there. Never show any anger toward or frustration with either the police officer or the judge. Rather, show the judge the logic of your defense, and you'll have a good chance of "beating the rap."

Example of Testimony in Speeding Case

In the following case, the defendant was cited for speeding while she and a friend were on their way home from work. The police officer who cited her has testified that as he was coming onto the freeway, he noticed a dark blue sedan going at a high rate of speed and weaving in and out of the fast lane. He gave chase and found the defendant proceeding along in the number-three lane at 55 miles per hour in a dark blue sedan. The defendant contends that she had been traveling in the number-three lane at this speed the whole time and that it was another car that the police officer observed speeding. Here is an example of some questions the defendant may ask of the police officer on cross-examination to support her theory that the officer saw another car speeding.

Q. How many lanes away from you was the dark blue car when you first spotted it?

A. Four.

Q. How would you describe the traffic at this time, light, moderate, or heavy?

A. Moderate.

Q. Were there any cars between yours and the dark blue car when you first observed it?

A. Yes.

Q. Approximately how many cars were there between your car and the dark blue car?

A. I would say about four or five.

Q. What made you notice the dark blue car?

A. I noticed it because it was weaving in and out of traffic and was going at a high rate of speed.

Q. Did you get a good look at the driver when you first saw it, or were you just looking at the car itself?

A. I was just looking at the car itself.

Q. So you didn't see the driver at that time?

A. That's correct.

Q. Could you tell at that time whether the driver was a man or a woman?

A. No, I could not.

Q. Did you see any passengers in the car at this time?

A. No, I did not.

Q. Did you see the license plate of the car at this time?

A. No.

Q. Did you notice anything on the back of the car when you first saw it, such as bumper stickers or dents?

A. No.

Q. Were you able to move in immediately behind the dark blue car and give chase?

A. No.

Q. Isn't it true that you lost sight of the dark blue car before you could get behind it?

A. That's correct.

Q. So you had never seen the driver up to this point?

A. That's correct.

Q. And you never saw a passenger?

A. That's correct.

Q. So it's possible that the car you first saw was only occupied by the driver, with no passengers?

A. That's possible.

Q. And it's possible that the car you first saw was driven by a man?

A. That's possible.

Q. How long did you chase the dark blue sedan?

A. I pursued it for about one mile.

Q. And during this time, you did not have it in sight, correct?

A. That's correct.

Q. How fast were you going during this pursuit?

A. I was going about 75 miles per hour.

Q. Isn't it true that you had already passed the car I was driving before you noticed it?

A. That's true.

Q. So up to that point, you believed the car you were pursuing was somewhere in front of you, perhaps far ahead of you?

A. That's true.

Q. What did you do after you spotted my car?

A. I applied my brakes, slowed down, moved in behind you, and put on the flashing lights.

Q. Did you notice anything on the back of my car?

A. I don't remember.

Q. I have here a picture of the back end of my car as it appeared on the date and at the time in question. I would like to show this to you to refresh your memory. [First show the picture to the representative from the district attorney's office, then hand the picture to the bailiff or ask permission of the judge to step forward and hand it to the police officer yourself.] Now can you tell us whether you noticed anything about my car?

A. Yes, I noticed that the right rear side appeared to have been damaged in an accident.

Q. And didn't you wonder why you hadn't observed that damage when you first spotted the blue car as you got onto the freeway?

A. I guess it may have struck me as a little strange that I didn't see it.

Q. Thank you. I have no more questions of this witness, Your Honor.

At this point, the defendant will testify that she had been proceeding in the number-three lane at 55 miles per hour the entire time and that she observed a similar car, but newer and not damaged, speeding along in the fast lane. The defendant will also testify that there was only one person in the other car and that the officer had passed her own car before slowing down. The defendant will also present the testimony of her passenger, who will corroborate the defendant's testimony.

This example demonstrates how being prepared and presenting your defense methodically will help you win the case. If you take the time to plan your presentation, you'll greatly increase your chances of walking out of the courtroom with a smile on your face.

3

ESTATE PLANNING

FOR MOST OF US, estate planning means planning for death. Who gets the property? How much will be due in taxes? Will the estate be tied up in the probate court for several years? Who will take care of the children? These are some of the considerations that motivate us to put our affairs in order. Estate planning can also involve complex strategies to reduce taxes during a person's lifetime, but this is generally only a concern of the wealthy.

This chapter focuses upon what the average American needs to know about estate planning: how to determine the size of your estate, what happens to your property if you fail to plan, the impact of taxes imposed after your death, and ways to avoid probate. The chapter that follows discusses wills—an integral part of any estate plan—and includes instructions for making your own.

People set up an estate plan to achieve a number of goals. For many the main goal is to avoid or minimize estate and gift taxes, so more of the estate goes to loved ones instead of to the government. Others are primarily motivated by a wish to avoid the expenses and delays of probate. Ensuring that there are enough liquid assets or ready cash to pay any estate or inheritance taxes and to provide for the surviving spouse and children while the estate goes through probate are other important concerns.

Determining the Size
of Your Estate

Before doing any estate planning, you need to determine the size of your "estate"—what you own and how much it's worth. When lawyers talk about estates, they speak of property: "real property" and "personal property." Real property is legalese for real estate. Personal property, or personalty, is everything else: cars, boats, airplanes, cash, stocks and bonds, clothing, furniture, jewelry, coin collections, dishes, antiques, and so on. This is an important distinction to make because the average person often thinks of "property" as only real estate. When a lawyer uses the word *property*, it usually includes every type of possession—real estate and personal assets—that a person has.

If you're like most Americans, the major assets of your estate are your house, perhaps a second piece of real estate (such as a vacation home or investment property), life insurance proceeds, retirement benefits, stocks and bonds, bank accounts, automobiles, furniture, and jewelry. The easiest way to get a handle on the size of your estate is to buy a thorough financial statement form at your local stationery store and complete it. Be sure to include all retirement plans and death benefits, such as life insurance benefits (include term insurance if you plan on keeping it in force), IRA accounts, Keogh plans, certificates of deposit, treasury bills, and pension plans. If your jewelry is worth a good deal of money or you have a valuable stamp or coin collection, consider getting an expert appraisal. (It's also a good idea to have an appraisal just in case you ever have to file an insurance claim.) Note that if a business is an important part of your estate, it requires special planning. What happens to the business after you die? Is it shut down, sold, or kept going—and if the last, by whom?

Title to Property

To determine the size of your estate, you need to find out how title to your various belongings is held. Title is also important in ascertaining what right you have to dispose of an individual asset. Obviously, you can't give something away if you don't own it. When you own property with someone else, the manner in which title is held can affect the type of planning you can do with it. The main forms of ownership and their distinguishing features are discussed below. To find out how title to something is held, you will have to see the document of ownership, such as the deed to a house; the certificate of ownership for a car, airplane, or boat; stock certificates; and bankbooks.

Separate Property

When title to anything is in your name alone, it is generally presumed to be your separate property, to do with as you see fit. You can sell it, you can give it away during your life, or you can give it to someone in your will. But if you own the property with someone else and title was taken in your name alone—say, for convenience—your right to sell or give the property away may be affected.

Joint Tenancy

Two (or more) people can hold title to property as joint tenants. Unless otherwise agreed, each joint tenant owns an equal share of the property and can dispose of only that share. The most important thing to know about joint tenancies for estate planning is that a joint tenancy carries with it an automatic right of survivorship. This means that when one joint tenant dies, the remaining joint tenant automatically receives the other's share. The property does not go through probate (although it is subject to estate tax, which is discussed later), and any provision in the deceased person's will relating to the distribution of the property is ignored by the court. If you own property in joint tenancy with someone else, be sure you want that person to get your share of the property when you die. If not, then you should change the title to tenancy in common (see below).

Tenancy by the Entireties

Some 20 states recognize a tenancy by the entireties, which is basically a joint tenancy that can exist only between a husband and wife. As with a joint tenancy, there is a right of survivorship, and the deceased spouse's interest automatically passes to the survivor, without the need for probate. One way a tenancy by the entireties differs from a joint tenancy is that some states have special rules limiting the ability of a creditor to satisfy one spouse's debt from property held in tenancy by the entireties.

Tenants in Common

A tenancy in common is another form of joint ownership that can exist between any two or more people. Each tenant in common owns an equal share of the property (unless they agree otherwise), and can sell or give away only that share. The major distinction between a tenancy in common and a joint tenancy is that in the former, there is no right of survivorship. When a tenant in common dies, his or her share of the property is distributed according to the wishes expressed in his or her will. If there is no will, his or her share goes to the heirs—the next of kin—entitled to it by state law.

Community Property

Nine states—Arizona, California, Idaho, Louisiana, New Mexico, Nevada, Texas, Washington, and Wisconsin—recognize a form of joint ownership between a husband and wife called community property. Holding title as community property for the most part gives a husband and wife the same rights as joint tenants. Each spouse owns one-half of the community property and generally can dispose of only his or her share. There is one major difference from a joint tenancy, however: one spouse's share of community property usually does not pass automatically to the other upon his or her death. The property is distributed according to the terms of the person's will, if there is one, and if not, it goes to the person's heirs, as discussed below.

What Happens If You Don't Plan

If you die without a will or other estate planning tool (such as a living trust), your property will be distributed according to the laws of "intestate succession" of the state where you were living at the time of your death. In this event, it is the state—not you, the owner of the property—that determines who gets what and how much. This may or may not be the way in which you would like to have your property distributed.

The laws of intestate succession vary greatly from state to state. The following examples show just a few of the ways in which property may be divided if a person dies without a will. (Keep in mind that if you own property with someone else, the title can affect who gets it. For example, if the property is held by you and another person as joint tenants, that person gets your share if you die first.)

When There Is a Surviving Spouse

It is a common misconception that when a married person dies without a will, the surviving spouse automatically gets all the property. In fact, the amount the surviving spouse receives depends upon whether there are any children or grandchildren and whether the parents or brothers and sisters of the deceased spouse are living.

In many states, when a married person dies without a will

and leaves a spouse and one child, the surviving spouse gets half and the child the other half. (If the child is a minor, someone will have to be appointed guardian of the property until the child reaches 18.) If there are two or more children, the surviving spouse receives only one-third of the estate, and the children divide the other two-thirds equally. Other states give the surviving spouse one-half or one-third of the estate regardless of the number of children. In some states, the surviving spouse receives cash up to a certain amount and then a percentage (typically one-half) of the rest of the estate.

In most community property states, the surviving spouse receives all of the community property but shares the deceased spouse's separate property (property he or she owned before marriage or received as a gift or inheritance during marriage) with the children.

In a few states, the surviving spouse gets a percentage of the personal assets and a life estate in anywhere from one-third to all of the deceased spouse's real estate. A life estate gives a person the right to live on the property and use it for the rest of his or her life. This is a remnant of old English law, when women had "dower" rights and men had "curtesy" rights.

If a child dies before a parent but leaves a child of his or her own (in other words, a grandchild), when the grandparent dies, the grandchild is entitled to the share of the estate that his or her parent would have otherwise received. Consider the following illustration: John Jones had two children, Larry and Dave. When John died, only Dave was still living; Larry had died several years earlier. Larry had a daughter, Kristen, however, who was living at the time of John's death. Dave and Kristen each get one-half of John's estate. If Larry had left two children, they would have divided equally the one-half share he would have received.

If a person dies leaving a spouse but no children or grandchildren, some states give the surviving spouse everything. Other states split the estate between the surviving spouse and the deceased person's parents (or brothers and sisters, if the parents are no longer living). In community property states, the surviving spouse usually gets all of the community property but must share the separate property with the deceased spouse's parents or brothers and sisters in the absence of surviving children. If there are no surviving parents or brothers and sisters, the surviving spouse generally gets it all.

When There Is No Surviving Spouse

If a person dies without a surviving spouse, then the property usually goes to the children (or grandchildren if a child has died). An adopted child is entitled to share in an estate to the same extent as a child born to the deceased person. (In some states, the adopted child shares in the estate of his or her biological parent as well.) Unadopted stepchildren ordinarily do not share in the estate of a stepparent. As for children born out of wedlock, the rule used to be that the child was entitled to inherit from his or her mother, but could inherit from his or her father only if the father had admitted in writing that the child was his. Today, a child born out of wedlock is entitled to inherit from both mother and father. Of course, the child still has to prove that a particular man was the father, which can be difficult if the father never acknowledged the child as his. Recent advances in blood testing, however, have made it possible to prove parentage with a very high degree of certainty. (See chapter 1 for a discussion of proving paternity.)

When there are no children, grandchildren, great-grandchildren, and so on (in law, "issue" or "lineal descendants"), the deceased person's parents usually each get one-half of the property. If only one parent survives, he or she gets all of the property in many states. Some states divide the property among the deceased person's parents and brothers and sisters. The deceased person's brothers and sisters split the estate if the parents are not living. When a person dies without close relatives, then the closest next of kin (such as nephews and nieces, cousins, and aunts and uncles) share the estate. What happens when no heir can be found? The state gets everything. If a relative of yours has died without leaving a will or close relatives (spouse, child, grandchild, parent, brother, or sister), it may be to your benefit to consult an attorney to investigate whether you have any rights to the estate.

Other Considerations

If you have any minor children, by not planning your estate, you throw away the chance to suggest a guardian for them. You also lose the opportunity to name the executor or executrix—the person you want to oversee the distribution of your estate. The court will appoint a guardian for your children and a person to administer your estate without your having a say about it. And if your estate is larger, your failure to plan may make the government tens of thousands of dollars richer—money your loved ones could have received.

Death and Taxes

Benjamin Franklin once wrote, "In this world nothing is certain but death and taxes." Could anything be more certain than a combination of the two, with taxes imposed upon your property when you die? And so it is that the federal government has a complicated estate and gift tax system. Most states also impose their own inheritance and gift taxes, but because these vary greatly from state to state, the following discussion is limited to federal estate and gift taxes. Fortunately, taxes upon a person's death are not quite as certain as old Ben Franklin would lead us to believe. Through proper estate planning, you can take all or much of the bite out of the taxes due upon your death. And the passage of new laws on both the state and federal levels have reduced the burden of death taxes considerably.

Thanks to the Economic Recovery Tax Act of 1981, fewer people now need to worry about federal estate and gift taxes.

Before that law was passed, you had to think about federal taxes if your estate was worth more than $175,000. Estates below that amount were entirely exempt from federal estate taxes. When you realize that any life insurance proceeds payable upon your death are normally included when the size of your estate is computed, it's easy to see that millions of Americans needed to do some estate planning. The new law raises the amount of your estate that does not get taxed. For persons dying in 1986, the first $500,000 of the estate is free from federal taxes. Beginning in 1987, this amount increases to $600,000. If your estate (including life insurance benefits) is less than this amount, then you needn't concern yourself too much with federal estate taxes—although you will want to find out how much your state taxes will be so you can plan accordingly.

If your estate is subject to federal estate and gift taxes, you can eliminate or minimize those taxes through proper planning. Two important planning tools in this regard are the marital deduction trust and giving gifts during your lifetime.

The Marital Deduction Trust

A married couple with an estate of more than $500,000 (or over $600,000, starting in 1987) can use a "marital deduction trust" to double the amount that is free of federal estate taxes. (Remember that you don't need to worry about this if your combined estate is worth less than $500,000 in 1986 or $600,000 beginning in 1987.) Suppose a married couple have an estate worth $1 million. When the first one of them dies—let's say the husband—he leaves his share of the estate ($500,000) to his wife outright; no federal estate taxes are due upon his death. If the wife dies later that same year, $500,000 of her estate (which now totals $1 million) is taxed. At the rates effective in 1986, $190,000 would have to be paid to the federal government in estate taxes. If she dies after 1986, then only $400,000—the amount over the $600,000 exemption that begins in 1987—would be taxed, and $153,000 in estate taxes would be due. (There's a lot more to figuring out federal estate taxes, but this gives you a rough idea of what's at stake.)

To avoid paying this large chunk to the government, the couple could set up a "marital deduction trust." Instead of the husband's share of the estate going to his wife, it is put into a trust for the benefit of his wife for the rest of her life; when she dies, the money and property are distributed to their children, grandchildren, or other beneficiaries named in the trust. During her lifetime, the wife gets to live in the house and receives all of the interest and income from the assets; she may even be able to reach part of the principal if she needs to. When the wife dies, her estate is now worth only $500,000—her husband's share is not included in her estate because she is only a beneficiary of a trust and not the owner of her late husband's property. And since the wife's estate is only $500,000, no federal estate taxes are due upon her death. The couple have managed to protect their entire $1,000,000 estate from all federal estate taxes—a savings of almost $200,000. Since either the husband or wife may die first, it is essential that both have a will or other plan (such as a living trust, discussed below) that creates a marital deduction trust in favor of the other.

If you are married and have sufficient assets to be concerned about federal estate taxes (or state inheritance taxes), you should see a lawyer about setting up a marital deduction trust. After all, who would you rather give your money to—Uncle Sam or your children?

Taxes on Gifts Made during Your Lifetime

Giving gifts during your lifetime can be an excellent way of reducing a large estate (and estate taxes) and avoiding probate at the same time. Currently you can make a gift of up to $10,000 per person each year to as many people as you want. For instance, you can reduce your estate today by $20,000 by giving two different people $10,000 apiece, or ten people $2,000 each, or 20,000 people a dollar each—or any other combination you can think of. A husband and wife can make a combined gift of up to $20,000 per person free from federal gift tax concerns. For example, if there are two children, each year the couple can give up to $20,000 to each child without worrying about federal gift taxes. In large estates, making gifts each year over a period of time can result in significant federal estate tax savings.

An important caution: Do not start making substantial gifts without first discussing it with a good lawyer, who can advise you on all of the implications, tax and otherwise. Remember that even if gift giving might benefit you taxwise, you have to be in the position to afford to give the gift. This depends in large part on your financial liquidity (ready cash or assets that can be sold quickly), your age, and your health. If you give away too much of your estate, and some of your major cash-producing assets (such as stocks and bonds) decline in value, your income—and standard of living—may drop dramatically. You could well find yourself having to ask for your property back. Be aware, though, that once you make a gift, you cannot revoke it, and you can't compel the beneficiary to return it—assuming he or she hasn't already spent it.

The Orphan's Deduction Trust

Before 1982, a special rule allowed parents to set up an "orphan's deduction trust" in their wills to soften the blow of estate taxes when a child was left orphaned upon the death of his or her parents. This trust let the parents put aside up to $5,000 for every year the child was under 21. If the child was six years old when both parents died, for example, the orphan's deduction trust could consist of up to $75,000 ($5,000 times 15 years). That $75,000 was not used in computing the size of the parents' estate for federal estate taxes. The Economic Recovery Tax Act of 1981 repealed the orphan's deduction trust. If your will contains an orphan's deduction trust, you should review it for a possible change.

Avoiding Probate

What Probate Is and How It Works

Probate is the legal process in which the probate court (called surrogate court in some states) authenticates a written document as the will of the deceased person and directs the distribution of the estate to the persons entitled to it according to the will. If there is no will or if the will is declared invalid, the probate court distributes the property to the heirs entitled to it under state law (discussed earlier).

Within a certain time after a person dies, usually 30 days, the person named in the will as executor or executrix must offer it for probate. He or she does this by filing the will, a death certificate, and a petition to administer the estate. These are filed in the probate court in the county where the deceased person had his or her principal residence, his or her "home." To probate the will, the executor usually hires an attorney, whose fees are paid by the deceased person's estate. If the person died without a will, the next of kin can file the same documents (except the will, of course).

The close relatives of the deceased usually must be notified of the probate proceedings. Later, a court hearing is held at which the executor must prove that the document is in fact the deceased person's will, that the person was of sound mind when he or she signed the will, and that the will satisfies all legal requirements. Most states permit a person who witnessed the will to sign an affidavit stating that he or she was present at the signing of the will, saw the testator (or testatrix)—the person who made the will—sign the will, and that the witness then signed the will. In some states, at least one witness may have to appear in court and testify that he or she witnessed the signing of the will. If none of the witnesses can be found and the will is proper on its face, the law presumes that the will is valid and places the burden to prove otherwise on any person objecting to it. If a holographic (handwritten) will is involved, someone familiar with the deceased person's handwriting can testify as to whether the handwriting is indeed that of the deceased person. If a forgery is suspected, known writing samples of the deceased person can be used for comparison, and professional experts in handwriting analysis and document examination may be called upon to assist the court.

After the will has been proved to be that of the deceased person, the court will give an order accepting the will for probate, and the executor is usually confirmed by the court. If the executor named in the will refuses to or cannot accept the position, the court will confirm the testator's second choice, if there is one or, if there is not, appoint another person. If the person died without a will or if the court rules that the will offered for probate is invalid, the court will appoint an administrator (or administratrix) of the estate, whose functions are the same as those of an executor. The administrator is usually the deceased person's next of kin—the person who will inherit all or the largest portion of the estate. Like the executor, the administrator generally hires an attorney to probate the estate; the fees, like those of the executor's attorney, are paid by the deceased person's estate.

The executor (or administrator, as the case may be) collects all of the deceased person's assets, inventories them, then has them appraised. Creditors of the deceased person are notified so they can file their claims with the probate court. If a creditor fails to file a claim within the specified time—say, four months—that claim is lost forever. If a creditor's claim is disputed, an amount sufficient to satisfy that claim may be put in a separate fund pending the outcome of the litigation, and the rest of the estate may be distributed. A large creditor's claim can hold up distribution of the entire estate until the dispute is settled.

After any challenges to the will and disputed creditor's claims have been resolved, the taxes, costs of administration (including fees to the executor or administrator and attorney), funeral expenses, creditors, and the like are paid. Finally, the remaining property is transferred to the persons named in the will or entitled to it by law.

Why Avoid Probate?

The rather serious disadvantages to probate prompt many people to seek out ways to avoid the probate process. The chief complaint about probate is the sheer length of time it takes— anywhere from a few months to several years, with an average in the area of one year. Restrictions are placed on dealing with and selling the estate assets while the estate goes through probate. If a surviving spouse or other beneficiary wants to sell a piece of property, he or she (or the executor) ordinarily has to seek permission of the court. The proceeds from the sale of an asset usually are placed in the estate's bank account until the judge orders the final distribution of the estate.

During the time an estate is in the probate court, a surviving spouse and children are given a reasonable allowance for living expenses. What amount is "reasonable" depends on the size of the estate, the circumstances of the survivors, the standard of living to which they are accustomed, and the solvency and liquidity of the estate.

Another reason many people want to avoid probate is the cost involved. The ordinary costs involved in probating an estate are the executor's (or administrator's) fee, the fee of the executor's (or administrator's) attorney, court filing fees, the cost of having the estate assets appraised, and advertising costs (to publish notices of death to allow creditors and others to file their claims or challenges). On top of this, there could be additional fees to the executor and the attorney to compensate for "extraordinary" services, such as defending the estate in a will contest or against disputed creditors' claims.

Some people wish to avoid probate because they don't want others to know the size of their estate or who the beneficiaries are. This usually occurs in the case of political figures, heads of large corporations, movie stars, and the like, who want to keep the size of their estates private. While the rich and famous may wish to keep secret the extent of their financial empires and who received what, to the average person, publicity is not a real threat or concern.

A final reason some people want to avoid probate is to reduce the emotional effect on the survivors, so they can get on with their lives. This can be very hard to do when they are constantly being reminded of the death of a loved one while the property is tied up in the courts. A bitter will contest between relatives can certainly leave deep emotional scars. A trust or other method that avoids probate can provide for the quick distribution of the assets and let everyone start making a new life as soon as possible.

Avoiding Probate May Not Mean Avoiding Taxes

Many people believe that avoiding probate means avoiding death taxes (federal estate taxes and state inheritance taxes). This is not necessarily true. It is possible to avoid probate and eliminate or minimize death taxes through proper planning. But just because some asset doesn't go through probate does not mean it isn't taxed.

An example: Bert, an elderly man in poor health, owns a piece of real estate that he wants his niece, Cory, to get when he dies. Bert knows that if the land passes through probate with the rest of his assets, it will be subject to death taxes. Thinking to avoid death taxes, Bert deeds the land to himself and his niece as joint tenants (below) and dies the next week. At the moment of Bert's death, the land automatically belongs to Cory; it does not go through probate. But the land is subject to the same amount of taxes as if it had gone through the probate process. Its value is included in the size of Bert's estate, and the federal estate taxes and state inheritance taxes are based on the total amount of Bert's estate, including the land. In short, Bert didn't save a penny in taxes. (Bert did, however, manage to speed up the transfer of the property to Cory and did reduce the fees the executor and attorney for the executor were entitled to collect by reducing the size of his probated estate.)

Ways to Avoid Probate

Here are some of the common methods for avoiding probate:

Joint Tenancy

As we discussed earlier, when two or more people own property as joint tenants, title automatically transfers to the surviving owner or owners upon the death of a joint tenant. A provision of a will or trust that attempts to dispose of the joint tenant's interest in the property in any other manner will not be enforced by the court. If your estate is large enough for you to think about reducing estate and inheritance taxes, holding property in joint tenancy may defeat the plan, since that property will not be available for a trust to take full advantage of the marital deduction discussed earlier in this chapter. (Proper estate planning with a living trust, discussed below, that includes a marital deduction trust, lets you avoid probate *and* save taxes.)

As observed earlier, holding title as joint tenant does not necessarily mean avoiding death taxes. Moreover, the creation of a joint tenancy could have some immediate gift tax implications. If one person owns a piece of property, for example, and adds another's name as a joint tenant, the owner may be deemed to have made a gift of one-half of the property to the new joint tenant. And by putting someone else's name on the deed as a joint tenant, the owner runs the risk that that person might try to sell his or her interest or bring a court action to partition (divide) the property. Although adding a person as a joint tenant seems a simple thing to do, you need to consult a lawyer on all of the potential ramifications and problems if the asset is something as major as a house or other piece of real estate.

Giving Gifts during Your Lifetime

Suppose you want to give $5,000 cash to a favorite nephew or niece. If you make that gift in a will, it may be quite a while before the nephew or niece ever receives it, and the amount will be included in determining the size of your estate for taxes and executor's fees. On the other hand, if you have enough cash on hand and can afford to do so, it may be easier simply to give your nephew or niece the $5,000 while you are still living. This sum does not pass through probate, nor is it included in determining the size of your estate for federal estate tax purposes. A growing number of people are making gifts during their lifetimes not only to avoid the delays and expenses of probate, but also to share the joy of the gift's recipient. If you plan on making a sizable gift, first consult a lawyer experienced in estate planning to see how the gift will affect your taxes. (Remember that a gift of more than $10,000 to one person is subject to federal, and perhaps state, gift taxes.)

Totten Trusts

If you'd like to give cash to someone but want to make that gift effective only upon your death and not before, then you should consider a so-called Totten Trust. This applies only to bank accounts and lets you open an account in your name as trustee for another person—and you keep the power to revoke this "trust" at any time before your death. The beneficiary of the trust has no right to withdraw any of the funds while you are living. You don't even have to tell the beneficiary that you have set up this trust. You can make deposits into or withdrawals from the account as you see fit during your lifetime. You can even close the bank account before you die, in which case the beneficiary gets nothing. But if the bank account still exists at the time of your death, the beneficiary receives everything in the account— and doesn't have to go through probate to get it.

Life Insurance and Retirement Benefits

If you purchase a life insurance policy and name your spouse or another person as beneficiary, the beneficiary is automatically entitled to the proceeds upon your death. The only time the money goes through probate is when the proceeds are paid to your estate. To avoid this, in your policy you should name not only a primary beneficiary, but also a secondary beneficiary. If you are married, for example, you would probably want to name your spouse as the primary beneficiary and your children as secondary beneficiaries in case your spouse dies before or with you. Don't name your estate as a beneficiary except as part of a broad tax plan or if there isn't anyone else you can think of. If the life insurance proceeds are paid to your estate, this could significantly increase the fees received by the executor (or administrator) and the executor's attorney, as well as the amount of time your heirs will have to wait before they get the money.

Like life insurance benefits, benefits paid to a deceased employee's beneficiaries under a pension or profit-sharing plan (or a deferred-compensation contract) normally do not go through probate. They are, however, subject to probate if the proceeds are paid directly to the deceased employee's estate.

Living Trusts

A living trust is a trust set up during the lifetime of the trustor (the person who makes the trust). A testamentary trust, on the other hand, is found in a person's will and takes effect only upon the person's death. Lawyers refer to a "living" trust as an "inter vivos" trust, *inter vivos* meaning "between living persons." A living trust may be either revocable or irrevocable. An irrevocable living trust is ordinarily a device only the very rich take advantage of, primarily to minimize tax liability. The person with an average-size estate is more interested in the revocable living trust, in which the trustor retains considerable control over the property, including the right to revoke the trust at any time.

A few basics about a trust: To form a valid trust, there must be a trustor, a trustee, a beneficiary, and the trust property ("res"). The trustor is the person (or persons) who initially owns the property and wishes to create the trust. The trustee is the person to whom title to the property is transferred and who is charged with managing and administering the trust. The beneficiary (or beneficiaries) is the person (or persons) for whose benefit the trust is created. A trustor cannot also be the sole trustee and sole beneficiary of the trust. The trust "res" is simply the property or assets that constitute the trust. Money, real estate, stocks and bonds, or almost any other property can be placed in trust.

Under a typical revocable living trust, a person places property that he or she owns in trust for the benefit of himself or herself and at least one other person, usually a child. A married couple will ordinarily place their property in trust for the benefit of themselves and their children. The trustor may name himself or herself as the trustee. A bank or other financial institution can be named as trustee or cotrustee. (Always discuss this with the bank first, to see if your estate is large enough for them to handle. Also find out how much the annual trustee's fee will be.) Frequently an adult child is named cotrustee or even sole trustee to see how well he or she will act as trustee after the parent's death. The parent can retain the power to remove that child as trustee at any time, without a reason.

If the trust is not revoked during the trustor's lifetime, then the trust property is distributed according to the terms of the trust when the trustor dies, thereby avoiding probate and its delays and expenses. In the case of a married couple, a living trust frequently provides that upon the death of one spouse, the trust remains in effect for the benefit of the surviving spouse. When the surviving spouse dies, the trust may provide that the property be distributed among the children, or it may provide that the trust remain in effect, with the children or grandchildren as beneficiaries. (But a trust can't last forever. As a handy rule of thumb, the longest a trust can continue is until the last of the trustor's grandchildren reaches the age of 21.)

Any property that isn't part of the trust is distributed according to the terms of the trustor's will, if the trustor has one, and if he or she does not, according to state law. When a person has a living trust, his or her will usually contains a provision that any property remaining at death becomes part of the trust property. This type of provision is called a "pourover" clause, as the property remaining at death is poured over into the trust.

Like wills, revocable living trusts can be structured to help minimize estate taxes. For example, just as a married couple can create a marital deduction trust (see discussion above) by their wills to save taxes, so too can they put a provision in their revocable living trusts that when the first of them dies, his or her share is placed in a marital deduction trust. (Remember that setting up any type of estate plan to minimize taxes is complex and requires the skill of a competent estate-planning lawyer.)

Life Insurance

Life insurance is an essential part of estate planning. Indeed, the proceeds from a life insurance policy frequently constitute the largest or second largest asset (after the house) of many estates. Life insurance provides ready cash to support the surviving spouse and children, pay the taxes, keep a business running, and more. When there isn't sufficient cash on hand to pay these things, other assets must be liquidated, often in a hurry and at bargain-basement prices.

In a family where one spouse works and the other stays at home taking care of the kids, life insurance is needed on both lives. It is clear to see why life insurance is necessary on the breadwinner's life; if he or she dies, the family will have no source of income. But if the spouse who cares for the children dies, many people overlook that outside help will probably have to be hired to assist with the household chores.

How much insurance coverage you need depends upon a

number of factors, including how much tax will be due upon your death, how many people you support and their standard of living, and your age and health. Several different types of life insurance policies are available, the most popular of which are whole life and term insurance.

Under a whole life policy, you pay a set premium every year for the rest of your life (or a specified number of years). The amount of the premium is based on your age and health at the time you buy the policy and the amount of insurance you get. A $100,000 policy is going to cost less than a $200,000 policy, and a younger person will pay a smaller premium than an older one will.

After a couple of years, your whole life policy will have a "cash value." If you want, you can terminate the policy and take the cash value instead. (The amount of the cash value depends on how much you've paid on the policy over the years. The longer you've had the policy and the more you've paid, the higher the cash value will be.) Or you can "borrow against" the cash value. This means that the insurance company lends you part or all of the policy's current cash value, at an interest rate usually lower than a bank's. You can pay this loan back but generally don't have to. If you don't pay it back, when you die, the amount of the loan and all outstanding interest charges normally are deducted from the policy's face value, and whatever is left is paid to the policy's designated beneficiary.

As people get older and retire, they sometimes find it is difficult to keep up the premiums. It is usually possible to modify the original policy so that you can stop paying the premiums in exchange for reduced coverage.

Term insurance pays out only if you die within a certain period of time—for instance, five years from the date you take out the policy. Unlike whole life insurance, you do not build up any cash value with a term policy. You can't trade your policy in for cash, and the insurance company won't lend you money against a term policy. But term insurance usually costs much less than whole life insurance for the same amount of coverage, and by wisely investing the money you save, you can build up an even greater "cash value" to borrow against or withdraw from.

Who gets the money is usually the most important consideration, apart from how much and what type of insurance to buy. The "primary beneficiary" of the policy is the person who gets the money when you die. If the primary beneficiary dies before you, and you don't get around to changing the policy to name someone else, the "secondary beneficiary" gets the money.

We have already seen that by naming someone other than your estate as the beneficiary of the insurance proceeds, you can avoid probate and its delays and costs. You can even make a trust the beneficiary of the policy, so that your spouse or children don't get a huge sum of money all at once. By using certain kinds of trusts, such as a marital deduction trust, you can also take advantage of tax savings. If you're worried about giving someone the entire amount of insurance money in a single cash payment but don't want to go to the trouble of setting up a trust, most insurance companies offer you the option of spreading out the payments over a period of years.

Another thing to consider is who owns the policy. If you own an insurance policy on your life, the proceeds are considered part of your estate when you die and are included for tax and other purposes. If, however, someone else, such as your spouse or child, owns the policy on your life, the money is not included in your estate, nor is it taxed. Even if you have a policy in force right now, you can transfer ownership to someone else, such as your spouse or children, to avoid estate taxes when you die. Your lawyer or insurance agent can counsel you on questions of ownership and how to change it.

The Dangers of Do-It-Yourself Estate Planning

There are a growing number of "do-it-yourself" books about estate planning and probate avoidance, many of which preach living trusts as "the" planning tool. Some of these books are basically compendiums of trust forms that you allegedly merely have to photocopy and complete for an instant estate plan. The problem is that every estate is unique, and every person's goals are different. Tax avoidance may be the prime goal of one person, probate avoidance the desire of another, ensuring that property is given to the correct persons the wish of another. A living trust is only one tool of the estate planner and might not be right for you.

Furthermore, there is much more to a living trust than filling out a few forms, filing them away, and forgetting about them. Probate will be avoided only if the living trust is set up properly *and* administered properly. Did you know that you are required to keep proper records and books for the trust, and, if the trust was created before January 1, 1981, you must file an information return (I.R.S. Form 1041) each year with the Internal Revenue Service? (Although you don't have to file Form 1041 with the I.R.S. if you set up the trust after December 31, 1980, you may still have to file an information return with your state.) If you don't follow the procedures to the letter, the courts may not recognize your living trust. And there's a lot more to it than this. By doing it yourself, you risk blowing the whole thing.

There are just too many pitfalls for the untrained person trying to do his or her own estate planning. We recommend that you not do anything more complicated than preparing your own simple will, according to the directions in the next chapter. If your estate can benefit from some estate planning, or if you want to avoid probate, discuss your needs and goals with a qualified professional estate planner. While there are some nonlawyers who advertise their services as estate planners, the first person to contact is a lawyer who is experienced in this field. Depending on the size of your estate and your objectives, the lawyer may work with other professionals, such as an accountant, a life insurance agent, or an investment counselor, to work out a complete estate plan for your needs. This really is the only way you can get the assurance—the peace of mind—that everything is in order.

4

WILLS

IN THIS CHAPTER, we discuss everything most people need to know about wills and other death-related considerations, such as funeral arrangements, organ donations, "living wills," and euthanasia. Many of you will even be able to write your own will with the directions and examples provided here. But before going any further, if you haven't already done so, read the preceding chapter on estate planning and probate avoidance. That chapter contains explanations and definitions that are necessary to fully understand the following material. It also has valuable information to help you determine whether you should write your own will.

Why You Need a Will

A will is a document that takes effect on the death of the person who made it—the "testator" if a man, "testatrix" if a woman. It directs who gets your real estate, automobiles, money, furniture, stocks and bonds, jewelry, and anything else you own. A will also carries out other final instructions, such as naming a guardian to care for your minor children. (It shouldn't, though, as discussed later in this chapter, include funeral arrangements.)

In effect, a will allows you to speak "from beyond the grave" to ensure that things are done according to your wishes.

But a will is much more than a cold legal document. It is truly an expression of love. You make a will because you care enough about someone to share the things that you treasured most during life. Which brings us to the main reason people make wills: peace of mind. Why take a chance on what will be done with your property? Dying without a will is one risk that just isn't worth it.

Who needs a will? Just about every adult. Of course, the reasons can be very different. Here are a few examples: A young couple who don't have much in the way of money and belongings need a will to appoint a guardian for their minor children if they die. A middle-aged couple with substantial assets can use a will to eliminate or minimize the taxes that may be due upon their deaths. Older persons prepare wills to ensure that their estates go to their children, grandchildren, or a favorite nephew or niece, or to make gifts to a hospital, religious institution, or disease research foundation. Another person might make a will to give a gift to someone who has been kind to him or her, especially during a time of illness.

Seventy percent or more of American adults do not have wills. If you talk to them, you'll find that most have been meaning to make a will for quite some time but keep putting it off. Ask them why, and they'll give you the same answers: "It costs too much to have a lawyer draw a will," or "I don't have enough property to go to the trouble." (Many, particularly older people, have more money and assets than they think. For example, a couple who bought their house for $20,000 or less may not realize that today, it could easily be worth $100,000 or more. And some of the "junk" they have collected over the years may prove to be considerably valuable.)

But the main reasons so many people don't have wills are psychological: people don't want to think about their own deaths. Or they believe that by making a will, it will somehow hasten death. Picasso, for instance, refused to make a will for this very reason. Granted, he did live to the venerable age of 91. But it took 4½ years of bitter fighting before his estate—worth about $300 million—was settled. This wasn't unexpected. Picasso himself once predicted that "the settling of my estate, I am sure, is going to be worse than anything you can imagine." Had he made a will, the estate no doubt would have been resolved sooner, with less of a toll on his family and loved ones—and he probably would have lived just as long.

One final observation: Of the 30 percent or so who do have wills, many have wills that are at least ten years old. If the person died today, the old will might not now dispose of the property in the way he or she would like. An old, outdated will often is as bad as, and sometimes is even worse than, no will at all.

Types of Wills

There are three types of wills: the formal witnessed will, the "holographic" (handwritten) will, and the "nuncupative" (oral) will. Of these, only the formal witnessed will is good in all situations. A number of states do not recognize holographic wills, and oral wills are permitted only in very unusual circumstances. We will therefore concentrate on formal wills, particularly with regard to making your own will.

The Formal Witnessed Will

A formal witnessed will is one that is typed up and signed by the testator or testatrix and by two witnesses (except in South Carolina and Vermont, which require three witnesses). We usually associate formal wills with those drawn up by a lawyer, but there's no reason why you can't make a simple one yourself (step-by-step instructions to help you write your own will are included below). But only you or your lawyer can prepare your will. A person who is not a lawyer cannot prepare a will for you, since drafting a will involves the practice of law, for which a proper license and admission to the Bar is required. If a nonlawyer prepares a will for you, you're taking a big chance that the court will throw it out or that the will is poorly drafted and doesn't dispose of your assets in the way that you'd like.

Holographic (Handwritten) Wills

A holographic (also called "olographic") will is one that is entirely in your own handwriting and that you have signed and dated. This type of will is usually not witnessed. Holographic wills can be made in the following states: Alaska, Arizona, Arkansas, California, Colorado, Idaho, Kentucky, Louisiana, Michigan, Mississippi, Montana, Nebraska, Nevada, New Jersey, North Carolina, North Dakota, Oklahoma, Pennsylvania, South Dakota, Tennessee, Texas, Utah, Virginia, West Virginia, and Wyoming. Three other states—Maryland, New York, and Rhode Island—permit only servicemen to make holographic wills, and even then only under certain circumstances.

If made according to the state's requirements, a holographic will is just as good as a formal witnessed will. This usually remains true even if you later move to a state that doesn't recognize holographic wills made in that state. If you decide to prepare your own will, however, we recommend that you type it up and then sign it and have it witnessed (in other words, make a formal will) in the manner described below.

Because holographic wills are more the exception than the rule, courts have traditionally been very strict in accepting them for probate. Since a holographic will must be *entirely* in the handwriting of the testator, courts have ruled holographic wills invalid where the testator used a rubber stamp to sign his name, where the date was typed in rather than written, where an address identifying a piece of property was inserted by rubber stamp, or where other provisions were not in the testator's own handwriting. A holographic will written by someone other than the testator is not valid. And if you buy a preprinted form at the stationery store, fill in the blanks, and sign it, most courts will not accept this as a holographic will. (Besides, with most preprinted forms, you're essentially buying just a blank piece of paper with a fancy title.)

Nuncupative (Oral) Wills

When a person doesn't have enough time to prepare a written will before he or she dies, many states recognize an oral, or "nuncupative," will. Oral wills, which are very rare, are valid only if made during the person's last sickness. In some states, for an oral will to be valid, the person must expect immediate death from an injury received the same day. Depending upon the laws of the particular state, the person must state the oral will in front of two or three witnesses. The oral will usually must be put in writing within a certain number of days and signed by the witnesses and must be offered for probate within a specified period, such as six months.

There are usually strict limits on the amount of money or types of assets that can be passed down through an oral will. For example, real estate cannot be disposed of by an oral will. And there may be a limit of, say, $5,000 on the money or assets a person can give away through an oral will.

Joint and Mutual Wills

Joint and mutual wills aren't really a separate category of wills, but rather are types of formal wills. Although these kinds of wills can be made by any two (or more) people, they are usually made by a husband and wife.

A joint will is a single will signed by two people (the husband and wife), in which each gives his or her share to the survivor; when both are dead, the property goes to their children or other designated beneficiaries. Mutual wills contain the same provisions a joint will would, but instead of just a single will, each spouse has his or her own will. For example, the husband's will might provide that all of his assets go to his wife, and if she is not living, to the children; the wife's will in return would give her assets to her husband, and to the children if he has died.

It is usually preferable to make mutual wills rather than a joint will. One reason is that the single joint will may become tattered going through probate on the death of the first spouse. Another reason is that problems may arise if one spouse wants to change the joint will but the other doesn't. A mutual will, on the other hand, ordinarily can be changed without the other spouse's consent.

What You Should Know about Wills

Age Requirements

In most states you must be at least 18 years old to make a will. In Georgia you only need to be 14, in Louisiana 16, and in Alabama and Wyoming, you must be 19 years old. There is no upper age limit; as long as a person has the proper mental capacity, he or she can make a will. A person under the required age usually must go to court and get a guardian appointed to make a will.

Sound Mind and Body

Every reading of a will in a movie begins "I, _____ , being of sound mind and body, hereby declare that this is my Last Will and Testament." The fact is that there simply is no such thing as a "sound body" requirement. Physical condition is not important, except to the extent it affects a person's mind and mental capacity. A paraplegic, amputee, or other person suffering from a physical disability is certainly not precluded from making a will.

When lawyers talk about "sound mind," they mean that a

person has the "mental capacity," or "mental competency," to make a will. Being of sound mind to make a will does not mean that you must be perfectly sane (if there is such a thing!), have a clear and unfailing memory, and otherwise have the mind you had when you were 18. You only need a general understanding of how much property you own and who the natural objects of your affection are—your children or grandchildren, for instance, or a favorite nephew or niece. And you must be able to put these two factors together and form an orderly plan for who gets what.

Your competency to make a will is determined by your mental state at the time you sign your will. A person who is insane may become sufficiently lucid to make a will and then again lose sanity. As long as the will was made during a period of mental lucidity, it is valid. Suppose a person makes a will, then goes insane. Is the will still good? Yes. That a person loses mental capacity at some time after the will is made and signed is of no consequence. It becomes important only if the person tries to revoke or amend the will after becoming mentally incompetent.

The person who indulges in alcohol or drugs, even to excess, the eccentric who exhibits bizarre behavior, the older person who has occasional lapses of memory—all may at times have sufficient mental capacity to make a will. For example, an alcoholic or a drug abuser can make a valid will when sober.

Another example: Lucy, an 89-year-old widow, has been in ill health for several years. She is occasionally forgetful but she is aware of the fact that she owns the house she lives in; that she holds some stocks and bonds in various companies (although she is not quite sure of what exactly she owns); and that she has some jewelry, furniture, and the like. Her only living relatives are a cousin she hasn't seen in 50 years and a nephew who visits her each month. She makes a will, giving her house, furniture, jewelry, and the like to her nephew, and her stocks and bonds to her favorite charity. Her will is valid because, under the legal test, she was "of sound mind."

Is a will made on a deathbed good? Again the real question is whether the person was of sound mind. The fact that a person is on the verge of death does not alone invalidate a will. If a disease has resulted in brain deterioration, however, then that person may not be of sound mind. What if the person was medicated when the will was made? If the person didn't know who or where he or she was and didn't know he or she was signing a will, then the will is no good. But if the medication only made the person tired or weak, and he or she fully realized what was going on, the will is valid. If a will is to be made on a deathbed, a lawyer should prepare the will after meeting privately with the person. A videotape recording of the signing of the will is highly recommended in this situation, as it will give the judge or jury a better picture of just how "sound of mind" the person was.

What You Can and Can't Give Away

Before sitting down to make your will, you have to figure out what you own and how you want to distribute it. Use the guidelines in the previous chapter to do an inventory of your assets. If something is your own separate property, you have the right to dispose of the whole thing any way you want. If you own the property with someone else as tenants in common, or if something is community property, you usually can give away only your share. Remember that if you own something with someone else as joint tenants (or tenants in the entirety), it automatically goes to the surviving joint tenant. That property does not go through probate, so any provision in your will does not apply to it. If you want someone other than your joint tenant to get your share of that property, you will have to change the title to, for example, tenants in common.

You cannot give away property that is subject to a contract. Say, for example, that you want to give the proceeds of your life insurance policy to someone other than the policy's named beneficiary. Even if your will gives the life insurance money to someone else, however, the beneficiary named in the policy gets the money. Why? Because the terms of the policy—a contract— control the money. If you want the proceeds to go to someone other than your currently named beneficiary, you'll have to contact your insurance agent and fill out the necessary forms. This same advice applies to retirement benefits, pension plans, IRAs (Individual Retirement Accounts) or similar accounts, and deferred compensation plans and other employee benefits.

Here is another example of how a contract can affect your right to dispose of your property: Donald, an ailing octogenarian, tells his niece, Linda, that if she will move in and take care of him for the rest of his life, he will leave her his house. Linda moves in and takes care of Donald until he dies six years later. But when Donald's will is read, Linda learns that he has given the house to someone else. Can she do anything? Yes. If Linda can prove that there was an agreement, a court will enforce it against Donald's estate, and Linda will get the house. For your own protection, if you ever find yourself in the position of making a deal to perform services in exchange for a gift by will, put that agreement in writing, and have the other party sign it. If it affects real estate, record the signed agreement in the county recorder's office.

Restrictions on Gifts

Generally speaking, you have the right to give your property to anyone you want. If you give property to a minor, however, a guardian may have to be appointed to hold title to the property for the minor until the minor reaches 18. Some restrictions may also be placed on gifts to charities or religious institutions and gifts to animals, and these are discussed below.

What happens when a person gets impatient and kills to speed up an inheritance? A murderer forfeits any gift that he or she would have received from the victim. But if the death is accidental or the result of negligence, such as carelessness while driving a car, the gift usually is not forfeited, even though the recipient was the direct cause of death.

Gifts to Charities and Religious Institutions

Some states do not allow gifts to religious or charitable institutions if the will was made less than a certain period of time (such as thirty days or six months) before the person died. What happens to the gift in that case? It goes to the person named in the residuary clause (see below) of your will or to your next of kin if there is no residuary clause. The state you live in may also have a law limiting the amount of your estate that the charity or religious institution can receive—for instance, one-fourth or one-third of the estate.

One usual restriction imposed on all gifts to charities or religious institutions is the requirement that the recipient be a bona fide, legitimate organization. A gift of $100,000 to, say, Sister Mary's Religious Sect for the Divine Rutabaga would probably be void in all states.

Gifts to Animals

Every now and then you read in the paper of the eccentric millionaire whose will gave all of his or her money to a parakeet, dog, cat, or other pet. (Imagine the surprise of the children or other heirs when they learn of this!) Is such a gift valid? No. A gift of money or property to a pet does not hold up legally, for the simple reason that a pet is incapable of holding title to property. A cat cannot own a house, a dog cannot own a car, and a bird cannot open a bank account in its own name for any amount. To get around this, some people appoint a human guardian for the pet, and occasionally a court upholds this. Instead of giving your property to your pet, something the courts probably will not recognize, consider making a gift of part of your estate to your local humane society.

Directing That Your Pet Be Put to Sleep

Many people provide in their wills that, when they die, their pets be put to sleep. At one time these provisions were enforced without question. Lately, however, animal protection groups have successfully challenged this practice. If you own a pet, the best thing you can do is arrange to leave the pet with someone who is fond of it, someone you are sure will care for the pet properly. Of course, first discuss this with that person. A small gift in your will to compensate that person for the pet's food, veterinarian bills, and the like would be a thoughtful gesture.

Providing for Your Minor Children

Parents with minor children should have a provision in their wills naming a guardian to take care of those children if both parents die. What should you look for in a guardian? Some important factors are the age and health of the guardian and the child, the religious beliefs of both, the guardian's standard of living, and whether the child will have to change schools or move a long distance from his or her present home. Many young parents name their own parents as guardians, without thinking that when their children reach their mid-teens, the grandparents may be a little too old to handle the natural energy of teenagers.

Before you name a guardian for your children, first discuss it with the person to make sure he or she is willing. You should also name an alternate guardian in case your first choice refuses or is unable to accept the position at the appropriate time because of, for instance, poor health. The probate judge will give your choice for guardian great weight and will usually follow it but is not bound by the law to do so. The "best interests" of the child— the same guideline used to resolve family law issues involving children—is the determining factor.

If your estate is large enough, it might be wise to set up a trust in your will for your children. Even though your estate is not large enough to worry about tax planning, it can be large enough to think about a trust for your kids. Suppose your estate is worth $50,000. If you take that amount and invest it at 9 percent interest per year, in ten years, you'll have over $118,000. In fifteen years, it will have grown to more than $182,000. In ten years, $100,000 invested at 9 percent yields over $236,000, and in fifteen years, it will total almost $365,000. If there is no trust, a guardian is appointed to manage the estate until the child reaches 18, at which time the child receives the whole thing. Unfortunately, many 18-year-olds who suddenly come into a large sum of money aren't as financially responsible as we'd like them to be.

To protect the child from himself or herself, a trust typically provides that the money is given out in two or more installments. For example, a trust might provide that the child receives one-third of the trust money when he or she graduates from college or turns 25; at age 30, he or she gets one-half of the remaining amount; and at age 35 the rest of the trust is distributed. Trusts for children are too complex to go into in any great detail here, and each situation is unique. Best consult a lawyer if you want to set up a trust.

Disinheriting Someone

The first thing you need to know about cutting someone out of your will is that the courts don't like it. They'll usually do anything possible to get around disinheritances. For example, suppose you want to disinherit someone, so you just don't mention that person anywhere in your will. Is that person disinherited? No. The law generally presumes that you simply forgot or overlooked the person and didn't intend to leave him or her out of your will. That person then receives the share of your property he or she would have received if you had died without a will. You must therefore make it clear in your will that you are deliberately disinheriting a person.

The only sure way to disinherit someone is to state expressly in the will something like: "It is my desire that _____ take nothing under this will," and then give all of your property to another person or other people. This leaves no doubt as to your intention. You don't even have to leave the person one dollar or other token gift. In one case, however, a bitter father's entire will (which he had prepared himself) read: "It is my greatest wish that my only child, my son Fred, get nothing, as he has turned out to be a worthless, good-for-nothing bum who squanders all of his money on women and gambling." Guess who wound up with all of the property? That's right, Fred. Why? Because the man did not give his property away to others. If not Fred, then to whom? The court couldn't guess at who should receive the property, so it gave it all to the man's next of kin—Fred.

What happens if a married person's will expressly disinherits his or her spouse and gives all of the property to others? Is the surviving spouse left with nothing? No. Most states give the surviving spouse a "right of election." The spouse gets to choose between what the will gives and an amount or percentage of the estate that the law provides to protect a married person in this very situation.

A final word about disinheritances: You only have to disinherit a person if he or she would get any of your estate if you don't leave a will. (Who gets your property if you die without a will is discussed in the previous chapter.) If someone isn't entitled to any of your property upon your death, then you don't have to worry about disinheriting that person. But if you're planning on cutting someone out of your will, have a lawyer prepare the will.

Appointing an Executor or Executrix

The executor (executrix if a woman) of a will has a demanding job: he or she must take possession of the deceased person's personal property; make an inventory of all property; probate the will; arrange for the support of the survivors; pay funeral bills; file insurance claims; pay debts; file all tax forms; and ensure that the beneficiaries get what is rightfully coming to them. Depending upon the size of the estate, the job of executor can be one requiring great business sense and experience.

A married person usually names his or her spouse as executor. But if your estate is large and your spouse does not have much business experience, consider appointing someone with more business acumen. Some people prefer to name a bank as the executor or to name their spouse and a bank as co-executors.

Others like to name their attorney, a parent or adult child, or a trusted friend. Whomever you decide to name as executor, talk it over with that person before making your will. Ideally, the executor should live in or near the same county as you, since your will will be probated in the county where you reside at the time of your death.

Unless your will states otherwise, the person you name as executor will have to post a bond to ensure proper, professional, and faithful fulfillment of the duties and obligations required by the position of executor. (The cost of this bond is paid by the estate, not out of the executor's own pocket.) If you're selecting your spouse, a close relative, or a trusted friend as your executor, you will probably want to consider putting in a clause that the executor doesn't have to post a bond.

The executor of the will receives a fee based on the size of the estate and the amount of work the executor does. This fee varies from state to state. The lawyer who probates the will on behalf of the executor also receives a fee, often equal to the executor's fee. If the estate is small and there are no problems, the fees of the executor and attorney will be relatively small. But if the estate is large, and there is a fierce will contest and several disputed creditors' claims that have to be defended, the fees will be considerably greater.

How to Write Your Own Will

In this section, we show you various clauses you can adapt and use to draw up your own will. Later in this chapter several sample wills are provided to assist you. You may want to take a moment now to look at them, if only because they will give you the complete picture. It's frequently easier to understand things when you see the assembled product before taking a look at the nuts and bolts.

When Not to Do It Yourself

Be forewarned that not everyone can or should make his or her own will. A lawyer is absolutely required in certain situations. Have a lawyer prepare your will if any of the following apply:

• You are unsure about anything or have a question that isn't answered here. By necessity, we address only the most common situations in this chapter. More complex matters have not been included. If your question is relatively simple, you might get the answer by visiting your local law library or calling the clerk at the probate court. Otherwise, consult a lawyer.

• Your estate is large enough to benefit from some estate planning to reduce death taxes. This requires the expertise of a lawyer experienced in this particular field.

• You own a business. What happens to a business when the owner dies? Is it kept running, sold, or simply shut down? If it is to be sold, to whom and for how much? Proper planning with the help of a good lawyer can mean the difference between closing the doors and liquidating the fixtures for next to nothing and selling it as a going enterprise at a fair price.

• You want to disinherit your spouse or a child, or your will is going to leave somebody terribly unhappy. In fact, if there's a chance that someone might challenge your will for any reason at all, a lawyer should draw up the will.

The Title of Your Will

The first thing your will needs is a title. Use:

"Last Will and Testament of
_____"

or simply:

"Will of
_____"

The Declaration

Immediately after the title, state who you are, where you live, and what you are doing (that is, making a will).

"I, _____ , a resident of the city of _____ , County of _____ , State of _____ , hereby make, declare, and publish this, my Last Will and Testament."

This paragraph does several things: First, it identifies who is making the will. Second, it indicates where you are living (your "domicile") at the time you make the will. Finally, it clearly states that the document is in fact your will.

Lawyers usually insert a clause stating that the person making the will is of sound mind and is acting free from the influence of others. If you don't include this language, it does not raise a presumption that you were not of sound mind or that someone was pressuring you to make a gift. If you want to include something along this line, use this clause:

"I, _____ , a resident of the city of _____ , County of _____ , State of _____ , being of sound and disposing mind, and acting of my own free will, hereby make, declare, and publish this, my Last Will and Testament."

Recital of Marital Status and Children

In this paragraph, state whether you are single or married, and if married, state the name of your spouse. If you have any children, biological or adopted, give their names and birth dates. If you have any children from a previous marriage, be sure to include their names and birth dates as well. Here are some examples:

1. Married, Have Children

"I am married to _____ , and all references to my [wife/husband] are to [him/her]. I have ____ children. Their names and dates of birth are:

| _[name]_ | Date of Birth: _____ |
| _[name]_ | Date of Birth: _____ |

2. Married, No Children

"I am married to _____ , and all references to my [husband/wife] are to [him/her]. I have no children or other issue, living or deceased."

3. Single (Including Widowed or Divorced), Have Children

"I am not married. I have ____ children. Their names and dates of birth are:

| _[name]_ | Date of Birth: _____ |
| _[name]_ | Date of Birth: _____ |

4. Single (Including Widowed or Divorced), No Children

"I am not married, and I have no children or other issue, living or deceased."

Revoking Prior Wills

If you have an earlier will, then you should expressly revoke it with a sentence such as:

"I hereby expressly revoke all wills and codicils that I have previously made."

Disposing of All Property

Somewhere in a will a lawyer usually puts in a sentence saying that you are disposing of all of your property. (Remember that in legalese, real property is real estate, and personal property is everything else—cars, clothing, jewelry, cash, stocks and bonds, and so on. "Mixed property" is a combination of the two, such as a house—real property—with easily removable fixtures—personal property.) This isn't really necessary, particularly if other provisions in your will make this clear. Still, if you want to include such a clause, here's one you can use:

"It is my intention to dispose of all property, whether real, personal, or mixed, and wherever situated, I own or which I have the right to dispose of by will."

Who Gets What

Now we've reached the heart of the will: who gets what. This is where most wills differ, so we have included a number of clauses to help you. The main thing to remember is to make your gift as clear as possible, so there is no question as to which item goes to whom. If you're giving someone a particular object, such as a painting, identify it completely. If you're giving your house to someone, identify it by its street address. Also give the name and address of every person who receives something.

You will see that some of the clauses require the beneficiary to survive you by 30 days in order to receive a gift. This is to cover the situation in which you and the beneficiary are injured in an accident together, and the beneficiary lives a few days longer than you. Without this provision, in this situation your gift would actually go to the named beneficiary's heirs instead of to your alternate selection.

1. Gift of All Property to Your Spouse

"I give all of my property, real, personal, or mixed, to my [husband/wife] if [he/she] survives me for thirty (30) days, and if [he/she] does not so survive me, then I give all of my property, real, personal, or mixed, to _____ [*children or other person*] _____ ."

2. Gift of Everything to Children in Equal Shares

"I give all of my property, real, personal, or mixed, to my children who survive me for thirty (30) days, in equal shares. If a child of mine does not survive me for thirty (30) days, and that child leaves any issue surviving, I give such issue the share my child would have received; and if there are no such surviving issue, then that share shall be distributed equally among my surviving children. If none of my children survive me, and they leave no surviving issue, then I give all of my property, real, personal, or mixed, to _____ ."

3. Gift of All Property in Percentages

"I give all of my property, real, personal, or mixed, as follows:
Forty percent (40%) to _____ ;
Forty percent (40%) to _____ ;
Twenty percent (20%) to _____ .
If one or more of them has died, then such share or shares shall be divided equally among the survivors."

4. Gift of Your House

"I give my house, located at 1234 Main Street, Springfield, to _____ , if [he/she] survives me for thirty (30) days, and if [he/she] does not so survive me, I give my house to _____."

5. Gift of Furniture and Furnishings

"I give all of my furniture and furnishings to _____."

6. Gift of Cash

"I give the sum of _____ dollars ($_____.00) to _____."

7. Gift of Stocks and Bonds

(a) Gift of All Stocks and Bonds   "I give all stocks and bonds that I own at the time of my death to _____."
(b) Gift of Particular Stock   "I give all shares of XYZ Corporation stock that I own at the time of my death to _____."

8. Gift of Automobile

"I give any automobile that I own at the time of my death to _____."

If you want to give a particular car to someone, identify it by year, color, make, model, and license plate number. But if you sell or give that car to someone else before you die, the gift in your will is void.

9. Gifts of Clothing, Jewelry, and Personal Effects

(a) Gift of All Personal Effects "I give all of my jewelry, clothing, furs, and other personal effects to _____."
(b) Gift of Particular Item "I give my four-carat diamond solitaire ring to _____."

Naming a Guardian for Minor Children

If you have minor children and want to name a guardian for them, use this clause:

"If my [husband/wife] does not survive me and at my death any of my children are minors, I nominate ___[name and___ __address]__ as guardian of my minor children. If_____ fails or refuses to qualify as guardian, or ceases to act as guardian, I nominate [name and address] as guardian of my minor children."

Remember to talk it over with the person before naming him or her as the guardian. Also, if you're married, first discuss your selection with your spouse.

The Residuary Clause

The residuary clause of a will is a catchall clause that essentially provides for the distribution of all property not otherwise specifically covered in the will. It also governs the disposition of any gifts if the intended beneficiary is dead or refuses to accept the gift. If your will gives all of your property to one person, a residuary clause is not necessary. But if you're making several gifts, a residuary clause is a good idea, as it directs who gets the property if a beneficiary of a specific gift dies before you. A typical residuary clause reads:

"I give the rest, remainder, and residue of my estate, real, personal, or mixed, to _____ , if [he/she] survives me for a period of thirty (30) days, and if [he/she] does not so survive me, then I give the rest, remainder, and residue of my estate, real, personal, and mixed, to _____ _____ ."

Naming Your Executor or Executrix

The first paragraph below is used to name the executor or executrix of your will. Be sure to get the person's consent before appointing him or her as executor. In addition to appointing the person as executor, the paragraph also waives the bond the executor otherwise would be required to post (at the expense of your estate). If you want the bond posted, simply omit the relevant sentence. The second paragraph gives the executor the right to deal with the property pretty much in the same manner as you could. Without this authority, the executor may constantly have to go back to court to get permission before doing many routine things. The extent of the powers you give your executor depends on how much you trust your executor. Since you usually trust the person you name as executor very much, we have assumed you want to give him or her broad powers. Omit the second paragraph if you don't want to give your executor this much power.

"I hereby nominate _____ to serve as the [Executor/Executrix] of this will. If _____ refuses to or cannot qualify, or ceases to act as the [Executor/Executrix], then I nominate _____ as the [Executor/Executrix]. It is my wish that no bond shall be required of any person named as Executor or Executrix in this will.

"I give my [Executor/Executrix] the power to act as I could act if living, including, but not limited to, the powers to invest and reinvest any surplus money in my [Executor's/Executrix's] hands in every kind of property and every kind of investment that persons of prudence, discretion, and intelligence acquire for their own account; to sell, with or without notice, at either public or private sale, and to lease any property, real, personal, or mixed, for cash, partly for cash and partly for credit, or entirely for credit; to partition, allot, and distribute my estate in kind, or partly in cash and partly in kind, or entirely in cash."

The Signature Clause

There is no particular wording that must precede your signature. In fact, you can simply date and sign the will. We do, however, suggest that you use the following:

"I subscribe my name to this will this _____ day of _____, 19 __ , at _____[city]_____ , County of _____, State of _____.

_____
[type your name here]

Keep in mind that your signature should be at the end of the will. Nothing—except the attestation clause and witnesses' signatures—should follow your signature. If you make any additions or notations after your signature, a court usually will ignore them. If you discover you forgot to put something in your will, either draw up a new will or prepare a codicil (see below) after the will is signed and witnessed.

The Attestation (Witnesses') Clause

As with the signature clause, there is no requirement that the signatures of the witnesses be preceded by any particular wording. Still, it is a good idea to have a witnesses' clause, if only because it reinforces that the signature and the witnessing of the will were done correctly. Use the following clause—called the "attestation clause"—in your will:

"On the date last above written, _____[your name]_____ declared to us, the undersigned, that the foregoing document

was [his/her] Last Will and Testament, and requested us to
act as witnesses to it. [He/She] thereupon signed this will in
our presence, all of us being present at the same time. We
now, at [his/her] request, in [his/her] presence, and in the
presence of each other, subscribe our names as witnesses.

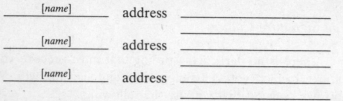

Make sure you know how many witnesses are required by your
state. As mentioned earlier, all require two witnesses, except
Maine, New Hampshire, South Carolina, and Vermont, which
require three witnesses; Louisiana requires that the two witnesses
sign the will in front of a notary public, who then attaches his or
her seal verifying that the witnesses are who they claim to be.
(You can check the current requirements by calling the clerk of
the probate or surrogate court.) Lawyers frequently have one
more witness sign than is necessary. For example, if the law requires two witnesses, a lawyer will have three witnesses sign. This
is to protect you in case the court rules that one person was
ineligible to witness your will. (Who your witnesses should be is
discussed below.)

Examples of Complete Wills

Here are examples of wills to use for guidance in writing
your own. The first two are the mutual wills of a husband and
wife, in which each gives the estate to the other, and to the
children when both die. If none of the children survives, the wills
provide accordingly. The third example is one that a single person
with no children or grandchildren might make. Remember that
these wills are only examples. You can adapt them to your own
situation by using the information and clauses provided above,

keeping in mind the cautions about doing it yourself found at the start of this chapter.

Example of a Married Couple's Mutual Wills

The Husband's Will

LAST WILL AND TESTAMENT

OF

JOE SMITH

I, JOE SMITH, a resident of the city of Hometown, Lincoln County, State of _____ , hereby make, declare, and publish this, my Last Will and Testament.

1. I am married to JANE SMITH, and all references to my wife are to her. I have two (2) children. Their names and dates of birth are:

> JACK SMITH   Born January 2, 1976
> SHERRY SMITH   Born April 4, 1978

2. I hereby expressly revoke all wills and codicils that I have previously made.

3. It is my intention to dispose of all property, whether personal, real, or mixed, and wherever located, I own or which I have the right to dispose of by will.

4. I give all of my property, real, personal, or mixed, to my wife if she survives me for thirty (30) days, and if she does not so survive me, then I give all of my property to my children who survive me for thirty (30) days, in equal shares. If only one of my children so survives me, then I give all of my property to that child. If neither my wife nor any of my children survive me, then I give all of my property, in equal shares, to my brother, WILLIAM SMITH, who lives at 1234 Main Street, Hometown, and to my wife's sister, MARGIE JONES, who lives at 987 Elm Street, Mayfield, or to the survivor of them.

5. If my wife does not survive me and at my death any of my children are minors, I nominate my brother, WILLIAM SMITH, as guardian of my minor children. If WILLIAM fails or refuses to qualify as guardian, or ceases to act as guardian, I nominate my wife's sister, MARGIE JONES, as guardian of my minor children.

6. I nominate my wife to serve as the Executrix of this will. If she refuses to or cannot qualify, or ceases to act, as the Executrix, then I nominate my brother, WILLIAM SMITH, as the Executor. It is my wish that no bond shall be required of any person named as Executor or Executrix in this will.

I give my Executrix or Executor, as the case may be, the power and authority to do all acts I could do if living, including, but not limited to, the powers to sell, with or without notice, at either public or private sale, and to lease any property, real, personal, or mixed, for cash, partly for cash and partly for credit, or entirely for credit; to invest and reinvest any surplus money in my Executrix's or Executor's hands in every kind of property and every kind of investment that persons of prudence, discretion, and intelligence acquire for their own account; and to partition, allot, and distribute my estate in kind, or partly in cash and partly in kind, or entirely in cash.

I subscribe my name to this will this 8th day of November, 1986, in the City of Hometown, Lincoln County, State of _____ .

_____

                                                        JOE SMITH

On the date last above written, JOE SMITH declared to us, the undersigned, that the foregoing document was his Last Will and Testament, and requested us to act as witnesses to it. He thereupon signed this will in our presence, all of us being present at the same time. We now, at his request, in his presence, and in the presence of each other, subscribe our names as witnesses.

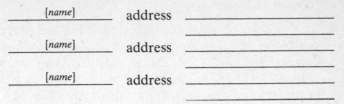

[name]   address _____

[name]   address _____

[name]   address _____

The Wife's Will

LAST WILL AND TESTAMENT
OF
JANE SMITH

I, JANE SMITH, a resident of the city of Hometown, Lincoln County, State of _____ , hereby make, declare, and publish this, my Last Will and Testament.

1. I am married to JOE SMITH, and all references to my husband are to him. I have two (2) children. Their names and dates of birth are:

JACK SMITH   Born January 2, 1976
SHERRY SMITH   Born April 4, 1978

2. I hereby expressly revoke all wills and codicils that I have previously made.

3. It is my intention to dispose of all property, whether personal, real, or mixed, and wherever located, I own or which I have the right to dispose of by will.

4. I give all of my property, real, personal, or mixed, to my husband if he survives me for thirty (30) days, and if he does not so survive me, then I give all of my property to my children who survive me for thirty (30) days, in equal shares. If only one of my children so survives me, then I give all of my property to that child. If none of my children survive me, then I give all of my property, in equal shares, to my husband's brother, WILLIAM SMITH, who lives at

1234 Main Street, Hometown, and to my sister, MARGIE JONES, who lives at 987 Elm Street, Mayfield, or to the survivor of them.

5. If my husband does not survive me and at my death any of my children are minors, I nominate my husband's brother, WILLIAM SMITH, as guardian of my minor children. If WILLIAM fails or refuses to qualify as guardian, or ceases to act as guardian, I nominate my sister, MARGIE JONES, as guardian of my minor children.

6. I nominate my husband to serve as the Executor of this will. If he refuses to or cannot qualify, or ceases to act, as the Executor, then I nominate my husband's brother, WILLIAM SMITH, as the Executor. It is my wish that no bond shall be required of any person named as Executor in this will.

I give my Executor the power and authority to do all acts I could do if living, including, but not limited to, the powers to sell, with or without notice, at either public or private sale, and to lease any property, real, personal, or mixed, for cash, partly for cash and partly for credit, or entirely for credit; to invest and reinvest any surplus money in my Executor's hands in every kind of property and every kind of investment that persons of prudence, discretion, and intelligence acquire for their own account; and to partition, allot, and distribute my estate in kind, or partly in cash and partly in kind, or entirely in cash.

I subscribe my name to this will this 8th day of November, 1986, in the City of Hometown, Lincoln County, State of _____ .

_____

JANE SMITH

On the date last above written, JANE SMITH declared to us, the undersigned, that the foregoing document, was her Last Will and Testament, and requested us to act as witnesses to it. She thereupon signed this will in our presence, all of us being present at the same time. We now, at her request, in her presence, and in the presence of each other, subscribe our names as witnesses.

_____[name]_____ address _____

_____[name]_____ address _____

_____[name]_____ address _____

Example of a Single Person's Will

LAST WILL AND TESTAMENT
OF
RHONDA JONES

I, RHONDA JONES, a resident of the city of Hometown, Lincoln County, State of _____, hereby make, declare, and publish this, my Last Will and Testament.

1. I am not married, and I have no children or other issue, living or deceased.

2. I hereby expressly revoke all wills and codicils that I have previously made.

3. It is my intention to dispose of all property, whether personal, real, or mixed, and wherever located, I own or which I have the right to dispose of by will.

4. I give the sum of one thousand dollars ($1,000.00) to GEORGE JOHNSON, whose address is _____ .

5. I give the sum of one thousand dollars ($1,000.00) to the American Heart Association.

6. I give all of my clothing, jewelry, and other personal effects to SUSAN STANTON, whose address is _____ _____.

7. I give any automobile that I own at the time of my death to GUS ADAMS, whose address is _____ .

8. I give the rest, remainder, and residue of my estate, real, personal, or mixed, to BEVERLY HANSON, whose address is _____ , if she survives me for thirty (30) days, and if she does not so survive me, then I give the rest, remainder, and residue of my estate, real, personal, or mixed, to MARGARET BATES, whose address is _____ .

9. I nominate BEVERLY HANSON to serve as the Executrix of this will. If she refuses to or cannot qualify, or ceases to act, as the Executrix, then I nominate MARGARET BATES as the Executrix. It is my wish that no bond shall be required of any person named as Executrix in this will.

I give my Executrix the power and authority to do all acts I could do if living, including, but not limited to, the powers to sell, with or without notice, at either public or private sale, and to lease any property, real, personal, or mixed, for cash, partly for cash and partly for credit, or entirely for credit; to invest and reinvest any surplus money in my Executrix's hands in every kind of property and every kind of investment that persons of prudence, discretion, and intelligence acquire for their own account; and to partition, allot, and distribute my estate in kind, or partly in cash and partly in kind, or entirely in cash.

I subscribe my name to this will this 8th day of November, 1986, in the City of Hometown, Lincoln County, State of _____ .

_____

RHONDA JONES

On the date last above written, RHONDA JONES declared to us, the undersigned, that the foregoing document was her Last Will and Testament, and requested us to act as witnesses to it. She thereupon signed this will in our presence, all of us being present at the same time. We now, at her request, in her presence, and in the presence of each other, subscribe our names as witnesses.

____[*name*]____	address	_____
		_____
____[*name*]____	address	_____
		_____
____[*name*]____	address	_____
		_____

Typing Your Will

Before typing your will up for signing, do a rough draft or two to make sure everything is in order. As for the paper to use for the final draft, either 8½″ × 11″ or 8½″ × 14″ is fine. The paper should be blank and white. The final draft should be as neat as possible. If you have access to a word processor or self-correcting typewriter, use it. Otherwise, avoid strikeovers, erasures, and use of any correction fluids. If you have to, retype it several times until it looks clean. You don't want the will to give the impression that someone may have altered it after it was signed.

The lines can be single-spaced or double-spaced, whichever you prefer. An extra line should be left between paragraphs so they can be easily distinguished. Lawyers usually number each paragraph, such as "FIRST," "SECOND," "THIRD," and so on. It's not a bad idea, but it's just as effective to use numerals, such as *1.* or *2.* Number each page at the bottom.

When numbers are used for amounts, lawyers generally write he number out and then place the numeral in parentheses. For example: "I give the sum of five hundred dollars ($500.00) o . . ." or "I give fifty percent (50%) of my estate to. . . ." You hould do this too, if only because it removes any doubt as to hat you meant and protects your will from tampering.

Don't start a page with your signature. Always have at least a line or two run over from the previous page. This too helps protect your will from someone trying to change it.

Before you staple your will together, make several photocopies of it. Then staple the unsigned original together, but only after making sure all the pages are in order.

The Signing and Witnessing of Your Will

Now you're ready to sign your will and have it witnessed—the "execution." We have already mentioned that two witnesses are required in all states except South Carolina and Vermont, which require three witnesses.

Who to Get as Witnesses

You can have just about any adult person who is 18 and older in most states, 19 and older in some, serve as a witness to your will, as long as he or she is mentally competent. You don't even have to know the person well, although it's usually better to have good friends witness your will. There are two reasons for this. First, a friend will be more willing to help you out and witness your will than a stranger might. The second reason is that when the time comes to verify a witness's signature on your will, it is usually easier for the executor's lawyer to track down a friend with whom you have kept in touch than it is to find someone you only met once or twice. One thing that may affect your choice of a witness is his or her age and health. As morbid as it may sound, you want to get someone who is probably going to outlive you, so that person will be around to verify ("attest") that he or she witnessed your signature on the will.

If a lawyer prepares your will, he or she will usually be a witness—a standard and proper procedure, assuming he or she is not receiving a gift under the terms of the will. (If you want to give something to your lawyer, another lawyer should prepare the will.) The lawyer's receptionist or secretary may also witness the will.

Who Should Not Witness Your Will

Anybody who receives a gift under the will should *not* be a witness to your will. Likewise, anyone who is entitled to a share of your estate if you die without a will should not be a witness. A husband and wife should not act as witnesses to one another's will, nor should their children be witnesses.

In most states, a witness named as a beneficiary in the will is disqualified from acting as a witness, and his or her signature is ignored. If this happens, the will becomes invalid, and the deceased person's property passes as though there were no will at all. Some courts may find that the will is good, but the witness will have to forfeit his or her share to the extent that it exceeds the estate he or she would have received if the deceased had died without a will. This is why lawyers usually have a will witnessed by one witness more than is required by law; if one of the witnesses is disqualified, the will still stands, as there remain two (or three, as the case may be) valid witnesses.

The Procedure for Signing and Witnessing Your Will

Here is the procedure that we recommend you follow in signing your will and having it witnessed.

Gather all of the witnesses around you, and tell them that the document is your will. (In Louisiana, you will also need a notary public present to watch the signing and witnessing of the will. The notary must then put his or her seal on the will after the witnesses' signatures.) Then ask them to serve as witnesses to it. Read aloud the attestation clause (the clause appearing above the place for the witnesses' signatures). While the witnesses watch you, initial each page of the will in the bottom right-hand corner. (This protects you from somebody trying to slip in a phony page.) Sign the will as the witnesses watch, then have each witness sign his or her name while the others look on. It is not necessary for the witnesses to read the will. You have every right to keep the contents of your will confidential.

Safekeeping, Reviewing, and Changing Your Will

Where to Keep Your Will

Don't handle your original will unless you want to revoke it or modify it. But you should keep a copy of your will handy so you can review it periodically—something that, as discussed below, we highly recommend. If a lawyer has prepared your will, he or she will keep a copy of it in your client file. Tell your spouse and the person named as executor where the will is kept, so that it can be obtained promptly when needed. It is also a good idea to give your executor a copy of your will and, if applicable, the name, address, and telephone number of the lawyer who prepared it. This way the executor can immediately notify the lawyer upon your death, obtain the original will, and get the probate proceedings under way as soon as possible.

After your will is signed and witnessed, put it in a place safe from fire, flood, loss, and theft. The best place for your original will is usually your safe-deposit box. If you prefer, you can keep it in your home in a fireproof safe. If a lawyer prepared your will, he or she may retain the original will for you. In that case, make sure that it is placed in the law firm's fireproof safe or safe-deposit box. In some states, you can deposit your will with the court. We advise against this in most cases, however, since if you want to change your will or revoke it, you will have to go to the court to get it.

Do you need a court order to get a will out of a safe-deposit box after a person dies? Generally, no. If the box is in your name and the name of the deceased person, then you have every right to enter it. And even if it is in the deceased person's name alone, in many states, you can open a safe-deposit box without a court order to get the original will or burial instructions. But not just anyone can open the safe-deposit box. You must have a logical reason to be looking for the will. This means that you must be the spouse, child, or other close relative of the deceased person. (If there are no close relatives, the deceased person's attorney or a court-appointed administrator can open the box.) Be prepared to show a death certificate or other evidence that the person who rented the box has died. The safe-deposit box will then be opened in the presence of a bank employee, and only the will, burial instructions, and related documents can be removed at this time.

When to Review Your Will

Once a will is made, it is good until you die, change it, or revoke it. If you make a will today and die 50 years from now without changing it, your property will be disposed of according to the will you made a half-century earlier. As you can imagine, a few changes might be in order over that time, and you should, in fact, review your will periodically to make sure that it carries out your current wishes. As a general rule of thumb, you should review your will at least every four years. Many lawyers recommend that wills be reviewed every two or three years, particularly in the case of an older individual. One thing is certain, though: you can't expect to make a will today and put it in your safe-deposit box and forget about it. It must be reviewed periodically to reflect the changes in your life.

Certain events in life especially demand that you review your will for probable revision. In the pages that follow, we will consider each factor separately. Later we will tell you how to make any needed changes.

The Birth of a Child

You need to update your will if a child is born (or adopted) after you make a will. You may want to appoint a guardian for your child, set up a trust, or otherwise make provisions for your child in the event of your death.

If you don't change your will after a child is born, the law will change it for you, and in a way that you might not like. In almost every state, a child born after you make a will is entitled to the same share he or she would have received if you died without a will. (The amount of this share is discussed in the previous chapter.) If you don't update your will after a child is born, the law ordinarily presumes that you simply hadn't yet gotten around to changing your will, not that you intended to disinherit the child. If you want to disinherit a child, you will have to make a new will doing just that. Adopted children are usually treated the same as biological children when it comes to omission. But if you fail to name an unadopted stepchild that stepchild usually gets nothing.

The Death of a Close Relative or a Beneficiary

You should also review your will when a close family member such as a spouse, child, or parent has died, or when a beneficiary under the will has died. If your will contains a gift to the deceased person, that gift will pass through the residuary clause if your will is not updated; if there is no residuary clause, that portion will be treated as if there were no will at all. Of course, your will can provide for an alternate disposition of a particular gift if the primary beneficiary dies, but even if it does, you should still review your will.

If You Get Married

When you get married, you will most likely want to change your will to provide for your new spouse. What happens if you don't? In many states, when you get married, any will you have at the time of the marriage is automatically revoked. If you die without making a new will, the property will be distributed as though there were no will at all, even if you didn't want to make any changes in the earlier will. If you get married but don't want to change your earlier will, you should at least execute a codicil stating that the original will signed before your marriage is to remain in effect.

If You Get Divorced

If you have obtained a divorce or are in the process of doing so, you should review your will for possible changes. In many states, the fact that a person has obtained a divorce does not automatically revoke a will. If you want to cut your ex-spouse out of your will, you should make a new will.

If You Move Out of State

You should review your will for changes when you move from one state to another. Usually a will that was valid in the state where it was made will be accepted in another state. But even if it is valid in your new state, you may still want to have a new will prepared if the gift and inheritance tax structures of the new state affect your will. You should also consider changing your executor or the guardian of your minor children to someone who lives closer to your new home.

Changes in Your Financial Position or in the Law

For a young couple without a family or much property, a simple will is usually sufficient. But as the size of their family and estate grows, they will need to change their wills to nominate guardians for the children and to set up trusts for them, or to do some estate planning to minimize the federal estate and state inheritance taxes payable upon a spouse's death. When the children are grown and have children of their own, changes in the will again are called for.

When there are major changes in the law, it is important to review a will. For example, if your will was prepared before the Economic Recovery Tax Act of 1981 was passed, you will want to review it now because there are a number of significant changes in the new tax laws that may have tremendous impact upon your will.

How to Change Your Will

Reviewing your will one day, you change your mind about giving someone a particular gift. Can you just draw a line through that person's name and write the name of the new beneficiary in the margin? No. In most states, this attempted change will be ignored completely because it doesn't meet the legal requirements, and the gift will therefore go to the person whose name was crossed out. In a few states, the gift to the original beneficiary is revoked, but rather than going to the new beneficiary, the gift will pass through the residuary clause.

If you want to make a change to your will, no matter how minor it is, you have two options: make a completely new will or make a "codicil" to your existing will. A codicil is an amendment to a will and must be prepared and executed (signed and witnessed) the same as a will. A codicil is usually appropriate only when the change is relatively short, say, changing the name of a beneficiary or the executor. If the changes are long or numerous, or if you have already made a codicil or two to your will, it is usually better to prepare a new will to prevent confusion.

In states that recognize a holographic will, you can make a holographic codicil (one entirely handwritten by you, and dated and signed). But as we suggested in the section on making your own will, whether or not your state recognizes holographic wills and codicils, we recommend that the codicil be formal—that is, typed out, dated and signed by you, and signed by the appropriate number of witnesses (three in Maine, New Hampshire, South Carolina, and Vermont, two elsewhere, although having three witnesses sign is advisable in every state). In Louisiana, a notary public must be present at the signing and witnessing of the codicil, and must attach his or her seal.

Here is a sample codicil:

CODICIL

I, Mary Baker, hereby make this Codicil to my Last Will and Testament dated July 1, 1986.

FIRST: I hereby revoke my gift to Sally Sand of all my clothing, furs, jewelry, and other personal effects, and instead give all of my clothing, furs, jewelry, and other personal effects to Jane Jackson, who lives at _____ .

SECOND: I hereby withdraw my nomination of Roger Reed as the Executor of my Will, and instead nominate Victor Vincent to serve as Executor. Victor Vincent's address and telephone number are _____ . It is my desire that no bond be required of Victor Vincent if he serves as Executor of my estate.

I subscribe my name to this Codicil this ____ day of _____ , 19__ , at __[city and state]__ .

_____

                                        MARY BAKER

Attestation Clause

On the date last above written, Mary Baker declared to us, the undersigned, that the foregoing document was a Codicil to her Will of July 1, 1986, and requested us to act as witnesses to it. She thereupon signed this Codicil in our presence, all of us being present at the same time. We now, at her request, in her presence, and in the presence of each other, subscribe our names as witnesses.

[witness]	[address]
[witness]	[address]
[witness]	[address]

The signing and witnessing of the codicil should follow the same procedure as that set forth earlier for a will. Make a pho-

tocopy or two of the codicil before you sign it to review periodically. After you and your witnesses have signed it, the codicil
should be stapled to the original will and put back in a safe place
(preferably your safe-deposit box or a home safe).

How to Revoke Your Will

If for some reason you decide to revoke your will completely
(perhaps it is 15 years old, and it would be disastrous if the
property were now distributed according to your outdated will),
there are several ways to do this. The simplest way is to rip up
the original will completely. A more dramatic but equally effective
way to revoke the will is to burn it. The destruction of the will
must be done with the intent to revoke it, and you must be of
sufficient mental capacity ("sound mind") to revoke it. A will
destroyed by accident or by a person who lacks sufficient mental
capacity to revoke it remains in effect. When this happens, a copy
of the original will could be used to verify the contents, or the
lawyer who drafted the will or anyone else who had read it could
testify to its contents.

Another way to revoke your will is to execute a new document stating that you revoke your will. When a new will is prepared, a clause is usually inserted stating that all wills and codicils
previously made by that person are revoked and ineffective. If
you are making your own will, you should include a similar provision.

Why and How Wills
Are Challenged

The most common grounds for contesting a will are that the
person wasn't of sound mind (discussed earlier), someone was
exercising undue influence or committed fraud, the will offered
for probate was revoked and replaced by a later will, the will

wasn't signed and witnessed according to the statutory formalities, or the will offered for probate is an outright phony, a forgery.

Undue Influence and Mental Duress

There are those who will do everything they can to coerce another person to will them property. A son, daughter, grandchild, nephew, or niece may be guilty of such behavior; there are even instances of nurses who have threatened a patient or withheld nourishment if the patient did not prepare a will giving the nurse all or most of the estate.

Undue influence and mental coercion are found most frequently when one child or grandchild wants all to himself or herself. Over a period of years, the child or grandchild may make subtle threats to an aging parent or grandparent in order to gain an unfair advantage over others. A court will set aside a gift on the grounds of undue influence only if a four-part test is satisfied. Under this test, a person claiming that another received a gift because of improper conduct must show that (1) because of advancing years or physical or mental infirmity, the person making the will could be influenced or controlled by those close to him or her; (2) the person who received the gift in question had the chance to use undue influence; (3) the person had a motive for using undue influence (usually to get a large part of the estate or to see that someone else was denied a fair share); and (4) the person making the will probably wouldn't have given this gift if somebody weren't putting pressure on him or her.

Fraud

Fraud in the preparation of a will can be of two types. The first is fraud in the execution: the person making the will is misled as to the nature of the paper being signed or the contents of the will. For example, an older person whose mind and vision are both slipping may be given a piece of paper to sign that, unbeknownst to him or her, is a will prepared by a conniving child or nurse. The "testator" signs the document, believing it to be something as innocuous as a letter. Another example: an invalid dictates a will, but the lawyer and a child conspire to change the contents and assure the testator that everything is as he or she wished, so he or she signs the altered will. In cases of persons whose health or memory is failing, it is a good idea, in order to reduce the chances of fraud, to have a videocamera record the will being read for the testator's approval.

The second type of fraud is fraud in the inducement, where the testator is misled about some fact that affects the provisions of his or her will. For example, one child may tell an ailing father that another child has died, to induce the father to give everything to his "sole surviving heir." A court would probably invalidate the will in this case, since it was the result of the child's deliberate misrepresentation.

The Forgotten Heir

Sometimes a person will forget to provide for a close relative—say, a child or a spouse—in his or her will. Failure to include someone so close to the testator may be a factor in determining the testator's soundness of mind at the time the will was made. But assuming that the testator was sound of mind, the question is, what does the omitted person get, if anything?

Earlier we discussed the rights of a disinherited spouse. When there is an omission, his or her rights are usually the same: the spouse has the right to elect between the share he or she would have received if the spouse had died without a will, and what the will gives.

A child not mentioned in the will is a "pretermitted" heir. (This generally includes adopted and illegitimate children as well as legitimate children, but not unadopted stepchildren.) In such a case, the law presumes that the testator merely "forgot" about the child when making the will and didn't intend to disinherit the child. But if the will makes any mention of the child, this is usually enough for a court to hold that the testator was thinking of the child when the will was made and intentionally failed to give the child any property. In most states, an omitted child is usually entitled to the same share he or she would have received if the parent had died without a will. This could be as much as one-third, one-half, or even all of the estate, depending on the state, the circumstances, and whether a surviving spouse or any other children are entitled to share in the estate.

Mistakes

What happens if someone mistakenly believes that the person to whom he or she was going to give all of his or her estate is dead and therefore gives all of the property to others? As long as no one intentionally convinced or tricked the person into believing that the intended beneficiary was dead, the will is generally carried out as written. A judge can, however, change the will if the will clearly shows both the person's mistaken belief as to the death of the intended beneficiary and what property the person would have given him or her had the intended beneficiary been alive. For example, if Becky's will reads "I would have given my house to my friend Dorothy, but unfortunately she is dead; I therefore give the house to my cousin Sam," the judge would probably award the house to Dorothy.

Now suppose that Becky's will merely stated "I give my house to my cousin Sam." There is no mention of Dorothy anywhere in the will. If Dorothy could prove that Sam (or someone acting on his behalf) deliberately led Becky to believe that Dorothy was dead so she would give the house to Sam instead of to Dorothy as Becky had planned, the judge would void the gift to Sam and give the house to Dorothy.

Here is a different type of mistake: Suppose a lawyer draws up mutual wills for a husband and wife. The husband inadvertently signs his wife's will, and the wife signs her husband's will. No one catches the mistake, and the witnesses sign the wills. When the husband dies, the mistake is discovered. Which will gets probated, the one the husband actually signed (his wife's), or the will he thought he was signing (his own)? Neither. The husband's innocent mistake in signing his wife's will (and her mistake in signing his) invalidates the will, as the husband intended to sign his will, not hers. And this intent cannot be transferred from one document to another. The husband's property is then distributed as if there were no will.

Procedure for Contesting a Will

It is during the probate process that the validity of a will can and must be challenged. The procedure for a will contest differs greatly from state to state. All states' procedures have one thing in common, though: they generally must be initiated promptly, or you will lose your right to challenge the will, regardless of how meritorious your challenge is. To find out the time limitations for filing a will contest, call the clerk at the appropriate probate court. If you are considering contesting a will, you should consult a lawyer immediately.

Preventing a Possible Will Contest

To prevent a possible will contest, many people insert a clause to the effect that if anyone challenges the will, that person automatically forfeits his or her gift. This clause is a good idea if there is a strong likelihood that a greedy person will instigate a will contest in bad faith, with no valid reason. But a no-contest clause can also dissuade a person with a legitimate challenge from pursuing it, for fear that he or she will lose what he or she already has if the challenge is not successful. Because of this, some courts do not enforce a no-contest clause if the challenge was undertaken in good faith. If a person successfully challenges the will or a provision of the will, the no-contest clause is not enforced. A no-contest provision should be prepared by a lawyer to increase the chances that a judge will enforce it.

Funeral Arrangements, Organ Donations, "Living Wills," and Euthanasia

In addition to your will, you may wish to prepare other documents relating to your death, including funeral instructions, a body or organ donation card, and a "living will." These documents should be kept in a separate packet or envelope from your will and should be readily available to your survivors. Why not attach these documents to your will? Because wills often are not found or read until after the person has been buried or cremated. When the will is finally opened and read, it is belatedly discovered that the person wished to be cremated, or that he or she wished to be buried elsewhere. Similarly, if you sign a "living will," you don't want it read after you die. And your signed organ donation card won't do much good if it's found with your will after you're buried.

Funeral Instructions

Funeral instructions should specify whether you wish to be cremated or buried, by whom, where you wish your ashes to be scattered or where (cemetery and plot) you wish to be buried, and any special arrangements. The original document containing your funeral instructions should be kept in a safe place, preferably your safe-deposit box or a fireproof safe at home. Keep a copy of the funeral instructions to refer to, and give a copy, along with information about the location of the orginal document, to your executor or excutrix, your next of kin, and your attorney. In the case of a single person, or a married couple who die together, the executor or executrix, who is typically a close friend or relative, would likely be the person to take care of or assist in the funeral arrangements. If you have made advance arrangements with a specific mortuary for burial or cremation, you should also give the mortuary a copy of your funeral instructions.

The following sample documents show examples of funeral instructions. The first includes instructions for a person who wishes to be cremated; the second includes instructions for a person who wishes to be buried in a certain plot.

Funeral Instructions for Cremation

FUNERAL INSTRUCTIONS

I, _____ , hereby direct the disposition of my remains upon my death as follows:

1. It is my wish to be cremated, and that the cremation and all other arrangements be handled by _____ Mortuary, located at _____ .

2. It is my wish that after cremation, my remains be disposed of as follows: _____ [for example, scattered in the ocean].

The original of my last will and testament is in _____ [for example, my safe-deposit box; give bank's name and address] [the possession of my attorney, _____ ; give attorney's name and address].

DATED: _____ , 19___

_____ [*signed*]

Funeral Instructions for Burial

FUNERAL INSTRUCTIONS

I, _____ , hereby direct the disposition of my remains upon my death as follows:

1. It is my wish to be buried in plot #___ of Peaceful Gardens, in the City of _____ . The deed to this plot is with the original of these funeral directions.

2. It is my desire that all funeral arrangements be handled by _____ Mortuary, located at _____ .

The original of my last will and testament is in _____
_____ [for example, my safe-deposit box; give bank's name and address] [the possession of my attorney, _____ ; give attorney's name and address].

DATED: _____ , 19—

_____
                                    [*signed*]

Your Rights under the Funeral Rule

When a loved one dies, it is a very trying time for the survivors. Emotions may get in the way of rational decision making about funeral arrangements (if the deceased person didn't take care of this beforehand). More than 2 million funerals are arranged each year in the United States, at an average cost of $2,400. To protect consumers from abuses by the funeral industry, the Federal Trade Commission instituted a regulation known as the Funeral Rule.

Under the Funeral Rule, if you call a mortuary (or funeral home) for information over the telephone, the mortuary must tell you the prices and give you any information about services. It cannot refuse to give out such information over the telephone.

If you visit the mortuary in person, you must be given a list that specifies the price of each funeral item and service offered. The list must also disclose certain legal rights and requirements regarding funeral arrangements, including information on embalming and caskets for cremation. Generally, you have the right to choose which items you want and do not have to buy services you don't want, unless state law requires it. In the event that the law does require the purchase of certain goods or services, the mortuary must give a written statement informing you of the specific law that mandates the purchase. If the mortuary adds a fee to its cost (or gets a refund, discount, or rebate) for items it buys for cash in advance, such as flowers, obituary notices, pallbearers, or clergy honoraria, this must be disclosed to you in writing. The mortuary must give you an itemized statement showing the total cost of the funeral goods and services you have selected.

The law generally does not require embalming, and the mortuary cannot falsely tell you that it is required by law. If the mortuary does embalm the body without your consent, it usually cannot charge you for this. The mortuary must inform you that if you want certain arrangements, such as a viewing of the body, embalming is a practical necessity and therefore a required purchase. If you do not want embalming, then you should opt for a direct cremation or immediate burial. If you select a direct cremation, one without a viewing or ceremony at which the body is present, the mortuary must offer you either an inexpensive alternative container (one made of pressboard, cardboard, or canvas) or an unfinished wood box.

If you have a question or seek further information about your rights, or if you have a complaint about a mortuary or funeral home, contact your state's office of consumer affairs or consumer protection. You can also contact the Conference of Funeral Service Examining Boards, 520 East Van Trees Street, P.O. Box 497, Washington, Indiana 47501; ThanaCAP, 135 West Wells Street, Suite 600, Milwaukee, Wisconsin 53203 (which arbitrates consumer complaints regarding funeral directors); or your regional office of the Federal Trade Commission.

Organ and Body Donations

All 50 states have enacted the Uniform Anatomical Gift Act, which makes it easy for a person to donate all or part of his or her body upon death. Generally, you need only fill out a donor card, have it witnessed by two people, and attach it to the back of your driver's license. A donor card can usually be obtained at the department of motor vehicles. A Uniform Donor Card that meets the legal requirements of all 50 states can also be obtained from The Living Bank, a nonprofit, national organization that registers donors and coordinates donations when death occurs. To get a Uniform Donor Card, send a self-addressed stamped envelope to The Living Bank, P.O. Box 6725, Houston, Texas 77265. The donor card should be kept with your driver's license. It is a good idea also to give a copy of it to your family physician and attorney.

Advances in medicine have made organ transplants more successful than before. One problem this has created is a lack of donor organs to meet the demand. In July 1985, Oregon became the first state in the nation to pass a law requiring hospital officials to ask the family of a person who dies whether they wish to donate the deceased person's healthy organs for transplant. (The law was passed in response to the death of a two-year-old girl who died after two liver transplants failed, the first because the organ was unsuitable, the second because the organ arrived too late.) One month later, New York adopted a similar law. Several other states have since passed comparable laws, and more are expected to follow.

Dying with Dignity—The Living Will

If, because of an illness or injury, you can be kept alive only with machines, do you have the right to order the machines shut off so you can die with dignity? Two things happened in 1976 that had a profound impact on this difficult question: the New Jersey Supreme Court recognized the right to disconnect life-sustaining equipment in the famous Karen Ann Quinlan case, and California became the first state in the nation to enact a right-to-die law, the California Natural Death Act. Twenty-one other states and the District of Columbia have since enacted laws recognizing a person's right to die rather than be hooked up to machines, and most remaining states are considering passing a similar law. A right-to-die law is on the books in Alabama, Arkansas, California, Delaware, Florida, Georgia, Idaho, Illinois, Kansas, Louisiana, Mississippi, Nevada, New Mexico, North Carolina, Oregon, Texas,

Vermont, Virginia, Washington, West Virginia, Wisconsin, Wyoming, and the District of Columbia.

The provisions of the laws and the form of the living will vary greatly from state to state. You should follow precisely the form for your state, as any deviation could result in a hospital or a court refusing to recognize your living will. You can obtain a living will form that complies with the laws of your state by sending your request and a self-addressed stamped envelope to: Society for the Right to Die, 250 West 57th Street, New York, New York 10107. (They can also provide you with up-to-date information on whether your state has passed a right-to-die law if it is not one of the states listed above.) If your state has not yet passed a right-to-die law, ask for the "Living Will Declaration" from the Society for the Right to Die. This declaration is essentially a generalized living will form that serves to express your wish not to be hooked up to machines when your condition is hopeless.

In most states, the living will is valid until it is revoked. California, Idaho, and Wisconsin provide that a living will is good for only five years; in Georgia it is good for seven years. In several states, a living will is binding if it is signed and witnessed after a person is diagnosed as terminally ill, but it is deemed only advisory if there has been no such diagnosis.

The issues surrounding a living will are not always clear-cut. Suppose, for example, that a pregnant woman is injured in an automobile accident and is declared brain dead. The doctors are given her living will. Do they shut off the machines, ending her life and the life of the fetus? In many states, the living will is suspended during a pregnancy. The woman can be kept alive by artificial means until the baby is born. Once the baby is born, the living will would take effect, and the machines would be disconnected.

A living will usually must be signed by two witnesses. When you request a living will form from the Society for the Right to Die, they will usually send you an instruction sheet that includes information on who can—and who can't—be a witness. Your spouse, relatives, heirs to your estate, and your doctor ordinarily can't be witnesses. Special rules may govern who must be the witnesses if the person making the living will is in a nursing home.

A physician who complies with the patient's wishes as set forth in the living will cannot be sued for honoring those wishes. If the physician refuses to comply with the directive contained in the living will, he or she may have to transfer the patient to a physician who will honor the living will.

Some states also have laws enabling you to give a "durable power of attorney" to someone else. This lets you appoint someone to act as your "attorney in fact" to make medical decisions (including the decision to withhold or withdraw life-sustaining procedures) on your behalf if you become unable to make decisions for yourself because of injuries or illness.

If you decide to prepare a living will, you should make your wishes known to your family physician and attorney, each of whom should be given a copy of your living will to keep in your file, along with instructions as to the location of the original living will. Many states require that a copy of the living will be included in your medical file. If you have prepared a will, the person who is named as executor should also receive a copy of your living will. The original of the living will should be kept in a safe-deposit box or fireproof safe in your home or office.

Mercy Killings—Euthanasia

A terminally ill cancer patient is in the final stages of the disease. The pain is insufferable. Even the most powerful pain-killing drugs do little to alleviate the suffering, and the side effects add to the patient's discomfort. It is only a matter of days or weeks before the patient dies. The patient has accepted the inevitability of death and wishes to hasten it because the pain is just too much to bear. Does the patient have the right to take his or her own life? Or can the patient ask his or her doctor or spouse to end the suffering with an injection that would provide a quick, painless death? The answer is no. The law does not permit the practice of euthanasia, or "mercy killing."

In the early development of the law, it was a serious crime to commit suicide. Since a person could not be prosecuted for successfully committing suicide, as punishment all of his or her property would be forfeited to the government. And anyone who assisted in the suicide could be convicted of aiding and abetting the suicide. In some cases, a murder charge was brought.

In the United States today, it is still a crime in most states to aid or abet a potential suicide. If a dying man asks his wife to supply him with some poison so he can take his own life, and she does so, she risks prosecution for abetting a suicide. If she administers the poison to her husband, she conceivably could be tried and convicted of first-degree murder, even if her husband would have died of natural causes the next day. Since the woman deliberately shortened her husband's life, even though it was at his express request, she has committed a crime.

In one well-publicized example, Roswell Gilbert, a 75-year-old Florida man, was charged with murder after shooting his 73-year-old wife twice in the head on March 4, 1985. Mrs. Gilbert had suffered from Alzheimer's disease and osteoporosis, which caused brain degeneration and painful bone disintegration. On the day of her death, Mrs. Gilbert was crying and in extreme pain and allegedly begged for death. The jury convicted Mr. Gilbert of first-degree murder, on the basis that his actions were deliberate and premeditated. Gilbert was sentenced to life in prison.

The issue of mercy killings is a difficult one—legally, medically, and morally. There is the danger that some killings may be done not so much to relieve the victim of any further suffering, but to remove a burden from another person's life. Alzheimer's disease, for example, may place a tremendous strain on the afflicted person's spouse or children, and the spouse or children could be motivated more by their own considerations in making the decision to end the life of the ill person. Some people fear that a terminally ill patient may persuade a healthy spouse to join in a double suicide. And persons who are only temporarily ill, or whose condition is not as serious, may be encouraged to end their lives when appropriate treatment could save them or lessen their pain.

Rather than turning their backs on this sensitive issue, legislators, lawyers, physicians, and representatives of various advocacy groups for senior citizens and teminally ill patients will, we believe, have to get together and form strict guidelines for permitting the practice of euthanasia in appropriate cases. The decision on whether to allow a person to end his or her life should involve the terminally ill person, the family physician, and family lawyer, plus an independent review board. This decision should never be in the hands of one person alone, particularly someone so close to the ill person that he or she is unable to look at the matter objectively.

REAL ESTATE

THE LAW OF REAL ESTATE ("real property" in legalese) covers a wide range of subjects, of which buying and selling a house are the most important for us. Other topics included in this chapter are trespassing, nuisance, and property condemnation. This chapter also discusses your liability as a homeowner for injuries others sustain on your land, although technically this is a part of tort law (chapter 8). Real estate law also covers leases and landlord-tenant relations, which because of their special complexities are treated in the next chapter.

Ownership of land has long been considered one of the fundamental rights we enjoy in America. In the early days of the United States, particularly in the West, you acquired title to land simply by living on the property and perhaps building a fence around it. If anyone dared challenge your title and claimed the land as his or her own, a shotgun decided the question, not a judge. Today, title to real estate is almost always obtained by acquiring a deed from the land's owner. And if a dispute does arise as to who owns the land, we now settle it in court, using legal precedents and title searches instead of bullets.

Buying and Selling a House

For most of us, a house is the largest and most important purchase in our lifetime. Unfortunately, all too often the purchase of that dream home turns into a legal and financial nightmare for buyer and seller alike. The buyer may be surprised, to say the least, to find out several months after buying the house that it is slowly sinking into the ground or that the plumbing is falling apart. For the seller, problems may arise because the real estate broker doesn't try very hard to find a buyer or misrepresents the condition of the house. Or the broker may claim that a commission is owed even if the sale falls through or the seller finds the buyer without the broker's help.

A brief overview of the events that take place between your first offer to buy a house and the time you take possession of it will make it easier to understand this chapter. First, a seller usually lists the house for sale with a real estate broker, who will advertise it and help negotiate a deal between the buyer and seller. When the buyer and seller agree on the price and terms, they will sign a binder, and the buyer will make a small deposit. A binder is a short form that basically states nothing more than that the seller agrees to sell the house—and the buyer agrees to buy the house—for a specified price. Several days later, the buyer and seller will sign a complete contract covering all of the terms of the agreement. The buyer may be required to make a larger deposit at this time. An escrow is then opened. This means that the contract and other documents and the buyer's deposit are entrusted to an independent third party, usually an escrow company or one party's lawyer.

Over the next few months, a number of things happen. The buyer obtains financing, arranges for house insurance, and has termite and building inspections done. A title insurance company or a lawyer will research the title to the property to make sure the seller in fact owns it, that no one else has an interest in it (such as an easement, which is discussed later in this chapter) that may affect its use, and that there are no judgments or liens outstanding against the property. This protects you from buying a house for, say, $100,000 and then learning that, for example, the government has a $50,000 lien against the house for back taxes the seller owes, giving the government the right to foreclose on the property.

If everything is in order—there aren't any termites, the house is sound, the title is good, and the buyer's loan application is approved—escrow will close. The close of escrow is commonly referred to as the "closing." At the closing, all of the parties— the buyer and seller, perhaps their attorneys, the bank's representative, and someone from the escrow company—assemble. The buyer shows the bank proof that the house is insured, the bank lends the buyer the money, the buyer gives the money to the seller, and the seller signs the deed and hands it to the buyer. The buyer now owns the house and is ready to move in.

Real Estate Brokers and Agents

Most houses in the United States are sold with the assistance of real estate brokers. It's all right to sell your own house without being a licensed broker. But if you're going to arrange the sale of someone else's house and charge a fee for your services, then you have to be either a licensed broker or a real estate agent working through a licensed broker. In several states, attorneys can act as brokers, but they can't hire real estate agents to work for them. A person who sells real estate without a license to do so not only risks being prosecuted for breaking the law, but also will not be able to sue for the commission if the seller refuses to pay it.

The real estate broker is supposed to use reasonable efforts to find a person who is interested in buying your property, help you negotiate a deal, assist in finding financing, and otherwise aid in the consummation of the sale. The seller normally hires the broker, and the broker is considered the seller's agent. If you're interested in buying a house, be advised that, while the broker must deal fairly and honestly with you, the broker's ultimate loyalty is to the seller.

The Listing Agreement

If you decide to sell your house through a broker, the broker will have you sign a written "listing agreement." This gives the broker the authority to find a buyer for your house and also obligates you to pay the broker a commission if the broker locates a willing and qualified buyer. There are several different types of listing agreements: the open listing, the exclusive agency listing, and the exclusive right-to-sell listing.

Open Listings

When you give a broker an open listing, you reserve the right to list the house with other brokers or sell it yourself. You only have to pay a commission to the broker who supplies the buyer. If you find your own buyer, you don't pay a commission to anyone. In an open-listing agreement, you can usually revoke the agreement at any time by giving written notice to the broker.

Exclusive Agency Listings

Under an exclusive agency listing, you agree to let only one broker sell your house. If you list the house with a second broker, and he or she sells the house, you'll have to pay two full commissions: one to the broker who found the buyer and one to the broker to whom you originally gave the exclusive agency listing. Although an exclusive agency listing prohibits you from listing your house with another broker, it does allow you to sell the house yourself, and you won't have to pay the broker a commission if you do.

Exclusive Right-to-Sell Listings

An exclusive right-to-sell listing agreement entitles the broker to a commission if the house sells during the term of the agreement, regardless of who sells it. Even if you find the buyer and handle all the details yourself, you'll still have to pay the broker's fee. An exclusive right-to-sell listing must clearly state that you are liable for the broker's commission even if you sell the house yourself; otherwise it is usually considered to be only an exclusive agency listing.

Which listing agreement is best? The open listing gives the seller the greatest rights, but real estate brokers rarely accept property on an open-listing basis. And if they do, they're not going to put in as much effort trying to sell the house if the seller can cancel the listing at any time. The exclusive right-to-sell listing is least advantageous to the seller because the broker gets a commission even if he or she doesn't do a single thing to sell the house. The most popular listing is the exclusive agency listing because it strikes a nice balance between the rights of the seller and the broker.

Most listings—even exclusive listings—give the broker the right to place the house on a "multiple-listing service." This is particularly true in metropolitan areas. The multiple-listing service is a directory of all houses for sale in the area, regardless of who the broker is. When a house is placed on the multiple-listing service, other brokers can try to find a buyer for the house but must go through the original broker to sell the house. The two brokers then split the commission any way they agree, although it is usually 50–50.

How long does a listing agreement last? Ordinarily the length of the listing is stated in the agreement, often 60 or 90 days. In open listings, as already noted, the seller usually can cancel it at any time. Suppose, however, you give a broker an exclusive right-to-sell listing for six months, but the broker doesn't do a single thing to find a buyer. Can you cancel the listing agreement? Usually you can, because the broker must make a reasonable effort to sell the property. But before canceling the listing, write a letter to your broker, informing him or her of your concerns. In the letter, state that unless you get some assurances in the next week or two that the broker is doing something to promote your property, you will consider the broker in breach of the agreement, leaving you free to list it with another broker.

Before signing the standard preprinted listing agreement form, read it over carefully. Take the agreement home to read if you feel pressured in the broker's office. These forms are prepared by the real estate industry and favor the broker over the seller. If you object to any provisions, discuss them with the broker and see if they can be deleted or changed before you sign it. And don't hesitate to call your lawyer if you don't understand anything in the agreement.

Brokers' Commissions

Brokers earn their living by charging a fee for selling your property. Usually the broker takes a percentage of the property's final selling price. Less frequently a flat fee is charged, regardless of how much the property sells for. Ordinarily the seller pays the broker's commission at the close of escrow (discussed later) from the money the buyer paid for the house.

Typical commission fees charged by brokers run from 4 percent to 8 percent of the selling price, with 5 and 6 percent being the most common. In more expensive properties, the commission percentage usually decreases as the price increases. For example, the broker's fee schedule may start out as 6 percent of the first $500,000 of the purchase price, 5 percent of the next $100,000, 4 percent of the next $250,000, and 3 percent of the rest.

Before signing a listing agreement, shop around and see what other brokers are charging. The percentage of the broker's commission is always negotiable; don't let anyone tell you otherwise. Any agreement between real estate brokers in an area to set a standard rate violates federal antitrust laws. If one broker refuses to bargain, find one who will. But don't opt for a low commission if the broker's not going to do much to find a buyer. Find out exactly what services the broker will be rendering and how hard he or she will work to find a buyer for you.

The following provisions of the broker's commission agreement should be included in the written listing agreement: what the amount of the broker's fee is (percentage or flat fee); how the fee is determined (normally from the actual selling price); who pays it (usually the seller); and, most importantly, when it is due. Keep in mind that unless a clause in the listing agreement states otherwise, the broker's fee usually is earned when he or she presents a person who wants to buy the property and who has the money or can qualify for a loan—someone who is "ready, willing, and able" to purchase your house. The commission is payable even if the sale is never actually consummated. Suppose you change your mind at the last minute and decide not to sell. Or suppose there is a problem with the title that causes the sale to fall through. Unless the listing agreement states otherwise, the broker is still entitled to the commission, because the broker has done what he or she agreed to do: bring you someone who wants to and is qualified to buy your house at an acceptable price.

Obviously, you should negotiate for a listing agreement more to your advantage. You can, for example, provide in the listing agreement that the broker's commission is payable only if and when escrow closes. This protects you from having to pay the broker's commission if the purchase doesn't go through. At the very least, you, as seller, should insist upon including a clause in the listing agreement stating that if the sale is not consummated because of anyone's acts other than your own, the broker does not get a commission.

Let's say that one day your broker comes by with a couple—the Robinsons—who look the place over, but they don't show any interest in buying. Two weeks later, the Robinsons drop in alone and offer to buy your house for 3 percent less than your asking price, saying, "Let's just forget about the broker and split the difference you'll save in the commission." You agree and sell them your house. A month later, your broker finds out and demands the 6 percent commission.

Or suppose your broker is showing the Hansens a number of houses. She drives them by your house, but they feign indifference. You know nothing of the whole matter. The next day, the Hansens knock on your door, say they heard about your house from a friend, and ask to look around. The Hansens decide to buy, and you close the deal yourself. No mention is made of your broker. Your broker gets wind of the sale and threatens to sue if you don't pay her fee.

In both of the examples above, your broker is entitled to the commission, even if you've reserved the right to sell the house yourself if you find the buyer. It was your broker's efforts that brought the buyer to your house, and that's what the listing agreement is really all about. Were it not for your broker, the buyers would not have seen your house. But if the buyers pretended they didn't go through your broker, and you lowered the price because you thought you were saving the broker's commission, ask the buyers to reimburse you for some or all of the broker's commission. If they refuse, consider seeing a lawyer or suing them in small claims court.

Duty of Seller or Broker to Disclose Defects

For centuries, the rule of caveat emptor—"buyer beware"—applied in the sale of real estate. If the seller or broker (or broker's agent) did not tell you, the buyer, of a defective condition in the house, such as a leaky roof, you had no recourse against the seller when you discovered the defect. The law traditionally required you to inspect the house carefully and thoroughly before buying it, and to ask specific questions relating to any defects.

Under the common law rules, there really were only two situations in which the seller or broker was liable for failing to disclose a defective condition. The first instance occurred when the seller or broker falsely answered a buyer's question—for example, if you asked whether there was any problem with termites, and the seller answered "no," even though he or she knew full well that a termite problem existed, having spent $10,000 in the last two years to eradicate—unsuccessfully—the menace. You could then sue the seller for intentionally misrepresenting the condition of the house.

The second situation occurred when the seller or broker deliberately concealed a defect to make it appear on the surface that there was no problem. For example, to hide the fact that the roof leaks, the seller painted over the water marks running down the walls. You looked at the ceiling and walls for evidence of leaks, and seeing none, assumed the house was watertight. When the first rains came, you learned just how porous the roof was and sued the seller. In this case, you would not have to ask any questions regarding the defective condition—the leaky roof—as the problem was not apparent and the seller intended to mislead you by concealing the problem.

Today, you also have legal recourse if the seller or broker negligently misrepresents the condition of the house. For instance, the seller might state that the electrical wiring is in good condition, without knowing one way or the other what condition the wiring is in. If it turns out that the wiring is bad, you can sue the seller for the cost of replacing it. The difference between a negligent misrepresentation and an intentional one is that in the intentional misrepresentation, the seller knows that he or she is lying. But to you, the buyer, it really doesn't matter if the misrepresentation was deliberate or not; the bottom line is that the house isn't as the seller said it was, and you got less than what you had bargained for.

Until recently, brokers could list a house and rely on what the seller told them about the condition of the house. They could take it for granted that what the seller was saying was true, and if they said the same thing to the buyer, the buyer couldn't sue the broker if it later turned out the information was false. A new trend in some states, however, requires a broker to inspect the property before making any representations. If there is a significant defect that careful inspection would have revealed, the broker must tell you about it. If the broker doesn't do this and if you buy the house, you can sue him or her when the truth comes out.

The Binder

Say you're shopping for a house, and you find one that you want to buy. You make an offer to the seller, the seller makes you a counteroffer, and the two of you negotiate from there. Once you strike a deal, you will probably be asked to sign a "binder," or "earnest money deposit receipt." This is usually a preprinted one-page form that the seller (or his or her broker) supplies. (Binders can be picked up at a stationery store that carries legal forms.) The binder essentially signifies that the buyer and seller have reached an agreement and that each is committed to going through with the deal.

The binder usually contains the barest of information: the names and addresses of the buyer and seller, the street address of the property for sale, and the purchase price. If a broker is involved, the binder will frequently specify the amount of his or her commission. The buyer is usually required to make a deposit when the binder is signed, anywhere from $100 to $1,000 or more. As the buyer, you should negotiate to pay as little as possible as the deposit. The amount of your deposit should, of course, be included in the binder.

A binder is usually not intended to set forth the complete terms and conditions of the agreement. In fact, it should contain a clause calling for a complete contract to be prepared and signed within a specific length of time (usually three to ten days) and stating that if the contract isn't drawn up, your entire deposit will be immediately refunded upon your request.

Before signing the binder, both the seller and the buyer should read it thoroughly. Generally, you don't need to have a lawyer review it, but if you don't understand something or if any questions do spring up, don't hesitate to get legal advice. As the buyer, you don't want to put your signature on something that's not complete. If you are making the purchase conditional on anything—such as your ability to obtain financing or a favorable termite report—you should try to hold off signing until you have the full purchase and sale contract to review.

The one chance you take by not signing a binder is that someone else will come along and sign it. The seller is then obligated to sell the house to that person. Since you had no written agreement with the seller, you can't sue the seller for selling the house to someone else. If you do sign a binder, remember—put as little information in it as possible, pay as little as possible, and make the sale contingent upon signing a complete purchase and sale contract within so many days, or you get all of your money back.

Option Contracts

Patty has just finished reading a book on making money by investing in real estate. Scanning the real estate section in Sunday's paper, she finds an older house offered at a low price. She looks the property over and decides she can quickly find someone to buy it for $10,000 more. Patty doesn't really want to buy the house herself, so she shouldn't sign a binder. But she wants to keep the property off the market for a month or two while she tries to find a buyer. She offers the sellers $100 if they will give her the exclusive option of buying the house for their asking price during the next 60 days. If the sellers agree to this, then Patty has 60 days to buy the property. This is an example of an "option contract." During this time, the sellers cannot sell the property to anyone else. If Patty exercises her option—agrees to buy the property—before 60 days go by, the sellers must sell it to her at the agreed-upon price. If Patty doesn't find a buyer, then at the end of 60 days, the sellers are free to sell the house to anyone else. The only thing Patty loses is the $100 she paid for the option.

Option contracts are used primarily in transactions involving commercial and industrial real estate. In recent years, however, many more people are using option contracts to do what Patty did: to buy time to find someone else who will purchase the property at a higher price, so they can make a tidy profit with little effort or risk. If no buyer is found, all that is lost is the money paid for the option.

What happens if the seller sells the property to someone else before the option has expired? If you can prove that you would have been able to sell the property to someone else at a higher price before the option was up, you can recover your "lost profit" and other damages. For example, if Patty had an option to buy the property for $75,000, and she found a person willing to pay $85,000 for it, she could recover $10,000 and other damages from the sellers. Even if Patty would not have found a buyer, she should still ask the sellers to return the money she paid for the option since they breached the contract by selling the property to someone else before Patty's 60 days had passed. She can also recover any out-of-pocket expenses, such as her advertising costs.

An option contract for the purchase of real estate should be put in writing and signed by both parties. It should include the names of the parties, the street address of the property, the selling price, when the option expires, and the amount of money paid for the option.

The Contract

Once you are ready to buy a house, all of the terms of the sale must be put in a written contract, usually called the "purchase and sale agreement." The provisions listed below should be in the contract to deal with the legal situations most likely to arise in the purchase of real estate. Don't sign the contract until you have thoroughly reviewed it. Get a copy of it and take it home to look it over before you sign. Compare the provisions in the contract with the information in this chapter to see what your rights are. And if you still have any questions, talk to a lawyer. An hour or two in legal fees now could save you thousands of dollars later.

Description of Parties and the Property

The contract should contain the full names and current addresses of the seller and the buyer and an adequate description of the property. The street address is usually sufficient to identify the property at this stage.

The Purchase Price and Deposit

The sales contract must include the purchase price of the property. Unless otherwise stated, the full amount is due when escrow closes. The contract should provide that the sale is contingent upon the buyer's ability to obtain financing (unless, of course, the buyer will be paying from cash on hand). If the seller will be financing any part of the price (see below), the contract should also state the amount financed and all terms of the loan. If you, as buyer, plan to assume the existing mortgage, this fact, too, should be noted in the sales contract. Because many mortgages are not assumable, you should insert a clause stating that the deal is canceled if the bank or savings and loan association refuses to let you assume the outstanding mortgage.

The amount of money you give as a deposit—usually 10 to 20 percent—should be noted in the contract. Don't trust this money to the seller. The money should be entrusted to your attorney, the seller's attorney, or a reputable escrow company. Suppose you hand the money over to the seller, who then uses it as a down payment on his or her next house. If your deal falls through, you'll probably find yourself waiting until the seller sells the house to someone else before you get your money back. (If this happens to you, consider seeing a lawyer immediately; otherwise, you might find yourself waiting months—even years—to get your deposit back.)

What Comes with the House?

Are the stove and refrigerator included in the sale? The washer and drier or other appliances? Any furniture, tools, or equipment? How about the lighting fixtures, drapes, and the like? Generally, except for built-in appliances, these things are not included in the sale of a house unless they are specifically included in the sales contract. Before you sign on the dotted line, identify in the contract each item that goes with the house.

Inspection and Repairs

If you haven't had the chance to inspect the house thoroughly before signing the contract, insist upon a provision stating that you can back out if a termite or building inspector's report shows any problem whatsoever. Do this even if the seller agrees to guarantee that the house is free from termite infestation, structural damage or weakness, and so forth. What happens if the seller refuses to make his warranty good after you buy the house? You'll have to hire a lawyer to sue him or her. Better to find out now, before you buy the house, if there are any problems.

Suppose that your inspection reveals a problem—say, a leaky roof. You like the house but don't want to buy it unless the seller fixes it before you move in. The seller agrees to do this but balks when you start to write it in the contract. In this case, either tell the seller that you won't sign the contract unless the provision is in there, or be prepared to pay for the repairs out of your own pocket. If such a clause is not in the written contract, the seller generally is not legally obligated to make any repairs to the property. Another alternative is to get a couple of estimates of what it will cost to fix the problem, then negotiate a corresponding reduction in the price and take care of the repairs yourself.

The contract should state that all repairs must be completed before escrow closes. If a repair cannot be made by that time, your best bet is to find out how much the repair will cost, then get the price of the house reduced by that amount. Don't rely on the seller to take care of these things once the money changes hands.

Damage to the House

One week after you sign the sales contract, the house burns down. You, the buyer, did not think about buying property insurance until escrow was due to close, another seven weeks away. Can the seller force you to go through with the deal? In some states, unless the contract provides otherwise, you become the owner of the house when the contract is signed, even though escrow doesn't close until two or three months later. As owner, you assume the risk of any damage to the property. In many states, however, you do not assume these risks until escrow closes and title passes. In any event, the sales contract should always include a provision stating that if the house is damaged before escrow closes, the seller must repair it, or the buyer can cancel the deal. Likewise, the contract should give the buyer the right to cancel if the house is destroyed. One thing you, as the buyer, should do to protect yourself is arrange for property insurance to take effect immediately when escrow closes (or as soon as the contract is signed, if you are assuming the risk that the house will be damaged or destroyed before escrow closes).

The Title, Deed, and Encumbrances

The sales contract should always state that the sale is contingent upon the seller's ability to give the buyer a "marketable title." The type of deed (such as a warranty deed or grant deed, discussed below) that the seller must give the buyer should be noted. If the contract doesn't specify the type of deed to be used, the law presumes that you intended to use the type of deed customarily used in your area. All existing encumbrances, liens, easements, covenants, restrictions, and so forth (which are discussed later) affecting the property should be included.

The Broker's Fee, Adjustments, and Escrow

If a broker is involved, the contract should state what the broker's commission is, when it is due, and who is responsible for paying it. Any adjustments that will be made concerning taxes, insurance, and other expenses already paid by the seller (see discussion below) should be noted in the purchase and sale contract. The contract should also set forth information concerning escrow, such as when and where it will be opened, who will pay the closing costs, and when and where escrow will close.

Making Sure the Seller Is Out When You're Ready to Move In

Escrow closes; your furniture is loaded onto the moving van and taken to your new house. But when you get there, the sellers and all their furniture are still there. They tell you that their new house won't be ready to move into for another two weeks or so. And when the sellers finally are out, you open the door and find it looks as though a tornado hit the place.

The sales contract should explicitly require the seller to move out and leave the house in a clean condition before escrow closes. Ideally you don't want escrow to close until the seller is out (unless you have agreed to lease the property to the seller for a while) and you have looked the place over. This gives the seller an extra incentive to be out of the property on time and to leave it clean. You will want to include a provision stating that if the seller is not out of the house on time, the seller has to pay your lodging and storage costs until the seller is out. If there is a tenant who has some time remaining on a lease, or there is some other reason why you won't be able to move in when escrow closes, this should be noted in the contract.

Signing the Contract

The seller and buyer must both sign the contract. If the buyer is married, his or her spouse should usually sign the contract as well. If the seller is married, both the husband and wife should sign the contract even if the title is in the name of only one of them. (The fact that title is in one spouse's name does not necessarily mean that the other spouse has no rights in and to the property.) The contract should require the spouse whose name does not appear on the deed to sign a "quitclaim deed" releasing all interest in the property before escrow closes.

If the property is being sold by a corporation or a general or limited partnership, the contract should state that the seller has the authority to bind the corporation or partnership. The buyer should request and review copies of all documents giving the seller this authority, and these documents should be incorporated into the contract. If two or more people own the property but do not have a partnership agreement (say, two friends who hold title to the land as tenants in common), have each of them sign the contract if you're buying more than one person's share.

Changing the Contract After It Is Signed

The building inspector you hired to check out the house tells you that everything is fine, except that a new heating system is needed. You get some estimates and learn that it will cost about $2,500 to install a new one. You call up the seller, who agrees to reduce the price by this amount. You figure you can trust the seller, so you don't ask to have this put in writing. The next week escrow closes, but at the original contract price. Why? Because you didn't change the contract properly.

Like any other type of contract, a contract for the sale of real estate can be changed at any time by mutual agreement of the parties. But ordinarily in real estate transactions these changes must be put in writing and signed by both buyer and seller to be enforceable. An oral modification is usually not sufficient, since the original contract—one for the sale of real estate—is required by the Statute of Frauds to be in writing and can be changed only by an instrument of "equal dignity."

Financing the Purchase Price

Most people who buy a home today don't have the money to buy it for cash and have to finance a large portion of the price. Most of the time, the loan comes from a conventional source, such as a bank or savings and loan association. Or, the financing of the house may be made possible through the FHA (Federal Housing Administration), which often loans money for homes at a lower rate than conventional sources. Qualified veterans may obtain a loan from the Veterans Administration (VA), which requires a minimal down payment and offers a lower interest rate than even the FHA loan. Sometimes the seller will finance all or a portion of the price.

You may want to take over ("assume") the existing mortgage on the property because it has a lower interest rate than today's loans. Loans are not as freely assumable as they once were, however. Most loans cannot be assumed without the bank's permission unless the loan agreement expressly states that it is assumable. (Loans with variable interest rates are most likely to contain this kind of provision than other loans are.) If you plan on assuming a loan, get the details worked out with the bank before escrow closes. You don't want to get caught in the situation of closing escrow and then finding the bank calling in the loan when it learns of the sale.

Suppose you let the buyer assume the outstanding mortgage on your home. Two years later, the house burns down. The buyer didn't have insurance on it and can't afford to rebuild. The buyer walks away and defaults on the loan, the bank forecloses, and the property is sold at auction, but the money isn't enough to pay the balance of the loan. The buyer can't be found or doesn't have the money to pay the balance. Can the bank sue you? Generally, yes. You are still liable for the loan, although the bank must first try to get the money from the buyer. But if the buyer doesn't have the money, the bank can come looking for you. Some states, however, have "antideficiency judgment" laws, which limit the bank to selling the property. If that isn't enough to cover the loan, the bank is stuck. Before agreeing to let the buyer assume your mortgage, see if the bank will release you entirely from your obligations under the loan. Otherwise, make sure the buyer is responsible and can be counted on to make the payments, keep the property in good shape, and maintain adequate insurance on it at all times.

When money is loaned to buy a house, a mortgage or deed

of trust is used to secure the lender's interest in the property. Although there are some differences between the two, the effects are the same: they give the lender the right to foreclose on the property if the buyer defaults on the loan.

If you are seeking financing from a bank or savings and loan, shop around to make sure that you are getting the best deal possible. Calling three different financial institutions on the same day may get you two or three different interest rates quoted. Carefully consider all costs of the loan and the period of time in which it must be paid back. Find out what the total cost of the loan will be, including "points," which is a fee based on a percentage of the loan amount. For example, if you are borrowing $100,000, and the bank charges 2 points, you have to pay a $2,000 "loan fee," which is usually due when escrow closes. Also find out whether there is a "prepayment penalty" if you refinance the loan when interest rates come down and pay it off earlier than it is due.

The term *creative financing* has become part of the real estate industry's vocabulary. Creative financing cannot be defined with any exactness, except to say that it is anything different from the traditional 20- or 30-year mortgage. For example, the loan may require the buyer to pay only interest for five years and then pay the entire loan back in one "balloon payment." Or, a bank may be willing to lend only a certain amount of money on the property, so the seller agrees to finance the rest ("carry paper").

Creative financing has allowed many people to purchase a home when they otherwise would not have been able to. But at the same time, creative financing has caused great suffering to some. For example, if the buyer can't make that balloon payment, the lender forecloses, and the buyer loses the house. Many sellers who finance the price face the expense and trouble of having to foreclose when the buyer defaults. If you will be using creative financing, make sure you know just what you're getting into. In some cases, for instance, the buyer's payments for the first few years are not enough even to pay the interest on the loan. When this happens ("negative amortization"), the interest that isn't paid off is added to the purchase price. In a few years, the amount of your monthly payment will increase—perhaps by as much as several hundred dollars—to cover both the principal and the interest. By that time, however, the price of your $85,000 house may have risen to $90,000 or more with the accumulated back interest.

The Closing

After the purchase and sale contract is signed by both the buyer and the seller, you, as the buyer, will need to do a number of things, including arranging financing, getting a title search done (see discussion below), having termite and building inspectors check the property out, obtaining insurance for the property, and perhaps having a survey done. As the seller, you may have to make some repairs to the house or clear up some problems with your title (such as paying the landscaper $250 to release the lien filed against your property).

Most contracts for the sale of real estate state that "time is of the essence." This means that escrow must close on the day and time specified, and not a minute later. If you won't be ready to close escrow on that date, call the seller or broker, let him or her know why you can't close escrow then, and state when you will be ready to close escrow. As long as you're making a solid effort to do what you have to do to close the deal, there shouldn't be any problem getting a reasonable extension of time to close escrow. Be sure to get the other party to sign a written document agreeing to the time extension and file it with the escrow company. Keep a copy for yourself in case a problem arises later.

When everything is finally in order, escrow will close. Several people may be present at the closing, including the buyer, the seller, perhaps their attorneys, the real estate broker, the bank's representative, and someone from the escrow company. A number of things happen in sequence. The buyer shows the bank the title insurance company's report (discussed below) and also proof of property insurance if this hasn't been given to the bank already. The bank lends the buyer the money to purchase the property.

The buyer gives the money to the seller, who in turn gives the buyer the deed to the land. The seller also pays off the balance of his or her mortgage on the property. If a broker is involved, the commission is paid at this time. Adjustments are made to reimburse the seller for various expenses that he or she has already paid but that will benefit the buyer. For example, if the seller has prepaid the full year's taxes of, say, $1,000, and there are six months left in the year, the buyer will give the seller an additional $500 to adjust the taxes. A closing statement listing all monies, costs, expenses, and deductions is prepared (usually by the escrow company or by one of the party's attorneys) and given to each party. The deed is then recorded in the county recorder's office.

If the Sale Falls Through

When a sale falls through for some reason—if, for example you can't get financing or your building inspector finds a big crack in the foundation—you can usually cancel the sale and get your deposit back. But what happens if either the buyer or seller backs out without justification and refuses to go through with the deal?

If the seller backs out, the buyer is entitled to recover any money he or she has actually paid, including the deposit, escrow expenses, and costs of a building inspector and title search. The buyer can also sue for the difference between the contract price and the cost of buying a comparable house from someone else. For example, if you agreed to buy the house for $125,000, and it costs you $140,000 to find a comparable house, you are entitled to recover the $15,000 difference. But what if you really want the property in question rather than another house? Frequently you can go to court to compel the seller to sell the house to you. This is known as "specific performance." Courts will routinely force a seller to sell the property to the buyer if the buyer has done everything the contract required but the seller reneges without justification.

Now suppose that you are the seller, and the buyer backs out for no reason. If you end up selling the house for a lower price, you can make the buyer pay the difference. You can also recover any additional out-of-pocket expenses, such as advertising expenses that would not have been necessary if the buyer had gone through with the deal. If you had to pay a commission to a broker when the buyer backed out, the buyer can be held liable for this, too. And just as a buyer can force a reluctant seller to sell the property, you can sometimes force the buyer to complete the deal by suing for "specific performance."

Here is the most commonly encountered scenario when the sale of a house is aborted: Sidney agrees to sell his house to Frank for $90,000, and they sign a written contract. The next week, Nancy offers Sidney $95,000, which Sidney likewise accepts, and a contract between Sidney and Nancy is signed. Sidney calls Frank up and tells him that he has changed his mind and is not going to sell the house after all. Frank tells Sidney they have a signed contract, and he will take the case all the way to the Supreme Court if Sidney backs out. When Frank learns of the deal between Sidney and Nancy, he calls Nancy and tells her that Sidney sold him the house first. Nancy says she doesn't know a thing about that, and as far as she is concerned, she owns the house. Both Frank and Nancy want the house, and each refuses to back down. Who wins? If Nancy knew of the signed contract between Frank and Sidney before she signed her contract, Frank will win. But if Nancy did not know of the earlier agreement, the issue may be resolved on the basis of who recorded a signed contract or a deed first. Many states hold that in this situation, who gets the house depends on who was the first to record a deed with the recorder's office. If Nancy recorded her deed first, she would win, even though she was the second buyer. One way to avoid this problem is to record the binder and purchase and sale contract as soon as they are signed. A final note: if separate brokers brought Frank and Nancy to Sidney, Sidney will probably wind up paying them each a full commission. (If the same broker that closed the deal between Frank and Sidney also closed the deal between Nancy and Sidney, Frank would be able to sue the broker for inducing Sidney to break the contract with him.)

New House Warranties

What happens if you buy a new home and later discover that the built-in dishwasher doesn't work, or the electrical wiring is all bad, or, worse yet, the house is slowly slipping into the ground, and huge cracks are developing in the walls and ceiling?

When the defect is in an appliance, such as the oven, dishwasher, water heater, air conditioner, microwave oven, or trash compactor, the first thing to do is check the manufacturer's warranty card, which should have come with the house. Is the appliance still covered by the warranty? If so, contact an authorized service company to repair or replace it according to the terms of the warranty. If the defect is due to an error in its installation, however, you'll have to look to the general contractor or developer to fix it. Call or write the contractor and identify the problem. If the manufacturer told you the problem was one of installation rather than manufacturing, be sure to tell this to the contractor.

If the defect is with the house itself, such as faulty electrical wiring or leaky plumbing, contact the general contractor or developer. If the wiring or plumbing needs replacing, this should be done as soon as possible, at no cost to you. You are entitled to be compensated for any inconvenience to you, including the cost of lodging if it becomes unbearable for you to stay in the house because of, for instance, a prolonged lack of water or heating. If the defect is structurally related and serious—say, the house is slipping down a hill, or the roof is slowly collapsing—you should hire a lawyer to represent your interests.

Condos, Townhomes, and Coops

Most of what has been covered already in this chapter also relates to buying a condominium, townhouse, or cooperative. But these involve a few different considerations—particularly as to just what you own.

When you own a "condominium" ("condo" for short), you generally own only the "living space" of a particular unit. Exactly what you own is determined by the deed, the declaration of covenants, conditions, and restrictions (CC&Rs), and other documents. Sometimes you own the inside walls. Other times, you own only the "airspace" inside the walls. The condominium homeowners' association owns all or most of the building and all of the land and communal structures, such as a clubhouse or swimming pool.

The main difference between a "townhome" and a condominium is that with a condominium, the homeowners' association owns all of the land, while with a townhome you own the land beneath your townhouse. You also own the walls, inside and outside, except for "party walls"—walls you share with your neighbor—which you only own the inside of.

"Cooperatives" ("coops") are chiefly found on the East Coast, particularly in the major metropolitan areas. A coop is unique in that the only thing you own is stock in a corporation. The corporation owns all of the land and the apartment building and gives you a "proprietary lease" to live in a particular unit. This lease lasts for as long as you own your stock in the corporation. If you want to live in a coop, you will have to submit the necessary application to the board of directors for review. You can be turned down for a variety of reasons but not because of your race, national origin, or religion.

A coop is managed by the corporation's board of directors, who usually hire a management company to take care of the building. Condos and townhomes are governed by a board elected by members of the homeowners' association. Regardless of whether you live in a coop, townhome, or condo, you'll probably have to live by a number of rules and regulations concerning the use of your unit and the common area, some of which may be contained in the corporation's or partnership's bylaws or the CC&Rs you received with your deed or stock.

In addition to the regular mortgage payment, you will probably pay monthly or annual dues to the homeowners' association or maintenance fees to the coop corporation. Before you buy, find out what the dues currently are and how much they have increased in the past two or three years, then figure this amount into your monthly payments to see if your budget can handle it. This money is used by the homeowners' association or coop to maintain and repair communal structures, to pay for gardening and the like, and to buy insurance for the building and land. Depending on exactly what you own, you may need to obtain property insurance to cover your particular unit in case of fire or other damage. (And in any case, you'll still need to buy insurance if you want your personal belongings—furniture, jewelry, appliances, and so forth—covered.)

Estates, Marketable Title, and Deeds

Estates—What You Get for Your Money

When purchasing land, you need to know exactly what you are buying. Not all "estates," or interests, in land are equal. You can have anything from the absolute right to do whatever you want with a piece of property to a mere license to come onto the land for a specific purpose.

Fees

The most common interest in land is the "fee simple absolute," or just "fee simple." When you buy a piece of land, you usually become owner of a fee simple absolute. This is the largest interest you can have in real estate. You own the property lock, stock, and barrel, no strings attached (except maybe a mortgage or trust deed). You are free to sell the land as you see fit. When you die, the property is passed according to the provisions of your will; if you die without a will, the land goes to your next of kin (see chapter 3). Sometimes the seller (or a previous owner) will retain certain rights, such as the rights to any gas or minerals under the property.

The other type of fee is the so-called defeasible fee. Unlike a fee simple absolute, which you own forever, you can lose a defeasible fee when a specified event or condition occurs. For example, the deed may give you the property "so long as liquor is never sold on the premises." If you open a market and sell liquor, you lose the land. The title to the land reverts to the original owner (or his or her survivors). Defeasible fees are not too common, but if you ever run across any type of restriction or condition on the title that could result in your losing it, you should talk to a lawyer before buying the land.

Life Estates

A life estate gives you the right to live on a piece of land for as long as you live. (A life estate can also let you live on a piece of land for as long as someone else lives.) The owner of the life estate is called a "life tenant." If you own a life estate, you can do what you want with it: you can live on the land, you can sell your interest, or you can give it away. But when you die, your life estate is automatically terminated. Life estates are usually found in the context of wills and estates, as when one spouse by will gives the other the right to live on any property for as long as he or she lives, and someone else (such as the children) gets it afterward.

When you own a life estate, you must leave the property in substantially the same condition as it was in when you received it. You can use reasonable amounts of the natural resources on the property—timber, water, minerals, and the like—but usually you can't exhaust them unless the deed granting you a life estate specifies differently. The person who is to receive the property after you can get a court injunction to stop you from unreasonably depleting the resources. You are also obligated to make ordinary repairs to the land and structures but don't have to spend more money in repairs than you receive in profits (from timber, gas, and mining, for example) and rent from the land.

Future Interests

A future interest gives you a right in the property at some later date. In the case of a life estate, for example, the person who gets the property after the life tenant dies has a future interest. Someone who owns a future interest must wait until a specified event happens—say, the life tenant dies—before taking possession of the property.

Easements, Profits, and Covenants

An "easement" involves the right to go onto another's property for some purpose. A common example of an easement is the right to use a road on your neighbor's property to get onto and off your own land. Easements are typically granted to public utility companies to run power, water, sewer, gas, and telephone lines over or through property. Easements can also prohibit you from using your property in some way. For example, if Marilyn divides her property in half and sells you one lot, she may place a restriction in the deed preventing you from building a house or other structure in a way that will interfere with the view from her property.

A "profit" gives you the right to take some resource, such as timber, minerals, dirt, gravel, or oil, from another's land. A profit necessarily includes an easement to go onto that person's land to get the resource. The profit may be an exclusive or a nonexclusive one. If you get an exclusive profit, you and you alone can take the resource from the land. But the profit can restrict how much of the particular resource you can take. In a nonexclusive profit, the owner of the land can give others the right to take the same resource from the land.

A "covenant" is a promise found in a deed concerning the use of land. An affirmative covenant requires that you perform a specified act—mow your lawn every week, for example. Far more common, though, are negative covenants, which prohibit certain acts or uses of property. For example, a covenant may prevent you from painting your house purple or operating a business out of your home. Covenants are particularly important in communal living arrangements, such as condominiums.

Easements, profits, and covenants ordinarily must be put in writing to be enforceable. The document giving you the right to use the land should be recorded in the county recorder's office, especially if you want to enforce it against future buyers of the property. If you don't record your easement or other interest, you may lose it when the land is sold. But if your use of the land is obvious from looking at the land itself, this is usually enough to notify a purchaser of your interest. To avoid disputes and costly legal proceedings, you should always record an easement, profit, or covenant.

If you misuse an easement or profit, you risk losing it altogether. Suppose Mary gives Jane an easement to drive her car over Mary's property so Jane can get to her own property. Jane opens a 24-hour convenience market on her land, and her customers use Mary's road to get to it. Can Mary sue to stop this? Yes. At the time she gave Jane the easement, Mary did not contemplate a steady stream of cars going over her property at all hours of the day and night.

Licenses

A license gives you permission to go onto another person's land for some reason without being a trespasser. When you go to the stadium to watch a football or baseball game, the ticket gives you a license to be on the premises. Without the ticket or other consent of the owner or lessee of the property, you would be a trespasser. When you let an advertising company put a billboard on your land, the advertising company has a license to keep its sign there. If the sign is put there without your consent or the advertising company fails to remove it when the license expires, the advertising company is trespassing on your land.

Marketable Title

When buying land, you want to make sure that the seller has a good, or "marketable," title. A marketable title is one free from problems—no one else claims to own the land; there are no outstanding liens, judgments, mortgages, or other encumbrances against it; and there are no easements other than the typical easements for power, water, sewer, gas, and telephone lines.

A title is rendered bad ("unmarketable") by such things as a defective deed (perhaps it was not notarized or the description of the property is incomplete or wrong), an easement, or an encumbrance—a mortgage, judgment, or lien—that the seller cannot or will not remove. Title can also be bad because of a "break" in the "chain of title"—somewhere along the line, somebody failed to record a deed.

There are two main ways to find out if a title is good. One is to obtain a title insurance policy from a reputable title insurance company. Prior to insuring the title, the title insurance company will have its employees thoroughly research the title to see if it is marketable. You need to be aware, though, that the typical title insurance policy only protects you against recorded documents. If someone claims ownership or an easement through adverse possession (see discussion below), the ordinary policy doesn't cover this. You should always personally visit the land before buying it to see if anyone else claims to own any part of it. A more expensive policy protecting you against things that are not in the official records can also usually be purchased.

The second method of ascertaining whether a title is marketable is by having a lawyer do a "title abstract." This was the uniform method of ensuring a marketable title before title insurance companies sprang up and is still the standard practice in some states. An attorney skilled in title searches will go through the official records and then issue an opinion as to whether or not the title is marketable.

The protection you get from an insurance company is usually greater than what you get from a lawyer who does an abstract. If a lawyer makes an error, you can recover damages only by proving that the lawyer was negligent in some way—that the lawyer overlooked something that a careful lawyer would not have missed. And if the lawyer does not carry adequate "errors and omissions" insurance (professional malpractice insurance), you might not be able to collect the full amount of your damages. On the other hand, if a title insurance company makes an error, it usually has to pay your damages, regardless of whether or not it was negligent.

If the title search reveals a defect a "cloud" on the title— the seller must clear this up before escrow closes. If the seller is unable to deliver a marketable title, however, you can either call the deal off or go through with the purchase and assume the risk of the defective title. Whether or not you should accept an unmarketable title depends on how serious the problem is. It's a good idea to talk to a lawyer before buying the property, even if the defect appears minor. In exchange for accepting a less than marketable title, you may wish to negotiate a lower price to reflect the risk you are taking.

The Deed

The seller's interest in the property does not pass to you until the seller signs a deed containing an adequate "legal description" of the land. The legal description, which governs what you own, is based on "townships," six-mile squares consisting of 36 sections. Reading a legal description can give you the same feeling Alice had when walking through the looking glass: "The northeast quarter of the southwest quarter of the southeast quarter of the northwest quarter. . . ."

You may want to have the property surveyed to make sure the visible boundaries (fences, for example) correspond with the legal description. A survey may reveal some problem—that the garage is encroaching two feet onto the neighbor's property, for instance. If this is the case, you will want to get an easement or other agreement with the neighbor before buying the land.

Here are the various types of deeds that are used to transfer ownership of real estate:

General Warranty Deed

In a general warranty deed, the seller promises that he or she owns the land, has the right to sell it, and that there are no encumbrances (mortgages, liens, judgments, and the like) against the property. The seller also promises to defend the title against third parties who claim to own all or part of the land, and to compensate the buyer if a third party manages to remove the buyer from the property. A "full warranty deed" includes the additional promise that the seller will do anything necessary to clear up any questions about the title. A warranty deed gives the buyer the greatest protection of all the deeds, but even so, this protection is no match for a title insurance policy.

Grant Deed

In a grant deed, the seller warrants that he or she has not conveyed the same property to anyone else and that the property is free from encumbrances other than those disclosed to the buyer. The seller does not, though, promise to defend the buyer if someone else claims ownership of the property.

Bargain and Sale Deed

In a bargain and sale deed, commonly used in the Northeast, the seller makes no express warranties. The law, however, imposes the warranties that the seller has a marketable title and is transferring all of his or her interest unless the deed states otherwise. A bargain and sale deed with a covenant against the seller's acts warrants that the property is not encumbered except as specified in the deed.

Quitclaim Deed

A quitclaim deed merely releases the seller's interest in the property, if he or she has any interest at all. If the seller is the sole owner of the property, and no one else claims an interest therein, the quitclaim is sufficient to transfer the title. Quitclaim deeds are usually the least preferred type of deed when land is being sold.

Forms of Ownership

When you are buying land with someone else, you need to consider how you will hold title: as joint tenants, tenants in common, community property, or tenants by the entirety. The differences between these are discussed in chapter 3. Suffice it to say here that tenancy by the entirety and community property (which exists in only nine states) can exist only between a married couple, and joint tenancies and tenancies by the entirety have an automatic right of survivorship. This means that when one owner dies, the surviving owner automatically owns the other's share of the property.

Adverse Possession

Usually you become the owner of a piece of land by buying it from the person who owns it. You can also become the owner simply by taking possession of the land and sitting there long enough. This is the doctrine of "adverse possession."

To acquire property by adverse possession, you must actually live on or use the property, and this fact must be clear if the owner inspects the land; it doesn't count if you're hiding your presence. You must be in continuous and peaceable possession of the property for the statutory period of time, which varies from five to twenty years, depending on the state. Some states also require that you pay taxes on the property for a certain number of years. Your possession of the land must be "hostile." This means that you must claim to be the owner of the property, even though there may be no justification for the claim. Once you have done all of this for the requisite length of time, you become owner in fee simple absolute of the property. But if you build a house on a far corner of a thousand-acre spread, you can't claim title to the entire property. You only get the property immediately surrounding the house, including the land you farm or have otherwise been using throughout the required time period.

If you own land somewhere remote from where you live, land that you don't get to very often, you should make it a point to check it out—either in person or through a local real estate agent—every few years to make sure people have not settled in. If they have, give them a written notice that you own the property, that they are trespassing, and that you demand that they move at once. If they don't, it would be best to hire a lawyer to start proceedings to remove them, rather than risk losing the property by doing nothing.

Trespass

A person who walks across your land without your permission is trespassing, even if the property isn't in the slightest way damaged. And a person doesn't actually have to walk on your land to commit a trespass. Throwing a rock or other object onto the land constitutes a trespass, as does firing a shot across the land, even though the bullet doesn't touch the ground or any structure on the property.

Consent of the property owner or other person in lawful possession of the land (such as a tenant) is a defense against a trespass action. The person must not exceed the scope of that consent, however, and if the consent is revoked, the person must promptly leave the grounds. An example: Charles gives permission to a local boy scout troop to spend one night camping out on a remote corner of his farm. The boys like it so much, they decide to spend a second night but don't bother asking Charles if it's okay with him. By staying a second night, the boys have exceeded Charles's consent to use the property and are now trespassing.

Necessity can be a valid defense against a trespass action. For example, if a weekend sailor is out on the lake when a storm suddenly threatens the safety of the boat and persons aboard, the sailor can tie up at a nearby pier. But if the boat does any damage to the pier during the storm, the sailor must pay for the repairs. On the other hand, if the pier's owner untied the boat before the storm ended, and the sailor or anyone else aboard was injured or if the boat was damaged, the pier's owner is liable.

In certain cases, you can go onto another's land to recover possession of something that was stolen from you. This is usually allowed only if you are in "hot pursuit" of the person who took it, and you generally can go only onto the land; you can't, for example, break down a door and enter the house.

The most pressing questions many people have about trespassing concerns how much force they can use to remove a trespasser from their land. You are entitled to use only "reasonable force" to remove the trespasser. What amount of force is "reasonable" depends on a number of things, including the danger the trespasser poses to your safety. If the trespasser is a harmless tramp, you can ask that he or she leave and gently escort him or her off your property. But you can't use excessive physical force to get someone off the land, unless he or she is threatening immediate serious harm—for example, trying to burn your house down. Ordinarily, you cannot shoot a trespasser unless it is a matter of justified self-defense. If someone refuses to leave your property after being asked to do so, it is usually best to call the police and have them remove the trespasser.

A trespasser is generally liable for all damage done to your property while trespassing upon it, even though the damage is accidental. If, for example, Tony decides to camp out on Victor's property and lights a campfire that, through no fault of his, spreads and burns down Victor's house, Tony is liable for the damage done, even though he did not intend to damage the house.

Ownership of Airspace and Subspace

Years ago, when you bought a piece of real estate, you became owner of more than just the house and the surface of the land. You also owned the air above ("airspace") as far as you could see and the ground below ("subspace") to the center of the earth. Anyone crossing above or below your land, no matter how far, was trespassing upon your land unless you permitted it. If your neighbor was mining under your house without your consent, for instance, you could sue to stop it and also to get paid for the minerals taken from your land.

Subspace rights have remained essentially the same over the centuries. Ownership of airspace, on the other hand, has changed considerably. Today, you own only so much of the airspace above your property as you can occupy or use in connection with the land—the "immediate reaches." If an aircraft flies over your land, the pilot is not committing a trespass unless the plane is flying below the altitude prescribed by federal laws or in a way that is dangerous to persons or things on the land.

Nuisance

Penny, your entrepreneurial neighbor, has come up with another scheme to make money: starting a chicken ranch in her backyard. She builds some cages and buys 100 chickens. Within days, your peaceful solitude is transformed into a dusty, smelly, noisy hell. You ask Penny to get the chickens off her land, but she refuses. What can you do about it? You can sue her for maintaining a nuisance.

There are two distinct types of damages you can ask for in nuisance actions: money damages to compensate you for any injuries or inconveniences you suffered from the nuisance, and an injunction ordering Penny to "abate the nuisance"—to stop the dust, smell, and noise, or completely and permanently shut down the chicken farm. If Penny fails to remove the chickens after being ordered to do so, she can be found in contempt of court and jailed until she gets them out of there.

Not every unpleasant smell or noise is a nuisance, however. The thing must be offensive to the point where it greatly interferes with your use and enjoyment of your property. Minor annoyances are just a fact of modern life that we all have to put up with.

Let's say that a new airport is built near you. The noise, smoke, and vibrations are more than you can stand, so you sue the airport for creating a nuisance. The airport contends that the government authorized the location, and therefore it cannot be held liable. Will that defense succeed? No. The fact that a business of any kind is operating under a government permit and in an area zoned for that kind of activity does not usually prevent you from suing it for being a nuisance.

Suppose that for 20 years, Filbert has been operating a dairy farm about 10 miles outside of Metropolis. Although the farm has produced a lot of noise and strong odors throughout its history, no one has ever complained, since the nearest neighbors are two miles away. Metropolis grows, a developer buys the land beside the farm, and a subdivision springs up. The owners of the new homes sue Filbert to abate the nuisance. Filbert argues that he should not be enjoined (stopped) from operating the farm because the developer and homeowners were fully aware of his farm when they bought the land. Will Filbert win with his argument that the people "moved to" the nuisance? No. Simply because he has used his farm in an offensive manner for many years does not give Filbert the right to continue the nuisance. His new neighbors are entitled to enjoy their property free from excessive noise and foul odors and can bring a lawsuit to stop the nuisance.

Water Rights

The two types of water disputes that arise most frequently are those involving surface water and those involving rivers, lakes, and streams.

Surface Waters

Every spring since he bought his house eight years ago, Mike's property has been flooded with the runoff from rains. He decides to take action and erects some barriers and digs some ditches to divert the water. When the rains come this year, Mike's property is protected. But the water now flows onto Kim's land, where it does considerable damage. Kim sues Mike to pay for the damage and to remove the barriers and ditches. Who wins?

In some states, Mike wins because surface waters—runoff from rain, melting snow, and springs—are considered a "common enemy." You can divert the water any way you want, without worrying about the effects on others. In other states, Kim wins because the law prevents you from doing anything that interferes with the "natural flow" of water—you generally must sit back and let the water run its course, even if damage to your property will surely result. Some states permit you to make reasonable changes in the natural flow of the surface water, so long as you avoid unnecessary harm to your neighbors' property.

Watercourses

Suppose that your land borders on a small river. For years, you have been using the water to irrigate your garden, water your cows—whatever. One day you go to dip your bucket in the river, only to find it's all dried up or polluted because of a new factory upstream. What can you do about it?

In many states, primarily those east of the Mississippi River, if you own property alongside a watercourse—a river, stream, or lake—you can take a reasonable amount of water from the river, so long as you don't interfere too much with the water supply to others along the river. In many western states, where water is scarcer, the rule is "prior appropriation"—essentially, "first come, first served." The person who uses the water first has priority. If you've been using the water, and someone new comes along and interrupts its flow to you, you can sue to stop that person from interfering with your rights. Regardless of which law is applied, you would most likely win a lawsuit to keep the upstream owner from interfering with your water supply.

Condemnation

Through its power of "eminent domain," the government can condemn your land—force you to sell it. But the government can't go around condemning land anytime it wants for just any purpose. There must be sufficient public interest, such as making way for a freeway, redeveloping a blighted area, or providing water or electricity to the community.

Usually the government deliberately condemns a house, as when it plans the route of a new road and then condemns the houses in its path. Sometimes, though, the condemnation is the unintended result of another act that effectively makes it impossible for you to live in your house any longer. For example, if the government builds a new airport, and your house is now right beside the runway, the noise and exhaust from the planes may make it unhealthy for anyone to live there. This is called "inverse condemnation."

All or only part of the property can be condemned. In either case, you are entitled to be paid the fair market value—"just compensation"—for the land (or portion of land) the government takes from you. Fair market value is the amount a willing buyer would pay a willing seller for the property, taking into consideration its development potential. If you don't think the government is offering enough, you can challenge the amount in court. At the trial, the evidence mainly consists of real estate appraisers testifying as to the value of the land based on sales of comparable parcels in the area. If your land is being condemned, and you want to challenge either the government's right to do so or the amount of money it wants to pay, you're usually better off hiring a lawyer to help you, preferably one experienced in this area of the law.

Lateral and Subjacent Support

Suppose that your neighbor decides to put a swimming pool in his or her backyard. One day you come home and find a big crack in your kitchen floor. Looking out the window, you see the cause: the hole for the pool has caved in, taking a good chunk of your property with it and undermining your house's foundation. Is your neighbor liable for the damage? Yes; your neighbor cannot do anything that adversely affects the stability of your land, either from the side ("lateral support") or beneath it ("subjacent support").

The right to lateral and subjacent support generally applies only to land in its natural condition—that is, a vacant, undeveloped lot. Your neighbor might not have to pay for the damage to your house if it can be proved that your land would not have collapsed were it not for the house.

If Someone Is Injured on Your Land

Suppose that one night your daughter leaves a roller skate on the walk leading up to your front door. A person walking to your door slips and falls on the skate and is injured. Are you liable for those injuries?

Historically, your liability to someone injured on your land has depended in large part upon who the person was—a trespasser, a visiting friend, a solicitor, the letter carrier, a business client, and so on. You generally aren't liable to trespassers, especially if you didn't know they were there. If the person was on a social visit or was a door-to-door solicitor, you aren't liable unless you knew the skate was there—in which case, you either have to make the walkway safe by moving the skate or warn the visitor of the danger. If the person was the letter carrier, a meter reader, a trash collector, a repair person, a delivery person, or a business customer, you are liable even though you didn't know the skate was there. To these "business visitors," you owe a duty to inspect your property for dangerous conditions and remove them or warn your business visitors of the danger. But you usually don't have to warn your visitor if the danger is obvious.

A growing number of states have abolished these classifications as arbitrary and hold that a landowner owes only one standard of care toward all people—the duty to exercise reasonable care depending on the situation. (Some states have, however, retained the distinction of trespasser.) Under the new rule, you must keep your land in a reasonably safe condition and warn anyone who comes onto your property of dangers that are not obvious.

Injuries to Passersby

If someone is injured on a public street or sidewalk while passing by your property—say, on foot, on a bicycle, or in a car— you're generally not liable for their injuries. There are several important exceptions to this rule, however. The first is that you must not do anything on your property that poses a danger to persons off your property. For example, when burning brush on your property, you must do it in a careful manner. If the fire goes out of control and injures others, you are legally responsible for the damage. Another exception is that if you dig a hole on your land next to a public street or sidewalk, you must take adequate precautions to protect passersby from falling into it.

Suppose, for example, that Melinda is walking on a public sidewalk in front of Eric's house, slips on a sheet of ice, and falls and breaks her arm. Can she make Eric pay? The general rule is that a landowner doesn't have to keep public sidewalks clean and free from danger. That is the city's job. So if the sheet of ice resulted from the natural run-off of water or melting snow from Eric's property, he is not liable. But if the ice sheet was formed by a structure on Eric's land—such as the discharge from the eaves—Eric is liable because he created the danger. Eric then has an obligation to keep the sidewalk free of the ice that forms beneath his eaves, and if he doesn't do so, he is liable for the resulting damage.

Fred is walking beside Joanne's property, when a branch from a tree in Joanne's yard falls on him. Fred inspects the tree and finds that it is old and rotted and should have been removed years ago. Is Joanne liable to Fred? If Joanne lives in a rural area, probably not, because a rural landowner generally does not have to inspect the trees growing naturally for disease, age, and weakness. On the other hand, if Joanne lives in the city, she must periodically inspect the trees to make sure they are not a danger to anyone. If she doesn't, she is liable for injuries to passersby. These same rules apply if the branch falls onto your neighbor's land and damages your neighbor's car.

Injuries on Recreational Land

Steve owns several acres of land that is used by off-road enthusiasts for motorcycle riding and such. Bert jumps his motorcycle over a small hill, lands in a deep hole hidden on the other side, and is seriously hurt. Bert sues Steve for failing to post a warning that the hole was there. Who wins the case? In many states, Steve will win because a person who lets others use his or her land without charge for recreation is not liable for their injuries. This rule encourages landowners to keep their property open for recreational use of every kind. Without it, landowners, fearing lawsuits, would fence off their property, and the public would suffer. But the landowner is liable for someone's injuries if he or she expressly invited the person onto the property, charged the person a fee for using the land, or deliberately injured the person.

Injuries to Fire Fighters and Police Officers

A policeman chasing a burglary suspect on the second floor of a building falls through a hole and is injured. Can he sue the building's owner? Usually not. Most states follow the "fireman's rule," which bars a fire fighter or police officer injured in the line of duty from suing a landowner for negligence. The reason behind this rule is that fire fighters and police officers have voluntarily chosen professions with all sorts of inherent dangers. In other words, they generally assume the risk that they will be injured on the job.

A few states have recently realized that, while they may assume the risk of being shot or burned, police officers and fire fighters do not usually assume the risk of being hurt because a building is unsafe. These states allow fire fighters and police officers to sue the building's owner for damages and injuries that result from a dangerous condition in the building.

6

LANDLORD-TENANT ISSUES

WITH INFLATION and the rising costs of construction, it is a sure bet that owning a house—long the American dream—will be beyond the reach of many. This means that the number of people who rent apartments, houses, condominiums, and townhomes is certain to keep increasing steadily.

In the landlord-tenant relationship, there are reciprocal rights and duties that each side should respect. Much too often, landlord, and tenant view each other as adversaries, to be hated and feared. As the tension mounts, problems seem to grow until finally one side explodes: the landlord orders the tenant to leave or changes the lock, or the tenant refuses to pay rent or abandons the apartment without warning and disappears.

Landlord and tenant should realize that each is dependent upon the other and should strive toward a businesslike—or at least tolerable—working relationship. A landlord wants the peace of mind that comes from knowing that the rent will be paid on time, that the tenant will keep the apartment clean and not damage it, and that the tenant will not interfere with the landlord's or other tenants' enjoyment of their units by, for example, excessive noise. The other side of the coin? A good landlord will lease the apartment in a clean condition and will ensure that all repairs to appliances, fixtures, and the building are made promptly. A good landlord will respect the tenant's right to privacy and not enter the unit without giving the tenant a day or two's notice, unless there is an emergency.

A landlord is generally free to accept or reject prospective tenants as he or she sees fit. The landlord's main interest, of course, is to find tenants who will be able to pay the rent on time and who won't damage the apartment. But there are some restrictions on the landlord's ability to refuse a prospective tenant. A landlord cannot refuse to rent the apartment to you because of your race, national origin, religion, or sex. In some states, a landlord usually cannot turn you down (or end your lease) just because you have children even if the apartments are advertized as adults-only. In other states, landlords have the right to do so.

Many leases prohibit animals without the landlord's written consent. Recent developments have somewhat restricted a landlord's arbitrary enforcement of a "no pets" provision (see chapter 7).

Types of Leases

The two most common types of leases are the "month-to-month" lease, and a lease for a specific period of time—often six months or a year. A month-to-month lease, or "periodic tenancy," is one that continues until the tenant or the landlord notifies the other that he or she is terminating the lease. A periodic tenancy can also be from, say, year to year or week to week, but these are not nearly as common as the month-to-month tenancy.

A periodic tenancy is automatically renewed for another term if neither party gives the other "timely" notice to end it. How much notice do you have to give your landlord—or does your landlord have to give you—to end the lease? If it's a month-to-month lease or greater (for instance, year to year), only 30 days' notice before the lease ends is usually required. But if it's a week-to-week tenancy, only seven days' notice is needed.

A tenancy for a definite time—a "tenancy for years"—is a lease for a certain period of time: one year, five years, two months, even fifteen days—*any* definite time period. (But when you go to a hotel, motel, or inn and request a room for, say, three days, this does not create a tenancy for years; you merely receive a "license" to use the room.) When the last day of this type of lease arrives, the lease ends automatically. Neither landlord nor tenant has to notify the other that the lease is over; the tenant is expected to be out of the apartment unless a new arrangement has been made.

Two other types of tenancies less frequently encountered are "tenancies at will" and "tenancies at sufferance." In a tenancy at will, you can live in the apartment for as long as the landlord says. (Some tenancies at will are at the will of the tenant; you can live there as long as *you* want.) A tenancy at will ends when either you or the landlord dies, when the landlord sells the property, when the landlord tells you to leave, or when you move out. Many states require that the landlord give you notification of a certain amount of time—such as 30 days—that the lease is over. Other states still apply the old common law rule that a tenancy at will ends immediately when the lease expires. In other words, you have to pack up and get off the property without delay when the landlord tells you to leave.

A tenancy at sufferance arises when you stay in the apartment without paying rent after the lease is over. You can stay as long as the landlord lets you, or until the landlord begins legal proceedings to evict you. When you stay on after the lease ends, you are a "holdover tenant." If the landlord accepts a rent check from you, however, you now have a periodic tenancy (usually a month-to-month tenancy), and your landlord will have to give you proper notice to end the lease. Say that you have leased an apartment for two years at $500 a month. Two years later, the lease automatically ends. The next day, you give your landlord a check for $500, which is cheerfully accepted. You now have a month-to-month tenancy. You must give your landlord 30 days notice if you plan to leave, and your landlord must likewise notify you 30 days if he or she wants to terminate your lease.

The Written Lease

Leases for one year or more generally are required to be in writing. Although month-to-month rentals don't have to be in writing, it is always best to have a written lease. The reason is that most of your rights and obligations as either a landlord or tenant are determined by the provisions of the lease agreement. A few rights—such as the right to a livable apartment—are implied by law regardless of what the lease says or doesn't say. Having the terms of the lease in writing and signed by both landlord and tenant reduces the chances for disputes over how much the rent was, how long the lease was, and who had to do what.

Most landlords use a standardized lease form bought from the stationery store, one prepared by the real estate industry to favor landlords. Before signing a lease and moving in, read it over carefully and thoroughly. Make sure that the lease you get is legible, not a copy of a copy of a copy that was bad to begin with. If you can't read the copy you're handed, ask for one that is clear.

As a tenant, it is to your benefit to negotiate the most favorable provisions before you sign the lease and move in. If you find something objectionable, mention it before you sign. But let's look at this realistically. If you live in a big city, where rents are high and vacancies low, when you find an apartment you like and can afford, the landlord is going to shove a lease under your nose with the admonishment, "Take it or leave it." Face it—the average person doesn't have much bargaining strength when it comes to leases. You either agree to everything the landlord says and sign the lease, or you keep looking. The only time you have a real shot at changing some provisions of an apartment lease is if you're in an area where the vacancy rate is high or if you're dealing with someone who is new to the business of landlording.

The lease should contain the basics: who the landlord is, who the tenant is, the address and unit number of the apartment, how long the lease lasts, and the amount of rent and when it is due (for instance, the first day of the month). If the tenant has the option to renew the lease at a set price, this too should be included.

The lease should specify everything that is included in the rental price. For example, is a garage or outdoor parking space included? If so, clearly spell this out in the lease. Who pays the apartment utilities—electricity, gas, water, and trash collection—the landlord or the tenant? If the landlord tells you that the rent includes, say, water and gas, make sure you get this in the lease. Other things, such as who has to make repairs, whether the tenant can paint or make other improvements to the unit, and what the landlord's rights are if the tenant abandons the apartment without paying rent should also be included in the lease.

If You Have a Roommate

If you're renting an apartment with someone else, the landlord will usually have each of you sign the lease. Both of you then become "jointly and severally" liable for the rent. This means that each of you is individually liable for the full amount of each month's rent. If your cotenant doesn't pay his or her share, you will have to pay it as well as your own share or face eviction. You can ask the landlord to include a clause in the lease that makes you liable for only your share of the rent, but few landlords will agree to this.

If you are planning on sharing an apartment with someone else, you should lay down certain ground rules—preferably in writing—to prevent disputes. First, reach an agreement about the amount of rent each will pay. Will it be split in half, or will some other arrangement be made? If there is a one-car garage, who gets it? Will utility bills be split in half? Take note that if you signed the utility service agreements, the utility company can seek full payment from you—even if it was your roommate who made all those long-distance calls.

Security Deposits

The landlord will require every new tenant to pay a certain amount of money as a security deposit before leasing the apartment. The purpose of the security deposit is to protect the landlord from tenants who abandon the apartment without paying the rent or to pay for damages tenants have done to the unit.

Most states now have laws regulating how much of a deposit the landlord can ask the tenant to pay for "security." In many states, a landlord of a residential unit can ask a new tenant to deposit an amount of up to two months' rent as security. This includes security however it may be disguised: as a security deposit, the last month's rent, or a cleaning deposit. For instance, if the monthly rent for the apartment is $500, the landlord can require the tenant to post up to $1,000 as a deposit. (This $1,000 is in addition to the first month's rent, so it will cost the tenant $1,500 to move in.)

The lease should clearly state how much money the landlord receives from the tenant and include an itemized account of what each sum represents. For example, if $500 was for the first month's rent, $500 for the last month's rent, $450 for a security deposit, and $50 for cleaning costs, this should be specified in the lease before you sign it. Any other sums paid by the tenant—as a key deposit, for example—should also be listed separately. Many states require the landlord to place the security deposit in a separate bank account, and some make the landlord pay the tenant interest of, say, 5 percent, on the money so deposited.

Rights and Obligations of the Landlord and the Tenant

Moving into Your New Apartment

The landlord must have the apartment ready for you to move in on the agreed date. If it isn't ready when promised, you are entitled to damages resulting from the landlord's breach of this duty. For instance, if it costs you $250 to live in a hotel and store your furniture while you wait for the apartment, the landlord has to pay this. The landlord can, however, deduct from this the amount of rent you would have paid for the apartment during this same period; so if you would have paid $125 in rent to the landlord for the time you spent in the hotel, the landlord owes you $125.

If the previous tenant refuses to move out, the landlord may have to start legal proceedings to evict him or her. If, for any reason, the landlord doesn't have the apartment ready for you within a reasonable length of time after it was promised, you can usually treat this as a breach of the lease. You are now free of your obligations under the lease and can even sue the landlord for any damages you suffer. If you had a six-month lease, for example, and it costs you an extra $150 a month to rent a comparable apartment, you can sue the landlord for the additional $150 per month for the length of the lease.

Before signing the lease and moving in, inspect the apartment to see if it is clean and undamaged. If you run across any defects, such as a hole in the wall or a leaking toilet, write them all down on a piece of paper, and ask the landlord to sign it. This protects you from a landlord who tries to charge you for "your" damage later on. Also get written assurance from the landlord that all of the problems will be corrected promptly. If the landlord refuses to sign your inventory of defects, seriously think about finding another apartment.

Making Changes to the Apartment

Most residential leases prohibit you from making any changes or additions to the apartment—painting, wallpapering, or paneling, to name a few. All you're usually allowed to do is move your furniture in and hang a few pictures on the wall. Before making any changes or improvements, carefully read your lease. Does it forbid alterations of "fixtures" without the landlord's prior written consent? A fixture is something that is attached to the building, such as a shelf that is nailed to the wall. (Fixtures are much more frequent in business leases, which are discussed below.)

When you move out, can you take your improvements with you? Again, what does your lease say? If it states that all fixtures become the property of the landlord, you must leave them there, even if you put them in with the landlord's permission. You can usually remove your own fixtures only if you can do so without much damage to the apartment. And if there is any damage to the apartment from the installation or removal of an improvement, you must pay to have the damage fixed.

Who Is Responsible for Making Repairs?

You've been living in your apartment for five months, when all at once everything seems to start falling apart; the air conditioner or heater stops working, there's no hot water, and the kitchen faucet is leaking. Whose responsibility is it to fix these things, yours or the landlord's? First look at your lease. What does it say? Whatever the lease provides is what a judge will ordinarily follow.

But if the lease doesn't mention a thing about repairs, then the first thing to consider is what is customary in the area. If tenants usually take care of leaky faucets and burned-out light bulbs, then you will probably have to do these things yourself. More major repairs are usually the responsibility of the landlord, although the extent of the landlord's duty to make repairs sometimes depends in part upon what is being rented. If the tenant is renting one apartment in a large apartment building, generally the landlord has to take care of all the repairs. But if the tenant is renting a house, the tenant may have to make minor repairs, such as fixing leaky faucets and small holes in the roof.

With apartment leases, a growing number of states have shifted the burden of making all but the most minor repairs onto the landlord. Without an agreement to the contrary in the lease (perhaps the tenant has agreed to make certain repairs in exchange for lower rent), for the typical apartment rental, the landlord usually must fix all damage and defects, except for that caused by the tenant. If you caused the damage, you must either repair it yourself or pay the landlord the cost of repairing it.

As a tenant, you have the responsibility to inform the landlord promptly when a repair is needed. If you wait a while before telling the landlord, and the condition gets worse, you may have to pay for some of the repairs. The landlord must make the repairs a reasonable time after being notified by the tenant. What is a reasonable time depends on the circumstances—for example, a heater failing in the dead of winter requires faster action than one that breaks down in the summer. If the landlord fails to make the needed repairs within a reasonable time after being notified of the problem, some states permit you to make the repairs yourself (or hire someone to do it for you) and deduct the cost of repairs from your rent.

Your right to make repairs and deduct the cost from the rent is limited; it may be as little as $100 a year, and the most any state allows you to deduct is not more than the equivalent of one month's rent each year. Before you resort to doing the repair yourself, notify your landlord in writing that if the repairs are not done within a certain period of time (for example, one week), you will go ahead and make the repairs yourself and deduct their cost from your rent. This is often enough to spur the landlord to action.

Many states do not let the tenant make the repairs and deduct the cost from the rent. In this situation, the only way you can get an unwilling landlord to make a repair is to bring a lawsuit against the landlord. Before suing your landlord, write him or her a letter specifying what the defect is and requesting that it be fixed. Keep a copy of the letter for your files. If you can, take several pictures of the defect, so you can show the judge what you're talking about if it gets that far. Have a repair company inspect the damage and give you a written estimate. If the defect threatens your health or safety, a call or visit to the health department may help you get some results. A complaint to the housing or building department may be in order if the problem is related to the structure.

Injuries to Tenants and Their Guests

As you climb the stairs leading to your friend's apartment, your foot hits a loose step. You fall and break your arm. Who is liable, the landlord or the tenant? Usually the landlord. Why? Because the injury occurred in the "common area." The common area is everything outside of the tenants' apartments: hallways, stairs, the grounds, the parking lot, the swimming pool—any place that other tenants or members of the public are permitted to go.

Unlike the individual apartment units, which the tenant has exclusive possession of, the landlord retains control of the common area. It is the landlord's duty to keep the common area in a safe condition so that tenants and their guests do not injure themselves. The landlord must, for instance, provide adequate lighting to illuminate walkways, maintain stairways in good repair, and keep the elevator operating safely. If there is a swimming pool, recreation facilities, and the like, the landlord must keep them clean, sanitary, and safe. The landlord must also keep the building safe and in good shape. If a tenant or guest falls from an unguarded second-story balcony or slips on a steep stairway that doesn't have a handrail, the landlord may be liable.

A tenant is not liable to a guest injured in the apartment's common area, unless the tenant created the danger. If you put your bicycle on the landing in front of your apartment, for example, and it falls on a guest who is walking up the stairs, you are liable. Although the guest was injured in a common area—

the stairs—you created the danger by putting your bike there.

Your friend Theresa is cooking dinner for you in your apartment. She pulls on the oven door, but it doesn't open. She tugs a little harder, and the door falls off its hinges and lands on her foot, breaking several toes. You forgot to tell her to be careful because the door is loose. Are you liable for her injuries, even though the stove belongs to your landlord? Yes. You must warn your guests of dangers in your apartment, even if the thing doesn't belong to you. Can Theresa sue your landlord as well? If you haven't yet told your landlord of the loose stove door, your landlord probably isn't liable to Theresa. But if you notified your landlord of the problem a while ago, and it still hasn't been fixed, your landlord may also be liable. Once informed that something needs repair, the landlord must repair it within a reasonable time, or risk being sued by someone who is injured by it.

Suppose that Tony has a vicious German shepherd, which he keeps at his apartment. One day Ted, a repairman, comes to fix the refrigerator. While Ted is working, the dog attacks and severely injures him. Tony is liable to Ted, since Tony owns the dog. But is Tony's landlord liable as well? In a growing number of states, a landlord is liable for injuries caused by a tenant's pet if the landlord knows the animal is dangerous before renting the apartment or renewing the lease yet still rents the apartment to the tenant. A few states hold that if the landlord has the power to end the lease, he or she must order the tenant to get rid of the animal or terminate the lease.

Leslie hires George as night janitor for his apartment building without checking into his past. A few weeks later, George uses his passkey to enter an apartment and rapes the tenant inside. It turns out that George had just been released from prison after serving several years for rape. Is Leslie liable to the rape victim for failing to investigate George's background before hiring him? Yes. A landlord must take care in hiring employees, particularly employees who will have access to the tenants' apartments. A landlord must make a reasonably thorough search of the prospective employee's background. In this case, a search no doubt would have revealed George's recent criminal history. A prudent landlord would not have hired George or at least would have supervised him closely, and not have given him free use of the passkey.

Suppose that a tenant is raped or robbed on the apartment grounds by an unknown assailant, someone who was not an employee. Is the landlord liable to the tenant in this situation? Some states hold that a landlord is not liable for criminal assaults by unknown persons. A number of other states, however, hold the landlord responsible if previous assaults or robberies have occurred on the grounds, yet the landlord hasn't done anything to discourage criminals. For instance, the landlord must see that the hallways and grounds are well lit at night. In some cases, the landlord must hire a security guard to protect the front door or to patrol the grounds and buildings.

If you are a landlord and are interested in protecting both your tenants' safety and yourself from a lawsuit, you can take several simple steps to reduce the risk of criminal attacks and your liability for them. First of all, every apartment door should be equipped with a dead bolt lock. Windows should also be equipped with some type of locking device. The stairwells and common area should be kept well lit at night. If the apartment building is in a high-crime area, you may wish to install a fence or other enclosure around the building and keep it locked. Give the tenants their own keys to it, and install a telephone or intercom system so guests can let tenants know they're there. You should also conduct a thorough check of the background of any person before hiring him or her and keep track of all master passkeys.

"Quiet Enjoyment": Your Right to Peace and Quiet

When you rent an apartment, you expect to have some peace and quiet. Whether it is stated or not, every lease comes with a promise of "quiet enjoyment"—that the tenant will be free from unwarranted intrusions by the landlord or other tenants. Certainly complete silence is impossible in today's society, particularly in

crowded cities. But you don't have to put up with a landlord who
barges in unannounced or neighbors who are exploring new deci-
bel levels with their stereos.

Does this mean the landlord can't ever enter your apartment? Not at all. Your landlord can enter the unit to inspect it
for damage, make repairs, or show it to a prospective tenant after
you have given notice that you are moving out. Before entering
the unit, however, the landlord must give you reasonable notice
of the entry. Unless it's an emergency, the landlord should notify
you at least 24 hours before the planned entry. A landlord who
enters without giving the tenant adequate notice may be committing a trespass and invasion of privacy. And if your landlord
continually enters your apartment without reason or notice, you
may have the right to end the lease, move out, and sue your
landlord for damages.

If another tenant in the building is driving you crazy with
noise, and your landlord has done nothing about it despite your
repeated requests, again you may have the right to move out and
sue your landlord. Likewise, if threats from other tenants make
you fear for your safety, and the landlord ignores your complaints,
you are being denied your right to "quiet enjoyment" of your
apartment.

Rent Increases and Rent Control

You have been living in your apartment for six months, when
your landlord slips a note under your door stating that beginning
next month, your rent is being increased. Do you have to pay the
increase? If your lease provides that you are renting the apartment
for, say, one year at $500 per month, your landlord cannot raise
the rent during that time. The landlord has made a contract to
rent you an apartment for a specified price for a definite term
and is bound by the terms of the contract. If, however, you have
a month-to-month lease, and it is silent as to any rent increases,
then in the absence of rent control laws, when your lease expires,
the landlord can raise your rent as much as he or she wants.

Because of escalating rents, a number of cities and counties have passed laws limiting rent increases to no more than a specified maximum amount, such as 8 or 10 percent per year. The amount of increase is supposed to give the landlord a fair return on his or her investment, taking into account the costs of repairs, improvements, and depreciation of the buildings, among other things. If the landlord wants to raise the rent more than the maximum amount allowed, he or she will have to get permission from the proper governmental agency. A public hearing may be required, at which the tenants can appear and voice their objections to the proposed hike. Many rent control laws apply only to apartment buildings of a certain size—more than four units, for example. If a building is exempt from rent control, the landlord can raise the rent as much as he or she wants.

Ceilings on rent increases usually apply only to tenants who remain in their apartments. Once a tenant moves out, under many ordinances, the landlord can raise the rent to what the market will bear. If you are a landlord or tenant in a district covered by rent control, you should carefully scrutinize all applicable rent control laws before increasing rent or challenging a rent increase. You will find the rent control laws in your city and county ordinances at the public library. There may be a rent control office at city hall that can also answer your questions.

Whether or not rent control is in effect, a landlord must give the tenants proper notice of the rent increase. Generally, the landlord must give each tenant 30 days' written notice before the increase takes effect. Suppose the landlord wishes to increase the rent on July 1. All tenants must receive written notice of the increase on or before June 1. If notice is given after June 1, normally the landlord is not able to enforce the rent increase until August 1.

Subleases and Assignments

Most residential leases prohibit a tenant from subleasing the apartment or assigning the lease without the landlord's prior written consent. A "sublease" involves a transfer of less than all the lease. For instance, if you're living by yourself in a two-bedroom apartment and decide to rent the spare bedroom out to someone else, that is a sublease. Or, if you rent the whole apartment to someone for a couple of months while you're traveling across the United States, that, too, is a sublease. In an "assignment," you transfer the entire lease to another person. For example, if a new job requires you to move out of state, and there are six months remaining on the lease, it is called an assignment if someone agrees to take over the lease for you.

Suzanne's lease prohibits her from assigning it without the landlord's written permission but doesn't say a word about subletting. Can she sublet the apartment to her friend? Yes; if the lease states only that an assignment is forbidden, the tenant can still sublet the apartment. Conversely, if the lease bars only subletting, the tenant can assign the lease without the landlord's approval. Both actions are prohibited only if the lease says that the tenant cannot sublease the apartment or assign the lease without the landlord's consent.

Unless it states otherwise, when the lease prohibits you from subletting or assigning without your landlord's consent, ordinarily the landlord can arbitrarily refuse to permit a sublease or assignment. Some states and many leases now provide that the landlord must not unreasonably withhold consent to a sublease or assignment, however. So if you find someone who will be at least as good a tenant as you—who will pay the rent on time, not play the stereo too loud, and so on—the landlord must accept your subtenant.

When you sublease your apartment, you remain liable for the rent. Your subtenant ordinarily doesn't have to answer to the landlord, only to you. Your landlord generally can sue only you for the rent. If your subtenant doesn't pay the rent on time, your landlord can start eviction proceedings against you. If several months' back rent is due, you are responsible for it, just as you ultimately remain responsible for keeping the apartment in good shape. What can you do if you end up paying the delinquent rent or for repairs on damage your subtenant did to the apartment? You can ask your subtenant to reimburse you for this money and take him or her to small claims court if he or she refuses to pay (or hire a lawyer if the amount is substantial).

Unlike in a sublease, in an assignment, if the subtenant (technically, the "assignee" of your lease) fails to pay the rent, the landlord can sue your assignee. The landlord can also sue your assignee for any damage to the apartment that he or she is responsible for. Be aware, however, that your landlord normally can still sue you as well, even if the landlord consented to the assignment.

Before you sublease your apartment or assign the lease, make sure your subtenant is a responsible person who will pay the rent on time and will not damage the apartment. In a sublease or assignment, you become a landlord to your subtenant. You should protect yourself just as any landlord would: demand a security deposit equal to at least one month's rent and put the terms of the sublease in writing, including the length of the sublease, the amount of rent, when and to whom it is payable, late charges, payment of damages, and so on. Many stationers have standard sublease and assignment forms that will cover you adequately. Make sure you read a form over carefully before using it, as the forms published by one company can be much different from those of another. If you are assigning your lease, be sure to include a provision that you have the right to reenter the apartment and retake possession of it if the subtenant fails to pay the rent. This gives you some additional protection if the subtenant defaults on the lease.

What if you have to move out of the apartment for some reason, say, six months before your lease expires but don't want to worry about a subtenant? Your lease may give you the right to cancel it by giving two or three months' notice. (In a month-to-month lease, you can usually end it by giving your landlord 30 days notice; see below.) If it doesn't, one thing to consider is offering to find a new tenant (subject to your landlord's approval, of course) at your trouble and expense. When you do find someone suitable, ask the landlord to sign a document releasing you from the lease. Arrange for the new tenant to pay the required security deposit, and ask that yours be returned. The landlord will want to have the new tenant sign a lease. If your landlord will do this, you are no longer liable for the rent or for the acts of the new tenant. This solution should be acceptable to a reasonable landlord.

If the Tenant Moves Out or Abandons the Apartment

When Your Lease Is Up and You Move Out

In a month-to-month lease, when you decide to move out, you will have to notify your landlord in writing 30 days ahead of time. If you have a tenancy for a certain period of time—say, one year—at the end of the year, you have to be out unless your landlord renews the lease. You should talk to your landlord about renewing the lease at least one or two months before it expires.

Suppose you took possession of the apartment on September 1, on a month-to-month lease. On December 15, you notify your landlord that you will be moving out in 30 days. Your landlord tells you that you have to pay rent through February 1 because you have to give 30 days' notice from the first of the month, since you moved in on the first. Is that true? No. Generally, you only have to give 30 days' notice, whenever you want—the beginning, the middle, or the end of the month, or anytime in between. Your lease then expires 30 days from the date you notified your landlord that you were leaving.

You must be out of the apartment on or before the date the lease expires. When you leave, the apartment must be in the same condition as it was when you moved in, except for normal wear and tear—some dirt on the carpet, a few small holes in the wall where you hung your pictures, and the like. If you aren't out of the apartment on time, the landlord can charge you rent for every day you or your furniture remains in the apartment. The landlord can also collect any other damages suffered because of your delay in moving out. For instance, if the landlord has to pay the next tenant for storing his or her furniture while waiting for you to leave, the landlord can seek reimbursement of these costs from you.

Suppose you have notified your landlord that you will be moving out at the end of next month. When the first of the month comes, your landlord knocks on your door, asking for this month's rent. You tell the landlord to use the security deposit. Your landlord refuses, threatening that if you don't pay the rent tomorrow, eviction proceedings will be started against you, and you'll be thrown out of there in a week. Who's right? It boils down to what the lease agreement provides. If a certain sum was designated in the lease as the last month's rent, then you have every right to tell the landlord to use that money to pay the last month's rent. On the other hand, if the lease refers only to a "security deposit" or "cleaning deposit," then you do have to pay the last month's rent.

Before vacating the premises and giving the landlord the key back, you should arrange to meet the landlord (or apartment manager) in the empty, cleaned apartment to discuss any deductions the landlord intends to make from the cleaning deposit. If you feel that the apartment is in the same or better condition than it was when you moved in, tell the landlord so. The landlord should be specific about complaints of damage or uncleanliness if all or part of the security deposit will be withheld. If you have the landlord inspect the apartment a day or two before the lease officially ends, and the landlord points out some problems, consider doing the extra work yourself. This way you can get back more or all of your deposit. If you don't agree with your landlord's assessment of the apartment's condition, a lawsuit in small claims court may be the best way of getting your money back. It is a good idea to take pictures of the apartment after you cleaned it to support your position to the judge.

State laws often require the landlord to return what's left of the security deposit within a certain time—say, ten days or two weeks after you move out. Some states require the landlord to include an itemized statement of damages or cleaning costs to account for the amount deducted from the deposit. If the landlord doesn't return your full security deposit, and there is no statement of charges, you should write the landlord and ask for a full explanation of how the money was used. If you don't agree with the itemized statement, your letter should be clear and specific as to why you disagree. A second letter demanding the return of your full security deposit may be in order if you're not satisfied with the landlord's response or if the landlord doesn't respond at all. If this doesn't solve anything, then filing a suit in small claims court may be your next step (see chapter 15).

If Your Apartment Becomes Unlivable

The landlord must deliver the apartment to you in a clean and sanitary and otherwise livable condition. And after you move in, the landlord must do his or her part to keep the apartment and building fit for human living: the trash must be removed from the hallway and other common areas; heaters and plumbing must be repaired when they break down; rats, mice, and other vermin must be controlled; and so forth. This is known as the "warranty of habitability." You must do your share to keep the apartment habitable by cleaning it regularly. You generally cannot claim that the place is unfit to live in if you are responsible for the unsanitary condition.

If the apartment becomes unfit for you to live in, you have several options. You can keep paying rent and sue your landlord for damages (ordinarily the difference between the amount of rent you are paying and what a fair rent is in light of the apartment's condition); you can terminate the lease and move out; or, in some states, you can stay in the apartment without paying rent for as long as the apartment remains uninhabitable. The apartment must actually be unlivable to take advantage of these

options. If living in the apartment is merely unpleasant or inconvenient, then your sole option generally is to sue the landlord for
a reduction in the rent.

Before taking any action, document your complaints as
thoroughly as possible. Send the landlord a letter or two clearly
identifying the problems and asking that they be corrected immediately. (Remember to keep copies of everything you send the
landlord so you can show them to a judge if you need to.) If
possible, take pictures of the problem; for example, show the
hallway with the mounds of garbage and the rats crawling over
it. Keep a journal of the problems and your efforts to get some
action. Get written and signed statements from friends, visitors,
and neighbors to support your complaints. Another thing you can
do is contact the local health department and complain to them.
This may be enough to motivate the landlord into resolving the
problem.

If you live in an apartment building, and the unsanitary
conditions are widespread, consider joining forces with the other
tenants in the building. There is strength in numbers, particularly
in landlord-tenant disputes. The landlord may not pay any attention to a single tenant, but you can bet your voices will be heard
if, say, 50 percent or more of the tenants get together to demand
action. If you still don't get any satisfaction, the tenants may be
able to go on a "rent strike." In a rent strike, all rent money is
placed in a special bank account, frequently under the supervision
of the court, rather than being paid to the landlord. The landlord
gets the money only when the repairs are made, or the money
can be used to make the repairs. Rent strikes should be undertaken only upon the advice of a lawyer, particularly since not all
states allow them.

Suppose your landlord is letting the building deteriorate; the
heating breaks down, the trash hasn't been taken out, and rats
are running all over the building. You have complained repeatedly
to your landlord, but nothing has been done, so you go to the
health department. Your landlord finds this out, tells you to leave
today, and changes the locks. Can your landlord get away with

this? No. A landlord cannot evict a tenant in retaliation for the tenant's attempt to enforce a legal right. This is called a "retaliatory eviction." If this happens to you, you should see a lawyer immediately. The lawyer may be able to keep you in the apartment. And even if you are forced out of the apartment, you can still sue your landlord for damages.

If the Tenant Abandons the Apartment

Six months remain on your lease, but you've decided to move. You talk to your landlord about it, but he or she refuses to let you out of the lease. So one night, without any warning to your landlord, you move all of your furniture out of the apartment and disappear. By abandoning the apartment, you "surrender" it to the landlord. The first question is whether the landlord accepts your surrender. If he or she does, you are completely out of the lease, although you are still obligated to pay any rent that is past due and for any damage to the apartment in excess of your security deposit. But if the landlord doesn't accept your surrender, you remain responsible for the full rent to the end of the lease. How do you know if the landlord has accepted your surrender? Sometimes the landlord will tell you directly—in person or by letter—whether or not he or she accepts the surrender and releases you from the lease. More often, the landlord's actions indicate whether or not your surrender of the apartment is accepted. If the landlord doesn't make any attempt to relet the unit, your surrender isn't accepted. But if the landlord does rent the apartment to someone else, this indicates that he or she has accepted your surrender.

A number of states require the landlord to make a good-faith effort to relet the apartment after a tenant abandons it. But if it takes two months to find a new tenant, and the landlord did not expressly accept your surrender when you left, you are responsible for the rent during those two months that the apartment remained empty. Suppose the landlord manages to rent the apartment to another tenant, but for, say, $50 less a month than you were paying. Can the landlord require you to pay that $50 for the months remaining on your original lease? Again the question is whether or not the landlord accepted your surrender. If he or she did, then you don't have to make up the difference in rent. But if your surrender was not accepted, you do remain liable for the $50 a month. In this situation, many states require the landlord to send you a letter informing you that he or she is not releasing you from your obligations under the lease and is reletting the apartment on your behalf. If the landlord doesn't send such a letter, you are released from the lease when it is relet.

Let's say you abandon the apartment with ten months remaining on the lease, at $500 monthly, and the landlord refuses to accept your surrender of the unit. Can the landlord file a lawsuit the next day for the balance of the rent—that is, the full $5,000? No. The landlord can sue only for rent that is past due at the time the lawsuit is filed. So when you don't pay your rent on the first of the month as required by the lease, the landlord can sue you, but only for that month's rent. To sue for the entire $5,000, the landlord could file ten separate lawsuits—one for each month—or wait and file one lawsuit for the full $5,000 ten months later. (Remember, in the meantime the landlord may have a legal obligation to attempt to find a tenant to take your place.)

Here is a practical note for landlords: If a tenant abandons the apartment without notice and without leaving a forwarding address, it can be more trouble than it's worth to find the tenant and get the rent. You may be better off simply applying the tenant's security deposit to the remaining rent and trying to lease the apartment to someone else. You may also be able to sell any furniture the tenant leaves behind and use the money toward the rent. Any costs you incur in storing the tenant's furniture can usually be deducted as well, as can your attorney's fees in many cases (see discussion below). If any money is left over after the balance of the rent is paid, you must try to return it to the tenant. Before selling a tenant's furniture, you should consult an attorney to make sure that you follow your state's procedure to the letter. If the sale of the property is unlawful, you may be liable to the tenant for conversion (theft) of the property. Always make sure that the tenant has in fact abandoned the apartment, never to return, before taking this kind of action.

If the Landlord Evicts
the Tenant

An eviction occurs when, for any reason, the landlord removes the tenant from the apartment before the lease is over. The eviction may be lawful, through the courts, or unlawful, as when the landlord changes the locks and throws the tenant's furniture into the street. In the event of an eviction, whether lawful or not, the tenant's obligation to pay rent ceases, except for any rent owed up to the date of the eviction.

The most common reason for eviction is the tenant's failure to pay the rent. But the landlord can also lawfully evict a tenant for major breaches of the lease. For example, if a tenant is using the apartment as an illegal drug factory or to run a prostitution ring, the landlord can evict the tenant.

Suppose that you've gotten a little behind in the rent. One day you return to your apartment to find your furniture on the front lawn and all the locks changed. Your landlord has taken the law into his or her own hands and has evicted you without bothering to go through the court system. Can your landlord get away with this? Not anymore. Almost every state has a statute expressly forbidding this type of "forcible entry." The only way a landlord can evict a tenant is to go through the legal system.

Most states now have a quick way—a "summary procedure"—for a landlord to get a court order to evict a tenant who is behind on the rent. Usually the landlord must notify the tenant to either pay rent within, say, three days or leave ("quit"). If, at the end of the three days, the tenant has done neither, the landlord can file an eviction proceeding in court. This type of action goes by several different names, the most common of which is an "unlawful detainer proceeding." Many states let the landlord sue the tenant for back rent as well as to evict him or her.

Shortly after the unlawful detainer action is filed and served on the tenant (within, for instance, 14 days), a court hearing is held to determine who has the right to the apartment—the landlord or the tenant. The judge may let the tenant remain in the apartment if the tenant brings the rent up to date at the court hearing. If you are the tenant and are claiming to have paid your rent on time, you will have to show the judge some cold, hard proof: your cancelled check, for instance, or a receipt from the landlord if you paid by money order, traveler's checks, or cash.

But let's say your landlord sues to evict you because you didn't pay the rent. Is there any way to get out of it? Yes—if you can convince the judge that you had a legal reason for not paying the rent. One such reason (discussed earlier) is that the apartment is uninhabitable. You'll have to show the judge adequate evidence of the apartment's unlivable condition. This is where pictures, testimony of friends and neighbors, and copies of your letters to the landlord come in handy. If the judge agrees with you, you may not owe anything. And even if the judge rejects your argument that the apartment was unfit for you to live in, you may still get a reduction in the rent of, say, 25 percent if the landlord refused to make repairs.

Another legal way to defend the eviction proceeding is by proving that you put the rent money toward necessary repairs that the landlord refused to make, up to the amount permitted by your state's law. Remember, though, that you can only count the money you actually spent to purchase the parts or to hire someone to do the job for you. You can't claim money for the hours of labor you put in fixing something yourself. A final way of stopping the eviction is possible in some states, which let you stay in the apartment if you pay all of the back rent (plus interest and other expenses of the landlord, including the landlord's attorney's fees) before the court orders the eviction.

Should the judge rule in favor of the landlord and order the tenant evicted, the tenant is usually given a day or two to move out. If the tenant still isn't out after two days, can the landlord physically remove the tenant? No. The landlord ordinarily must have the sheriff do the actual evicting if that becomes necessary.

Constructive Evictions

Not all evictions result from the landlord getting a court order to remove you, or throwing you out and changing the locks. Sometimes the eviction happens because something makes it impossible for you to remain in the apartment. When, through no fault of your own, the apartment becomes dangerous to your health or safety, you are forced to move out the same as if the landlord had picked you up and thrown you into the street. This type of eviction is called a "constructive eviction."

As an example, suppose the ceiling in your apartment is old and weak. When it rains, the ceiling sags, and the water pours through. You have complained a number of times, but your landlord refuses to do anything about it. A particularly heavy rainstorm comes, the weight is too much for the ceiling, and the ceiling collapses. Your living room is now under two feet of rubble and water. There are another six months to go on the lease, but you want to end the lease and move out today. Can you? Yes. You can terminate the lease and move out without worrying about the remaining rent. You can also sue your landlord for any damages you suffer from the constructive eviction, including damage to your property. Some things that can constitute a constructive eviction include the landlord's prolonged failure to provide water or heat, failure to stop continuous loud noise or threats of other tenants, and an apartment that is often flooded.

Making the Other Party Pay for Attorney's Fees

Suppose you have to hire a lawyer to sue your landlord to get repairs made. Or suppose your landlord has to sue you to evict you or to collect money to pay for damage to the unit. Can you collect your attorney's fees from your landlord, or vice versa? That depends on what your lease states. If the lease doesn't say a thing about attorney's fees, most courts will not award attorney's fees to either side. Many leases specify only that if the landlord has to sue you in court to collect the rent, evict you, or make you pay for damages to the apartment, you must pay the landlord's attorney's fees. The courts will enforce this provision against the tenant only if the landlord wins. And even though the lease mentions only the landlord's right to recover attorney's fees from the tenant, many courts will apply it both ways: if you win, the landlord will have to pay your attorney's fees. Many leases now state that if either party brings a lawsuit against the other, the loser must pay the winner's attorney's fees.

Landlords are usually in a position to afford a good lawyer to advise them. But what about tenants who can barely afford to pay the rent and buy food, let alone pay a lawyer a retainer? For many tenants, good and inexpensive legal advice can be found at the local Legal Aid office. Try to contact the Legal Aid office while a problem is still developing—before it gets out of hand and you find yourself being evicted.

Business Leases

There is a world of difference between leasing a building or suite for a business and leasing a house or apartment to live in. Generally, the residential tenant has greater rights in most respects. The business tenant is treated much the same as the residential tenant was treated in the days of old: once the landlord gives the business tenant the keys to the front door, and the tenant takes possession of the building, the landlord ordinarily is relieved of any further duties. Why? Because a commercial tenant frequently makes extensive changes to the interior of the building to accommodate particular needs. In fact, the whole nature of the building may change drastically after the business tenant moves in.

The business tenant has the burden of making more repairs to the property than the residential tenant does. The extent of the repairs the business tenant must make depends on such factors as the terms and length of the lease, the extent of any improvements made by the tenant, what needs repairing, and whether the tenant's alterations or use of the building caused or contributed to the faulty condition. Because the business tenant usually has a greater duty to maintain the premises and make repairs, there generally is no warranty of habitability in the lease of business property. The tenant must keep the building clean and free of health code violations.

Some states have begun to expand the rights of commercial tenants, particularly if the tenant makes few or no changes to the building after taking possession. A self-employed person who rents a small office in a large building, for example, should be entitled to expect that the landlord will keep the premises relatively safe and clean, keep the heating and air conditioning working properly, and so on. In this situation, the landlord should be required to make most repairs to the building. It is not fair to require the tenant to make extensive repairs—to fix a leaky roof, for instance, if the tenant didn't cause the damage.

Provisions regarding installation, removal, and ownership of fixtures are found much more often in business leases than in residential leases. For example, a retail business may install display racks on the wall, attach lighting fixtures to the ceiling, and so on. It is important that the lease lay out the rights of the tenant to remove the fixtures when the lease ends. Generally, a business lease provides that the tenant can remove all fixtures the tenant installed but must repair any damage to the building caused by the fixtures. In many cases, it is well worth having a lawyer review a business lease before you sign it.

ANIMALS

WITH PET OWNERSHIP come a number of legal responsibilities. In chapter 4, we discussed two legal considerations regarding animals: whether a pet can inherit your estate, and your right to order that your pet be put to sleep when you die. This chapter discusses the legal problems most commonly faced by pet owners.

If You Discover the Pet You Bought Is Diseased or Sick

Suppose you buy a pet—let's say a dog—from a pet shop for $250. Three days later, the dog seems ill. You call the pet shop, but they brusquely inform you that "All sales are final; the dog is now your problem, not ours." You take the dog to a veterinarian, who informs you that it is diseased. In fact, it was diseased long before you bought it and is now so sick that it should be put to sleep. You tell the vet to go ahead and pay the bill of, say, $50. You return to the pet store with copies of the store's receipt for the dog and the vet's bill and demand $300. The pet shop refuses, so you sue it in small claims court. Will you win? Yes. When a store sells a pet, the law assumes that the pet is healthy at that time, unless the store clearly tells you otherwise before you buy it. Since the dog was diseased when you bought it, the pet shop should have refunded your money or given you a new dog when you first told it of the problem. If the illness is not life-threatening, the pet shop should pay the vet's bills.

Now suppose that instead of buying the dog from a pet store, you buy it from a private party we'll call Jane. Is Jane liable under the same circumstances? If she regularly sells this type of animal—for instance, if she routinely breeds her own dog and sells the litter—she is considered a "dealer" and generally has the same obligations as a pet store. On the other hand, if Jane doesn't make a business of it—this is just a one-time sale, perhaps because she is moving—Jane is liable for your damages only if she knew the animal was sick or diseased when she sold it to you. If she had no idea the animal was ill, you are stuck with it.

Note that the above rules apply only when the animal was diseased or otherwise defective at the time of purchase. If the animal was healthy when you bought it and contracted a disease later, you usually cannot sue the person who sold it to you, whether a dealer or a private party.

Restrictions on Keeping a Pet

As an animal owner, you need to be aware of applicable zoning laws so you do not violate the law by keeping a particular animal in a prohibited area. Zoning laws are especially important if you live in an urban area and want to keep, for example, a horse or cow on your property. While certain domesticated animals, such as dogs, cats, and birds, are permitted (in reasonable numbers, of course) in any neighborhood, horses, cows, chickens, pigs, sheep, goats, and so forth are not ordinarily allowed in urban neighborhoods. (Dangerous wild animals such as lions, tigers, alligators, and piranha fish are generally barred from being kept on private property anywhere without a special permit.) Before buying a horse, cow, or other such animal that you intend to keep on your land, check with the city or county authorities or the public library to see if any local ordinance prohibits it.

Leases often ban the tenant from keeping an animal on the premises. Historically, the tenant's only choice was to give up the animal or find another apartment. Some tenants have successfully challenged this arbitrary ban on animals, especially when the landlord knew of the pet for some time but said nothing about it. A few states now have statutes that protect elderly people who own pets. Also, the National Housing Act prevents owners or managers of federally-assisted rental housing from discriminating against elderly or handicapped tenants who keep common household pets.

Condominium associations and cooperatives often restrict your right to keep a pet in your unit, such as limiting you to one cat or a dog weighing not more than, say, 25 pounds. These restrictions are generally enforced by the courts if they are not unreasonable. If you have several pets or a large dog and plan on buying a condo or a coop, carefully read all of the conditions, covenants, and restrictions (the CC&Rs), rules, regulations, and other legal documents pertaining to the unit before signing anything. The advice of a lawyer experienced in this area may be called for if it comes down to choosing between the pet or the condo or coop.

Dog Licenses

Most areas require dogs to be licensed annually. (Other domesticated pets ordinarily don't have to be licensed.) Two things are usually necessary to get the license: you must present a veterinarian's certificate showing the dog was given a rabies shot, and you must pay the license fee. Do you *really* need to license your dog? Unequivocally, yes. Failing to renew your dog's license each year will surely subject you to a fine if you're caught. (It's surprising how well the animal control authorities can track down owners of unlicensed dogs.) As a practical matter, you should get a license so your dog can be identified in case it is ever picked up by the animal control authorities.

What happens if your dog is found roaming the streets without a dog license tag or other identification? It will be impounded at the animal shelter nearest to where the dog was found. If you don't contact the shelter within a specified number of days—say, three—the dog can be destroyed or offered for adoption. Suppose you learn a few weeks later that someone else has adopted your dog. Can you get it back? Usually not. You can tell the person your story and hope he or she is sympathetic and returns the dog, but you can't force the new owner to give it up. By failing to license the dog and claim it within the prescribed time, you forfeit your ownership rights.

Another thing to consider if you don't bother to license your dog or get it immunized against rabies: you might be held liable for the damages if your dog bites someone and infects him or her with rabies. In some states, you are guilty of a crime if you know your dog is rabid but do nothing about it, and your dog bites somebody.

Injuries by or to Animals

If a Dog or Cat Hurts Someone

Under the traditional rule, the owner of a dog or cat is not liable for the injuries the pet causes unless the owner knew or should have known of the animal's dangerous propensity to do the type of act in question. Take, for example, a dog that chases after a boy riding his bicycle down the street and knocks him over. If the dog had never before done anything like this, its owner is probably not liable for the boy's injuries. But if the dog had previously chased other bicyclists, and the dog's owner saw the incident or learned about it from others, the owner is probably liable if he or she didn't take adequate precautions to restrain the dog. As the following examples demonstrate, many states now have laws that make the owner liable in many situations for injuries inflicted by a dog or cat even though the owner had no idea the pet would do this sort of thing.

Let's say that you're walking by your neighbor Hank's house when his dog Rex runs over and bites you in the leg for no reason. Sixteen stitches are required to close the wound, and your doctor orders you to take the next week off from work. You ask Hank to reimburse you for the medical costs and your lost wages, but Hank refuses, saying that Rex has never bitten anyone. If you sue Hank in small claims court, who will win? In a few states, Hank will win, because they apply the old law: the owner is not liable for the dog's bite unless the owner knew the dog had already bitten at least one other person. In other words, the first bite is free. Many states, however, now have laws that make the owner liable for all bites: the first as well as the last—regardless of whether the owner knew if the dog had ever bitten anyone before.

Now suppose Rex comes bounding at you, but, instead of biting you, leaps at your chest and knocks you down. Is Hank liable for your injuries if Rex had never done anything like this? In many states, no. If Hank was unaware that Rex had a tendency to jump on people, he doesn't need to take precautions to prevent it. Some states, however, now have laws that make the dog's owner liable for all injuries and damage the dog inflicts, regardless of whether the dog had done anything similar before.

Let's say that you are attacked and clawed by your neighbor's cat. Does your neighbor have to pay for your injuries? Again, the question is whether your neighbor should have realized the cat's propensity to attack and claw people. If the owner knew that the cat had a history of clawing people, he or she is obligated to take reasonable precautions against it—for example, declawing the cat, keeping it in the house, or putting it in another room and closing the door while people are visiting. Some states also have a statute that makes the cat's owner liable for all injuries it inflicts, regardless of whether the animal had ever done anything like it before.

One day you're walking toward Carla's front door, when her dog leaps at you, its teeth bared in a threatening manner. Afraid that the dog is about to attack, you jump out of the way, fall, and break your arm. Carla contends that she isn't liable for your injuries, because the dog didn't actually touch you. Besides, the dog was chained and couldn't get to you if it wanted. Can you make Carla pay for your injuries, even though the dog didn't—and couldn't—touch you? Yes. Since you honestly thought the dog was going to attack you, and you didn't know it was chained, Carla is responsible for your injuries.

Does it make any difference if a dog or cat attacks you while you are in a public place or on its owner's private property? Generally not—at least not if you are on the land with the owner's permission. In many states, even trespassers can recover their damages from the pet's owner, unless the person trespassed in a way that would normally excite and provoke the pet—by climbing through a window, for instance.

Your six-year-old daughter is clawed by a cat, and you sue after the owner refuses to pay for the damages. The owner claims the cat injured the child because she was pulling its tail. Who wins in this situation? Generally the cat's owner does, if he or she can prove that the girl was in fact pulling the cat's tail. By pulling its tail, the girl provoked the cat to take some defensive action. In other words, she asked for it. If the girl was very young, though—so young that she couldn't understand what the cat might do if she pulled its tail—the owner may be liable for her injuries. And if the girl was just petting the cat when it clawed her, and was not teasing or taunting it, this ordinarily is not considered "provocation." These same rules of provocation apply equally to injuries caused by dogs.

In some states a dog's owner usually is not liable for injuries the dog inflicts to persons on the owner's land if a large "BEWARE OF DOG" or "GUARD DOG ON DUTY" sign is posted in a conspicuous place on his or her property. A person who sees the sign and disregards it is held to have assumed the risk of being bitten or attacked by the dog. But the sign may not apply to children who can't read, or who can read but really don't understand the full import of the warning.

Damage to Another's Property—Leash Laws

You look out your window one day and see your neighbor's dog digging up your prize begonias. By the time the dog leaves, your flowers are ruined. Does your neighbor have to pay you for the damage? This usually depends on whether your neighbor knew that the dog had a habit of digging up yards. If this is the first time the dog has ever done something like this, your neighbor normally isn't liable. But if the dog had dug up someone's yard before, your neighbor is liable to you for the damage.

Many cities now have leash laws that require dogs to be on a lead no longer than, say, five or six feet when they are on public property. (Some places require cats to be on leashes, too.) Not only can you be fined for violating the leash law, but also, under many of these laws, you are liable for all damages your dog causes while wandering about the community unleashed. You can't get out of the fine by arguing that your dog is trained to obey your voice, hand, or whistle commands. A number of cities also now require pet owners to pick up their animals' waste from public streets, sidewalks, and parks and to dispose of it properly.

Let's say that you're taking your daily constitutional with your dog on its leash, when another dog attacks your dog, injuring it. Must the dog's owner reimburse you for your vet's bills? Yes. But if both dogs were roaming the neighborhood unleashed, the other dog's owner is usually not liable for your damages, unless you can clearly prove that the other dog attacked your dog and your dog was acting purely in self-defense.

Suppose that your dog is in heat. You have been very careful about keeping it away from other dogs, but one day your neighbor's dog jumps your fence and gets to your dog. Is your neighbor liable for the veterinarian costs, food for the litter, and so forth? Yes. But if your dog was roaming the streets, then the answer is no. (As a practical matter, you should have your pets—male and female— neutered if you don't intend to breed them.)

Damage Done by Horses, Cattle, and Livestock

The owner of a domestic animal—a horse, cow, sheep, pig, turkey, chicken, and so forth—is not liable for injuries to people inflicted by the animal, unless the owner knew that the animal was likely to do this kind of harm. The injured person normally must prove that the animal had done this type of thing before and that the owner knew of it. For instance, if you were bitten by a horse, you would have to prove that the horse had bitten others before. Proving that the horse had injured others by, say, kicking them ordinarily would not be sufficient.

What if a neighbor's cow, horse, or chicken strays onto your land and damages your property? In that case, the animal's owner is usually liable for the damage, regardless of whether the owner had any idea that the animal was likely to do such a thing. For example, if your neighbor's cow comes onto your land and eats your crops or infects your animals with a disease, your neighbor must pay you for the damage. The reason that horses, cows, chickens, and the like are treated differently from cats and dogs when it comes to trespassing upon another person's land is that cats and dogs are unlikely to inflict serious damage to property. Also, dogs and cats by custom have enjoyed considerable freedom to roam about the community.

Suppose that one day while driving down a country road, you turn a corner, see a cow standing in the middle of the road, swerve to avoid it, and hit a tree. Can you sue the cow's owner for your injuries and the damages to your car? In most states, the cow's owner is liable only if he or she knows the animal is likely to get out, yet fails to take adequate precautions to prevent it. For example, if the cow escaped through a hole in the fence that the owner had been meaning to fix for some time, the owner is probably liable. But if the hole is new and the animal's owner didn't know about it, the owner is probably not liable.

Injuries Inflicted by Wild Animals

The owner of a wild animal—a bear, lion, tiger, elephant, wolf, monkey, zebra, elk, moose, leopard, and so forth—generally is liable for all injuries inflicted by that animal, regardless of how hard the owner tries to protect others from the animal. The reason for this rule is that wild animals are instinctively dangerous and cannot truly be tamed. If you're going to take a dangerous animal out of the wild and put it where it can hurt people, you will have to pay the price.

Zoos and circuses are liable when a caged animal escapes or reaches through the bars and injures a visitor standing in the public area. But suppose a young child crawls under a bar to get near a tiger's cage, and the tiger claws the child's face. Is the zoo or circus liable, even though the child would not have been injured if he or she had not crawled under the barrier? Yes—at least if the child didn't understand the danger of being so close to the animal. But if an adult does the same thing and is injured by the tiger, the zoo or circus probably is not liable. The adult assumed the risk of being injured and therefore cannot recover damages.

If Your Pet Is Injured or Killed

When someone is at fault and kills your pet—shoots it without reason, perhaps, or runs over it because of careless driving—how much money does he or she have to pay? Usually all you can recover is the value of the animal at the time it was killed. For instance, if your cat was worth $100 when it was killed, that is all you can get. If the person deliberately killed your pet, you can also ask for "punitive damages" to punish that person (see chapter 8).

Suppose that your dog is run over and injured by a driver who wasn't paying attention. The driver of the car admits responsibility and agrees to pay you for the damages. What are the types of damages you can recover in this situation? Veterinarian bills ordinarily constitute the bulk of damages when an animal is injured. But let's say the dog loses a leg in the accident. In that case in addition to the vet's bills, you are entitled to recover the difference in value between what the dog was worth with four legs and what it is worth with three. If you're talking about a champion show dog or a trained dog used in the movies, then the damages may be substantial. But for the average dog, the damages (exclusive of veterinarian bills) are usually not going to be very much. If the dog was worth, say, $100 with four legs, it will be worth about $75 with three.

As callous as it is, the law still views animals as inanimate objects—just like cars, furniture, or bowling balls—for purposes of valuing their injuries. If you used the dog for a special reason—to guard your factory, for example, or for hunting trips—and the dog can no longer adequately do its job, you can recover the full value of the dog at the time it was injured, the same as if it had been killed.

Many people who have pets treat them as one of the family. And when the pet is injured or killed, they suffer almost as much as if it had been a child that was hurt. But you usually cannot make the other person pay for your mental anguish when your pet is injured or killed. Even if you see the accident happen, most courts refuse to let you recover damages for your own mental anguish when your pet is injured or killed. A few courts, however, let you recover damages for your emotional distress when someone unlawfully and deliberately kills the pet without justification—if a person shoots it for no reason, for instance.

Removing a Trespassing Animal from Your Yard

You are entitled to use a reasonable amount of force to get your neighbor's dog or cat off your property. What is reasonable depends on the circumstances, however. Hitting the animal on the haunches with a broom or spraying it with a hose is usually reasonable, since the animal won't be seriously hurt. On the other hand, shooting the animal or hitting it over the head with a heavy piece of wood is usually excessive force, unless the animal was threatening to attack you. If you use too much force to remove the animal and injure or kill it in the process, you may have to pay the owner for the damages.

If a dog bites you or a cat claws you while you're trying to shoo it away, does the animal's owner have to pay for the damages? Most courts hold that you are well within your rights to try to remove the animal, and the animal's owner must pay your damages. Some courts, however, will not let you recover your damages from the animal's owner because you assumed the risk that it would turn on you. Before trying to physically remove a potentially dangerous animal from your yard, you should first contact the owner if possible and ask that he or she come get the animal off your land. If you don't know the owner or if a call to the owner would be futile, a call to the animal control department is in order, especially if the animal is large, vicious, or possibly rabid.

Veterinarians

Suppose that you take your dog in for its annual vaccination shot, and it bites off the vet's ear. Can the vet sue you? No. Veterinarians and their assistants generally assume the risk that they may be bitten, clawed, or otherwise injured by the animals they treat. But if your pet is unusually vicious, you must warn the vet about it or you could be liable to the vet.

In many states, a veterinarian who treats your pet has a lien on the animal to the extent of the services rendered. If you refuse to pay your bill, the vet can keep the pet as collateral until you do pay. And all the while the vet is keeping your pet, you may be incurring additional fees for boarding. The vet can sell your pet to pay the bill but first must usually notify you in writing of that intention so you can pay the balance and get the pet back. If you get into a dispute with your vet over a bill, it is usually best to pay the bill in full, get your pet back, and then file suit in small claims court or complain to the consumer affairs agency.

Destruction of Dangerous Pets

A dog escapes from a person's yard and for no reason attacks and mauls a child walking down the street. Can the dog be destroyed against the owner's will? Yes—but only after the dog has been found to be a danger to society. The animal control board will first investigate the facts to determine whether the animal is indeed a public danger. If it finds the animal dangerous, it will then refer the case to the office of the district attorney, who will file a complaint to have the dog declared a menace and destroyed.

A court hearing will be held to decide the dog's fate. The pet's owner must be given notice of the hearing so he or she can present evidence to refute the charges. If the judge declares the pet to be vicious and dangerous to society, the pet usually will be destroyed. In lieu of ordering the animal destroyed, the judge may order the owner to take sufficient safety precautions to prevent the same thing from happening again—such as putting the animal in a large enclosed cage to keep it from getting out. Rabid and other seriously diseased animals can also be destroyed in the interests of public safety.

Cruelty to Animals

We usually think of cruelty in terms of mercilessly beating or torturing an animal. But cruelty is not limited to these "affirmative" acts; it also includes failing to give your pet proper care and attention. For example, if you underfeed your pet, if you don't supply adequate water, if you keep the animal in a closed hot shelter (even in a car with the windows rolled up in summer), if you don't give it prompt medical attention when needed—these, too, constitute cruelty. At the very least, you must give your pet sufficient food, water, exercise, and fresh air. And you can't simply abandon your pet when it becomes sick, injured, or old. Dog fighting is prohibited by state law in all states and is also illegal under federal laws. Many states also prohibit cock-fighting.

Where is the line drawn between cruelty and allowable discipline or punishment of a pet? The question generally is one of excessiveness. Striking a dog a time or two with a newspaper because it soiled the carpet is reasonable punishment. Brutally kicking it a number of times or hitting it with a heavy branch is too much. If you think someone is being cruel to an animal you should contact the local police or district attorney immediately.

If you are suspected of being cruel to your pet, you can be charged with a crime (usually a misdemeanor), and your pet can be taken from you. Usually the pet cannot be taken away until after a court hearing at which it has been determined that you are guilty of animal cruelty. But when the animal's life is threatened, it can be taken away immediately and the hearing held afterward. If you are found innocent of cruelty, the animal must be returned to you. If you are found guilty, not only can the animal be taken away, but you can also be fined and even sentenced to jail. If the judge is satisfied that you will change your ways and care for the animal properly, you may be allowed to keep it, subject to periodic visits by the animal control authorities to make sure you are taking good care of the animal—a "probation" of sorts.

Animals and Scientific Research

Medicine and other disciplines have long used animals for various purposes. For example, at one time, rabbits (and other animals) were routinely sacrificed to diagnose whether women were pregnant or not. Urine was taken from a woman suspected to be pregnant and was injected into a female rabbit. Several days later, the rabbit was killed and its ovaries examined for telltale signs that the woman was pregnant. Tests have since been developed that can diagnose pregnancy without using animals.

The use of animals undeniably has led to important medical advances. Without it, important discoveries in the treatment of diabetes, polio, and heart disease would never have been made. Not only do animals continue to be used to aid in disease research, they are used in many other experiments, such as in testing the toxicity of new cosmetic products. Much of the nonmedical research seems particularly needless and cruel. One example is rubbing new cosmetic compounds into rabbits' eyes to see what reaction follows.

What happens when the rights of animals to be free from cruelty clash with the use of animals in scientific research? This is a difficult question. Certainly animals should not be subjected to needless experimentation and its attendant tortures and injury. On the other hand, animal research can expand man's knowledge and lead to medical breakthroughs. Recognizing that some experimentation on animals is unnecessary or unduly harsh, in December 1985, Congress passed a law that strengthened the Animal Welfare Act of 1966. Among other things, it requires researchers to consider alternatives to any procedures that are likely to cause pain or distress in an experimental animal. As a result of growing community awareness of what the animals are sometimes subjected to, the use of animals in many fields is being reduced. Also, the use of alternative methods, including tissue and cell cultures, computer simulations and analyses, models, and genetic engineering, makes it possible to do much research without animals.

When animals are used in research, the federal Animal Welfare Act requires the scientists to adequately feed, house, and give medical attention to the animals. The Animal Welfare Act also requires that dogs be exercised and primates be kept in a physical environment adequate to promote their psychological well-being.

CIVIL WRONGS: TORTS

WHEN YOU ARE INJURED or your property is damaged, your rights are determined by the law of torts. The English word *tort* is taken from a French word that means "wrong." The most common example of a tort is the automobile accident caused by one driver's carelessness. A driver who is speeding and causes an accident commits the tort of "negligence" and must pay for the personal injuries and property damage resulting from this conduct.

What Is Tort Law?

The law of torts can be boiled down to this: When someone is in the wrong and injures you or damages your property, that person must pay you for the damage done. This is only fair; we expect others to pay for any damages they cause us, just as they expect us to pay if we harm them.

But the mere fact that someone injures you or damages your property does not automatically mean that that person has committed a tort and must pay for your damages. A person must pay for your damages only if he or she was somehow at fault. Some accidents are truly unavoidable; they happen even though everyone involved was paying attention, and no one was at fault. When that happens, each party involved bears the cost of his or her own injuries and damage. A person is responsible for your injuries and damage only if his or her conduct is "tortious"—of such a nature that it is fair to make him or her pay for your damages. The three types of tortious conduct, discussed below, are (1) negligence, (2) intentional misconduct, and (3) strict liability.

Most of the time, the victim of a tort is compensated by a sum of money for the injuries and damages he or she suffers. Usually the sum includes damages for any medical expenses, lost wages for any time the person is out of work, "pain and suffering," and the cost of repairing or replacing the damaged property. Money is admittedly a poor substitute for some things—a lost arm, for instance—but what else is there? In some cases, such as a nuisance or trespass, you can go to court to get an injunction ordering the person to stop committing the tort.

Some specific tort situations are dealt with in other chapters of this book. For instance, the right to sue members of your family is discussed in chapter 1; automobile accidents are covered in chapter 2; trespassing and nuisance are explored in chapter 5; suing a landlord for injuries is discussed in chapter 6; chapter 7 covers injuries caused by animals; chapter 9 deals with medical malpractice; chapter 10 concerns defective products; and employee-related torts are contained in chapter 11. If the particular topic you are looking for is not in this chapter, a review of the index will guide you to the proper page. Even though the specific tort you are interested in is dealt with in another chapter, however, you should still review this chapter in full in order to get a complete picture of your rights when you are the victim of another's tort.

How Torts and Crimes Differ

What is the difference between a tort and a crime? In tort law, it is you, the individual, who have been wronged; you seek damages for your own injuries by filing a lawsuit in your own name in civil court. In criminal law, by contrast, the community as a whole seeks justice. Crimes like murder, arson, rape, and burglary, to name a few, cannot be tolerated by society, and one who commits such acts must be dealt with appropriately. A criminal complaint is filed in the name of the people (or the state), not the victim's name. While tort law compensates the victim by awarding a sum of money designed to make him or her "whole," criminal law punishes the criminal, usually by imprisonment or fine or both.

The fact that some crimes are also torts is one reason for much of the confusion between a tort and a crime. Battery, for instance, is both a crime and a tort. If someone hits you, you can sue the person in a civil court for the tort of battery to recover your damages. The state can also prosecute that person for the crime of battery. Many crimes do not have a specific tort counterpart, but you can still sue the person in civil court for your injuries. For example, there is no tort called "rape." But a rape victim can sue her assailant in civil court for the torts of assault, battery, false imprisonment, and infliction of emotional distress.

Should You See a Lawyer?

When you're injured by someone else, should you see a lawyer? Generally yes—even if your injuries seem relatively minor to you. Most lawyers don't charge for the initial consultation fee in personal injury cases, so you can usually get at least a half-hour's worth of free legal advice for your problem. That half-hour combined with the advice in this book may be all you need to see just where you stand. And if you do hire a lawyer for a personal injury case, it normally is on a contingency fee basis; you pay the lawyer a fee only if you win the case. The lawyer's fee comes out of the money that you receive, often paid by an insurance company. The contingency fee basis relates only to the lawyer's fees. It does not apply to the "costs and expenses" of litigation, such as the cost of filing the complaint. You are liable for the full amount of all costs and expenses (to the extent they are reasonable) incurred by your lawyer, regardless of whether you win or lose the case. (Finding the right lawyer and fee arrangements are discussed in chapter 19.)

One definite advantage to hiring a lawyer is that even after paying the lawyer a fee, the chances are that you will get more with a lawyer than you will if you try to represent yourself in injury cases. A 1985 study of automobile accident victims conducted by the Rand Institute revealed that without an attorney, the average person wound up with $1,844, while with an attorney, the average person got $2,396—after the attorney was paid. The study also showed that your chances of getting anything at all increased from 83 percent if you did it yourself to 95 percent if an attorney represented you.

Negligence

The most common tort is the tort of negligence. Negligence can be defined simply as carelessness: failing to pay sufficient attention under the circumstances. Some everyday examples of negligence include automobile accidents caused by speeding, disobeying traffic signs and signals, tailgating, making an unsafe left turn, driving while drunk, and not keeping the brakes in good shape; falling in a store, theater, or even your neighbor's house because of a loose stair or carpet or a slippery floor ("slip and fall" cases); being injured by the carelessness of a doctor or dentist; or being hurt when the bus you're riding in makes a jolting start or an unexpected sudden stop.

How can you tell whether the person who hurt you was negligent or not? The standard used is whether that person was exercising a reasonable amount of "due care" under the circumstances. What due care is depends upon a number of factors—the circumstances, the age of the parties involved, whether anyone has a physical or mental disability, and the like. Conduct is measured against what a "reasonable person" would have done in the same situation. For example, a reasonable person would not make a left turn until it was safe to do so; negligence occurs when someone tries to make the turn when it is not safe.

This "reasonable person" against whom your conduct is measured is generally considered to be an adult of unspecified age who has no physical or mental disabilities and who is careful without being overly cautious. (The exceptions to this are discussed below.) Is reasonable conduct always the same? No, it changes from situation to situation. For instance, you are not expected to act the same in an emergency as you would in a nonemergency, when you had time to assess the situation and weigh the alternatives.

Children and the Elderly

The standard of conduct expected of a child is measured by what a reasonably careful child of like age, intelligence, and experience would have done under the same circumstances, not by what an adult would have done. A two-year-old child may not realize the danger in pulling a dog's tail, but a seven-year-old should. Very young children—usually under seven years old—are legally incapable of being negligent in many states. In other words, you can't sue a child under seven for injuring you. (Some states do not have a set age limit, but the courts often tend to settle on four years as the age at which a child becomes liable for negligence.) You can, however, sue a child under the set age limit for an intentional tort, such as battery, if the child understood the wrongfulness of the act, yet still went ahead and did it.

When a child engages in an activity traditionally reserved for adults—driving a car, for example—his or her conduct is measured by the higher adult standard. So if a 13-year-old boy takes his parents' car for a spin and gets into an accident, his conduct is measured by what an adult would have done while driving. The boy is not liable just because he was driving without a license. You still must prove that an adult driver would not have done what the boy did under the circumstances.

What difference does it make how old a child must be before

you can sue him or her or what the applicable standard of conduct is, since a child ordinarily doesn't have the money to pay any judgment even if you win? The difference is that, if you can sue the child, you may be able to collect under the parents' insurance policy. (In actuality, the issue of whether a child was negligent is more often raised when the child is injured and sues someone. The person being sued may claim that the child's own negligence caused or contributed to the injuries and therefore any monetary recovery by the child should be denied or reduced.)

At the other end of the spectrum, advanced age alone does not have any effect on the general standard of care applicable to all adults. An 85-year-old driver, for instance, must use the same degree of care that a 25-year-old driver must use while driving a car.

Physical and Mental Disabilities

A person who has a physical disability is not held to the same standard of care as a person without any disabilities. A physically disabled person is required to use only that degree of care and caution which a reasonable person with the same disability would use. A blind man, for instance, must exercise the same degree of care that a reasonably prudent blind man would use in crossing a street, and a paraplegic must use the same care in his or her activities as a careful paraplegic would. It would be unfair to require people with physical disabilities to act the same way as people with no disabilities where it is physically impossible for them to do so.

Although the law makes a concession for physical limitations, no allowances are made for people who suffer from mental disabilities or retardation. A person who is insane or mentally retarded generally is held to the same standard of care as the person of average intelligence. An insane person who injures another person or damages another's property is liable for the damages, even though the person doesn't know what he or she is doing at the time. (But the law relieves a person of criminal responsibility if he or she was insane at the time of the act; see chapter 18.)

Proving Negligence

How much care a reasonable person would use in a given situation is usually decided by a jury, based on all of the facts presented during the trial. Frequently, the process involves an inexact analysis: one could argue that a reasonable person would have done this, or a reasonable person would not have done that. And in fact, the standard of care is often supplied by custom and common sense. Many times, however, it is imposed by a statute. All states, for example, have laws for driving a car: you must stop for a red light; you can't exceed the speed limit; and so on. These laws set the minimum standard of care that you must follow. If you break any of these laws and cause an accident, you are usually liable for the injuries and damage. You are presumed negligent because you violated the law.

Sometimes an accident is so unusual that the mere fact that it happened is enough to infer that someone was negligent and must pay you for your injuries. This is the doctrine of "res ipsa loquitur," which literally means, 'the thing speaks for itself." It applies only when the defendant had the exclusive control of the thing that hurt you, you did not contribute to the accident, and the accident normally wouldn't have happened unless somebody was negligent.

The classic case involved a man who was walking down the street when a barrel of flour rolled out of a window above a shop, seriously injuring him. The man could not prove exactly how or why the barrel fell from the window, and the owner of the shop wouldn't admit to any fault. Because this type of accident normally would not have occurred unless someone was negligent, and since the store owner had the means to discover why the accident happened, it was up to the store owner to prove that he was not negligent. Without this rule, the store owner—who could get at the truth much more easily than the injured person could—

would be able to avoid responsibility simply by remaining silent and pretending to be ignorant of what caused the accident.

Another example: Sara goes into the hospital to have some surgery done on her knee. When she wakes up after the operation, she discovers a serious burn on her chest. None of the doctors, nurses, or other staff will admit knowing anything about how the burn got there. The hospital and its employees are presumed at fault: a patient normally wouldn't be burned like this unless someone was negligent; the hospital employees had exclusive control of the operating room; and Sara, who was unconscious when the accident happened, in no way contributed to her own injury.

Res ipsa loquitur is also applied to cases involving airplanes that suddenly drop out of the sky on a sunny day. The law presumes negligence of some kind—any kind—on the part of the airline; maybe there was pilot error, or the mechanics were careless. It is up to the airline to refute any possibility that it was negligent—by presenting the testimony of its mechanics that everything was done properly and by offering flight recorder data showing that the pilots didn't do anything wrong, for example.

Proving Notice of a Dangerous Condition If You "Slip and Fall"

If you injure yourself on someone else's land, is that person liable for your injuries? The answer depends on whether the person had notice that a dangerous condition existed on the land, and if so, whether he or she had a reasonable amount of time either to remove the danger or to warn persons on the land that the danger was there. (Other issues relating to a landowner's liability to persons injured on his or her land are discussed in chapter 5.) Say that Peggy is doing her weekly grocery shopping at the supermarket, when she slips on a piece of fruit that had fallen out of its bin and breaks her arm. If she sues the store for payment of her doctor bills and other damages, will she win? It depends on how long the fruit had been on the floor before Peggy stepped on it. If the fruit had fallen out of the bin only moments before Peggy walked down the aisle, the supermarket probably is not liable; it did not know the fruit was there. But if she could prove that the fruit had been lying on the floor for an hour or two, Peggy would most likely win her case.

How do you prove how long the fruit has been on the ground? Asking other shoppers who had been in that area before Peggy is a start. If nobody saw anything on the floor before Peggy fell, or if a supermarket employee had cleaned the area only minutes before, it is likely that the fruit had fallen out of the bin only moments before the accident. But if several shoppers noticed the fruit on the ground and told the manager about it half an hour earlier, this shows that there was enough time for the store to clean it up.

Another example: Mike leaves the balcony at the movie theater to go to the lobby for refreshments. On the way down the stairs, he trips over a loose piece of carpet and is seriously hurt. Again the question of whether the theater is liable depends on whether the theater knew or should have known that the carpet was loose, and had a reasonable amount of time to correct the dangerous condition, put a barrier around it, or post a warning until the carpet was fixed. One way to prove that the theater knew of the dangerous condition is by previous reports of people tripping over the carpet at an earlier show. Another way is to prove that someone had informed a theater employee that the carpet was loose or that a theater employee saw the loose carpet but did nothing about it. Yet another way to prove the theater should have known the carpet was loose is by analyzing the loose carpet and surrounding area for signs that the carpet had been loose for a while. But if Mike is the first one to report the danger, and all the evidence shows the carpet had not been loose for very long, the theater is probably not liable for Mike's injuries.

Defenses to Negligence

Even though someone has been negligent and hurt you, there are several defenses that can relieve him or her of having to pay

for part or all of your damages. These are the defenses of contributory negligence, comparative negligence, assumption of risk,
and releases.

Contributory Negligence

At one time, all states held that if you were at all responsible
for your own injury, you usually could not collect a dime from
the other party. If you were in an automobile accident, for instance, and were 25 percent at fault and the other driver was 75
percent at fault, you could not recover anything from the other
driver. This is the rule of "contributory negligence," and it is still
applied in a few states.

Comparative Negligence

Most states have abandoned the strict rule of contributory
negligence in favor of the doctrine of "comparative negligence."
Under comparative negligence, your negligence is compared to
the other party's negligence, and the damages you are entitled to
recover are reduced by your own percentage of fault. Say you
suffered $10,000 worth of damages in an accident in which you
were 25 percent responsible and the other party was 75 percent
at fault. You can sue the other party for your damages, but your
damages will be reduced by $2,500 (25 percent of $10,000). Who
determines the amount of your fault, and how? The jury decides,
based on all of the evidence presented during the trial.

Suppose you were injured in an automobile accident, and
the jury rules that you and the other driver were each 50 percent
at fault. Does the other driver have to pay you anything? The
answer depends on what state you're in. Some states have a "pure"
system of comparative negligence, which lets you sue the other
party no matter how much you were at fault. If you were 99
percent negligent and the other party was only 1 percent negligent,
you could sue the other party; of course, you'd only collect 1

percent of your damages. So when you're 50 percent at fault, the other driver has to pay for half of your damages.

Other states let you collect from the other party as long as you weren't more negligent than he or she. In this case, since you were 50 percent at fault, the other driver must pay for half of your damages. But if you had been 50.01 percent or more responsible for the accident, you couldn't recover any damages.

Finally, some states make the other party pay only if you were less at fault than he or she. Since you were equally at fault, the other driver owes you nothing. In those states, you can only recover if you were no more than 49.99 percent responsible for the accident.

Assumption of Risk

You generally cannot sue a person for injuring you if you knowingly and voluntarily assumed the risk that you might be injured. This is the legal doctrine of "assumption of risk." Suppose you're leaving your friend's house one winter day. She walks you to the door, looks at the walkway, and says, "You'd better not go out that way because there's ice all over the walk. Use the back door." You reply that you'll be okay and use the front walk—and then slip, fall, and hurt yourself. You have assumed the risk of being hurt because you knew the danger (ice) was there and voluntarily approached it, even though there was a way of avoiding the danger.

If you participate in a sport, you assume the risk that you may be injured. This is true whether you are a professional, a high school or college athlete, or a novice playing a sandlot game on Sunday. Suppose you are playing in a basketball game at the local park, when a player on the other team comes up from behind and deliberately pushes you into the pole holding the backboard. Does assumption of risk bar you from suing that player? No. You only assume risks that are inherent in the sport—a "part of the game." Assumption of risk does not prevent you from suing a player who intentionally injures you.

What if you're a spectator? Do you assume the risk of being struck by an errant baseball or hockey puck? By sitting near a tight corner at an automobile race, do you assume the risk that a car may crash into the barrier, sending up debris that can injure or kill you? Ordinarily, you do assume these risks at a sporting event, but only if the arena has provided a sufficient number of screened or otherwise protected seats for fans who could be expected to ask for them. About the only way you could recover damages is by proving that you asked for a protected seat, but they were all sold out. You can sue the stadium if you think you have found safe refuge behind the screen, but, for instance, a ball is hit through a hole in the screen and injures you.

Releases

Suppose you are hit by a baseball while attending a professional game. The stadium claims that you not only are barred from suing them because you assumed the risk, but you are also barred by the "release" on the back of the ticket, which states that you agree that the stadium cannot be held liable for any injuries you suffer on the premises. Does this release prevent you from suing the stadium? The answer can depend upon a number of things. First of all, it depends on whether the release was conspicuous and clear. If you didn't see it because, for example, it was in fine print, it doesn't count. Neither does a release that is so poorly written that you can't understand it. Another important factor is how you were injured. If you were struck by a foul ball, the release may be valid. But if you were injured by a defective seat or loose railing, for instance, you can sue because a facility that is open to the public ordinarily cannot disclaim liability for its negligence. And a release also will not be enforced to block your suit against someone who deliberately hurt you.

Intentional Torts

An "intentional tort" is one in which the person deliberately means to hurt you or damage your property. If someone punches you, purposely rams his or her car into yours, threatens to shoot you, throws a bottle or a rock at you—all of these are intentional torts. In intentional torts, the person's state of mind when he or she was performing the act is the critical element. If, for instance, the person meant to hit you, it is considered battery. But if the person was merely careless and didn't intend to hit you, then the tort is "negligence."

The most important legal difference between an intentional tort and negligence is that if you are the victim of an intentional tort, you are entitled to recover an award of punitive (or "exemplary") damages in addition to all of your other damages. Punitive damages are designed to punish the person for doing the wrongful act and to deter him or her from doing it again in the future. How much in punitive damages can you get? That's really up to the jury; it could be as little as $1 or as much as $100,000 or more, depending upon the facts of the case.

Suppose you are standing near Bob. Hal throws a rock at Bob, Bob ducks, and the rock hits you. Can you sue Hal for an intentional tort (battery) even though he meant to hit Bob, not you? Yes. Since Hal intended to hit Bob with the rock, that intent is "transferred" to you. The legal effect is that Hal is liable just as if he had meant to hit you with the rock in the first place.

Let's say that one night, Ernie sees his girlfriend on the other side of the street. He crosses the street, sneaks up behind her, abruptly grabs her, turns her around, and kisses her. He then realizes that the woman isn't his girlfriend but another woman who resembles her. If the woman sues Ernie for battery, can Ernie get off the hook by proving that he was mistaken—that he didn't intend to kiss this woman but his girlfriend? No. The fact is he *did* intend to kiss this woman. His mistake as to the woman's identity is of no legal consequence.

Assault

In tort law, an "assault" consists of a deliberate act that causes you to fear that you are in imminent danger of being struck—by a fist, a bullet, or whatever. If, for example, a person starts to take a swing at you or pulls a gun out and threatens to shoot you, the person is guilty of an assault because you reasonably feared that you were going to be hit or shot right away. Actual physical contact is not required for an assault to be committed. If you manage to step out of the way of the fist, for instance, or if the person doesn't fire the gun, it is still an assault.

You also do not have to fear that you will be injured from the contact. Suppose that Tiny Tom, standing 3′8″ and weighing all of 85 pounds, gets mad and takes a swing at Ken Norton, former heavyweight boxing champion. Is this an assault, even though Norton was in no danger of being hurt by the blow? Yes. Norton needs only to realize that Tiny Tom is about to hit him.

In fact, for an act to be an assault, you need only have a reasonable belief that the other person intends to hit you. The person's outward actions, rather than his or her subjective intent, are what determine an assault. If John takes a swing at Alan, even though he intends only to scare Alan and not actually hit him, John commits an assault. To Alan it looked as though John was going to hit him. Likewise, if John points an unloaded gun at Alan and threatens to shoot him, in most states, John commits an assault. Although John knew the gun was unloaded and couldn't possibly hurt anyone, Alan had no way of knowing whether the gun was loaded or not. He believed—as would most anyone else in his place—that the gun was loaded. In a few states, John is not liable for an assault unless there were bullets in the gun. John must have had the "actual ability" to commit the battery. But Alan could still sue John for the tort of intentional infliction of emotional distress (see discussion below).

Suppose Howard shakes his fist at Martha, saying, "If you weren't a woman, I'd hit you." Is this an assault? Probably not, since his words contradict his actions. But this is not always true.

If Howard was shaking his fist so vigorously and his face was so flushed that Martha justifiably feared an immediate strike—despite what Howard was saying—Howard is liable for an assault.

Battery

A person who deliberately hits or touches you without your permission commits the tort of "battery." As with other intentional torts, the person's mental state is all important. Accidentally jostling someone in a crowded hallway while you're in a hurry is not battery, but purposely shoving a person out of your way is. Whether something constitutes battery is often determined by socially acceptable standards of conduct. Certain deliberate physical contact, even with a stranger, is not battery if it is commonplace. For instance, tapping a person's shoulder to ask for directions or the time is not battery. But if the contact is harmful or offensive, it is battery.

Suppose Beth walks up to you and knocks your hat off your head. Is she guilty of battery, even though she didn't touch your body? Yes. Anything you are wearing or holding is so closely identified with your body that it is considered battery to touch it. So if a person intentionally grabs your coat while you're wearing it or yanks your briefcase from your hand, that person has committed battery. What if you're sitting in your car and someone deliberately runs into you? This too is battery; the car is considered an extension of your body while you are in it. But if your coat and briefcase were lying on a bench when they were grabbed, or you were across the street from your car when it was hit, there is no battery. (The person may still be liable for a "trespass to chattels" or even "conversion," discussed below.)

You do not have to suffer any injury in order to sue for battery. Any unlawful touching, regardless of how slight, is all that is required. If a man lightly brushes his hand over a woman's breasts without her consent, he is liable for battery, even though the woman isn't physically injured. But the absence of physical injury is germane to the question of how much money you can ask for—indeed, whether it is worth it to sue the person in the first place. You will probably get a lot more money if someone breaks your leg than if someone knocks your hat off your head. In some cases, however, such as where the conduct is very offensive, you may get a large award of punitive damages even though your physical injuries were next to nothing.

Assault and battery seem to go together like ham and eggs; you usually don't think of one without the other. But just as an assault can occur without battery, battery can happen without an assault. Suppose you're asleep, when someone you don't know kisses you. There is no assault because you weren't aware that the person was going to kiss you. But there is battery because the person touched you without your permission—you don't have to be aware of the contact when it happens. Another, perhaps more readily imaginable, example of battery without an assault would be if someone sneaked up from behind and hits you. Since you did not suspect anything until you were struck, there was no assault, but there was battery.

It is not battery if you permit someone to touch you. A man who kisses a woman with her consent, for example, does not commit battery. But the consent must be voluntary. If a man holds a knife to a woman's throat and says, "Kiss me, or I'll kill you," and she complies, it is still battery; the woman did not freely consent to the contact. The person must be legally and mentally capable of consenting to the act. The consent of a child, a drunkard, or an insane or mentally retarded person may not be good.

Let's say that Ron is drinking in a bar and gets into a shouting match with Mike, another customer. Mike asks Ron to step outside so they can settle their dispute in the alley. Ron says, "That's fine with me; let's go." Mike breaks Ron's nose in the fight; Ron sues Mike for battery. Mike contends that Ron consented to the fight and therefore can't sue him. Who wins? In some states, Ron wins because you can sue your opponent even if you were a willing participant in the fight. This is because you can't consent to an illegal act—here, a fight. Other states recognize consent to a fight as a valid defense; by voluntarily engaging in fisticuffs, you know you are going to be hit and likely injured and therefore can't sue the other person.

Someone is about to hit you, but you strike first, breaking his or her nose. Do you have to pay the other person for the damages? Not if you were acting in self-defense or to protect someone else. The one restriction on this is that you are only permitted to use "reasonable force" to defend yourself. How much force is reasonable depends on the situation. You can use deadly force—force capable of inflicting death or serious bodily harm, such as wielding a gun or a lead pipe—only if it is necessary under the circumstances. If you use too much force—if you shoot someone to prevent him or her from merely touching you, for instance—you can be held liable for battery. (You may be guilty of a *crime* if you use excessive force and hurt or kill someone.)

One day Ken starts insulting Rodney. Rodney tells him to stop, but Ken keeps egging Rodney on. Rodney finally says, "Listen, if you don't shut up, I'm going to belt you one." Ken doesn't stop, and Rodney hits him, breaking his jaw. Ken sues Rodney for battery; Rodney contends that Ken provoked him. Who wins? Ken. Verbal provocation is normally not considered to be a good reason to commit battery.

False Imprisonment

"False imprisonment" occurs when someone intentionally confines you against your will. We ordinarily associate false imprisonment with being locked in a room or a cell. But it can also occur, for example, when someone grabs you outside and prevents you from getting away. The confinement can also be psychological—if someone tells you that he or she will shoot you or a loved one if you try to leave an unlocked room, for instance.

You are not imprisoned if there is a reasonable way to escape from the confined area. If you can safely escape from a locked room through an open window, for example, there is no false imprisonment.

False imprisonment is frequently alleged by a person who feels that he or she was unlawfully arrested. If the police did not have "probable cause" to arrest you (see chapter 18), you can sue them for false imprisonment. ("False arrest" is really just a type of false imprisonment.) If someone files a false police report that ends in your arrest, you can sue that person for false imprisonment. For example, Dennis calls the police and informs them that he saw Ted committing a burglary. Dennis knows that this is untrue and is filing the false report to get back at Ted. The police arrest Ted and put him in jail. Ted can sue Dennis for false imprisonment because it was Dennis's act—filing a false police report—that got Ted arrested. The police are liable for false imprisonment if they knew Dennis was lying when he made the report but still went ahead and arrested Ted.

Suppose you're walking out of a store, when the manager asks you to follow her to a back room. Once there, she informs you that the store has had a problem with shoplifters and that she would like to take a look inside your shopping bag. You tell her that you have nothing to hide and dump the bag's contents onto a table. The manager goes through everything, finds nothing, thanks you, and tells you that you're free to go. The whole thing takes about five minutes. Can you sue for false imprisonment? Probably not. A store owner or employee who suspects a person of shoplifting generally can detain that person for a reasonable time to investigate a possible crime. But what if you refuse to let the manager look inside the bag; can she do it anyway? Generally not. About the only times the manager can look inside the bag over your objections is if she or another employee actually saw you steal something and put it in the bag, or if a stolen item is in plain view (a stolen sweater is sticking out of the bag, for example). Otherwise the manager would have to let you go or call the police to conduct any further investigation.

The investigation must be done in a reasonable manner; the owner or employee cannot loudly accuse you in front of other customers and must not be rude or offensive while questioning you. And the investigation must not take an unnecessarily long time—10 to 15 minutes is often the most that is needed. The owner or employee generally cannot search you or your shopping bag or purse without your permission unless he or she actually saw you steal some merchandise.

Damage to Personal Property

The act of deliberately damaging or interfering with the use of another's personal property is called a "trespass to chattels." Personal property (chattel) is anything other than real estate— your car, books, clothing, and furniture, to name a few examples.

Suppose you see someone sitting on the hood of your car. Can you sue that person for a trespass to chattels? No. The interference with your car is minimal. It's not enough to worry about, so the law doesn't. But if the car is damaged in any way— for instance, if the hood gets scratched—you can sue for a trespass to chattels.

When a person damages your property, ordinarily he or she must pay you the cost of having it repaired. If someone dents your fender, and it costs you $250 to get it fixed, that person has to pay you $250. Suppose that Ellen runs into your car and does $1,250 damage to it, but your car is old and worth only $850. How much does Ellen have to pay you, the full $1,250 to get it fixed or only $850? The answer is $850. If it costs more to repair the property than the thing is worth, you get the smaller value— the value of your car before it was damaged. Another way of calculating damages is the difference between the value of the property before it was damaged and what it is worth afterward. For example, if you could still sell the car for $300 after the accident, then Ellen only has to pay you $550—the difference between what the car was worth before the accident ($850) and what it was worth after ($300).

Theft or Destruction of Personal Property

Someone who steals or deliberately destroys your personal property is liable for the tort of "conversion," and you are entitled to be compensated for the value the property had at the time and place of the conversion. For example, if someone smashes your watch with a hammer, he or she has to pay you the value of the watch at that time. If the watch cost you $250 two years ago, and a new one costs $300 today, but yours was only worth $100 when it was destroyed, that's all you can get for it. (You can, however, also sue for punitive damages.)

Suppose your television set is stolen from your house. Two months later, you find it for sale at a swap meet. You tell the man selling it that it is your stolen set and that you want it back. He tells you that he bought the set at a garage sale and that it's now his to do with as he wants. Who is in the right? You are. A thief does not acquire title to stolen property and so has no title to give to someone who buys the property from him or her. In other words, a person who buys something that was stolen owns nothing. You are entitled to get your property back without paying the seller a dime. This is true even if the seller is totally innocent, had no idea that the property was stolen, and paid good money for it. His only recourse is to try to get the money back from the person who sold it to him. What if he refuses to return the property to you? Can you just pick it up and take it away? No. Ordinarily you must go through the courts to get the property back. The best thing to do in this situation is to call the police and tell them that you've located your stolen property and ask for their assistance. They'll impound the set, and if you can prove that it's yours, they'll return it to you when they no longer need it for the criminal case.

Let's say that in the middle of the night you're awakened by a noise in your driveway. You look out the window and see somebody stealing the tape player from your car. Can you shoot that person to prevent the theft? No. You can use reasonable force to defend your property from theft or damage. But the right to use force to protect your property does *not* include the right to use deadly force. Why? Because when it comes down to choosing between human life and property, human life always wins. It's another matter, however, if a burglar breaks into your house and confronts you, threatening your safety and the safety of your family. You may be justified in using deadly force in that situation, because you're protecting more than just your property; you're protecting yourself and your loved ones as well.

Misuse of the Judicial System

Suppose you are a tenant and your landlord files eviction proceedings against you, knowing that there is no reason to do so. Or suppose someone signs a false criminal complaint against you, knowing that you haven't committed a crime. In either case, you can sue the person for the tort of "malicious prosecution." Malicious prosecution is the filing of a civil lawsuit or the making of a criminal complaint against someone without "probable grounds" for doing so. (In the second example, if you are arrested and taken into custody, you can sue the person for false imprisonment as well.)

You cannot sue for malicious prosecution until the original bogus case is terminated, and then only if the case ends in your favor. If the other person wins, the law presumes that he or she had sufficient reason to bring the complaint in the first place. This is true even if the case is reversed on appeal and you ultimately prevail.

Let's say that you file a lawsuit on the advice of your attorney, but you lose the case, and the other person sues you for malicious prosecution. You contend that you brought the suit because your attorney told you that you had a good chance of winning. Who should win the lawsuit? You should. As long as you told your attorney all the facts of the case before he or she advised you to file it, you are deemed to have probable cause to file the suit. But if you withheld some important facts from the attorney, you cannot hide behind the attorney's advice to sue the other person.

Another tort involving the misuse of the judicial process is "abuse of process," which is the misuse of the court system to achieve an improper goal. Unlike in malicious prosecution, where there is no justification to file the lawsuit, in abuse of process the lawsuit is justified, but one party uses the court's power to achieve an impermissible result. For example, after a lawsuit is filed against you, the other party starts harassing you with court motions and procedures to coerce you into settling the case, rather than using them for the purposes they were intended to achieve.

Fraud

Let's say that you're interested in buying a horse and find one that you like. The owner tells you that the horse is only four years old and is in excellent health. In reality—as the owner well knows—the horse is eight years old and sickly. You buy the horse but a month later you take it to the vet because it seems ill. Your vet looks the horse over and tells you the truth about it. Is there anything you can do? Yes. You can sue the person who sold you the horse—for fraud. Fraud is committed when a person tells you something that he or she knows to be untrue, knowing that you will rely on this falsehood in making your decision.

The falsity usually must be one of fact, not opinion. For instance, if a used-car salesman tells you a car is a 1985 model when in fact it is a 1983 model, that is a misstatement of fact. But if the salesman tells you the car is good and will last a long time, this is only an opinion or permissible exaggeration—"sales talk" or "puffing."

Invasion of Privacy

The First Amendment to the Constitution guarantees the right to free speech. But what if you don't want to listen? Do you have the right to be left alone? Yes. You have the right to privacy, and if someone invades your privacy, you can sue to recover damages for any harm you suffer. And if the person threatens to continue invading your privacy in the future, you can get a court order to prevent it.

The tort of invasion of privacy really comprises four separate and distinct torts: (1) The unreasonable intrusion into your private life; (2) the public disclosure of private facts; (3) portraying you in a false light in the public eye; and (4) using your name or likeness for a commercial purpose without your consent.

Intrusion into Your Private Life

You have the right to be free from unwanted invasions into your privacy. Someone who breaks into your home is clearly guilty of invading your privacy (and of trespassing as well). But the intrusion doesn't have to be physical. The unauthorized use of wiretaps or other electronic listening devices to listen in on your private conversations is also an invasion of privacy, even if all the equipment is across the street on public property. Other examples of invasion of privacy include bill collectors and others who harass you with persistent telephone calls or knocks at your door, or someone who goes onto your lawn and looks through the window—a "peeping Tom."

Suppose a stranger takes a picture of you while you are in a public square or on a public beach. Is this an invasion of your privacy? Not by itself. You don't have as much right to privacy in a public place as you do at home. A person can follow you around in public, even take your picture without your consent and over your objections, since everyone has a right to be on a public street or sidewalk. (It becomes an invasion of privacy, however, if the picture is used in a way that portrays you in a false light or if the person uses the picture for commercial purposes without your consent, as discussed below.) There is one important limitation to the rule that you can be followed or photographed in public: If the trailing or shadowing turns into harassment, it becomes an invasion of privacy, and you can sue to stop the person from following you and to collect damages. Jacqueline Kennedy Onassis, for example, obtained a court order requiring a particular photographer who continuously overstepped the bounds of reasonableness to keep his distance. Private detective agencies have been successfully sued when their tailing operations of subjects proved less than clandestine.

Public Disclosure of Private Facts

What rights do you have if someone learns of a private fact about you and tells it to others? This is a form of invasion of privacy called a "public disclosure of private facts." You have a right to sue the person for your embarrassment and other damages that you suffer from it.

The most common example of a public disclosure of private facts involves debts. The fact that you owe somebody money is generally a matter between only you and your creditor. A creditor cannot tell others that you owe money, in order to humiliate you or to coerce you into paying it back. For example, if a store tapes your bad check to the cash register—in plain view of the customers—with your name and address and the words "Returned for Insufficient Funds" marked in bold red letters, that is an invasion of privacy. Likewise, posting a list of names on a piece of paper headed "No Checks Accepted" where other customers can see it is also an invasion of privacy.

Public disclosure of private facts constitutes an invasion of privacy only if the information is offensive and objectionable to a person of ordinary sensibilities. You can't sue for an invasion of privacy if the information is innocuous or flattering. If you did a good deed—returned lost money or saved a child from drowning—and someone told others about it, that isn't an invasion of your privacy. Telling others information that is contained in public records—a court file or the county clerk's office, for instance—also does not constitute an invasion of privacy.

The press can report "newsworthy" events, even though the facts are private. For example, murder cases, divorces, deaths from drug overdoses, or children with rare and unusual diseases—these are all considered newsworthy, and can be written about even if the person does not consent to the story.

Portraying a Person in a False Light

Suppose that near election time, you are reading the paper, when you see a political advertisement containing your name among the list of supporters for a particular candidate—a candidate you can't stand. Is this an invasion of your privacy? Yes. The ad places you in a "false light in the public eye" by making it appear that you endorse someone you abhor. This form of invasion of privacy originated in England in the early 1800s, when Lord Byron sued to stop the circulation of a bad poem that was falsely attributed to his pen. It is still an invasion of privacy to credit a person with writing a book he or she did not write or to state that a critic recommends a certain book, film, or play when it is not true.

Someone's use of your photograph to illustrate certain types of stories can also place you in a false light in the public eye. For example, suppose you are a used-car salesman—an *honest* used-car salesman. A magazine uses your picture without asking you, to illustrate an article on used-car salesmen who lie and use every dirty trick in the book. Can you sue the magazine for an invasion of privacy? Yes. A reader who sees your picture will naturally think that you are a dishonest salesman.

Appropriation of a Name or Likeness for Commercial Use

Suppose a soft drink company uses in its advertising campaign, without your permission, a picture of you drinking its product. Is this an invasion of privacy? Yes. No one can use your picture, name, or likeness for commercial purposes unless you agree. But a newspaper or television news story might be able to use the same picture in a report on the soft drink industry—the picture isn't being used to promote a particular brand but is merely used in connection with a newsworthy story.

Celebrities, who work hard to have their faces and names known to millions of people, have a "right to publicity." You can't use a celebrity's name or likeness without his or her consent.

If you do, the celebrity can sue to stop it and can also recover damages—including any money you made from the unauthorized use. Movie stars and rock stars, for example, have successfully sued to stop companies from selling without their consent novelty items featuring their names or likenesses.

Slander and Libel

"Defamation" is a false statement that tends to diminish your reputation so that other people think less of you and don't want to associate with you. They key word is *false*; you can't sue for defamation if the statement a person makes is true. (You may, however, still be able to sue for an invasion of privacy or infliction of emotional distress, depending on the nature and content of the statement.)

There are two types of defamation: slander and libel. Slander refers to spoken words, while libel encompasses written communications. A hundred or so years ago, it wasn't too difficult to tell whether a false statement was slander or libel. But the invention of television, radio, the phonograph, motion pictures, computers, and other kinds of modern technology has brought new problems in determining whether something is libel or slander. If a person ad-libs a defamatory statement on radio or television, for example, it is slander. But if the defamatory statement is read from a script or other prepared text, it is libel.

Say you're all alone in your office, when someone comes in and starts calling you a crook, a liar, and a cheat. Can you sue that person for defamation? No—even if you aren't a crook, a liar, and a cheat. Why can't you sue? Because the defamatory remarks must be heard (or read, in the case of libel) by someone besides yourself.

Now suppose that your secretary heard the person call you a crook and such but didn't believe a word of it. Does this prevent you from suing the person for defamation? No. It doesn't matter whether the person who heard the false remarks believed them or not. All that matters is that he or she heard the untrue statements and knew that they referred to you. The fact that nobody believed the false statements does, however, have a bearing on how much you will recover in damages. If no one believed the remarks, your business didn't suffer, and you lost none of your friends, your damages are minimal. On the other hand, if a major client of yours took his or her business elsewhere after hearing the statement, you'll collect much more in damages.

Can you sue if somebody makes a defamatory remark concerning a dead relative? Usually not. Under the current law, you generally can say anything you want about someone who has died, no matter how vicious and untrue it may be, and not have to worry about defamation.

Sometimes a statement is defamatory only if you are able to put two and two together. If, for example, the local society columnist reports that Mrs. Janice Jones is pregnant with her second child, this may seem innocuous enough on its face. But if the statement is untrue, and Mrs. Jones has been widowed for two years, the statement takes on new meaning. A person who knows Mrs. Jones can put the missing facts together to get the underlying—and defamatory—meaning of the statement.

Public figures—politicians, celebrities, star athletes, and so forth—have a tougher time suing a newspaper, magazine, or radio or television station than the average person does. In addition to proving that the statement was false and defamatory, the public figure must prove that it was made with "malice." Malice here means saying something that you know is false or making the statement with reckless disregard for the truth; you say it even though you have no idea whether it is true or not.

The difficulties a public figure faces in trying to win a defamation suit against the media received international attention when former Israeli Defense Minister Ariel Sharon sued *Time* magazine. In its February 21, 1983, issue, *Time* published an article that included a paragraph describing Sharon's alleged role in the 1982 massacre of 700 Palestinians in two Beirut refugee camps. The jury found that the paragraph in question was false and that it did defame Sharon. But the jury also concluded that *Time* did not act with malice, so Sharon lost the case. (In an unusual move that highlights the problems in this area of the law, the jury wrote a note stating that *Time* had acted carelessly and negligently in reporting and not verifying the story. But carelessness and negligence are not enough to make the media liable to a public figure for false statements.)

Infliction of Emotional Distress

One area of personal injury law that has undergone significant expansion in the last 20 years is your right to recover damages when you suffer emotional or psychological injuries because of another's wrongful act. This development in the law has paralleled the developments in psychology and related disciplines. An early fear of the law was that psychological injuries could be easily faked. Because there were no sure means of verifying these injuries, the danger was that many sham claims would be successful. Today psychological and emotional injuries and other mental disorders can be diagnosed with a good deal of certainty, so the chances that a fraudulent claim for emotional distress will succeed are no greater than for any other type of injury.

Emotional Distress Resulting from Another Person's Negligence

Say that Denise is stopped for a red light when Stan runs into her car from the rear. Stan clearly is at fault. Denise is not physically injured, and the damage to her car is only a few hundred dollars' worth. But Denise soon develops a fear of driving, of even being a passenger in a car. Treatment for her psychological injury runs into thousands of dollars, and Denise endures several months of severe anxiety. Must Stan pay for these injuries as well as for the damage to the car? Yes. When you are injured by the negligence of another, you are entitled to be compensated for your emotional distress as well as the physical injuries or property damage you may suffer.

Suppose you are looking out the window, watching your five-year-old daughter, Louise, playing on the lawn. Suddenly, a car screams around the corner, jumps the curb, and runs over Louise, seriously injuring her. The shock of seeing your daughter run over is more than you can bear, and you suffer deep psychological problems. There is no question that the driver was at fault and must pay for Louise's injuries. But does the driver have to pay for your emotional injuries as well?

Under the old rule, which is still followed in some states, you cannot recover damages for your emotional injuries because you were not struck by the car. You can only recover damages for your emotional injuries if the car actually touched you—even if the contact was very slight and didn't physically injure you. If you were in actual physical danger of being hit—in the "zone of danger"—many states now permit you to sue even though you weren't actually hit. But in the example above, you couldn't sue because you were inside the house and well away from the street.

Today, however, a growing number of states allow you to recover damages for your emotional injuries if you witnessed the accident involving your daughter—even if you weren't in the zone of danger. But you must witness the actual accident; learning about it afterward is normally not enough. You cannot recover for your emotional damages if you heard about your daughter's accident while you were at work and first saw her in the hospital emergency room. But "witnessing" an accident does not necessarily mean you have to see it. Say that you park your car on the street outside your house. You and your son walk to the back of the car to get the groceries out of the trunk. You pick up a sack, turn your back, and start walking away. Seconds later—while your son is still standing behind the trunk—you hear the sounds of brakes squealing, bones crunching, and a car hitting another car.

Instantly you know what has happened: your son has been struck by another car. You turn around, but by that time the accident is over. Can you sue? Yes. Although you did not see the other car hit your son, you knew as it was happening just what was going on.

Can you sue anytime for emotional injuries you suffer from seeing someone injured or killed by another's negligence? No. You must be a close relative of the victim—usually limited to a spouse, parent, child, or brother or sister. And it must in fact be your relative who is injured. You can't sue if you mistakenly believe the victim is your son or daughter, when in fact it is someone else's child.

When Someone Deliberately Causes You Emotional Distress

Suppose a coworker tells you that he will break your arm or kill you if you don't agree to go on strike with the rest of your colleagues. Afterward, you dread going to work; you lose weight, can't sleep at night, and can't keep your mind on your job. You even become physically ill and can't go to work. Can you sue your coworker for your injuries, for missing work, and other damages? Yes. A person who deliberately causes you to experience severe mental anguish ("emotional distress" or "mental suffering") is liable for your injuries.

This doesn't mean, however, that you can sue anyone who insults you or calls you a name. You are allowed to recover only for "outrageous" conduct—conduct that nobody should have to tolerate. Modern life requires all of us to have a certain amount of hardness; we must brush off mere insults, profanities, and minor annoyances.

Suppose you are an extra-sensitive person. Someone says things to you that an ordinary person could simply shrug off, but the remarks cause you serious mental anguish. Must that person pay for your damages? Only if he or she knew that you were unusually sensitive and would probably suffer emotional injuries upon hearing the remarks.

Strict Liability

"Strict liability" is usually applied only to situations that are extraordinarily dangerous and that pose a great likelihood of harm, particularly when something goes wrong. Unlike negligence and intentional misconduct, which look at the conduct and mental state of the person doing the act, strict liability is concerned only with the nature of the activity. Extraordinarily dangerous activities include chemical spraying and crop dusting, conducting blasting operations, operating nuclear power plants, running an oil well, and the like. The broadest application of strict liability is in cases of persons who are injured by defective products, which is discussed in chapter 10.

If you are injured as a result of another person's extraordinarily dangerous activity, you are usually allowed to recover your damages without proving that he or she did anything wrong. The nature of the activity is so inherently dangerous that it alone is sufficient to impose liability. For instance, if your neighbors are doing some blasting on their property, and some debris injures you or damages your property (or you are injured or your property is damaged from the shock waves), your neighbors must pay for your damage. They cannot get out of it by saying that they did everything correctly and were as careful as anyone could be. In strict liability cases, how careful a person is generally is irrelevant to the question of whether or not he or she is legally responsible for your damages.

9

MEDICINE, MALPRACTICE, AND YOU

THE LAW now recognizes that modern medicine is more than just the science of healing; it is also big business. Some of the most important developments in law in the last 50 years have been in the area of your rights as a patient, particularly your rights to quality medical care and to sue when you are injured by a doctor's carelessness.

A discussion of your rights as a patient necessarily revolves around "medical malpractice." Medical malpractice is simply the negligence (carelessness) of a doctor in diagnosing or treating your condition, which results in injury to you. A few examples of malpractice include reading an X-ray backward so that your healthy left kidney is removed rather than the diseased right one or your good right knee is operated on instead of your bad left one; using an unsterilized needle or thermometer, resulting in an infection to you; leaving a sponge or surgical instrument in a patient after an operation; injuring an infant during delivery because of too much pressure on the forceps; misreading an X-ray so a broken bone goes undetected; performing unnecessary surgery; failing to advise you of the possible consequences of an operation or the side effects of a drug; carelessly performing surgery so that an artery is severed or an organ is damaged; allowing a semiconscious or elderly patient to fall out of a hospital bed because the guardrails were down; and subjecting a patient to too much radiation.

Not every untoward result means the doctor has committed malpractice. Unexpected things sometimes happen despite the best of care. The doctor is liable for injuring you only if he or she used less skill and care than other doctors use in doing the same thing. In legal terms, the question is whether the doctor failed to "possess and use that degree of learning, skill, and care in diagnosing and treating the patient's condition that a reasonably competent doctor would employ in the same circumstances." In plain English, the question is whether the doctor made a mistake that any other doctor would not or should not have made.

Medical malpractice isn't limited just to doctors. It applies to "health care providers" of every kind—hospitals, nurses, medical technicians, dentists, psychiatrists, psychologists, optometrists, chiropractors, osteopaths, acupuncturists, and others. For ease in reading, throughout this chapter, "doctor" will be used to include all other types of health care providers.

The Physician-Patient Relationship

Must a Doctor Accept You as a Patient?

Suppose you consult a doctor for the first time but after several minutes, the doctor tells you that he or she cannot or will not accept you as a patient and advises you to find another doctor. Can the doctor do this? Yes. A doctor generally need not accept every new patient that comes to him or her. A doctor might refuse to accept a new patient for a number of reasons: the doctor is too busy to take on new patients; your ailment is beyond the doctor's competency; or there is a personality clash between the two of you. A doctor's right to reject potential patients is endorsed by the American Medical Association, whose Principles of Medical Ethics state, "A physician is free to choose whom he will serve."

On the other hand, a hospital emergency room cannot turn you away if your problem is serious or life-threatening and you need immediate care. While doctors are essentially free to decide whom they wish to treat, hospitals with emergency rooms open to the general public must treat anyone needing emergency care for a serious injury or illness. An emergency room that refuses to examine or treat you in a true emergency is liable for your damages if you suffer further injury because of the delay in treatment that results from having to go to another hospital. For example, suppose that Collette takes her daughter to an emergency room after the girl falls off her bike and strikes her head. The girl complains of dizziness and vomits several times—signs of potentially serious head injuries. Collette tells the emergency room admissions nurse what has happened and describes her daughter's symptoms. The nurse refuses to have the girl examined, forcing Collette to take her to another hospital 30 minutes away. By the time they get there, the girl's condition is much worse, and she dies shortly after arrival. An examination shows that the girl would have lived if the first emergency room had treated her. The hospital that refused to treat the girl is liable for her death because it rejected her in an obviously serious emergency.

Now suppose that Collette receives welfare and is eligible for Medicaid, but in her haste to get to the emergency room, she forgets to bring her Medicaid identification. The admissions nurse is interested only in how Collette plans to pay the hospital's bill and refuses to let a doctor examine the child until Collette proves that she is covered by Medicaid. Collette returns home to get the identification, taking her daughter with her; the girl dies in the car on the way back to the hospital. Was the nurse wrong? Yes. In a true emergency, an emergency room cannot refuse to examine or treat you for any reason, including your inability to show proof that you will be able to pay the bill. The hospital must treat you first; later it can worry about how you're going to pay the bill. The nurse clearly should have realized that the injuries could be very serious and should have called for a doctor to examine the girl as soon as she was brought in. The doctor's examination would have revealed that the child had suffered severe head injuries that required immediate treatment. Collette would have a good case against the hospital for malpractice.

Your Right to Confidentiality— The Physician-Patient Privilege

Your doctor cannot properly treat your condition unless he or she knows all of the symptoms and possible causes—regardless of how embarrassing or "shameful" they may be. But you're not going to tell your doctor something delicate unless you are absolutely certain it will remain confidential. What legal assurance do you have that the doctor won't tell others what you say? The law requires the doctor to keep in strictest confidence anything you say for the purposes of treatment. Ordinarily, the doctor cannot reveal anything you say unless you permit him or her to do so. This is known as the "physician-patient privilege."

What can you do if a doctor tells others your confidences without your consent? You can sue for the damages and humiliation you suffer. In one case, a psychiatrist who had treated a husband and wife wrote a book containing verbatim reports of their thoughts, emotions, sexual fantasies, and the disintegration of their marriage. Although the book did not identify the patients by name, the court held that the psychiatrist breached his promise to hold in confidence all disclosures made by his patients. The psychiatrist was also guilty of invading his patients' privacy by writing the book.

Is a physician ever required by law to disclose to others a patient's confidences? Yes. Occasionally society at large has a special interest that is greater than the patient's right to confidentiality—such as protecting the public from injury or from serious communicable diseases. Many states, for instance, require a doctor to report cases of suspected child abuse to the police. If the police question the doctor, the doctor must tell them anything the patient said relating to being a child abuser. Another example: if a patient has infectious hepatitis—particularly if he or she works at a job involving food—the doctor may be required to report it to the health department. In addition, when you file a lawsuit claiming that you were physically or emotionally injured by the defendant, your medical history may be opened to the person you are suing so he or she can determine whether your injuries are real.

Diagnosis and Treatment

Diagnosing Your Condition

A doctor must use due care in diagnosing your illness, so that appropriate treatment can be prescribed without undue delay. To diagnose your condition properly, the doctor generally must take an adequate history of your previous health and medical conditions, as well as significant medical conditions of your relatives—cancer, diabetes, heart disease, and the like. The doctor must get a detailed description of your current symptoms and must examine you and order any diagnostic tests that are reasonably required to diagnose your condition.

The failure to perform certain tests can sometimes be malpractice in and of itself. Suppose, for instance, a middle-aged, overweight man complains to his doctor of heaviness and severe pain in his chest. The doctor doesn't order an electrocardiogram— which would reveal that the man had suffered a heart attack— and sends him home with a diagnosis of "heartburn." That evening the man dies from the heart attack. Or suppose a woman who was injured in a car accident complains of a serious leg injury, but the doctor doesn't take an X-ray, telling her the leg is just bruised. An X-ray would have shown that the leg was broken. Because the bone isn't set properly, the leg becomes deformed. In both of these examples, the doctor is guilty of malpractice for failing to order diagnostic tests that were called for under the circumstances.

When a doctor commits malpractice and misdiagnoses your condition, you can sue for any and all injuries that result from being given unnecessary or harmful treatment and for any injuries you suffer because proper treatment was delayed. For example, a doctor carelessly diagnoses your rather harmless condition as a serious form of cancer. Chemotherapy and radiation treatment are started immediately, and you suffer serious side effects: nausea, pain, vomiting, hair loss, and so forth. Three months later, the doctor realizes the mistake, and the cancer therapy is stopped. In your malpractice case against the doctor, you can recover damages for all of your hospital, doctor, and other medical expenses; for lost wages from time off work; and for any injuries you suffered. You are also entitled to compensation for the pain and suffering you experienced—not only for the suffering as a result of the radiation and chemotherapy, but for the mental anguish of being wrongly told you had cancer as well.

Now consider the reverse situation: a doctor negligently diagnoses a mole as benign, when it really is cancerous. Because of the erroneous diagnosis, no treatment is prescribed, and the cancer worsens. By the time the doctor realizes the mistake, the cancer has spread to the point where radical and dangerous treatment is necessary. Had the doctor recognized the mole as cancerous earlier, it could have been excised with little risk to you. You could sue the doctor for the injuries you suffer because the doctor didn't diagnose the condition correctly earlier.

Referring You to a Specialist

When your condition is beyond the competency or expertise of a particular doctor, that doctor must refer you to another doctor or a specialist for diagnosis or treatment. If the first doctor continues to treat you anyway, he or she is liable for any injuries you suffer from inappropriate treatment and the delay in getting proper treatment. Suppose, for example, you visit an optometrist,

who finds evidence of possible disease in your eye. The optometrist concludes that it isn't serious, however, and doesn't refer
you to an ophthalmologist. But the disease turns out to be more
serious than the optometrist thought, and you eventually lose your
eye because proper treatment was delayed. If the optometrist had
referred you to an ophthalmologist, your disease would have been
treated, and your eye would have been saved. Is the optometrist
liable to you? Yes. Although optometrists are trained to recognize
symptoms of many eye diseases, they are not allowed to make
definite diagnoses of those diseases. That is the responsibility of
a qualified medical doctor—an ophthalmologist.

Providing You with Effective Treatment

Once your condition has been diagnosed, the doctor must—
to the extent possible by modern medicine—prescribe an effective
method of treatment to cure or alleviate the ailment. Does the
doctor guarantee to cure you? Usually not. The doctor promises
only to use his or her medical training, skill, and best efforts to
treat your condition.

Once in a while, a doctor will promise to cure a patient. If
that is the case, the patient can sue the doctor for breaking that
promise, even though the doctor did not technically commit malpractice. Some states require such guarantees to be in writing in
order to be valid. But telling you that you will be pleased with
the results of surgery or will feel like a new person afterward is
not a guarantee of any kind but, rather, merely a general ther-
apeutic assurance. If you aren't happy with the results, or if you
feel like your old self afterward, you can't sue your doctor if he
or she has done nothing wrong.

Suppose there is more than one approved way of treating
your condition. Is the doctor guilty of malpractice for choosing
one method over the other, even though the chosen method later
proves less desirable? Usually not. The doctor has the right to
use his or her "best judgment" to determine which course of
treatment appears best for you, based on your condition and

medical history. The doctor doesn't even have to use the method preferred by a majority of other doctors; only a "respectable minority" of physicians need endorse the type of treatment used. So long as the doctor follows the treatment procedure correctly, there is no malpractice, even if you do not respond as the doctor had hoped. When it becomes evident that you aren't responding to the treatment, however, then the doctor may be required to change course. Indeed, it may be malpractice if the doctor doesn't try something else if your condition doesn't show any improvement within a reasonable time.

Suppose your doctor has been treating you for six months, but you aren't getting any better. As a matter of fact, you feel worse now than you did the first time you saw the doctor. You decide to consult another doctor, who tells you that the other doctor has been using an unaccepted and experimental method of treating you. The second doctor prescribes an established treatment program for you, and within days your condition begins to show great improvement. Is your first doctor guilty of medical malpractice? Yes. Medicine must experiment to progress—that cannot be denied. But this does not give a doctor license to use you as a human guinea pig to try out experimental techniques, only to discover too late that the techniques are ineffective—even downright harmful. Your rights as a patient dictate that accepted, effective, and safe treatments be used first. Only after established treatments fail should experimental treatment be considered— and then only if there is some reasonable medical basis for believing that it may work without unnecessarily endangering the life or health of the patient. Before the doctor can administer an unproven treatment, he or she must tell you that it is new and experimental and that neither its effectiveness nor its side effects are fully known.

Your Right to a Second Opinion

Before undergoing any type of surgery, you should usually seek a second opinion from another doctor. (But never postpone an operation to get a second opinion without first asking your doctor if the delay may worsen your condition.) Each year unnecessary operations needlessly subject many patients to the risks and complications inherent in every surgery. You have a right to a second opinion, and if the first doctor is put off by this, so be it. Most patients, however, will be pleasantly surprised to find how receptive their doctors are to their getting a second opinion. In fact, many doctors suggest that their patients get a second opinion, particularly if the patient has any doubt about whether the operation is necessary. Sometimes the doctor, on his or her own initiative, will ask another doctor to evaluate a patient's condition to confirm the need for surgery.

Many insurance companies now encourage you to get second opinions and even pay some or all of the cost of having another doctor review the case to see if surgery is necessary. This benefits the insurance company because it saves money by reducing the number of unnecessary and expensive surgeries. Review your policy to determine whether it covers second opinions, and contact your health insurance representative if you're not sure. Medicare pays for second opinions at the same rate that it pays for other services, and most state Medicaid programs also cover much of the cost of second opinions.

Your Right to Know the Risks

Before performing any diagnostic procedures or offering treatment of any kind, the doctor normally must have your consent. You can give your permission to the doctor in writing or orally. Frequently your permission is implied by your conduct: you call the doctor's office, make an appointment, show up, and let the doctor examine and treat you, even though you never once expressly tell the doctor that he or she can examine you. In the case of a minor or mentally incompetent person, the consent of a parent or legal guardian is usually required. A minor may not need parental consent to obtain an abortion (see chapter 1) or a birth control device. If the doctor touches or treats you without your consent, he or she may be liable for committing the intentional tort of battery (see chapter 8).

One instance when a doctor can treat you without first getting your consent, however, is when you are unconscious and in need of emergency treatment to save your life. The law assumes that you would have consented to the treatment had you been conscious, and therefore your consent is implied. For example, Sally is severely injured and knocked unconscious in a car accident. She is rushed to the hospital, and emergency treatment is administered to save her life. When Sally regains consciousness, she is distraught to learn that she received a blood transfusion, since this is contrary to her religious beliefs. If she sues the doctor, however, the doctor will win. Even though Sally would not have permitted the blood transfusion if she had been asked, the doctor was unaware of her religious beliefs, and the blood transfusion was needed to save her life.

Consent is much more than just saying yes or no to a proposed treatment. If you don't understand the risks involved, your consent isn't worth much. You must give the doctor an "informed" consent, one based on all the facts. To enable you to do this, the doctor must explain the risks of the procedure to you, as well as the alternatives: what other procedures are available and what their risks are. The doctor must also inform you of the dangers of not treating the condition.

Suppose a doctor prescribes medication to a pregnant woman but fails to warn her of one important side effect: the drug can cause birth defects. The woman later gives birth to a deformed baby, and a thorough investigation establishes that the drug caused the deformities. The woman did not give an informed consent to the drug treatment because she wasn't aware of all important facts and risks. If she had known of the hazards to the child, she could have chosen a less dangerous drug or some other type of treatment. Or, if her condition was not life-threatening, she could have postponed treatment until after the baby was born.

If you were facing surgery, and there was a less drastic alternative—drug therapy, for example—you'd want to know. And if that is a reasonable alternative, the doctor must tell you so, even if the doctor prefers surgery. The doctor can recommend one procedure over the other but must at least explain both alternatives, what their dangers are, their rates of success, and the like. The final decision, however, is yours and yours alone to make.

A doctor must even inform you of the risks of refusing to submit to a risk-free diagnostic examination. In one incident, a woman decided not to undergo a Pap smear, a simple and painless procedure designed to detect cervical and other vaginal cancers. Although the doctor recommended the procedure, he did not tell the woman why it was important and what could happen if she turned it down. The woman later died of cancer of the cervix. The court held that the doctor should have advised the woman of the risks of declining the Pap smear. Since she had no idea why the test was important, the woman did not give an "informed rejection."

Who determines how much information you need to be told, you or the doctor? In some states, your doctor must disclose only the amount of information that *other* doctors disclose to *their* patients. Other states apply the rule that the amount of information the doctor must disclose is set by the patient's needs and desires. Under this standard, the doctor must inform you of all "material" risks—risks that a reasonable person would consider important in deciding whether or not to proceed with the proposed treatment. What are considered material risks? Death, loss of limb, paralysis, brain damage, or any other serious injuries certainly are material and must always be disclosed to the patient if they are a possibility.

Say that before surgery you sign a written informed consent form handed to you by the doctor, a nurse, or a hospital administrator. Does this prevent you from later suing the doctor or hospital for operating without your informed consent? No. The issue isn't whether or not you signed a piece of paper. Rather, it is whether the risks of and alternatives to the treatment were fully explained to you. Blanket consent forms often do not apprise you of just what risks apply to your treatment. A written consent form is no substitute for a doctor's complete explanation of the risks of the proposed treatment and the alternatives. In fact, the doctor may even tell you that signing the form is "just a formality." If the doctor assures you that nothing will go wrong, and something does go wrong, you can sue and win despite what the form you signed states.

As another example, suppose your doctor tells you that there is a 90 percent chance that a proposed operation will be successful and a 10 percent chance that it will not improve your condition. You sign an informed consent form, and the doctor operates, but your condition is worse after the operation than it was before. Your doctor never said the operation could make your condition worse, and had you known there was that danger, you never would have agreed to the operation. You can sue your doctor for operating without your informed consent, despite the fact you signed the consent form.

A doctor isn't always required to inform you of the risks before treating you, however. If it's an emergency, the doctor can go ahead and treat you without advising you of the risks. As one court noted, a doctor need not discuss possible consequences and methods of treatment with a snake-bite victim while the venom is being pumped through the victim's body.

If you are likely to become so upset by news of the risks that you won't be able to make a rational decision or it would hinder treatment, the doctor again does not have to tell you of those risks. For example, a patient who was paralyzed from an operation for a suspected aneurysm (a bulge in an artery caused by a weakening of its wall) sued his doctor for failing to inform him that the operation could paralyze him. The information had been withheld because the patient was extremely nervous and suffered from coronary and kidney disease, and the doctor feared that the patient's health would be seriously jeopardized if he were told of the risks. The court dismissed the patient's lawsuit because under the circumstances, the doctor was clearly justified in withholding the information from the patient.

Your consent to an operation can be conditional, and the doctor must honor those conditions. Suppose a pregnant woman tells her doctor to perform a sterilization procedure (tubal ligation) after her child is born—but only if the baby is healthy and free of any abnormalities. The doctor delivers an obviously deformed child but does the tubal ligation anyway. Will the woman win if she sues the doctor? Yes. The doctor has committed malpractice because the woman's consent was based upon the birth of a healthy, normal baby. Some states hold the doctor liable for the intentional tort of battery (see chapter 8) in this situation.

Let's say that you've agreed to an operation to remove a gallstone. While you're under the knife, the surgeon decides to remove your appendix. Is the surgeon liable to you for removing your appendix without your consent? That depends on whether the appendix posed an immediate threat to your life or health. If your appendix was healthy, the surgeon was legally wrong in taking it out. But if your appendix was diseased and ready to burst, jeopardizing your life, the surgeon would be justified in removing it.

Suppose that the day after surgery, you learn that a medical student or a doctor you never heard of actually performed the operation, rather than the surgeon you thought was going to do it. Can you sue the person who did the surgery for operating without your consent? Yes. Ordinarily you must be informed of exactly who will be doing the surgery. If someone else steps in without your knowledge and consent—so-called ghost surgery—he or she can be held liable for committing battery on you.

Ending the Physician-Patient Relationship

If you are not satisfied with your doctor and decide to find another, your doctor can't stop you from leaving. You can uni-

laterally terminate the doctor's services, with or without a reason—
—even without notifying the doctor. Your doctor must forward
your medical records to your new doctor at your request. All your
old doctor is entitled to is to be paid for all medical services
rendered up to the time you leave.

But just as you have the right to end the doctor's services
unilaterally, the doctor has a right to unilaterally stop treating
you. There is, however, one important restriction on the doctor's
right to cut you off: he or she cannot simply abandon you if you
still need treatment. The doctor must give you a fair amount of
time to find a new doctor and must continue treating you until
that time passes.

Getting Copies of Your
Medical Records

Suppose you want to look at your medical records. Or suppose you want your lawyer to review them to see if you have
grounds to sue your doctor or a hospital for malpractice. Must
the doctor or hospital honor your request and give you your
records or copies of them? Until recently, you ordinarily couldn't
just go in and ask to see your records, let alone copy them. About
the only time you could get access to your medical records was
if you sued your doctor for malpractice. Why couldn't you see
your records? Doctors felt that medical records were beyond the
understanding of the average patient, and reading them could
unnecessarily frighten the patient. Doctors also contended that
the records and charts were prepared only as work sheets for
medical personnel and were never intended for review by the
patient. Some doctors feared that the patient—or the patient's
lawyer—would find some mistakes or omissions and would respond with a malpractice suit.

Today, many states let you obtain copies of your medical
records simply by making a written request to the hospital or your
doctor and paying a reasonable charge to have them photocopied.

Patients in Veterans Administration hospitals have had this right since 1974, when the Federal Privacy Act was passed.

How Malpractice Affects You and Your Doctor

The Medical "Conspiracy of Silence"

Since the average juror usually can't tell whether a doctor was careless or if the injury was just "one of those things" that occasionally happen, in most malpractice lawsuits you must have a doctor testify on your behalf that the doctor who treated you committed malpractice. Before 1970, this requirement stopped many potential malpractice suits dead in their tracks. It wasn't that the cases were unfounded; rather, it was nearly impossible to find a doctor who would criticize a colleague, in or out of court, even if the claim of malpractice was fully justified. The hesitancy of doctors to criticize colleagues has come to be known as the "conspiracy of silence." This conspiracy is not imaginary. Back in 1956, the Supreme Court of Kentucky acknowledged its existence when it observed: "The notorious unwillingness of members of the medical profession to testify against one another may impose an insuperable handicap upon a plaintiff who cannot obtain professional proof."

Why are doctors unwilling to speak badly of a fellow doctor's performance? The main reasons are fear of ostracism by colleagues or medical societies; "professional courtesy" or loyalty to fellow practitioners; a belief that if they protect their colleagues, their colleagues will protect them if necessary; and fear that even if they never commit malpractice, their medical malpractice insurance rates will get out of hand as a result of large verdicts against doctors who have erred.

How strong is this conspiracy of silence today? Generally, not as strong as it used to be. In metropolitan areas, it is relatively easy to find a doctor to testify against a colleague who has committed malpractice. But in rural areas, it is still difficult to get a local doctor to testify against a fellow practitioner in the same area, making it necessary in many cases to get a doctor from another city to testify.

The Medical Malpractice "Crisis"

The mid-1970s saw the beginning of the widely publicized medical malpractice "crisis," with insurance companies, hospitals, and doctors claiming financial hardship from the growing number of malpractice lawsuits. The crisis subsided for a bit but reared its head anew in 1983. What exactly is this crisis?

Insurance companies, hospitals, and doctors contend that because of a startling increase in both the number of medical malpractice lawsuits and the amounts of money sympathetic juries are awarding, medical costs and malpractice insurance premiums are rising out of sight. At one point, threats abounded that unless something was done, insurance premiums would soar to the point where many hospitals would be forced to close their doors and thousands of doctors would quit practicing medicine. Some doctors have gone "bare" and are practicing medicine without malpractice insurance. (These doctors are taking a big chance: if they are sued by a patient and lose, their life's savings could be wiped out.)

Obstetricians especially have felt the brunt of higher insurance costs, for their position has been complicated by the already high costs of medical care and advances in medicine. Take, for example, the case of an obstetrician who commits malpractice while delivering a baby. Say the umbilical cord gets wrapped around the baby's neck and cuts off the flow of oxygen to its brain. Not long ago, the baby might have died; today, however, life-saving techniques can save many babies, but sometimes at a high price. Often a child in this situation suffers serious brain damage; the child may never be able to care for itself and may require frequent medical care and round-the-clock nursing care for the rest of his or her life. These costs are enormous, amounting to millions of dollars over the child's lifetime.

On the other side of the fence, lawyers for malpractice victims claim that the only "crisis" is that so much medical malpractice is happening in the first place. They claim that the problem of increasing costs stems not so much from sue-happy patients as from shoddy medical treatment. The focus, they contend, should be on getting rid of bad doctors and on improving medical care—not on adding to the malpractice victim's burden by making it harder for him or her to sue a careless doctor.

How the Malpractice "Crisis" Affects You

Whether or not there ever was a true "crisis," the fact remains that insurance companies, hospitals, and doctors began an intensive lobbying effort at national and state levels to make it more difficult for you to sue a doctor for malpractice. These efforts have proven quite successful, resulting in the passage of many laws favorable to doctors and insurance companies. These laws vary from state to state and cover a wide range of subjects. Here are a few examples: requiring you to submit your case to arbitration before you can file suit in court; limiting the amount of money you can recover for some types of damages, such as "pain and suffering"; requiring that your lawyer send the doctor a letter informing him or her a certain amount of time—say 90 days—beforehand that you will be filing suit; requiring you to get a certificate from another doctor stating that he or she has reviewed the facts of your case and feels that the malpractice suit is warranted; and limiting how much the attorney who represents the victim can charge (though there are no limits on how much the lawyer representing the doctor or insurance company can charge).

Many of the laws were passed ostensibly to weed out non-meritorious cases against doctors. But two reasons unconnected with insurance costs have already greatly reduced the threat of spurious lawsuits against physicians: (1) Lawyers representing victims on a contingency fee basis will not accept a case if it doesn't appear that the doctor was negligent and that there's a reasonable chance of success, and (2) doctors are fighting back by suing patients and lawyers for malicious prosecution (see chapter 8) if the malpractice suit was unjustified.

How has the medical malpractice crisis changed the practice of medicine? Some doctors now view every patient as a threat, a potential adversary in a malpractice suit. New patients may be evaluated for "litigiousness"—will they be likely to sue the doctor? There is even a company doctors can call to find out whether a new patient has ever sued a doctor before. (Lawyers who represent victims of doctors' negligence are responding with lists of doctors who have been sued for malpractice.) Some doctors are becoming more detached from their patients, dealing in a colder, more businesslike manner than before. Some are even practicing "defensive medicine," with an eye as much toward defending a lawsuit as toward whether the treatment is appropriate or necessary in a particular case.

10

PRODUCTS LIABILITY

A FAULTY ELECTRIC HEATER causes a fire; a house burns down, and the family inside is killed. A man walking behind a car that is idling in park is run over when the transmission slips into reverse. A five-year-old girl is paralyzed when the heavy lid on her toy trunk falls onto her neck as she is reaching inside it. A teenager's arm is severed when the soda pop bottle he has just taken from the refrigerator explodes in his hand. A young woman's nightgown brushes against a stove burner and bursts into fire, severely burning her; she is permanently disfigured.

Hundreds of millions of products of every type and description are made each year. Mass production and mass consumption of products has also meant mass injuries. Statistics released by the Consumer Product Safety Commission (CPSC) show that 28,000 Americans die and 33,000,000 others are injured annually in accidents involving consumer products. Many others are harmed by products that do not come under the jurisdiction of the CPSC—industrial and farming machines, for example. Sometimes the injuries are the fault of the person using the product; other times, the injuries are purely accidental, the fault of neither man nor machine. Many injuries, however, are caused by products that are defective in one way or another—products that, if they had been made safely, would not have caused the injury.

A hundred years ago, if you were injured by a defective

product, you were pretty much left out in the cold when it came to trying to collect damages for your injuries from the manufacturer or seller. Caveat emptor—buyer beware—was the order of the day. The law assumed that you had ample opportunity to inspect the product for defects before buying it; if you decided the product was safe enough when you bought it, you could not later claim otherwise.

Caveat emptor developed in a time when products were much simpler than they are today. There were fewer products, with fewer moving parts. You could usually tell if something was built well by looking it over carefully, even trying it out a time or two. You didn't have to be a mechanical engineer to inspect a buggy for sound construction.

The average modern consumer is generally incapable of determining whether many products are safe and sound—even if given the chance to inspect and test them prior to purchase. Often, many components are hidden from view and can't be inspected without taking the whole product apart. And even if you could take the cover off, say, a television set or other product before buying it, you would need degrees in electrical engineering and many other disciplines to determine whether the product was safely designed and built. (You'd also probably void any warranty that came with the product if you took it apart before buying it to see if it was made properly.)

Liability of a Product Manufacturer or Seller

The Law of Strict Products Liability

One of the most important developments in the law regarding consumer protection is the birth of the doctrine of "strict products liability," which makes it much easier for you to recover damages from a manufacturer or seller when you are injured by a defective product. Strict products liability has also served as a strong incentive for manufacturers to design and make safer products.

Under strict products liability, a product manufacturer or seller is liable for marketing a defective product that is "unreasonably dangerous" and causes injury to the unwary consumer or user. All you need to show is that the product was defective and was allowed to get into the stream of commerce and that your injuries were caused by the product's defect. You normally do not have to prove that anyone was negligent. (Negligence—someone's specific and identifiable carelessness in designing or making the product—remains important only in the few states that have not yet adopted the law of strict products liability. In all other states, negligence is usually nothing more than a lawyer's academic addendum to the complaint.)

The rationale behind strict liability is that, as a part of its cost of doing business, a manufacturer must compensate consumers for injuries sustained from a defective product. The manufacturer can pass along the expense to the consumer by increasing the price of each unit sold. The consumer bears the ultimate cost, but when that cost is spread among hundreds of thousands or even millions of consumers, it is minimal as far as each consumer is concerned.

Say that you buy a new air conditioner at American Hardware Store and have it installed in your house by Tom's Air Conditioning Installation and Service Company. The first time you turn the air conditioner on, it blows up and injures you. It turns out that when the air conditioner was made, someone at the factory reversed two wires. American Hardware Store is strictly liable to you, since it sold you the unit. The company that made it is strictly liable as well. But how about Tom's? Is it also strictly liable for your injuries? No. The law of strict products liability does not apply to persons who are primarily engaged in the business of providing a service—installers, repairpeople, cleaners, doctors, lawyers, accountants, and so on. Tom's did not sell you the air conditioner; it merely provided the service of installing it.

Tom's would be liable for your injuries only if it installed the air conditioner incorrectly, and that mistake caused your injuries.

Suppose you buy a used toaster from Andy's Thrift Store, take it home, plug it in, and it blows up. Your house burns down, and everything in it is destroyed. Does strict liability apply to Andy's? In most states, no; strict liability applies only to those who deal in new products. Andy's is liable to you only if it was negligent in some way—if, for instance, Andy's had repaired the toaster, and its faulty repair work caused the fire. Some states do apply strict liability to persons who regularly sell used merchandise, and would make Andy's pay you. This rule does not apply to a person who occasionally sells his or her unwanted items at a garage sale or swap meet, for example.

What Makes a Product Defective

There are three broad types of product defects: (1) defects in making the product—"manufacturing defects"; (2) defects in the product's design; and (3) failure to give the consumer adequate instructions concerning use or assembly of the product or sufficient warnings concerning its dangers.

Manufacturing Defects

A "manufacturing defect" is one that happens when the product is being produced. Something happens so that the product that hurts you is made differently from the others: a nut isn't tightened, a weld is missed, the wrong type of metal is used, a smaller screw or nut and bolt are substituted for the proper size, the product is subjected to too much (or not enough) heat or cold, a piece is missing, or the product is assembled improperly. The result is that the product is not made according to specifications and leaves the factory in a faulty and dangerous condition.

Design Defects

A design defect exists when something is wrong in the specifications for the product; the product is inherently dangerous even when made according to the plans. An example will help explain the difference between a manufacturing defect and a design defect. Suppose that you are injured when your car axle breaks. Metallurgists examine the axle and find that the metal was too weak to support the weight of the car. If the design for the car called for a stronger metal to be used—one that would have supported the weight of the car—the defect is one of manufacturing, because an inferior grade of metal was in fact used. But if the design called for the grade of metal that was actually used—the inferior grade—then the defect is one in design. All cars made according to the design would share the same defect: a weak axle that is likely to fail.

A product's design can also be defective because it omits adequate safety devices to protect against injuries. A power saw, for instance, must be equipped with a guard over the top part of the blade to prevent injuries. Lack of safety devices is especially important in commercial, industrial, and farming machinery. One slip by the worker or other user could mean the loss of an arm, a leg—even his or her life. Machines must therefore be designed with an eye to protecting the user from accidents that are likely to happen.

Since hundreds of thousands of automobile accidents occur every year, an automobile manufacturer can expect its products to be involved in an accident. A motor vehicle must therefore be designed to withstand a certain amount of contact with other vehicles and stationary objects, such as telephone poles. Because of the foreseeability of accidents, an automobile manufacturer must design its products to be reasonably "crashworthy." For example, cars flip over in some accidents. Accordingly, the manufacturer must make the roof of the car strong enough to support the weight of the car, to prevent it from collapsing and allowing the occupants to be crushed should the car roll over. The car only has to be crashworthy, not crashproof. A manufacturer is not required to design a car that will provide protection in all situations. For instance, no car is expected to withstand crashes and flips at, say, 100 miles per hour.

Lack of Adequate Instructions or Warnings

A product can be defective because it does not come with complete instructions on how to use it correctly or because consumers aren't sufficiently warned of its dangers. Products that the consumer assembles must include clear and complete instructions to ensure that the product is put together properly.

Certain dangers are inherent in some products, and removing the dangers would remove the effectiveness—indeed, the purpose—of the products. Drain cleaners, for instance, often contain caustic chemicals without which they couldn't do their job. When a product has a danger that cannot be removed, the manufacturer must warn purchasers and users of the product of its dangers. The warning must be specific. A generalized statement such as "Warning: Dangerous If Used Incorrectly" isn't enough; it doesn't tell you why or how the product is dangerous. A warning that doesn't expressly designate each and all of the product's dangers that can cause serious injury is not legally adequate.

Does a manufacturer have to place a warning on a knife stating that the blade is sharp and could cut somebody, or that a bow and arrow can hurt others? No. A manufacturer need not warn of dangers that are obvious and understood, even expected, by everyone. In one case involving the sale of a slingshot to a young boy, the manufacturer was not liable for failing to include a warning of the dangers of a slingshot. The court stated: "Ever since David slew Goliath, young and old alike have known that slingshots can be dangerous and deadly. There is no need to include a warning. . . ." Similarly, it has been held that there is no need for a manufacturer to warn of the dangers of shooting a BB gun at another person.

The warning on a product must be conspicuous; it must catch

the attention of the average person and must be written in language that is readily comprehensible to the average consumer. When non-English–speaking people can be expected to use the product, the manufacturer may be required to communicate the warning by signs or even in other languages.

Inadequate Packaging

An important development in the law of products liability involves defects in packaging. (Technically, this is a subcategory of design defects.) For example, dangerous household chemicals should be sold in childproof containers; if they are not, the manufacturer may be liable if a child gets into the product and swallows it, for example. If the product cannot be made child-safe, it must be accompanied by clear warnings of its specific dangers and cautions that it should be kept out of the reach of children.

In 1982, seven people in the Chicago area died after taking the pain reliever Tylenol, which had been laced with cyanide. The bottles had been deliberately contaminated by an unknown person sometime after they left the factory. As a result of this tragedy, manufacturers have become increasingly aware of the need to make a tamper-resistant product. Most packages of headache relievers and similar products are now sealed in various ways to reduce the possibility of undetected tampering. Some manufacturers, for example, place a plastic seal around the box or a seal over the lid of the bottle, or both. But there are still thousands of other products on the supermarket shelves that are vulnerable to tampering that leaves no signs behind to arouse the innocent shopper's suspicions.

How far must a manufacturer go to protect its product from intentional outside interference? This question is far from resolved. But one thing is certain: the manufacturer must take some precautions to prevent tampering with its product after it leaves the factory. The question is really one of cost versus benefit. The manufacturer's cost to make each package tamper-resistant is minimal and can be passed on to the consumer by an insignificant increase in the price of each product. On the other hand, there is a great benefit to the consumer—protection against serious injury or death.

When a Manufacturer Knowingly Markets a Dangerous Product

Sometimes a manufacturer or seller knows that its product is likely to cause great harm but still lets it reach the public without removing or warning of the danger. This was the charge against Ford Motor Company in a suit involving the Ford Pinto. Richard Grimshaw was a passenger in a Pinto when it stalled on the freeway. Another car rammed into it from behind. The Pinto's gas tank exploded, and Grimshaw was severely burned. Grimshaw and his lawyers contended that Ford had known of the dangers associated with the gas tank, yet had not taken prompt steps to correct the problem or at least warn the public. Grimshaw's attorneys discovered that Ford had conducted a cost-analysis survey that compared the costs of lawsuits against Ford for deaths and injuries resulting from the gas tank with the cost of eliminating the problem. The analysis concluded that by leaving the problem uncorrected, Ford would save $100,000,000, and this even after paying for expected deaths and injuries. To correct the problem—at the expense of $11 per car for 12,500,000 cars—would have cost Ford $137,500,000. Other documents showed that Ford decided to delay changing the fuel tank to save over $20,000,000. The jury awarded $2,800,000 in compensatory damages and $125,000,000 in punitive damages. The judge reduced the award to $3,500,000, and the case was later settled out of court while on appeal.

Express Warranties and Defectiveness

Express warranties are the bases for some lawsuits when a person is injured, even though the product is not defective in the usual sense. An express warranty is created when the manufac-

turer or seller makes a specific promise or representation concerning the quality or ability of its product. Manufacturers often
make certain statements in their advertisements to entice you to
buy their product, and you naturally rely on the truth of these
statements when buying the product. Suppose you weigh 225
pounds, for example, and need a ladder. You want to make sure
that the ladder you buy will support your weight, so you buy the
one whose label states that it can hold 250 pounds. But back at
home, the ladder buckles under your weight when you climb it.
You fall to the floor and are injured. The manufacturer must pay
for your injuries even if the ladder was designed and made properly, because the label constitutes an express warranty. The ladder
could not do what the manufacturer distinctly said it could, and
this is why it is "defective."

Suing for Your Injuries
If You've Been Hurt by a
Defective Product

Can You Sue?

At one time, you could sue a product manufacturer or seller
only if you were in contractual "privity" with it. This meant that
you had to have bought the defective product directly from the
manufacturer or the seller to be allowed to sue for your injuries.
This requirement came from the historic 1842 English case of
Winterbottom v. Wright. Mr. Winterbottom was seriously injured
when the mail coach he was driving broke down because it had
not been kept in good repair by Mr. Wright, who had a contract
with the postmaster general to keep the coaches in safe condition.
Mr. Winterbottom sued Mr. Wright, but the judges threw the

case out of court because Mr. Winterbottom did not have a contract (was not "in privity") with Mr. Wright. The postmaster general, the court declared, was the only party who could sue, because it was to him that Mr. Wright had promised his services. One judge commented that if Mr. Winterbottom were allowed to sue, then "every passenger, or even any person passing along the road, who was injured by the upsetting of the coach, might bring a similar action. Unless we confine the operation of such contracts as this to the parties who entered into them, the most absurd and outrageous consequences, to which I can see no limit, would ensue."

American courts generally required privity until 1916, when Judge Benjamin Cardozo of the New York Court of Appeals (New York's highest court) handed down the decision in the famous case of *McPherson v. Buick Motor Co.* Mr. McPherson was injured when the wooden wheel on the car in which he was riding crumbled and he was thrown from the car. Judge Cardozo decreed that if the manufacturer knows that its product will be used by persons other than the purchaser, the manufacturer owes a duty to these persons to make the product carefully, lack of contractual privity notwithstanding.

Today the purchaser of a defective product can sue the manufacturer even though he or she didn't buy it directly from the manufacturer. You can also sue if you weren't the actual purchaser of the product but were an "ultimate user" of it. An ultimate user is someone who is likely to use the product: a member of the purchaser's household, a friend, an employee, or a person who buys the product from the original purchaser, among others. But what if you neither bought the product nor were using it, but you were merely a bystander injured by the product? For example, you are walking down a sidewalk. The steering linkage of a car breaks, sending the car out of control. The car jumps the curb and hits you, or you are injured when you fall jumping out of the car's way. Is the manufacturer strictly liable for your injuries? In most states, yes. A few states, however, have refused to extend strict liability beyond consumers and users of the prod-

uct. (You might, nevertheless, be able to collect from the manufacturer if you can prove that it was negligent in making or
designing the product.)

Who Is Liable for Your Injuries?

If you are injured or your property is damaged by a defective
product, you can sue the manufacturer, distributor, wholesaler,
retailer, and anyone else involved in the chain of distribution—
the "stream of commerce"—for your damages. Let's say that you
are injured by a defective lawnmower. The lawnmower was made
by X Corporation and is distributed nationally by Y Company.
Z Wholesalers markets it in your state, and you bought it at Joe's
Lawn and Garden Shop. You can sue all of them for your injuries.

Suppose Acme Department Store markets its own brand of
clothes. The clothes are made by Fashion, Inc., which also sells
clothes nationwide under its own name. You buy a sweater with
the Acme label (made by Fashion, Inc.) and are hurt when an
errant cigarette touches the sweater and it goes up instantly in
flames. Is Acme strictly liable to you because the sweater was not
sufficiently fire-retardant, even though Fashion, Inc., not it, actually made the sweater? Yes. A company that puts its label on
a product made by another and markets it as its own is deemed
a manufacturer. Some department stores, for example, put their
own names on tools, appliances, and clothes made by other companies. When they do, they are liable as if they had made the
products themselves. Would Fashion, Inc., the actual makers of
the defective sweater, also be liable for your injuries? That depends on the type of defect and Fashion, Inc.'s involvement. If
it is a manufacturing defect—the wrong material was used, or the
fabric was doused with some highly flammable liquid—then Fashion, Inc. is jointly liable with Acme Department Store. But if
Acme furnished the specifications for the product, and Fashion,
Inc. made it according to the designs, Fashion, Inc. usually isn't
liable. In some states, Fashion, Inc. would be liable if the design

was clearly dangerous, and it did not eliminate the danger or put an adequate warning to consumers on the product.

Limitations on the Manufacturer's Liability

If you are injured by a defective product, there are several factors that can relieve the manufacturer or seller of liability in whole or in part. One restriction is that the product must reach the consumer in substantially the same condition as it left the factory. If the product was significantly altered by a supplier, seller, or the consumer himself, the manufacturer ordinarily is not liable if the injury is attributable to the change. This rule does not apply to products that require some alteration after they leave the factory so they can be used, however—in particular, products that you must put together before you can use them. Also, the manufacturer remains liable if the alteration had nothing to do with the cause of the injury.

Suppose the head on your new hammer is loose and flies off while you're using it, hitting you in the face and knocking out an eye. Whether the manufacturer is liable for your injuries depends on whether you knew the head was loose before you used it. If you didn't know it was loose, you can collect damages from the manufacturer, even if an inspection of the hammer before you used it would have revealed the defect. But if you realized the head was loose and still went ahead and used the hammer, you may be barred from suing the manufacturer because you assumed the risk that the head could come off.

Now suppose that you are an employee and you realize that the machine you work with is defective. You inform your boss that the machine is dangerous and that you don't want to use it. Your boss tells you that if you don't get back to work on it immediately, you'll be fired on the spot. You go back to the machine and 20 minutes later are hurt. Is the machine's manufacturer off the hook because you assumed the risk that the defective machine could hurt you? At one time you *would* have been barred from recovering your damages from the manufacturer. Today, though, the courts are beginning to recognize that employees who use machines may be doing so not because they assume the risk of being injured, but rather out of fear that they will be fired if they don't. When it comes right down to it, the employee really doesn't have much of a choice. Therefore, an employee who continues to use a defective machine rather than face unemployment often can sue the manufacturer if the machine injures him or her. (Workers' compensation laws usually prevent the employee from suing the employer; see the discussion in chapter 11.)

The fact that you assume some risks of being hurt by a product does not prevent you from suing if your injury was caused by a risk you didn't expect. When you use an ax, for instance, you assume the risk that if you are careless, you can injure yourself or others. But you don't assume the risk that the ax is defective in any way. Suppose you are chopping wood with a new ax, and the wooden handle breaks, and the blade cuts your leg. The manufacturer is liable for your injuries. Similarly, if the blade is made from an inferior material and breaks or splinters while you're using it correctly, the manufacturer must pay for your injuries. Clearly, these dangers are beyond what you normally expect when using an ax.

To avoid or reduce their liability, manufacturers frequently assert that the person was misusing the product at the time he or she was hurt. But just because you were using a product for something other than its primary function when you were injured doesn't mean that you can't sue the manufacturer. Suppose you want to hang a picture high on the wall—too high for you to reach—so you stand on a chair. The chair breaks under your weight, and you are injured. Are you barred from suing the manufacturer or seller because you were using the chair in other than its intended manner? No. The issue is whether your misuse of the product was "reasonably foreseeable" or not. A manufacturer of a chair can expect someone to stand on its product, so a chair must be designed and made strong enough to withstand a person's full weight. On the other hand, the maker of, say, a glass soda bottle would not expect people to use it as a hammer. If someone does and the bottle shatters and hurts persons nearby, the manufacturer of the bottle is not liable. Even if the manufacturer could expect that someone might use the bottle as a hammer, it would be impossible to make a glass bottle that could survive such a use intact.

The growing number of lawsuits against product manufacturers and sellers has prompted action by the product industry to put limitations on consumers' lawsuits. The most common restriction is on the length of time (the "statute of limitations") you have to sue the manufacturer, wholesaler, or seller. Usually statutes of limitations address how long you have to sue after you have been *injured*—one or two years after the date you were hurt, for example. The new laws, however, speak to when suit must be brought after the product was *first sold*. For instance, the statute may require you to sue the manufacturer no more than four years after the product was sold to the original purchaser. But if you're hurt five years after it was first sold, you can't sue, even if you'd never used the product before. There have also been efforts—so far unsuccessful—by the product industry and their insurance carriers to get a federal products liability act passed, which would make it harder for injured consumers to sue and would place restrictions on the damages they could recover.

What to Do If You Are Hurt by a Product

The most important thing to do when you are hurt by a product—after getting proper medical attention, of course—is to keep the product. For example, if a bottle explodes, keep all of the pieces; if a child gets into a dangerous chemical, keep the container; if you are hurt by a machine that you rented, take pictures of it, write down the name of the manufacturer, the model, and the identification number and keep your receipts from the rental company. The product that hurt you is obviously a critical piece of evidence that may have to be analyzed by experts to determine exactly how the injury happened. But don't despair if you've already disposed of the product or if the product was consumed in the accident. In many cases, it is possible to construct the cause of the injury by analyzing other similar products.

When a defective product injures someone, a lawyer should usually be consulted as soon as possible. (Chapter 19 tells how to find a lawyer if you don't have one.) Don't hesitate to see a lawyer even if you think the injury was your fault. Frequently it turns out that many injuries that appear on the surface to be the user's fault are really due solely to a defective product. And even if the injury was partly your fault, under the rules of comparative negligence (see chapter 8)—called "comparative fault" in strict liability cases—you may still be able to collect part of your damages from the manufacturer, wholesaler, or seller.

11

EMPLOYEES

EMPLOYEES ARE COVERED by a wide range of laws dealing with many subjects: minimum wages, safe working conditions, the right to form a union, and so on. This chapter discusses the areas that today's working man and woman most frequently consult an attorney about: compensation for on-the-job injuries; race, sex, and age discrimination; sexual harassment; rights when a worker is fired without reason; ownership of patents and inventions made on the job; misuse of confidential information; and agreements not to compete.

Job Discrimination and Harassment

People should be hired, fired, and promoted on the basis of their ability to do the job—not because of their sex, their race, the color of their skin, their religious beliefs, and their national origin. Nor should they be subjected to intolerable working conditions and harassment because they are different from other workers. Many laws at both the federal and the state level guarantee just this.

The following discussion is limited to federal laws, which

generally apply only to employers who have more than 15 or 20 workers. Many states have their own laws (usually modeled on the federal laws) extending the same rights to employees of smaller businesses or to those not engaged in interstate commerce.

If You Are Discriminated Against Because of Your Race, Religion, or Sex

The federal Civil Rights Act of 1964 and the Equal Employment Opportunity Act of 1972 guarantee to all workers the right to be free from discrimination because of race, color, national origin, sex, and religious beliefs. In addition to protecting you from being fired or not being hired or promoted because of any of these things, these laws also ensure that you will be given the same training and opportunity for advancement, and equal pay for equal work.

Not all discrimination is unlawful. An employer can refuse to hire or promote you if a different race, color, national origin, sex, or religious belief is a "bona fide qualification" of the job. For instance, a woman cannot sue for sex discrimination if she is turned down for the job of men's locker room attendant, since being male would be a legitimate qualification for the job. True instances of permissible discrimination are rare, however.

Often discrimination takes a subtler form. Women have been discriminated against by job qualifications that specify certain minimum requirements regarding height, weight, and physical abilities that are not reasonably related to the job. The qualifications usually favor the average American male over the average American female. Many police forces, for example, used to have rather strict minimum requirements concerning height, weight, and physical abilities, which tended—intentionally or unintentionally—to discriminate against women who wanted to become police officers. But since many women could still do a police officer's job without meeting the minimum requirements, the requirements had to be revised so women were not discriminated against.

Suppose that you are black, and your boss wants to fire you because of your race. Your boss knows that it's against the law to fire you because of your race, so he or she waits for you to do the slightest thing wrong. And when you do, your boss immediately calls you into his or her office, tells you that the company can't tolerate employees who foul up, and fires you. You later discover that other workers—all of them white—had done the same thing wrong but weren't fired for it. If you sue your employer for unlawful discrimination, will you win? Yes. The fact that other workers of a different race were not terminated for the same mistake shows that your race and not your job performance was the motivating factor behind the decision to fire you.

If you claim that you were not hired or promoted because of your sex, you need to prove that you were qualified and that you applied for the job or promotion in question, that you were not hired or promoted although a vacancy existed, and that similarly situated members of the opposite sex with comparable qualifications were hired or promoted at the time your request for promotion was denied. Likewise, if you claim you were not hired or promoted because of your race or religion, you must prove that you were qualified for the job in question, that you applied for the position, and that other workers with comparable qualifications—but of a different race or religion—were given the job while you weren't. The first time you are passed over for a job, it may be difficult to prove that your employer was motivated by the wrong reason. But the second or third time the same employer passes you over, the intent will usually become clear.

Age Discrimination

The Age Discrimination in Employment Act, passed by Congress in 1967, makes it unlawful for employers of 20 or more employees to discriminate against you because of your age if you are between the ages of 40 and 70. If you fall within this bracket, an employer cannot refuse to hire you solely because of your age, nor can you be terminated or refused a promotion for this reason.

If you are under 70 years old, you cannot be forced to retire against your will unless a younger retirement age is a legitimate qualification of the job.

An obvious instance of age discrimination occurs when your boss tells you to your face that you are being terminated because of your age and that a younger employee is taking your place. Or an employer may tell a prospective employee that he or she is qualified for the position but is a "little older than we want." More often, however, claims of unlawful age discrimination are proved by circumstantial evidence: you are fired for no reason and a week or two later learn that a younger worker has replaced you. But just because your employer replaces you with a younger employee does not make your termination unlawful. Your employer can do this if there is a legitimate reason for firing you—if your job performance is substandard for a long period of time, for instance.

Sexual Harassment

As an employee, you have the right to be free from unwanted sexual advances and offensive or obscene remarks that make your working conditions uncomfortable or intolerable. We generally think of sexual harassment in terms of a female employee who is the target of the sexual advances or lewd behavior of male co-workers or bosses; this is certainly the most common type of sexual harassment. But sexual harassment also exists when a male employee is sexually harassed by a female supervisor or when any worker is sexually harassed by a fellow employee (or boss) of the same sex.

What type of conduct constitutes sexual harassment? The federal Equal Employment Opportunity Commission defines sexual harassment as any verbal or physical conduct of a sexual nature that unreasonably interferes with the performance of your job or that creates an intimidating, hostile, or offensive working environment. The conduct must be both undesirable and offensive. And it must be so significant and pervasive that it creates an abusive working environment, one that seriously affects your emotional or psychological well-being.

The clearest example of sexual harassment takes place when your superior requires you to submit to his or her sexual advances in order to keep your job or get a raise. Touching your genitals is also sexual harassment (and battery as well). If your boss or coworkers continuously make lewd comments and sexually offensive suggestions or jokes to you or frequently touch you in a sexually suggestive manner, that too is sexual harassment. In the case of coworkers who are sexually harassing you, your employer usually is not liable for sexual harassment unless he or she directly participates in the harassment or knows that other employees are sexually harassing you but doesn't do anything to correct the situation.

Casual or trivial events usually are not enough to constitute harassment; neither are most isolated events, such as a single obscene joke. But if your boss or coworkers persist in telling such jokes, it can be harassment—particularly if you make it clear that you are offended by lewd jokes and ask that they not be told in your presence. The more offensive the conduct is, the less frequency is required to constitute sexual harassment. For instance, if your supervisor asks you once to have sex with him or her to keep your job, that is sexual harassment even if the request is never renewed.

An essential element of sexual harassment is that it must be unwelcome. You can't complain of sexual harassment if you invited or otherwise encouraged the sexual advances or lewd remarks of your boss or coworkers. But this doesn't mean that you must put up with offensive conduct indefinitely. Even though you originally encouraged the remarks or conduct, you can change your mind and request that it now be stopped.

If the sexual harassment is less serious—say, crude jokes rather than pressure to have sex with your boss—you should talk to the offender directly or complain to both your supervisor and the offender's supervisor. Your employer must take prompt action to stop the harassment after you complain. If this doesn't make a significant difference or if the harassment is of a more serious nature, then other action (discussed below) is appropriate. You don't have to get used to the offensive conduct or lewd language; nor can your employer simply tell you to laugh it off, that your coworkers don't really mean anything by it.

What to Do If You Are a Victim of Discrimination or Harassment

If you feel that you have been the victim of unlawful discrimination or harassment, you should promptly file a complaint with the local office of the Equal Employment Opportunity Commission. Even if the commission doesn't have jurisdiction over your employer, it can usually advise you which federal or state agency to contact. Talk to your shop steward or union office if you belong to a union, and file a complaint there as well. It is usually a good idea to contact a lawyer to learn of your full rights and to consider other appropriate action, including a lawsuit, against the offender. You should take action as soon as you suspect that you are being unlawfully discriminated against. If you wait too long, you may lose the right to complain.

If you have been unlawfully fired, demoted, or not promoted because of your race, color, national origin, religion, or sex, you are entitled to be reinstated and to receive back pay starting with the date of your termination or demotion or the date when you should have been promoted. You may also be entitled to recover lost benefits, damages for your emotional suffering, and punitive damages as well. (You may also be eligible for workers' compensation benefits if you are unable to work because of the stress you suffered.) If, for some reason, you are fired and can't get your job back, you can recover damages in lieu of reinstatement. Your employer may also have to reimburse you for your attorney's fees.

Workers' Compensation Laws

A waitress carrying a tray slips on a loose tile, falls, and hurts her wrist; she is out of work for three weeks. A maintenance worker changing a light bulb falls off a ladder and is paralyzed, never to work again. A loading dock worker is run over by a forklift and killed. All of these workers have one thing in common: they or their families are probably entitled to receive workers' compensation benefits.

Workers' compensation laws are designed to provide an expeditious system of compensating an employee who was injured—or the family of an employee who was killed—in a work-related incident. Employers are required to purchase workers' compensation insurance to protect their employees. (Some states require employers to contribute to a state fund, out of which the benefits are paid to the injured employees.) In return, employers receive the guarantee that they generally can't be sued by their employees and exposed to the higher amounts a jury might award. Employees are guaranteed that they will receive benefits if they are injured on the job, regardless of who causes the injuries (unless the employee deliberately hurts himself or herself). Workers' compensation acts are also intended to reduce the role of attorneys, so that all or most of the benefits go to the injured employee.

Workers' compensation laws are based on the belief that "the cost of the product should bear the blood of the workman." In other words, as a cost of doing business, an employer is required to pay for injuries its employees suffer on the job. The employer offsets this increased cost of doing business by raising its prices to the general public. Spread out over thousands or millions of consumers, the increase is generally rather small.

Before there were workers' compensation acts, employees had a tough time collecting any money for their injuries or for the wages they lost when they were injured on the job and couldn't work for a time. It was true that they could sue their employers, but winning was a different story. First a worker had to prove that the employer caused the accident, which was not easy to do. And even if the worker succeeded, the employer still won many cases by claiming that the employee had assumed the risk of injury or had partially caused his or her own injuries. The so-called fellow servant rule usually barred the employee from suing co-workers who injured him or her.

Recognizing how unfair this situation was to injured workers, New York enacted the first workers' compensation act in 1910. Within the next ten years, most of the other states had passed similar laws. Today all 50 states and the federal government have workers' compensation laws, protecting about 90 percent of the nation's work force.

Have workers' compensation laws lived up to their goals? Not really. The biggest complaint is that the benefits paid to the injured worker are woefully inadequate, especially when the injuries are extensive. One court acknowledged this fact when it stated: "It is common knowledge that workmen injured or killed in construction work do not receive full compensation under the Workmen's Compensation Act for damages that they sustain, notwithstanding the commendable purpose of such legislation." In many cases, there are no time savings in processing an injured worker's claim because of administrative delays and lengthy appeals. And many employees—particularly those who are seriously injured—find that being represented by an experienced lawyer is essential to getting maximum benefits. So rather than alleviating the problem, in many cases, workers' compensation laws have made it worse.

Who Is Entitled to Receive Benefits

To be eligible for workers' compensation benefits, you must be an employee of a company at the time of the accident. All employees are presumed covered unless the law specifically excludes their class of workers from coverage. Farm workers, domestic help, voluntary workers, and people who work for nonprofit organizations are excluded from coverage in many states. Occasional temporary employees are not usually entitled to benefits, but regular part-time employees are. In some states, employers of only a small number of workers (usually fewer than three, four, or five) do not have to provide workers' compensation protection for their employees.

Suppose that you have your own air-conditioning business and are hired by Sunset Construction Company to install air conditioners in a new building. While doing so, part of the ceiling falls and injures you. Can you collect workers' compensation benefits? No. You are considered to be an "independent contractor" rather than an employee of the contracting company. If someone's negligence caused your injury, you can, however, sue the person who was negligent.

Limitations on Your Right to Benefits

Workers' compensation benefits are payable only if your injury is related to your job. The clearest example of a work-related injury occurs when you are hurt on your employer's premises during working hours, while you are doing your job and getting paid for it. You are also usually entitled to benefits if you are injured in the company lunchroom during a break.

Can you get benefits if you're injured in a traffic accident on the way to work? Usually not. Under the so-called going and coming rule, you generally are not entitled to workers' compensation benefits if you are injured while commuting to and from work. If, however, you are an outside salesman and call on clients between your home and the office, you are probably eligible for benefits in this situation.

You can't get benefits if you deliberately injure yourself. (But you can if you were injured by your own carelessness.) Many states deny you benefits if the injuries happened because you were drunk or high on drugs. But the intoxication must have been a cause of the accident. If you are walking down an aisle when a light bulb explodes and injures you, for instance, you can recover compensation benefits even if you were drunk, since your drunkenness had nothing to do with the accident.

Most workers' compensation acts also limit benefits to cases where *physical* injuries are suffered. Disease and illness often aren't covered by workers' compensation laws (but other laws may cover industrial diseases). Things like emotional distress and mental suffering, violation of your civil rights, defamation, or invasion of privacy are also beyond the scope of many workers' compensation acts, although, as discussed below, you may have the right to sue your employer or fellow employees.

How Benefits Are Determined

Each state has an exhaustive schedule regulating how much money is paid for a given type of injury. The benefits you receive depend on the seriousness and permanency of your injuries and the amount of your weekly salary. You'll get less for a temporary partial disability than for a complete and permanent disability. If you break your arm, for instance, you will be given a certain percentage of your weekly wage for a specified number of weeks. If you lose a foot, you will receive a larger amount for a longer period of time.

You are considered totally disabled if you can't work at your old job or at another job for which you are suited without experiencing substantial pain. But if you're able to work at another job without too much discomfort, you are only partially disabled. A temporary disability is one that is likely to last a certain period of time, whether several days, weeks, or months. You are permanently disabled when your physical condition, combined with your age, training, and experience, prevents you from obtaining anything more than sporadic employment for an indefinite period of time.

If you are killed in a work-related accident, your dependents are entitled to death benefits under the workers' compensation act. A "dependent" is typically defined as anyone living under the same roof as you and who received most of his or her support from you. Does this mean that your spouse doesn't get anything if he or she earned more than you? No. Your spouse is entitled to full death benefits (up to the maximum) regardless of whether he or she made more than you.

How to Claim Your Benefits

When you suffer a work-related injury, you should notify your employer or supervisor as soon as possible and ask for a claim form to fill out. You will have to report the basic information—where, when, and how you were injured—and submit proof of your injury, including doctor's bills. If your claim is accepted, your benefits should commence promptly, usually on a weekly basis. If your claim is partly or completely denied, you can have it reviewed by the workers' compensation appeals board. You can sue the workers' compensation appeals board if you don't agree with its decision, and have the extent of your disability and the amount of your benefits decided in court.

You usually don't need an attorney to help you with your workers' compensation claim, at least not if your injury is relatively minor and you are out of work for only a short time. This type of claim is processed routinely and quickly, and you should get full benefits with no problem. But if the injury is fairly serious, or the worker was killed, it is best to be represented by an attorney. You should certainly hire an attorney if problems arise in the processing of your claim or if you plan to appeal your claim.

When Even Maximum Benefits Are Too Small

Anytime workers' compensation benefits don't adequately protect you, you should consider whether your employer, a fellow employee, or a third party was responsible for the accident and is liable for the rest of your damages. This is an especially important concern in cases involving serious injuries or death. For example, a widow and three children would be hard-pressed to live on the maximum death benefits of, say, $50,000 for more than a few years. The following situations are among the more common ones when you can sue others for job-related injuries.

Suing Your Employers

Worker's compensation benefits are usually referred to as the employee's *exclusive remedy* against the employer. This means that you can receive only the workers' compensation benefits and are barred from suing your employer, even if the injury was the employer's fault. In a number of situations, however, you can sue your employer in addition to or in place of collecting benefits under the workers' compensation act.

No Workers' Compensation Insurance. If your employer fails to carry workers' compensation insurance, you usually have the choice of collecting workers' compensation benefits from the state compensation fund or suing your employer in court. In some states, you can do both: you can collect benefits *and* sue your employer. Whether you should just take the workers' compensation benefits or sue your employer depends on a number of factors, including whether your employer was at fault, whether there are any defenses that may bar or substantially reduce the amount you can recover in damages, whether your injuries are serious, whether workers' compensation benefits are sufficient, and whether the employer can pay the judgment if you win. You should discuss the matter with an attorney before making your decision.

Excluded Employment or Injuries. Earlier we noted certain types of workers (farm workers, domestic help, temporary workers, and others) and injuries (emotional suffering and invasion of privacy, for instance) that are often excluded from coverage under workers' compensation acts. If you or the particular injury you suffer isn't covered, you can sue your employer.

If your injury occurs outside the course of employment, you can sue your employer. For instance, let's say that your employer invites you to a baseball game on a Sunday. On the way to the game, you are hurt in an automobile accident that was your employer's fault. Since the baseball game had nothing to do with your job, you can sue your employer and have his or her automobile insurance company pay the damages.

Intentional Misconduct of the Employer. Suppose your employer punches you in the face and breaks your nose. Can you sue your employer, or are you limited to workers' compensation benefits? Some states let you sue your employer for deliberate injuries. Other states, however, prohibit you from suing your employer even in this situation. A few states that do not let you sue your employer will award you additional workers' compensation benefits, such as 50 percent more up to a certain point, (say, $10,000), in this situation.

The "Dual Capacity" Doctrine. Let's say that you work for American Ladder Company, which makes ladders that are sold to the public. While using one of American's ladders at work, the ladder breaks; you fall and are seriously injured. Can you sue American Ladder, or are you limited to workers' compensation benefits? Many states let you do both under the "dual capacity" doctrine. The ladder company wears two hats with respect to its employees—that of employer to employee and that of product manufacturer to consumer. The ladder company has a duty to the general public—for whom its product is intended—to make a safe product. You have the same right to a safe product that any other member of the general public has.

The dual capacity doctrine is not restricted to employers who make products for public sale. It applies anytime your employer treats you as he or she treats a member of the public. Suppose, for example, you are a nurse and strain your back on the job. Your employer-doctor treats you but is negligent (medical malpractice), and your condition gets worse. You can sue your employer-doctor for the worsened condition because he or she assumed a dual capacity toward you—that of employer and that of doctor. As a patient, you have the same rights as any other patient, even if you happen to work for the doctor.

Fellow Employees

Fellow employees generally have the same immunity from a lawsuit as your employer. In other words, you usually cannot sue a coworker who accidentally or carelessly injures you, and you are limited to workers' compensation benefits. Most states, however, let you sue fellow employees who deliberately hurt you.

Let's say that you're riding to work with a coworker and are injured in an accident caused by your coworker. Do workers' compensation laws bar you from suing your coworker? Generally not. (But in some states, a "guest statute" may still bar your suit; see chapter 2). Now suppose that you are injured by a coworker in an automobile accident in the company parking lot. You are probably entitled to workers' compensation benefits in this situation. But can you sue your coworker as well? The states are split on this: some let you sue your coworker, while others don't.

Third Parties

Although you are generally barred from suing your employer and coworkers for on-the-job injuries, you can usually sue anyone else (a "third party") who injures you. You may also be able to sue that person's employer if the person was acting within the course of his or her job when you were hurt. For example, if another company's delivery van backs into you because the driver was negligent, you can sue the driver and the company he or she works for. Likewise, if you are a traveling salesman and are injured on a business trip in an automobile accident caused by another person, you can sue that person for your injuries in addition to collecting workers' compensation benefits. Suppose you work for Acme Tool and Die and are injured by a defective machine made by ABZ Corporation. Although you can't sue your employer, Acme, you are free to sue ABZ Corporation.

You Can't Get Paid Twice

Suppose you sue your employer, a coworker, or a third party for your injuries, and the jury awards you $50,000. You have already received $10,000 in workers' compensation benefits. Does this mean you net $60,000? Usually not. In some states, the judge will reduce the jury's award to $40,000. In other states, you will get the full $50,000 but will have to pay back the $10,000 in workers' compensation benefits you received to the insurance company. This prevents you from being paid twice for the same injuries.

If You Are Fired or Laid Off

If you are terminated by your employer, that doesn't mean the end of your rights. In fact, getting laid off may activate a whole new set of rights. We have already seen, for example, that you can't be fired because of your race, color, national origin, sex, or religious beliefs, and you can take action against your employer if you are. And even if you are terminated for a lawful reason, you may still have some rights, such as the right to collect unemployment insurance. If you discover that you are being terminated, and you belong to a union, you should immediately contact the union; a collective bargaining agreement may give you some rights to job security, reinstatement, or benefits—rights that a nonunion employee ordinarily doesn't have.

Unemployment Insurance

Suppose you are terminated through no fault of your own—you are laid off during a slow period, for instance, or fired without cause (that is, you didn't do anything wrong, like stealing or being habitually late). Do you have any rights? If you have worked at your job long enough and have earned enough, you ordinarily are entitled to receive unemployment benefits. The amount depends on how long you were working for the company and how much you earned. One thing is certain, though: unemployment benefits do not replace your earnings in full. And if you are self-employed, you cannot collect unemployment benefits. You only get unemployment benefits if you worked for someone else.

You likewise usually cannot collect unemployment benefits if you voluntarily quit your job, regardless of how long you were employed. But if your employer coerced you into quitting—by making working conditions so intolerable for you that you were forced to leave, for example—you may still be able to collect unemployment benefits. Unemployment benefits may also be available if you have to quit your job for health reasons.

Ordinarily, you have to be out of work for at least one week before you can receive unemployment benefits. (Apply for the benefits at your local unemployment office as soon as you can.) Benefits usually last for up to 26 weeks. But if unemployment levels are exceptionally high, you can sometimes get benefits for up to 13 weeks more. If you go back to work—even if to just a low-paying part-time job—unemployment benefits usually stop; in most states, you must be totally unemployed to be eligible for unemployment benefits. A few states, however, give you reduced benefits if you take a part-time job that doesn't pay much.

What are your rights if the umemployment office turns down your claim because it feels your employer had cause to fire you, but you disagree? The procedure varies greatly from state to state, but generally you are entitled to an administrative hearing in front of someone who was not involved in the denial of your application for benefits. The hearing is informal, and you (or your attorney) can present your side of the dispute, including witnesses and other evidence. If your claim is still denied, you may be able to sue in court.

You have to make an effort to find a job while you receive unemployment benefits; in fact, if you don't look for a new job, your benefits can stop. Usually you've at least got to go to the unemployment office once a week to check the job list. Suppose you're offered a job, but you turn it down because it's not quite what you are looking for. What then? Your benefits can be cut off if the job was reasonably suited for you, taking into account your education and skills and the type of work you've been doing.

Retaliatory and Wrongful Discharge of Employees

There are many valid reasons for which an employer can fire an employee: the employee is caught stealing, the worker's performance is poor, or the employee is habitually late and does not change that habit despite fair warnings, for example. Or business is slow and the employer has to lay off some workers to survive. An employer who discharges an employee for any of these or other legitimate reasons usually does not have to worry about being sued by the former employee.

But what if your employer doesn't have a good reason to fire you and fires you anyway? Your rights depend in part on whether you have an employment contract guaranteeing your job for a certain period of time. Suppose your employment contract provides for you to be employed for five years. If you are dismissed without good cause before the employment period ends, your employer must still pay you the wages and other benefits you would have earned if you had not been terminated. But if, say, you're caught embezzling money from the company, your employer would be justified in terminating you immediately.

Let's say that like so many other workers, you don't have an employment contract. You have been working for the same employer for 15 years, and one day your supervisor tells you that you are being terminated. There is no reason for you to be fired; you have always been a hard and honest worker, and business is good. What rights do you have here? Traditionally, even though you have worked for the same employer for many years, have always been a loyal employee, and have done a good job, your employer basically has had the absolute right to discharge you at any time, with or without a reason (as long as the reason wasn't an impermissible one, such as your race or sex). You are an "at-will" employee, which means that you can be fired at the will of your employer. (A collective bargaining agreement may protect union members from being fired without reason.)

In recent years, some courts have limited an employer's right to fire at-will employees. There are now certain reasons for which you can't be terminated, and if you are, you can turn around and sue your employer for "wrongful discharge." You can't be fired (or demoted) in retaliation for filing a workers' compensation claim, for filing a complaint of unlawful discrimination or sexual harassment, or for complaining of unsafe working conditions. You can't be terminated for refusing to participate in illegal activities or to commit perjury or for reporting the criminal acts of your fellow workers or employer ("whistle-blowing"). If you work around food, you can't be fired for reporting to the health department that your employer is selling tainted food. If you work in a state that prohibits employers from requiring employees to submit to a lie detector test, you cannot lawfully be discharged for refusing to take the test. Your employer also can't fire you close to your retirement just to avoid paying your pension or other retirement benefits.

Suppose that you're an at-will employee and have been working at your job for a number of years, and your employer fires you for no reason. You had planned on staying with the company until you retired. In fact, you were told a number of times that your job was guaranteed as long as you did it well (which you have). The personnel handbook the company gave you even states that all employees can look forward to "long-term employment" and will only be fired for just cause. Can you sue your employer for wrongful discharge? Courts in several states have recently recognized your right to sue your employer for wrongful discharge in this situation. You relied on the company's representations of job security, and it is only fair that it be held to its word. (Unfortunately, the effect of these rulings may be short-lived. Many companies are revising their hiring procedures and personnel manuals to remove any references to "long-term" employment and the like so their right to terminate at-will employees is not jeopardized.)

A few courts have restricted the employer's right to fire long-term employees who have always done satisfactory work—even though the employer never made any promises that the employee could stay with the company as long as he or she wanted. These courts hold that even though the employer never made any promises, the employer is required to deal fairly with you. If you have worked hard for many years and legitimately expected some job security, some courts will now see that you get it.

Does it make any difference to your wrongful discharge case if you quit as opposed to being fired? Not necessarily. You can still sue your employer for wrongful discharge if your employer intentionally made the working conditions so intolerable or unsafe for you that you had no choice but to quit. Your leaving is considered involuntary, the same as if you had been fired—a "constructive discharge."

What should you do if you feel you have been wrongfully discharged? Since this is a new and expanding area of the law, and any real relief is likely to come only through the courts, you should consult a lawyer as soon as possible. Filing a complaint with the Equal Opportunity Employment Commission is often in order, as is notifying your union if you belong to one. If you win your case, you are entitled to recover all wages and benefits from the date you were unjustly terminated. You may also be able to recover other damages, including punitive damages, from your ex-employer. One thing you ordinarily must do after being unjustly fired is try to find a comparable job. You don't have to accept just any job, though; it must be similar in skill requirements and pay to your old job. But if you make no attempt to get new work (to "mitigate your damages"), you may be prohibited from recovering damages from your former employer, or your damages may be reduced by the amount you probably would have made if you had actively sought and obtained another job.

Who Owns Inventions or Copyrights Developed at Work?

Suppose you develop a patent, an invention, or copyrighted material during the course of your job. Who owns the rights to it, you or your employer? To determine the answer to this question, first look at your employment contract, if you have one, to see what it provides. For example, the employment contract may state that all inventions, patents, and copyrighted material that you develop on your employer's premises belong to your employer. If you are hired to assist in the development of something specific, say, a particular product, computer program, or book, the employment contract will normally provide that all rights in the end product are the exclusive property of the employer.

Let's say that a computer software company hires you to develop a new data management program. At night, in your own home, using your own computer, you create a game program that turns out to be quite successful. Your employment contract states that all inventions, patents, and copyrights you develop belong to the employer. Does your employer have any rights to the game program? Probably not, since the game program does not relate to the terms of your employment, and you developed it at home, on your own time and with your own equipment. But if it was a data management program you developed at home, your employer probably owns it, since this was exactly what your employer hired you to write.

A "work-for-hire" is copyrighted material that you are specifically commissioned to create: for example, a magazine hires you to write an article on a specific subject, or a company employs you to create a computer software program. Copyright law (see chapter 16) provides that in a work-for-hire situation, the employer is considered the author of the copyrighted work. Accordingly, the employer generally owns all rights to the work, including the right to publish it whenever, wherever, and as often as he or she wants and receive all the profits from the work. Your only compensation, unless your agreement states differently, is the money you were paid to create the work. Work-for-hire agreements must be in writing; otherwise the copyright may belong to the person who created the work rather than to the employer.

If you have developed or are interested in developing an invention, patent, or copyrighted material, consider talking to an attorney experienced in these areas to see whether your employer may have any rights to it. As an example, if you don't have any type of agreement with your employer and you invent something on company time, you own the invention; your employer, however, usually has the right to use it without having to pay you any royalties or other expenses ("shop rights").

Misuse of an Employer's Confidential Information

Your job may give you access to confidential information—information that is vital to your employer's continued success in its field. Inside information is the most valuable asset of many businesses, which take numerous precautions to ensure that it does not fall into the hands of competitors. When you leave a company, inevitably you take with you some knowledge and skills you acquired from your job. The longer you work in your field, the more you learn about the ins and outs of the business. The law will not deprive you of the right to use the skills and experience you gain by working in the profession over the years.

The law draws a distinction, however, between using your new skills and experience and exploiting your former employer's confidential information. Suppose you leave a company and take some confidential information with you; you start your own firm or take a position with a competitor and use your former employer's information to compete with it. Your former employer can sue to prevent you from using any "trade secrets" and to force you to pay it any money you made from using the secret information.

A trade secret is something that gives one company an edge over its competitors. It can be a number of things: a formula (such as the recipe for Coca-Cola), a manufacturing process, a product design, a list of customers (see discussion below), or a private computer program, to name a few examples. Whether something is in fact a trade secret depends on the novelty of the idea. Is it really the trade secret of one company, or is it a general secret of the whole industry? If the latter, there is no protection for the "secret."

The most important trade secrets of many businesses are the customer lists they have developed through the years. If an employee leaves and starts soliciting the customers on the ex-employer's secret list, the company will do what it can to stop this. A company can stop an ex-employee from using a list of customers only if that list meets the requirements of a "confidential customer list." *Confidential* here means that the names are not available to a reasonably diligent competitor or salesman. The list is not considered confidential if the names are readily accessible from sources outside the former employer's business—the telephone book or a business directory, for instance. But even if the names of potential customers are accessible to others in the business, a company's confidential customer list can sometimes still be protected. A list of customers who have actually purchased the product or service in question is considerably more valuable than a list of people who only might be interested in buying it.

Patient and client lists are of the utmost importance to doctors, dentists, accountants, and other service professionals. If you use your former employer's confidential list to solicit patients and clients, your former employer may be able to get an injunction to stop you. But merely sending an announcement that you have left your previous employment and are now with another employer or are on your own usually is not considered an unlawful solicitation. Another important factor: the courts recognize that the customer has the right to hire whatever company he or she wants. So long as your conduct is not unfair, and you do not use trade secrets or confidential customer lists, the court will not stop you from competing with others in the same business, including your ex-employer.

Agreements Not to Compete

When you buy a business, you don't want the seller to open a new shop across the street from you and put you out of business before you get a chance to establish yourself. Usually when a business is sold, the contract requires the seller not to engage in the same business in a certain geographical area for a specificd length of time. This is called a "covenant not to compete."

Occasionally, in offering you a new job, an employer will require you to agree not to accept similar employment in the same geographical area for a specified number of years after leaving. A court will more readily enforce an agreement not to compete involving the sale of a business than one that an employee is required to sign. Why? Because when you apply for a job, the employer generally has the advantage. You are usually offered the job and the agreement not to compete on a "take it or leave it" basis. But when you buy a business, the law assumes that the two of you stand on relatively equal footing. Each of you knows what you are getting into and can protect your interests accordingly.

Agreements not to compete arc enforced only if the restrictions are reasonable in terms of time, activity, and geographical area. An agreement that bars you from engaging in any type of business in any given part of the United States for the rest of your life is invalid; you've got to be able to make a living.

Let's say that you want to buy a restaurant, but only if the seller promises not to open another restaurant in the area for several years. The contract provides that the seller agrees not to operate another restaurant within a five-mile radius for a period of three years. But six months later, the seller opens a new restaurant half a mile from your restaurant, and your business drops to nothing; many of your customers have gone to the seller's new place. You would most likely be successful in a lawsuit against the seller, because the restrictions as to time (three years) and place (a radius of five miles) are reasonable to protect your legitimate business interests. What type of damages could you recover in your lawsuit? You could get an injunction to stop the seller from operating the new restaurant in violation of your agreement. You could also ask for damages for business the seller took away from you and other damages you suffered as a result of the seller's violation of the agreement.

12

SOCIAL SECURITY, MEDICARE, AND SSI

THE GREAT DEPRESSION completely wiped out the savings accounts and stocks that many Americans were counting on to provide security for their retirement. The young were relatively fortunate; they could start over and build anew. But the elderly did not enjoy this luxury; many lived out their last days in poorhouses. To prevent the elderly from ever facing this prospect again, on August 14, 1935, President Franklin D. Roosevelt signed into law what has come to be widely regarded as the most important program spawned by this tragic period in American history: the Social Security Act.

Social Security consists of several different plans. The main one is Old-Age, Survivors, and Disability Insurance (OASDI), which provides benefits when a worker retires, becomes disabled, or is killed. Unlike workers' compensation benefits (see chapter 11), the worker's disability or death does not have to be job-related in order for the worker or his or her family to be entitled to Social Security benefits. Social Security also provides health insurance through Medicare, discussed later in this chapter, and unemployment insurance, discussed in chapter 11.

Just how important are Social Security benefits? About one in every six persons in America currently receives monthly Social Security checks. For two-thirds of them, Social Security benefits account for 50 percent or more of their total yearly income. And for 25 percent of all who receive Social Security, the benefits constitute 90 percent of their entire income. Without Social Security, an estimated 60 percent of the elderly would be living in poverty. (As it is, 14.1 percent of older Americans fall below the poverty level.) Social Security does not replace all of your earnings when you retire, so you should have additional retirement plans— savings accounts, Individual Retirement Accounts (IRAs), stocks, and so forth—to supplement Social Security when you retire.

This chapter discusses your legal rights to Social Security benefits, Medicare, and Supplemental Security Income (SSI). As with many government programs, your rights are determined by a maze of regulations. The material that follows will help you discover just what your rights are in many areas involving Social Security, Medicare, and SSI.

How Social Security Is Financed

Who pays for Social Security? If you are employed (or self-employed), the chances are that you do. Nine out of every ten workers contribute regularly to Social Security through a tax on their earnings. Your employer deducts a certain percent of your wages (7.15 percent in 1986 and 1987, 7.51 percent in 1988 and 1989, and 7.65 percent thereafter) from your paycheck and then matches this from his or her own pocket. If you're self-employed, you pay the entire amount yourself, although a tax credit reduces the rate a bit (under present law, the tax credit will be replaced in 1990 by deductions). Self-employed persons must file Schedule SE (Form 1040), Computation of Social Security Self-Employment Tax, with their annual federal income tax returns.

As of 1987, the maximum earnings taxed for Social Security total $43,800. Anything you make over that is free from Social Security taxes (but you still have to pay income taxes on it). This amount automatically increases each year as earning levels throughout the nation rise. If you work for two or more employers in one year and earn more than the maximum amount, be sure that you don't wind up paying too much to Social Security. For instance, suppose you worked for Company A for the first six months of the year and made $20,000. You then worked for Company B for the last six months and earned $25,000—a total of $45,000 for the entire year. If both companies deducted Social Security taxes from your wages, you can claim a refund of the overpayment when you file your tax return. (If you worked for only one employer and too much was deducted, ask your employer to refund the excess.)

Most jobs in the United States are covered by Social Security and are subject to the same rules. If your type of employment is covered, you don't get to choose whether or not you want to participate in Social Security; your participation is mandatory. There are a few employees who are subject to special rules. These include persons who do housecleaning, gardening, or baby-sitting in private homes; students who are employed by their school or college; farm workers; members of religious orders; persons who get cash tips on the job (waiters and waitresses, for instance); employees of international organizations; and persons who work outside the United States. If you fall into any of these categories, contact your local Social Security office for information regarding your situation. Railroad workers and federal employees are covered by their own plans but may have some rights to Social Security and should also contact the Social Security office to see what their rights are.

Qualifying for Benefits

You are entitled to Social Security benefits only if you have earned sufficient "work credits," or "quarters of coverage." How many quarters of coverage you need depends on how old you are and what the benefits are for—retirement, disability, or survivor's benefits. The number of quarters of coverage you need to be eligible for retirement benefits is shown in Table 12.1, and the number of quarters of coverage necessary for disability and survivor's benefits is shown in Table 12.2. (Depending

If you reach age 62 in:	Quarters of coverage needed:
1981	30
1982	31
1983	32
1984	33
1985	34
1987	36
1991 or later	40

Table 12.1

Quarters of coverage you need in order to qualify for Social Security retirement benefits.

upon your financial condition, if you aren't eligible for Social Security benefits, you may be able to get welfare or other public assistance.)

In 1987, you received one quarter of coverage for each $460 you made, up to a maximum of four quarters of coverage for the whole year. (The amount you need to earn for a quarter of coverage goes up each year.) You can earn four quarters of coverage in one month, or you can work all year long and still not get a single quarter. For instance, if you made $1,840 or more in January of 1987, you earned four quarters of coverage for that year, even if you didn't work another day. If you made only $35 a month, you wouldn't get a single quarter of coverage, since your total earnings for all of 1987 would be only $420. If you earned $100 a month— $1,200 for the year—you would receive two quarters of coverage for the whole year.

Would you have gotten additional quarters of coverage if you earned more than $1,840 in 1987. No. The most quarters of coverage you can get in a single year is four. That doesn't mean your earnings above $1,840 aren't taken into consideration. They are used to determine the size of your Social Security check. The greater your earnings, the larger your Social Security check will be—up to a point.

If you are born after 1929 and become disabled at age:	If you are born before 1930 and become disabled before age 62 in:	Quarters of coverage you need in order to qualify for benefits:
44		22
46		24
48		26
50		28
52	1981	30
54	1983	32
56	1985	34
58	1987	36
60	1989	38
62 or older	1991 or later	40

Table 12.2

Quarters of coverage you need in order to qualify for benefits if you become disabled at age 44 or older.

Suppose Heather has been working for several years and has earned ten quarters of coverage. She decides to have a baby and quits work for a time. Does she lose those ten quarters of coverage? No. Once you've earned a quarter of coverage, it's yours for good. You don't lose any quarters of coverage, even if you stop working before you qualify for Social Security benefits. When you go back to work, the new quarters are added to what you already have.

It's a good idea to check your Social Security record every three years or so to make sure your earnings are being reported correctly. You can get a free postcard form for this at any Social Security office. Be sure to notify your local Social Security office promptly if you change your name (for example, when you get married or divorced) to insure that you receive credit for your earnings under your new name. You will have to show sufficient proof to establish your identity, such as a driver's license, marriage certificate, or court order granting a name change.

Retirement Benefits

The bulk of Social Security benefits paid out in retirement benefits to workers who earned enough "quarters of coverage," as previously discussed. Table 12.1 shows how many quarters of coverage you must accumulate in order to be eligible for Social Security retirement benefits.

If you have earned enough quarters of coverage, you can retire and receive Social Security benefits as early as your sixty-second birthday, although your benefits will be permanently reduced if you retire before 65 (see discussion below). But you won't get any benefits unless you apply for them. You can work hard all your life and retire at age 65, but the Social Security office is not going to start sending you checks automatically. Ideally, you should notify your local Social Security office three months before you retire. Even if you won't be retiring, you should still contact your Social Security office three months before your sixty-fifth birthday in order to get Medicare coverage.

Suppose you retire on your sixty-fifth birthday but forget to apply for Social Security benefits for three months. Do you lose the benefits for those months? No. You can receive back payments for up to six months after you turn 65. But if you retire before you're 65, generally you can only get benefits starting with the month in which you apply for them. So if you retire at, say, age 63 in March but wait until August to apply for retirement benefits, your benefits start with August.

When applying for retirement benefits, have your Social Security card or a record of your number, proof of your age (your birth certificate is best), and your most recent W-2 form or a copy of your federal income tax returns for the last two years (so Social Security can update its records and include these earnings in computing the amount of your benefits). If you are applying for benefits based on your spouse's record, you'll need your spouse's Social Security number and perhaps your marriage certificate. You'll need your children's birth certificates if you're asking for benefits for them.

Amount of Your Retirement Benefits

When you retire at age 65, you are entitled to full retirement benefits (if you have earned enough quarters of coverage to qualify). The amount of your monthly check depends on how much, on the average, you made each year; the more you made, the higher your benefits will be (up to the maximum). You can retire as early as your sixty-second birthday, but if you do, your monthly checks will be permanently reduced to 80 percent of the full benefits. For example, the maximum monthly retirement benefit check for a worker who retired in 1987 at age 65 was about $789, but only $635 if he or she had retired at 62—a difference of $154 a month. But for the worker who retired at age 65 it will take 12 years to make up the difference. If you retire at age 62, for instance, and receive $635 a month, by the time you reach 65, you will already have collected $22,225 in retirement benefits. If you retired at age 65, it would take 12 years for your checks ($154 larger) to make up this difference.

If you retire before your sixty-fifth birthday, the amount by which your monthly check is reduced depends on how many months short of your sixty-fifth birthday you retire. The earlier you retire, the smaller your check will be. If you retire at 62, you will receive a smaller check than if you retired at 64.

By the same token, if you decide not to retire when you reach 65, your benefits will increase for each month that you continue working. Currently they go up 3 percent for each year that you don't collect Social Security retirement benefits. So if you wait until you're 67 to retire, your benefits will be 6 percent larger. (Your earnings for those two years may also cause your benefits to rise because they will be added to your work record.) Under present law, beginning in 1990, this figure will gradually increase until it eventually reaches 8 percent a year.

Your monthly checks will automatically increase each year as the national cost of living goes up. Under the current regulations, if the cost of living increases by 3 percent or more, your benefits will usually rise by the same amount.

Retirement Benefits to Spouses and Children

If you have been married for at least one year when your spouse retires and begins receiving Social Security retirement benefits, you may also be entitled to spouse's benefits (also called "auxiliary benefits"), even if you don't qualify for benefits on the basis of your own work record. You can apply for benefits as early as age 62, but, as with a worker who retires before 65, your benefits will be permanently reduced. If you wait until you are 65 to apply for your benefits, you will get one-half of the amount your spouse receives. You can also receive retirement benefits based on your spouse's record if you are under 62 and are caring for a child who is under 16 or disabled and who is receiving Social Security benefits based on the retired worker's earnings. If you also worked and earned enough quarters of coverage to qualify for retirement benefits on your own record, but your benefits as a spouse are larger, you will get the larger amount.

Even though you are divorced, you may still be eligible for retirement benefits based on your ex-spouse's record. If you are 62 or older, single, and were married to your ex-spouse for at least ten years, you can receive retirement benefits when your ex-spouse starts to collect them. Since January 1985, if you have been divorced for at least two years, you can receive retirement benefits as early as age 62 even if your ex-spouse isn't receiving them (but your ex-spouse must be eligible to receive retirement benefits). Although your retirement benefits based on your ex-spouse's record end when you remarry, they can start again if your new marriage ends in divorce or annulment.

When a worker who is receiving retirement benefits has unmarried children—including stepchildren, adopted children, and dependent grandchildren—under age 18 (or under 19 if they are full-time high school students), those children can receive supplemental benefits, as can single children 18 or over who were severely disabled before age 22 and who continue to be disabled. Illegitimate children may also be eligible for benefits. Social Security benefits to a worker's child generally end when the child marries and commence again only if the marriage is annulled.

If You Go Back to Work While Receiving Retirement Benefits

What happens to your Social Security retirement checks if you go back to work? That depends on how old you are. Nothing happens to them if you're at least 70 years old when you go back to work; your benefits remain the same regardless of how much you earn after reaching 70. But if you're under 70, your checks may be reduced, depending on how much you make. In 1987, for example, if you were between 65 and 70, the first $8,160 you made did not affect your Social Security check. If you were between 62 and 65, you could earn up to $6,000 and still receive your full retirement benefits.

If you make more than the base amount, the government deducts $1 from your retirement check for every $2 you earn above the limit. Suppose that in 1987 you are 66 and make $9,600 at your job. Under current law, since you made $1,440 over the limit ($8,160), your retirement benefits will be reduced by $720 for that year. Beginning in 1990, $1 in retirement benefits will be deducted for each $3 above the limit earned by persons 65 and over. (The rate will remain the same—$1 deducted for every $2 earned over the base amount—for persons between the ages of 62 and 65.) Note that if you go back to work after getting some retirement checks, your new earnings may result in higher benefits, as they will be credited to your record, and Social Security will automatically refigure your benefits.

What kind of income is taken into account? Money paid to you as an employee—including cash tips, bonuses, vacation pay, and severance pay—and your net profit from self-employment are counted. If you do work in exchange for room or board—if you manage an apartment building, for instance, or do maintenance work in return for a free apartment or reduced rent—you must include the value of that in your total earnings. The monthly income from your "nest egg"—things like savings accounts, IRAs, stock dividends, annuities and other insurance, gifts or inheritances, rents from real estate, and other investments—ordinarily does not count against you.

Suppose that in 1987 you turn 63 and decide to retire in July of that year, but you've already made more than $6,000 the maximum amount a person receiving retirement benefits could earn in 1987 without a reduction in benefits). Does this mean that your retirement benefits will be reduced for the rest of that year? No. You can still retire and collect your full benefits for each month your income falls below a certain amount. If you retired in 1987 after making more than the base amount for the year, you can get full benefits for any month your earnings do not exceed $680 if you are 65 or older, or $500 if you were between 62 and 65. This way you can retire in the middle or near the end of a year and still receive full retirement benefits for the remaining months. This special monthly test is applied only in the first year you retire. After that, your benefits are determined by your total annual earnings.

Disability Benefits

You and your dependents are entitled to receive Social Security disability benefits if you are disabled before your sixty-fifth birthday and have earned enough quarters of coverage (see discussion below). If you are disabled after your sixty-fifth birthday, you will receive retirement benefits rather than disability benefits. The amount of your disability benefits is based on your age, how long you have worked, and how much you earned before becoming disabled.

You are considered disabled when you suffer from a physical or mental condition that is terminal or expected to last at least 12 months and that prevents you from doing any "substantial gainful activity" (see discussion below). You are considered blind and disabled if, even with glasses, your vision is no better than 20/200 of your field of vision is 20 degrees or less.

Qualifying for Disability Benefits

As with other Social Security benefits, you must earn sufficient quarters of coverage to qualify for disability benefits. The number of quarters of coverage you need in order to be eligible for disability benefits is determined by how old you are when you become disabled.

If you are disabled before age 24, you only need to have earned six quarters of coverage (1½ years) in the three years before you become disabled. If you are between 24 and 31 when you become disabled, you must have earned quarters of coverage for half the time between your twenty-first birthday and the time when you become disabled. For example, if you are disabled on your twenty-eighth birthday, you need fourteen quarters of coverage—one-half of seven years—to qualify for disability benefits. If you are disabled at age 31 or later, you generally need at least twenty quarters of coverage in the ten years preceding your disability. The number of work credits you need in order to qualify for disability benefits if you become disabled at age 44 or older is shown in Table 12.2.

Disability benefits may also be available to a disabled widow or widower (and in some cases, to a disabled surviving divorced spouse) who is 50 or older, if the worker was insured at death.

Applying for Disability Benefits

If you can't work because of a physical or mental disability that is expected to last at least 12 months or to result in your death, you should apply for benefits without delay. Although you usually won't receive any benefits until you've been disabled for five full months (see discussion below), it is better to apply right away so Social Security can verify your disability and send you your checks as soon as you are eligible for them. You will need to give Social Security the names, addresses, and telephone numbers of the doctors, hospitals, and clinics that have treated you for the disability, and the approximate dates of treatment. (An easy way to provide this information is to supply copies of your medical bills.) You will have to tell Social Security what your illness or injury is, when the illness started or the injury was sustained, how it keeps you from working, and the date you stopped working. Be prepared to tell the Social Security office the restrictions your doctor has placed on you and the names and dosages of medicines you are currently taking.

The Social Security office will request all medical evidence from you regarding the doctors, hospitals, and clinics that treated you. Your claim will then be sent to the Disability Determination Services office in your state, where a disability evaluation specialist and a physician will review the evidence. They may ask your doctors about your condition, the diagnosis, the extent to which your working ability is impaired, the treatment that has already been provided, and what treatment may be required in the future. You may have to submit to a special examination or test—at no cost to you—to verify your claim.

Disability claims are ordinarily processed in three to four months, after which you will receive written notice informing you of whether your claim has been approved. If it is approved, the notice will show the amount of your monthly payments and the date when they start. For most people, there is a five-month waiting period after they are disabled before the payments start. No wait, however, applies if you are disabled before your twenty-second birthday and qualify for Social Security benefits on the record of a parent. If your disability claim is rejected, the written notice must explain why. You have the right to appeal the decision if you don't agree with it (see discussion below).

Why and When Disability Checks Stop

Disability checks continue for as long as you can't perform any "substantial gainful activity." Each case is reviewed periodically—usually every three to seven years—to determine whether the worker is still disabled. Should Social Security determine that your condition has improved to the point where you are ready to go back to work, you will be notified of that decision. You will then receive three more checks. You have the right to appeal this determination, and you can ask that your benefits continue in the meantime. But if you lose your appeal, you will be asked to repay the benefits. You do, however, have the right to ask that you not have to repay the benefits. (This applies only to disability decisions made through 1987 but is permanent for people who receive Supplemental Security Income [SSI] benefits due to disability.)

You usually can go back to work for as long as nine months (sometimes longer) on a trial basis without losing any disability benefits. A trial work month is one in which you earn over $75 or work more than 15 hours at your own business. The trial work months do not have to be consecutive; they can be separated by months or even years during which you don't work. When the trial period is over, the Social Security office will decide whether you can go back to work. If it determines that you can, your disability benefits will stop after another three months.

You are generally considered to be doing "substantial gainful work" if you make over $300 a month in gross wages ($610 if you are blind). In figuring your gross wages, you are allowed to deduct certain expenses related to your disability that you need in order to work—such as medical equipment, drugs, services, and nurses or attendants. For instance, if for March you were paid $600, but you spent $350 on medical equipment and drugs so you could work, your gross income would be $250. If you are self-employed, the amount you make is not the sole consideration. Other factors, including the general state of the economy, the type of work you did, and your ability to manage your business, are also taken into account.

If you are still disabled and go back to work, then stop working less than one year after your disability checks have stopped, you don't need to make a new application for disability benefits. But before the checks will be renewed, you do have to inform your local Social Security office that you have stopped working. And you may be required to undergo a new medical evaluation.

Suppose you are disabled, recover and go back to work, but become disabled again two years later. Do you have to make a new application for disability benefits? Yes. But if you are disabled within five years after your disability benefits stop, you won't have to wait five months for the disability benefits to start the second time.

Survivors' Benefits

When a worker dies, his or her spouse, children, and other dependents may be eligible for monthly survivors' benefits if the worker had earned enough quarters of coverage. In addition to the monthly benefits, a one-time lump sum death benefit of $255 is available to an eligible surviving widow or widower or child. Usually the worker must have earned the same number of quarters of coverage needed for disability, as shown in Table 12.2 (page 367). Under a special rule, the minor children and their mother or father can receive survivors' benefits if the worker had earned at least six quarters of coverage (1½ years) in the three years before his or her death. The wife and children of a deceased worker can usually get benefits if the marriage lasted at least nine months.

A surviving widow or widower under age 60 can generally

receive survivors' benefits only if he or she is caring for the worker's child under 16 (or the child is disabled), and the child is receiving benefits based on the record of the deceased worker. But when the child's benefits stop (discussed below), so do the benefits of the surviving widow or widower. The widow's or widower's survivors' benefits also stop if the child moves out. Survivors' benefits are also available to a surviving widow or widower who is 60 or older (50 or older if the surviving spouse is disabled within seven years of the worker's death), regardless of whether he or she is caring for any children.

If you are divorced, you can still receive survivors' benefits when your ex-spouse dies if you are not married, are 60 or older (50 or older if you are disabled within seven years of the worker's death), and were married to your ex-spouse for at least ten years. A divorced spouse under 60 who meets the other qualifications may be eligible for survivors' benefits if he or she is caring for the worker's child (who is receiving Social Security benefits based on the deceased worker's earnings). But, as with the benefits received by a widow or widower who is caring for a child, the benefits stop when the child turns 16 or the child moves out. The child's own benefits, however, continue until the child reaches 18 (19 if he or she is a full-time high school student), or longer if the child is disabled. Survivors' benefits to widows, widowers, and divorced spouses usually stop if they remarry before they are 60, but start again if the remarriage ends.

Unmarried children—including stepchildren, adopted children, even illegitimate children—under 18 (19 if they are full-time high school students) are usually entitled to survivors' benefits when the worker dies. Benefits are also payable to unmarried children 18 or older who were severely disabled before age 22 and who continue to be disabled. For most children, survivors' benefits stop when they marry and start again only if the marriage is annulled.

The parents of a deceased adult worker can receive survivors' benefits if the parent is 62 or older and received at least half of his or her support from the adult child. A grandchild who is living with and being supported by a grandparent who is covered by Social Security may be eligible for survivors' benefits when the grandparent dies. This applies only if the grandchild is under 18 and his or her biological parents are dead or disabled.

If your spouse or parent (or child or grandparent on whom you were dependent) dies, you should contact your local Social Security office as soon as possible. Widows and widowers can apply for survivors' benefits in the month after the worker's death and still receive benefits for the month of death. (The one-time death benefit can usually be applied for up to two years after the worker's death.) You will need the deceased worker's Social Security card or a record of that number, your marriage certificate, and the birth certificates for your children. If you are applying for benefits as a dependent parent of a deceased child or as a dependent grandchild of a deceased grandparent, you will have to prove that you were in fact being supported by the worker. Your local Social Security office can tell you what type of documentation you need to prove your dependency.

Some Things You Need to Know about Social Security

How Payments Are Handled

Benefits are paid only for a full month. Normally you should receive a given month's Social Security check in the mail on the third day of the next month. (For example, the check dated April 3 is really payment for March.) Notify your local Social Security office if you don't receive your check by the sixth day of the month.

You can arrange to have your monthly Social Security checks deposited directly into your checking or savings accounts by going to your bank and filling out the proper form—Form SF-1199. How can you be sure that the bank has received your check? The bank can do one of the following things: Within two business days of receipt, it can notify you that your check was received; it can notify you that your check was *not* received within two business days after it should have been received; or it can set up a telephone number for you to call to find out whether your check was received and deposited (this number must appear on your bank account's periodic statement).

When to Notify Social Security

If you are receiving benefits, here are some of the times when you need to contact your local Social Security office:

• If you move, change your mailing address, or change your name. (Be sure to report your address change even if the checks are deposited directly into your bank account, because the checks can be stopped if Social Security can't get in touch with you.)

• If the person receiving the benefits dies. If the Social Security checks are sent directly to a bank, the bank should also be notified. Since benefits are payable only for a full month, the check dated the month after the recipient dies should be returned to Social Security. For example, if a person dies during March, the Social Security check dated April 3 should not be deposited or cashed, since it is for the month of March. But if the person dies April 1 or 2, the check dated April 3 need not be returned. If your spouse dies, and the check is made out to the two of you, contact your local Social Security office to find out what to do with the check.

• If the person receiving the benefits becomes physically or mentally incapable of managing his or her funds. (Social Security can arrange to send the checks to a "representative payee," such as a relative or friend.)

• If you get a divorce or an annulment and receive benefits as a husband or wife, a surviving or divorced spouse, a parent, or a child of the worker.

• If a child receiving benefits becomes disabled or is a full-time high school student (otherwise, benefits automatically terminate when the child turns 18). Also notify Social Security if a child over 18 who receives benefits as a full-time student leaves school.

• If you are receiving retirement benefits, are under 70, and go back to work and expect to make more than the annual exempt amount for the year. If you are under 70 and work or are self-employed outside the United States, you must notify the nearest U.S. embassy, consulate, or Social Security office promptly and inform them of this fact.

• If your condition improves or when something happens that could affect your status as a disabled person (if you receive disability benefits). Also notify Social Security if you go back to work, regardless of how much or how little you expect to earn.

• If you will be traveling abroad for more than 30 days. Also notify your local Social Security office if you will be visiting Albania, Cuba, Democratic Kampuchea (formerly Cambodia), East Berlin, East Germany, North Korea, or Vietnam, even if the trip will be shorter than 30 days. Your local Social Security office can provide you with the pamphlet "Your Social Security Checks—While You Are Outside the United States," which discusses how traveling abroad affects your Social Security check.

• If a person receiving benefits is convicted of a felony and sent to prison. Although benefits ordinarily are not payable while a person is in prison, benefits to family members do continue.

Your Right to Have Someone Act for You

You have the right to appoint an attorney, a relative, or even a trusted friend to act on your behalf with the Social Security office if, for example, you are bedridden or just don't want to do it yourself. Your representative can do just about anything you can. To arrange for a representative, you must fill out and sign Form SSA 1696-U3, "Appointment of Representative" (available from your local Social Security office).

Most people are usually able to deal with Social Security without much problem. But if you're having trouble getting a claim accepted—particularly if the claim is a major one—you should seriously consider hiring an attorney experienced in Social Security claims to represent you.

Before you give anyone the authority to represent you, however, find out what fee, if any, he or she intends to charge you, and make sure you get this in writing. Will you have to pay a fee only if the person is successful with your claim? If so, make sure that, too, is written down. Before you have to pay anything, the person who represented you must file a petition with Social Security showing the fee requested, the nature and extent of the services performed, and the dates the services started and ended. Social Security usually decides the amount of the fee, but if you have to go to court, attorney's fees cannot exceed 25 percent of what you recover. If you disagree with the fee approved by Social Security, you can ask your local Social Security office to review it. You must make this request in writing within 30 days of the time you receive notice of the approved fee. Your representative likewise has a right to have the fee reviewed if he or she feels that it is too small.

If you are represented by an attorney, and your claim is successful, Social Security usually withholds 25 percent of your back payments for the attorney. If this is not enough to pay all of the attorney's fee as approved by Social Security, you must make up the difference from your own pocket. If the amount withheld is too much, you will be sent the excess. If your representative is not an attorney or if your claim is unsuccessful, you usually must pay your representative the fee directly.

Appealing Social Security Decisions

What can you do if your Social Security claim is denied or if you feel the amount of benefits you are given is too little? Within 60 days after you receive notice of the decision on your claim, you can send a written request for reconsideration to your local Social Security office. You can do this on a form available from Social Security, or you can simply write a letter. Your Social Security office can tell you what information your letter should contain and to whom the letter must be addressed. The main objective should be to present enough solid evidence to support your position.

If you disagree with the decision after reconsideration, your next step is to make a written request for a hearing before an administrative law judge of the Office of Hearings and Appeals of the Social Security Administration. (If your claim involves a Medicare hospital insurance claim of less than $100, you do not have the right to a hearing; your only recourse is to ask for reconsideration of the claim's denial.) You can represent yourself at this hearing or appoint someone to represent you. Or you can waive the hearing and have the case decided on the basis of the written evidence submitted to the judge. If you still aren't satisfied after the administrative law judge makes a decision, you can request a review by the Appeals Council. The Appeals Council will hear your case only if it wants to. If the Appeals Council refuses to hear your case or hears your case but rules against you, you can then file suit in federal court. Generally, you have only 60 days to appeal each action to the next stage, and appeals to Social Security usually must be made on a special form available at your local Social Security office. Appealing denials of a Social Security claim often requires the assistance of an attorney experienced in this area of law.

Taxation of Social Security Benefits

In 1984, something happened to Social Security benefits for the first time ever: they became subject to federal income tax. Most people who receive Social Security benefits will not have to pay any taxes on them. But if you are single and make more than $25,000 in a year (including half your Social Security benefits) or are married and, with your spouse's income, earn more than $32,000 and file jointly, you will most likely pay tax on some of your benefits. You are also subject to the tax if you are married and lived with your spouse at any time during the year but file separate tax returns.

Each January, the government will send you Form SSA-1099, "Social Security Benefit Statement," showing the benefits you received in the previous year. You will also receive a worksheet (IRS Notice 703) that you can use to determine whether you have to pay taxes on those benefits. More information on whether your Social Security benefits are taxable is available by calling or writing to your local Internal Revenue Service office and asking for I.R.S. Publication 915.

Medicare Benefits

Medicare provides health services for people who are 65 or older, people who are disabled for a certain length of time, and people who suffer permanent kidney failure. Medicare consists of two parts: hospital insurance and medical insurance. The hospital insurance is paid for from your Social Security taxes. The medical insurance is supported in part (one-third) by the small monthly premiums required of each person who enrolls. The remaining two-thirds comes from general federal revenues.

You are eligible for Medicare hospital insurance if you are 65 or older and are entitled to monthly Social Security benefits (you don't have to be receiving any benefits, though). Your spouse, divorced spouse, widow or widower, or dependent parents are also eligible for Medicare hospital insurance at age 65. If you are under 65, you are eligible for hospital insurance if you have been receiving Social Security disability benefits for 24 months or more.

Widows and widowers between 50 and 65 who have been disabled for at least two years may be eligible for Medicare hospital insurance, even if they have not applied for disability benefits because they were receiving other Social Security benefits. Disabled surviving divorced spouses under 65 and disabled children 18 or older are eligible for hospital insurance in some cases.

Even if your work record does not qualify you for Medicare hospital insurance, you can still enroll in the program and pay a monthly premium ($226 a month in 1987) if you are 65 or over. If you do enroll, you will have to enroll in the Medicare medical insurance plans as well.

Applying for Medicare Benefits

Some people are automatically enrolled in Medicare; others are not covered unless and until they apply. You are automatically enrolled in Medicare when you turn 65 if you are receiving Social Security checks or if you are under 65 and have been receiving Social Security disability benefits for 24 months.

If you plan to keep working after 65, you need to apply to be covered by Medicare. It is a good idea to apply three months before your sixty-fifth birthday so your benefits will start as soon as you are eligible. Disabled widows and widowers between 50 and 65 must also apply to be covered. If you have any question about whether you need to enroll in Medicare in order to be covered, contact your local Social Security office.

Medicare Hospital Insurance

Medicare hospital insurance helps pay for treatment in participating hospitals and skilled nursing homes. It also covers services for in-home care and, under certain conditions, hospice care.

Medicare will only pick up a portion of the "approved costs" of services. Approved costs are based on what charge is reasonable in your area for the same procedure. For instance, if your doctor charges you $250 to do something, but the average cost in your area is only $200, the "approved cost" of $200 will be used to determine the amount of your Medicare benefits.

Should you need inpatient care in a hospital, Medicare helps pay the cost during the first 90 days in a participating hospital. In 1987, Medicare paid for all but the first $520 of the covered medical services during the first 60 days you were hospitalized. "Covered services" include a semiprivate room, your meals, regular nursing services, operating and recovery room costs, intensive care and coronary care, drugs, lab tests, medical supplies and appliances, and rehabilitation services. For days 61 through 90, you pay $130 each day, and Medicare pays the rest of all covered services.

The above benefits are paid by Medicare for each "benefit period." A benefit period begins the day you enter the hospital and stops 60 days after the medical services end. For example, if you're in the hospital for 60 days, you're discharged, and then six months later you're back in the hospital for another 60 days, the second hospitalization constitutes a new benefit period. Instead of combining your two hospital stays into a single benefit period of 120 days, your two separate stays are counted as separate benefit periods of 60 days each.

Let's say that during one benefit period you're in the hospital longer than 90 days—120 days, for instance. Since Medicare covers only the first 90 days of hospitalization in a single benefit period, do you have to pay for the other 30 days? No—at least not if you haven't used up your 60 "reserve days." These reserve days were designed to help you during longer periods of hospitalization. But there's a catch: the reserve days are not renewable. That means that once you use one, it's gone forever. By using 30 of your reserve days to cover your 120-day hospital stay, you're left with 30 reserve days. For reserve days, you must pay $260 a day, and Medicare pays the rest.

If you need in-patient skilled nursing care or rehabilitation services after you leave the hospital, Medicare may pay benefits for up to 100 days in a participating facility. In 1987, Medicare paid for all covered services a person received in the nursing home the first 20 days and paid all but $65 a day for the next 80 days. Covered services in a nursing home include a semiprivate room, all meals, regular nursing services, rehabilitation services, drugs, and medical supplies and appliances.

When people are confined to their homes and meet other conditions, Medicare pays the full approved cost of home visits from a participating home health agency. Medicare also pays benefits for hospice care provided by a Medicare-certified hospice to eligible terminally ill beneficiaries, to a maximum of two 90-day periods and one 30-day period.

Medicare Medical Insurance

Medicare medical insurance helps pay for doctors' services, outpatient hospital services, and other medical items and services not covered by Medicare hospital insurance. If you are 65 or older or are eligible for Medicare hospital insurance, you are usually eligible for Medicare medical insurance. When you apply for Medicare hospital insurance, you are automatically enrolled in the medical insurance unless you tell the people at Social Security that you don't want it. The basic premium for Medicare medical insurance in 1987 is $17.90 a month. There is also a small annual amount (a "deductible") you must meet each year before Medicare medical insurance takes over. In 1987, the annual deductible was $75.

Medicare medical insurance pays 80 percent of covered services. Among them are treatment by a doctor anywhere in the U.S., including surgery, diagnostic tests, and X-rays; medical supplies (if furnished in a doctor's office); services of the office nurse; emergency room and outpatient clinic services; and home health visits (if you meet certain conditions). Other services covered under certain conditions include ambulance transportation; artificial eyes and limbs; home dialysis equipment, supplies, and periodic support services; laboratory tests; outpatient maintenance dialysis; outpatient physical therapy and speech pathology; and X-rays and radiation treatment. Prescription drugs, however, are *not* covered.

Permanent Kidney Failure

If you are insured under Social Security (or are receiving monthly Social Security benefits), and you, your spouse, or your children suffer from permanent kidney failure, Medicare medical insurance covers the costs of maintenance dialysis or a kidney transplant. If anyone in your family suffers from permanent kidney failure, contact your local Social Security office to see if you are covered by Medicare.

Supplementing Your Medicare Coverage

Because Medicare does not pay 100 percent of your hospital and medical bills, you should seriously think about supplementing your Medicare protection. Most people on Medicare need to consider additional protection, but some don't. For example, low-income people who qualify for Medicaid can usually do without protection from a private insurance company. (Medicaid is a joint federal and state program, administered by the state, which provides medical care to the poor. Eligibility for Medicaid is based on your income and assets, not your age. You can obtain information on or apply for Medicaid at your local welfare office.)

Many private insurance companies offer insurance plans to supplement Medicare. Before you buy from any company, compare the price of the policy and its benefits with those of the policies offered by other companies, since the benefits and cost of a policy can vary widely from one company to the next. Social Security has a pamphlet—"Guide to Health Insurance for People with Medicare"—that you should read before buying a policy.

Supplemental Security Income (SSI)

Supplemental Security Income—SSI for short—is a special program to help out aged, disabled, or blind persons with low incomes and limited assets. Although SSI is administered through Social Security, in many respects, it is considerably different from retirement, disability, and survivors' benefits. For example, your eligibility for SSI doesn't hinge on whether you've earned a certain number of quarters of coverage; you can be eligible for SSI benefits even if you've never worked a day in your life. And unlike Social Security, the money for SSI comes from the general funds of the U.S. Treasury, rather than a special tax on your earnings.

Who Is Eligible for SSI

You are eligible for SSI benefits if you meet the financial limitations discussed below and are at least 65 years old; are any age and can't work for 12 months or more because of a physical or mental impairment (or you are expected to die from the condition); or are visually handicapped—you cannot see better than 20/200 with corrective lenses or have a visual field of 20 degrees or less. (Even if your sight is not that bad, you may still qualify for benefits as a disabled person.) In some states, if you qualify under more than one category—if you are over 65, for example, and blind—you get the higher benefits—in this case, the benefits for being blind. Your local Social Security office will help you determine which category will give you the higher benefits.

To be eligible for SSI benefits, you must be a citizen of the U.S. or a lawfully admitted immigrant, and you must be a resident of the U.S. or the northern Mariana Islands. You are generally not eligible for SSI benefits if you live in a public institution, such as a jail or certain hospitals. You may, however, be eligible for SSI if you live in a publicly operated community residence of no more than 16 people. Temporary residents of a public emergency shelter may also be eligible for SSI payments for up to three months during any 12-month period.

The Amount of Your Assets and Income

Since SSI is designed for people who have low incomes and limited assets, how much property you own and the money you make are of the utmost importance. Currently, you are eligible for SSI only if your assets do not exceed $1,800 if single, and $2,700 for a married couple. Things that are counted include any wages you earn, bank accounts, Social Security checks, alimony, cash, workers' compensation benefits, retirement benefits, stocks and bonds, insurance annuities, and real estate (other than your home).

Items that are *not* used to determine the extent of your assets include your home, burial plots for your immediate family, and, depending upon their value, your personal and household items, a car, your insurance policies, and burial funds. Food stamps are not counted either. Although you can receive SSI benefits even if you are also getting Social Security benefits, you can't receive benefits from both SSI and the Aid to Families with Dependent Children (AFDC) program at the same time.

The standard federal SSI payment for an eligible single adult or child is $340 a month, and, for an eligible couple, $510 a month. Your income (or the parents' income in the case of a child) for the month may prompt a reduction in the amount of your check. The first $20 of income you have each month usually is not counted, regardless of where it comes from. All "unearned income" (such as stock dividends or interest from your bank account) over the first $20 of income ordinarily will reduce the amount of your SSI check. But the first $65 of "earned income" (wages) you have each month are not counted against you in determining your SSI benefits. If you earn more than that in a single month, your SSI payment is then reduced by $1 for every $2 you make above $65.

If you think that you may qualify for SSI benefits, you should immediately apply for benefits at your local Social Security office. SSI benefits can only begin with the day on which you apply for them (or the date you become eligible for SSI benefits, if that is later than the date you apply).

13

CONTRACTS

MENTION OF THE WORD *contract* often conjures up terrifying visions of endless pages of yellowed parchment written in obscure legalese. Nothing could be further from the truth. Of all the areas of law, none is encountered more frequently in day-to-day living than the law of contracts. Contracts are everywhere. You've probably made at least ten contracts this week without even thinking about it. You made a contract when you bought your groceries at the supermarket. If you ate at a restaurant last night, you had a contract; you paid money in return for food. Your savings account is the subject of a contract between you and the bank. Your credit cards are another example of a contract. Your electricity and gas are provided by the public utilities under a contract: you have agreed to pay them the going rate for the services they furnish. The same is true of the telephone company. In fact, when you bought this book, you entered into a contract. You gave the salesperson a certain amount of money and in return received this book.

What is it about the word *contract* that so intimidates the average person? Perhaps it is because we usually reserve its use for more significant things—buying real estate or cars, for instance, or employment contracts. But the general rules of contract law that govern your relationship with the person who delivers your daily newspaper are the same as those that protect your rights when you, say, hire a company to do extensive and costly home improvement work for you. The law of contracts, as you'll soon discover, is one of the most methodical areas of the law. It flows logically and chronologically from the time an offer is made until the contract is breached or successfully and unproblematically concluded. This chapter gives you the information you need to understand your basic rights when making an agreement. After reading the following material, you'll never again cringe upon hearing the word *contract*.

First, several introductory words about contracts are in order. Except for a few types of contracts (discussed below), an oral contract is just as good as a written contract. But it is always preferable to have the contract in writing and signed by each party. The terms of the contract should always be spelled out with specificity so the other party can't claim that there wasn't a contract or that the terms were different from what you think. If it comes down to a lawsuit—even if it's only in small claims court—it's much easier to prove the terms of a written contract than those of an oral one.

We've all been warned never to sign a contract without reading it. Just how important is this? It can be very important. Suppose you sign a contract without reading it and later discover that some of the provisions are different from those you thought you had agreed to. Can you get out of it? Generally not. You normally are bound by the terms of the contract you signed. So before you sign your next contract, take whatever time you need to read it carefully, and ask for explanations if you don't understand something. And if you don't get a satisfactory explanation, talk to a lawyer first. Above all, don't feel pressured into signing a contract without being given the chance to read it.

Making a Contract

Four things are essential for a contract to be legally binding: both parties must have the legal capacity and authority to make a contract; there must be an offer; there must be an acceptance of that offer; and there must be "consideration"—something you give (money, for instance) or do (such as provide a service) in return for something else.

Legal Capacity and Authority to Make a Contract

Having "legal capacity" to contract means in part that you are old enough to make a contract. A minor (in most states, a person under 18) is legally incapable of making a binding contract. A minor who enters into a contract with an adult really has the best of both worlds. The adult cannot enforce the contract against the minor, but the minor can enforce it against the adult. The minor can reap the benefits of the contract while avoiding any obligations. If an adult sues a minor for breach of contract, the minor can simply assert his or her minority as a complete defense. One exception is that a minor is usually liable for the reasonable value of any necessities of life—food, clothing, shelter, and medical care—given directly to him or her. What happens after the minor comes of age? The contract can be enforced against the minor if he or she does not "disaffirm" (cancel) it within a reasonable time after reaching the age of majority. In a few states, however, the only way a minor can ratify (affirm) a contract after coming of age is in writing. When a minor cancels a contract, he or she ordinarily must return what was received (or what is left of what was received) from the other party.

Legal capacity to contract also means that you have sufficient mental ability to understand what the contract is all about. A person who is insane, mentally retarded, or suffering the ravages of Alzheimer's disease, for instance, ordinarily lacks the mental ability to enter into a contract. If a guardian has been appointed for a person, only the guardian can make contracts on his or her behalf. Contracts made by insane persons are usually void and unenforceable. A number of courts, however, hold that if you don't know that a person is mentally incompetent (and the person doesn't exhibit bizarre conduct or do anything else to indicate a problem), and you fulfill your part of the agreement, you can enforce the contract against him or her. And, like a minor, a mentally deficient person can still be liable for the necessities of life that he or she receives.

A person who is so drunk or high on drugs that he or she doesn't understand the nature and effect of the contract is not bound by it. When the person sobers up, he or she has the option of canceling or ratifying the contract. If the person chooses to cancel the contract in this situation, he or she must return any money or property received from the other party.

"Legal authority" to make a contract is important when you or the person you are dealing with represents someone else. Suppose, for example, a friend asks you to sell her car while she is in Europe and gives you the necessary papers to transfer title. You now have the legal authority to make a contract on her behalf to sell her car. When you give someone the authority to make contracts on your behalf, you are the "principal"; the other person is your "agent." If the Statute of Frauds (see discussion below) requires the contract to be in writing, as when real estate is the subject, your authority permitting the agent to act on your behalf must also be in writing.

Whenever you are dealing with an agent, ask to see written (preferably notarized) authority from his or her principal. And when giving someone the right to contract for you, put in writing exactly what authority your agent has. For example, if you're giving someone the power to sell your car for you, describe the car and state the lowest price that he or she can sell it for and the terms (cash only, for instance). That way, should your agent sell your car for less than you authorized or on different terms, the other party may not be able to enforce the contract against you if you object to it.

The Offer

The first step in making any contract is the "offer"—a proposal to buy, sell, or do something. The person who makes the offer is the "offeror"; the person to whom it is made the "offeree."

The most important thing to know about an offer is that the proposal must be sufficiently clear and definite as to its terms. Four things should be spelled out in the offer: the names of the parties, the subject matter of the contract, the price, and how soon the contract must be performed. In order to avoid problems of fraud or misrepresentation, which can give the other person a way out of the contract (see discussion below), the offer should accurately and honestly describe what you are selling or promising to do. If you forget to agree on when the contract is to be completed—the money given, the work performed, and so forth—the law implies a reasonable time, usually no more than 30 days.

Suppose Joanne tells Elizabeth that she will sell Elizabeth her $15,000 car for $1,000. Elizabeth goes to the bank and withdraws the money, but when she tries to give Joanne the money, Joanne refuses to take it, saying she was only kidding. Can Elizabeth hold Joanne to her "offer"? No. An offer made in jest is not binding if a reasonable person would have realized it was in fact made in jest. The price Joanne was asking was clearly out of line, and anyone in Elizabeth's position would have known that Joanne was not serious. But if someone makes an "offer" to you that he or she secretly intends as a jest, but the offer outwardly appears reasonable and serious, and you accept that "offer," a valid contract is formed. And even though, to a reasonable person, the offer would seem adequately fair, you cannot enforce it against the person making the offer if you subjectively knew it was made in jest.

When Does an Offer End?

To determine how long an offer is good for, first look at the offer itself to see if it states how long it is open. For instance, if Jane offers to sell you her car for $2,500 and gives you a week to think about it, the offer is good for one week. But what if Jane doesn't say anything about the time that the offer is open? When no time limit is stated, the offer expires within a reasonable time. What constitutes a reasonable time depends on the circumstances.

Offers made face to face generally can be accepted only on the spot if no time limit is specified.

Suppose Jane told you that she'd keep the offer open for a week but the next day informs you that she's changed her mind about selling the car. Can you force her to sell you the car since the full week hasn't yet passed? No. Jane was within her rights to revoke the offer before you accepted it. But if you had given her, say, $25 to keep the offer open for the week, she could not revoke it before the week was up. You would have an "option contract" that allowed you to buy the car at the set price for the entire week.

What happens to Jane's offer if she dies or the car is destroyed in an accident while the offer is still open? The offer automatically ends. Likewise, if someone offers to sell you an animal, but it dies before you accept the offer, the offer dies with it.

Let's say that when Jane first offers to sell you her car, you decline. A few hours later, though, you change your mind, call her up, and tell her that you'll buy it. She informs you that the price has gone up $500 to $3,000. Can she do this? Yes; when you said no to the original offer, you rejected that offer, and it legally died at that instant. There was no longer any offer for you to accept. When you called Jane later, you were making your own offer—an offer to buy her car—which she was free to accept or reject. What Jane actually did was make you a "counteroffer." The legal effect of that counteroffer was to reject your offer of $2,500 for the car and make you a new offer to sell the car for $3,000.

The Acceptance

Once there is an offer, a contract is made only if the person to whom the offer was made accepts it while it is still open. Normally, only the person to whom the offer is made has the power to accept the offer. If Doris offers to sell you her stereo for $250, you and you alone can accept that offer. Suppose that

Peter is also present when Doris makes you the offer. Can he accept it? No. If Peter hands Doris the money, Doris is not obligated to accept it. But when an offer is made to the public in general, anyone has the right to accept it.

An acceptance must be unconditional and unequivocal—that is, with no strings attached. Suppose Bert says to Les, "I offer to sell you my sailboat for $5,000," and Les replies, "You have a deal, but only if you outfit it with a new mainsail first." Has Les accepted Bert's offer? No. Les has changed the terms of the offer by adding a new condition. Les's "conditional acceptance" has the same legal effect as a counteroffer; it terminates Bert's original offer and acts as a new offer, which Bert can accept or reject as he pleases.

A "grumbling acceptance" is one in which the offeree accepts the offer but makes a statement of dissatisfaction. For example, suppose Bill is interested in buying a 1955 Ford Thunderbird, a collector's item. In his part of the country, 1955 Ford Thunderbirds are a rare commodity. After six months of searching the classified ads and making weekly visits to used car lots, Bill finally finds one advertised for $25,000, well above the going rate, given the condition of the car. Bill buys the car but says, "I think the price is outrageous, and I'm only buying this car because I want one so badly." This is a classic example of a grumbling acceptance. Bill has purchased the car for $25,000, and his grumbling neither adds to nor takes away from the validity of the contract.

Unilateral and Bilateral Contracts

A "unilateral contract" is one in which someone promises to give you something or do something for you in exchange for your doing a specified thing. For example, if someone offers to sell you a table for $200, this is a unilateral contract: you accept the offer only by giving the $200. A "bilateral contract," on the other hand, is one in which both sides *promise* to do or give a certain thing. If the person selling you the table had said, "I'll sell you the table if you promise to pay me $200 next Tuesday," it is a bilateral contract: the contract is made as soon as you promise to pay the money next Tuesday. The distinction between a unilateral contract and a bilateral contract is not always an easy one to make, but it can be critical in determining the rights of the parties if a disagreement arises before both parties have completely performed their obligations.

Unless the offer states otherwise, you can accept a bilateral contract in person, over the telephone, by mail, or by telegraph, by promising to do what the offer requires, and your acceptance is good at the time it is dispatched via any reasonable means of communication. If you mail your acceptance, most courts hold that the acceptance is effective once you drop a properly addressed and stamped envelope into the mailbox. If you put too little postage on the envelope or make a mistake on the address, the acceptance is good only when it reaches the other person.

A unilateral contract is accepted only when you do what the offer calls for. For example, if Pam tells you that she will give you $150 for your bookcase if you deliver it to her house on Saturday, you can accept the offer only by delivering the bookcase to her house on Saturday. It is not necessary, nor does it have any legal effect, for you to say something like, "You have a deal; I'll be there Saturday morning." You don't have to say anything; all you have to do is show up at Pam's house on Saturday with the bookcase.

Suppose that Brad offers to pay Gene $750 if he digs a hole for a spa in Brad's backyard—a unilateral contract. Gene can accept Brad's offer only by digging the hole. Does that mean that Brad can revoke his offer before the work is completed, even if Gene has already started digging and is, say, half done? No. Once Gene begins work, Brad must give him a reasonable time to finish the work and accept the offer.

Consideration: The Heart of the Contract

The final thing a contract needs in order to be legally binding and enforceable is "consideration." Consideration is something you give or do in return for something; it is the heart of the contract, the very reason for its existence. You give up something to get something. Suppose you buy a sofa for $750. Your consideration is giving $750; the other person's consideration is giving you the sofa. Or suppose you get your car washed. Your consideration is paying money, and the other person's consideration is washing your car. Money is frequently one party's consideration in a contract, but bartering goods or services is just as valid.

The amount of the consideration given is generally not important, except to the extent it bears on whether the offer was made in jest or whether it wasn't a contract at all but really a gift. For example, if you pay $1,000 for a painting worth $15,000, the contract is binding, unless the other person claims to have been "only joking" when he or she made the offer. In some states, contracts in writing are presumed to be supported by consideration and are therefore enforceable.

You can enforce a contract, but you ordinarily cannot enforce a gift against the person who promised it. If, for instance, a solicitor from Community Chest, a charitable group, calls you on the phone, and you agree to give $10, are you legally obligated to pay that amount? No. This is not a legally binding contract because although you're giving up something, you aren't receiving anything in return. As it is only a gift, it cannot be enforced against you in court. Once you make the gift, you normally don't have any right to force the recipient to return it to you.

Sometimes a contract can be enforced against you even though you didn't receive any consideration in return for what you gave. Suppose, for example, that your niece wants to open her own business but doesn't have enough money. She needs $20,000 to get it off the ground but has only $10,000. You tell her that you'll give her the rest. She buys equipment, signs a lease, and otherwise gets things moving. Can you back out of your offer now, on the basis that you're not getting anything in return? No. You could have gotten out of it if you had told your niece you'd changed your mind before she bought the equipment and signed the lease. Since your niece relied to her detriment, on your promise, it is only fair and just that you be held to your word. This is the rule of "promissory estoppel."

When a Contract Must Be in Writing

In England in 1677, a statute of frauds and perjuries was enacted that required certain contracts to be in writing in order to be enforceable. Because some agreements were more susceptible to fraud than others, they had to be in writing to protect the parties involved. If the contracts were not in writing, the courts would not intervene.

All 50 states and the District of Columbia have adopted versions of this law, which has come to be known as the "Statute of Frauds." The main types of contracts that must be in writing in order to be enforceable in court are:

• Contracts dealing with interests in real estate, except for leases of less than a year;

• Contracts for the sale of goods priced at more than $500;

• Contracts that cannot be performed within one year from the date when the contract is made or that require services for the lifetime of either party;

• Contracts in consideration of marriage, such as premarital agreements and property settlement agreements;

• Promises to pay another's debts.

To be enforceable, the written contract need contain only the bare requirements: the names of the parties, the subject matter, the price, and when the contract is to be performed. Most states require that the contract be signed by the other party before a court can enforce it against him or her. (On the other hand, if you don't sign it, the other party can't enforce it against you.) A few states require that both parties sign the written contract. The written agreement can be made and signed after an oral agreement is reached. But until the essential terms are in writing and signed by the other party, you can't enforce it in court against him or her.

Under certain circumstances, a court will enforce an oral contract for the sale of goods for more than $500. If you've already paid for the goods, you can enforce the contract against the seller. Conversely, if you accept the goods, the seller can enforce the contract against you; you can't take the goods and then get out of paying for them because the contract isn't in writing.

If your contract requires you to perform services for more than one year, after you do all that the contract requires of you, you can enforce it against the other party even though it's not in writing. If you've only partially performed, you can still recover the reasonable value of any benefits that the other party received from your work.

Modifying a Contract after It Is Made

Once a contract is made, it usually can be changed only if both parties agree; ordinarily, neither party can unilaterally change the contract. For example, if Bill has agreed to sell his car to Virginia for $1,000, then calls her several days later and says he now wants $1,500, Bill is not entitled to the extra $500. Most of the time, even if both parties agree to change the terms of the contract, the change is not effective unless it is supported by new consideration—until the parties give and get something more than the original contract called for. So even if Virginia initially agrees to pay the higher amount, if she later changes her mind, she

doesn't have to pay the additional money. Bill is already con-
tractually obligated to sell her the car for $1,000.

Nothing, however, would prevent Bill from calling Virginia
and telling her that he wants to raise the price to $1,500 and in
return will add four new tires. If Virginia agrees, she is bound by
the new terms because she would be getting more than she was
originally entitled to. Of course, Virginia does not have to accept
Bill's proposal and can demand that the contract be carried out
as they originally agreed.

Once in a while, one party can make a unilateral demand
that the contract be changed. This happens when something comes
up that neither party could have anticipated when the contract
was made. Say that you hire Reliable Pool Company to put a
swimming pool in your backyard for $10,000. Soon after it starts
digging, Reliable discovers that instead of the typical dirt and clay
found in the area, your yard has a layer of solid granite. Reliable
informs you that it will cost $1,000 to get the granite removed
and that unless you agree to pay this extra amount, it will walk
off the job. Is Reliable bound to do the work for $10,000 as
originally agreed, the granite notwithstanding? Generally, no. In
this case, Reliable can demand that the contract be changed to
provide for the new difficulty, since neither of you could have
expected it at the start. To require Reliable to do the work at
the original price would impose a substantial hardship on the
company.

A written contract can usually be modified by an oral agreement, even if the contract expressly provides that it can be changed
only by a written modification. A written modification is normally
required only when the Statute of Frauds requires the original
agreement to be in writing, or if a statute (a law passed by Congress or a state legislature) expressly provides that written contracts can be changed only by written modifications. But even if
a statute does require a written modification, an oral modification
is valid and enforceable once it is completed. The other person
can't then get out of the terms of the modification by claiming
that the contract required all changes to be in writing. It is usually

best, however, to put the modification in writing and have both parties sign it to avoid later misunderstandings.

Here are some examples of the rules regarding contract modifications:

1. Dennis hires Phil's Construction Company to add a new room onto his house. The original contract calls for a single 10′ x 15′ single-story addition for $6,500. After the contract is signed, Dennis decides that he wants a larger room, and with a bathroom. Phil tells Dennis it will cost $12,500 to install a 15′ x 20′ room with a bathroom. Dennis agrees. In this situation, the modification is effective, since each party has given new consideration: Phil must now build the larger room with a bathroom, and Dennis must now pay $12,500.

2. Let's say that the contract for the construction of the 10′ x 15′ room addition for $6,500 is signed, and Phil has started work. Dennis now tells Phil that he wants an extra window in the new room. Phil refuses to do this because it would require considerable time and effort to change the plans and have them approved by the city building department, and work would be delayed several weeks while they waited for the framing. Dennis tells Phil that he will pay Phil a fair amount to cover the cost of the window and related expenses, but Phil still refuses to agree to the change. Phil does not have to accept Dennis's offer to change the contract and can continue work according to the terms of the original agreement. If Dennis tells Phil to stop working, Dennis will be in breach of the contract.

3. Ace Painting Company agrees to paint Patty's house for $1,000. When the job is about half done, Ace tells Patty that it will finish the job only if Patty agrees to pay $500 more and threatens to walk off the job if Patty refuses. Telling Ace that it is "putting a gun to my head," Patty reluctantly agrees to pay the additional amount, since she wants the work completed before her family arrives for a visit. After the job is finished, Patty refuses to pay Ace the extra $500. If Ace sues in court for the $500, who will win? Patty. She only has to pay the $1,000 as they originally agreed, because she is not receiving anything more in return for the additional $500. The terms of the original contract entitled Patty to have her house painted a certain color with a certain paint. Under the "modification," Patty receives the same thing, only now at a higher price.

When a Party Breaches the Contract

A contract is "breached" when one party unjustifiably refuses to do something that the contract requires of him or her— if, for example, the work you contract for isn't done correctly or on time, if the other person refuses to pay you, or if the thing you buy is defective or not what the seller represented it to be. What are your rights when the other party is in breach of the contract? If the breach is a minor one, the contract remains intact—you must still do what the contract requires you to do—but you are entitled to be compensated for any damages you suffer from the breach. If the breach is a major one, you have a choice: you can treat the contract as continuing and seek reimbursement for your damages, or you can treat it as completely breached, in which event the contract is over, you are relieved of your obligations, and you can demand compensation from the other party for the damages you suffer.

When the other party is in breach of the contract, you have a few other alternatives: you can forgive ("waive") the breach; you can agree to modify the old contract; or you can release the other from all or part of the contract. In some situations, you can unilaterally cancel ("rescind") the contract and get your money (or whatever) back.

Money Damages

When the other party breaches a contract, you are entitled to money damages to compensate you for your losses. The idea is to give you the "loss of your bargain" and put you in the position you would have been in if the contract had been carried out to the letter. For example, suppose the Standard Paint Company agrees to paint your house for $3,000, then backs out on the deal, and you have to pay $3,500 to get someone else to do it. You are entitled to recover $500 in damages from Standard Paint—what it cost you extra to get the job done.

Now consider the opposite side of the coin. You are the painter and have a signed contract to paint the house for $3,000. The day before you start, the homeowner calls you and cancels the contract. How much can you recover in damages? You are entitled to your lost profit. Say the paint and other materials for the job would have cost $1,000; you would be entitled to $2,000 in damages. What if you had already bought the paint for the job; could you recover the extra $1,000 for that as well? That depends on whether you can use the paint for another job. If you can, you can't recover its cost. But if you placed a special order for it, and no one else wants it, you can recover the $1,000 you paid for it as well.

When the other party breaches the contract, you must make a reasonable effort to "minimize your damages." Suppose you have an employment contract for two years and are fired without reason after six months. You must minimize your damages by attempting to find a comparable job—one doing similar work for similar pay. If you make no effort to reduce your losses, you may not get anything.

Suppose you buy a new bicycle made by American Bike Company. The first time you ride it, the wheel collapses, and you are thrown to the ground and injured. The registration card that came with the bike states that if the bike is defective, American Bike's sole liability is to repair or replace it and that this warranty is in place of any and all other warranties. In accordance with the warranty, American Bike Company offers to give you a new wheel but refuses to pay for your medical bills and other expenses. Can American Bike do that? No. A manufacturer cannot disclaim liability for personal injuries resulting from its defective products.

Say, though, that the bike broke down on your way to work. You weren't injured, but you missed work and were docked the full day's pay. Whether American Bike has to reimburse you for those lost wages depends initially on whether you saw the warranty disclaimer on the registration card before you bought the bike. A disclaimer is usually effective only when it is "conspicuous"—in larger type than the rest of the information—so that your attention is naturally drawn to it. A disclaimer in fine print doesn't count, so American may have to pay for your lost wages. But if the disclaimer is in large type, American Bike may not have to reimburse you for your pay, since this is a purely economic loss. Had you missed work because of personal injuries suffered in the accident, then you could recover damages for your lost wages.

Some contracts provide for a certain amount of money to be paid as "liquidated damages" in lieu of any other damages if either party breaches the contract. Many contracts for the purchase of real estate, for example, provide that if the buyer backs out of the deal, the deposit is forfeited to the seller as liquidated damages. A court will enforce a liquidated-damages clause only when the actual damages are difficult or impossible to ascertain, and the amount of the liquidated damages are reasonable under the circumstances; otherwise, the judge will ignore the liquidated-damages clause and set the amount of damages. Say you signed a contract to buy a $100,000 house, put down 20 percent, then changed your mind a week later. The seller refuses to return your deposit on the basis of the contract's liquidated-damages clause. If you sue the seller, who will win? You will. The $20,000 is clearly out of line with the seller's actual damages. The judge will most likely rule that the liquidated-damages clause isn't really a provision for damages but a penalty against you, the buyer. Courts will enforce liquidated-damages clauses, but never something that is clearly a penalty.

Specific Performance: Ordering You to Uphold Your Part of the Bargain

Sometimes the judge will order the party in breach to do what the contract requires of him or her, to "specifically perform." Specific performance is granted only when money is not adequate under the circumstances. Suppose, for example, you agree to buy an original painting from Gloria's Art Mart for $5,000. Before you pick the painting up, Gloria receives a higher offer from someone else and refuses to go through with your deal. Because original paintings are "one of a kind," no amount of money can really replace them. Unlike a mass-produced product, you can't just go to another art gallery and buy the same painting. You can therefore sue in court to force Gloria to sell you the painting for $5,000.

Specific performance is often ordered by courts when one party backs out of a contract that required him or her to sell land to someone else. The law views each piece of land as wholly unique and different, even if parcels stand side by side. So if someone contracts to sell you his or her house, then tries to back out and sell it to someone else at a higher price (or decides not to sell it at all), you can sue to compel the sale of the house to you (see chapter 5).

One important limitation on specific performance is that a court cannot order a person to work under a personal services contract, because of the Thirteenth Amendment to the Constitution, which abolished slavery and involuntary servitude. For example, suppose Tony's Italian Restaurant hires an acclaimed chef to work for it for two years. After eight months the chef quits. The court will not order the chef to work for Tony's because that would amount to forced labor. But one thing the court can do is prohibit the chef from cooking for any other restaurant. The chef is given a choice: cook for Tony's Restaurant or cook for no restaurant until the two years are up. The court could not, however, prevent the chef from working at a different type of job, such as selling insurance or repairing cars. In effect, the court can say to the chef, "You can do any type of work you want, but if you want to cook, then you can cook only for Tony's until the period of time specified in the contract expires."

Rescission and Restitution

In some situations, a contract can be canceled ("rescinded"), and each party gives back anything received from the other party ("makes restitution"). This serves to nullify the contract; it is as if the contract never existed. An everyday example of rescission and restitution: suppose you buy a pair of shoes without trying them on. You get home, put them on, and discover they're too small. You go back to the store, and since it doesn't have a pair that fits you, you return the shoes, and the store gives you your money back. It is now as though the contract never existed: you have your money and the store has the shoes.

Before a court will order rescission and restitution, you must return or attempt to return anything you received from the other party unless it is worthless. One exception, however, is that if you received money from the other party, you can credit it against the value of any services you performed or any property you gave. You must offer to make restitution promptly after learning of the other party's breach, or you may forfeit your right to this remedy. Do you have to give the other party what you received if he or she refuses to return what you gave? No. You can make the other party's restitution a condition of your own.

Accord and Satisfaction

An "accord and satisfaction" takes place when you and the other party disagree on what the contract requires to be paid or done and then you compromise. The terms of the compromise, not those of the original contract, then govern your rights and duties. For instance, suppose you owe Harry money for some work he did. You claim the amount owed is $350; he claims it's $500. If you send a check for $350 and write "Payment in Full" or something similar on the back, does that mean you don't have to pay the other $150 if Harry endorses the check and cashes it? Yes. Because the amount owed is in dispute, Harry is accepting the accord by endorsing the check. It will have no effect if Harry crosses out the words *Payment in Full* and writes something like "Compromise not accepted" before signing it; he has accepted the accord by cashing the check, regardless of what he writes on the check.

Suppose, though, that you don't dispute the amount of the debt but still send a check for only $350 and write "Payment in Full" on the back. If Harry endorses the check, will that release you from having to pay the other $150? No. Accord and satisfaction applies only if there is a dispute. When there is no dispute, in most states, Harry can endorse and cash the check and still collect the remaining $150 from you.

When you want a check to act as an accord and satisfaction of a disputed amount, write on the back of it something like "Accepted as Payment in Full of the Disputed Debt Involving the Contract Dated _____ ." With it, include a cover letter stating why you feel you owe the smaller amount and informing the other person that by endorsing the check, he or she accepts it as an accord and satisfaction. Keep a copy of the letter.

How a Judge Interprets a Contract in a Dispute

What happens when you and the other party disagree on the meaning of a word or sentence and can't work it out yourselves? In resolving disputes of how the words and terms of a contract should be interpreted, a judge uses the following guidelines. The contract is construed as a whole. An individual provision, sentence, or word is read in relation to the entire contract and the expectations of the parties. Nothing is considered alone or out of context. Words are given their ordinary meaning unless a special business or technical usage is apparent from the contract. Previous dealings between the parties are taken into consideration, as are trade customs in appropriate situations. Doubts and ambiguities in terms are resolved against the party who prepared the contract, since that party was in a better position to avoid them.

A special rule applies to written contracts that the parties intend as the "complete and final expression" of their rights and obligations. This is the "parol evidence rule," which generally prohibits the judge from considering earlier agreements or understandings that would change the terms of the written contract. Under this rule, the judge ordinarily cannot look beyond "the four corners of the contract" to resolve the dispute. This rule does not apply to modifications made after the contract was signed, however. Judges are hesitant to rule that a contract is the final and full expression of the agreement and usually will do so only when the contract contains a provision to that effect and the contract lays out the whole agreement.

Things That May Go Wrong

Satisfaction Guaranteed?

Can you get out of paying on a contract if you're not satisfied with the work? That depends on the nature of the contract. Unless they explicitly state otherwise, most contracts require only that the performance be acceptable to a reasonable person. If a reasonable person would be satisfied with the results, you cannot refuse to pay even if it wasn't up to your own standards. You can change this guideline by specifying in the contract that you must be personally satisfied with the other party's performance. You can even provide in the contract (if the other party agrees) that it must meet with the satisfaction of a certain third person.

When the subject matter is personal, it must meet *your* standards, unless the contract specifically provides otherwise. If you hire a photographer to take wedding pictures, for example, you must be happy with the final product. If you aren't, you don't have to pay the photographer. (Of course, you won't get the pictures, either.) It makes no difference that a reasonable person would accept the work. This is because the subject matter of the contract—the pictures—involves personal taste.

How Mistakes Affect a Contract

Suppose Molly sells you a champion male show dog for $1,000, and you have plans to breed it. After several months of failure at breeding it, your vet tells you the dog is sterile. If Molly knew why you were buying the dog but didn't know it was sterile, you can rescind the contract based on your mutual mistake and get your money back. (If Molly knew her dog was sterile before selling it to you and knew why you wanted it, you would have a good case for fraud.)

Not every mistake is enough. It must go to the heart of the matter. For example, Susan has inherited her uncle's estate. She holds a garage sale to clear out what she doesn't want to keep. One of the items is an old clothes wardrobe her uncle had for years. Because it is old and needs refinishing, Susan puts it up for sale at $50. You buy the wardrobe, take it home, and later learn that it is a rare antique worth several thousand dollars. If Susan finds out about this, can she demand that you return the wardrobe or pay more for it? No. This type of mistake is not enough to invalidate the contract, because you got what you both thought you were buying: an old wardrobe. In the example with the dog, by contrast, you thought you were getting a dog capable of breeding, when in fact it was sterile.

Your Rights When a Contract Is Grossly Unfair

Sometimes a court will not enforce all or part of an agreement against you if it is "unconscionable"—grossly unfair and oppressive. Suppose you buy a sofa from Jack's Furniture Store for $500, on time. After paying off all but $50, you buy a stereo from Jack's for $250, also on time. You pay Jack's another $150, then miss a few payments. Jack's attempts to repossess both the stereo and the sofa, claiming that the credit contract gives it this right. Can it do this? No. This is an example of a once prevalent practice that has been denounced as unconscionable—giving the seller an indefinite security interest in all property it ever sells you. You've more than paid off the sofa, and it would be patently unfair to let Jack's take it away from you now. The remaining security (the stereo) is enough to protect Jack's interest.

Unconscionability can be a number of things: high-pressure sales tactics; a seller's unfair security interests or repossession rights; sales contracts that result in your paying much, much more than the thing is actually worth (say, three or four times its value); excessive penalties or charges if you default on your payments; or long, confusing contracts that can't be understood even by the average lawyer. Unconscionability is particularly important in consumer transactions, since the ordinary consumer has little or no bargaining power and is handed the contract on a "take it or leave it" basis.

Suppose you quit making payments on a contract you believe is unconscionable, and are sued. If the judge agrees with you, he or she will do one of three things: (1) enforce the contract without the unconscionable provision; (2) limit the unconscionable provision to a more reasonable standard; or (3) completely refuse to enforce any part of the agreement.

Fraud and Misrepresentation

Let's say that you buy a used car. The seller falsely states that it is a 1983 model, when in fact it was made in 1980. The seller also tells you the car has only 15,000 miles on it, but what he doesn't tell you is that he disconnected the odometer for a couple of years, and the true mileage is closer to 50,000. What can you do when you learn the true facts, and the seller refuses to return your money? You can sue to rescind the contract and get all of your money back. You can also sue the seller for the tort of fraud (see chapter 8). If the seller honestly, though mistakenly, believed the car to be a 1983 model, you can still rescind the contract and get your money back on the grounds of misrepresentation; what you bought was not what the seller led you to believe you'd be getting. If you decide to keep the car, you can ask the seller to refund you the difference in price between the value of the car as he represented it and its actual value. If you paid $5,000 for the car (thinking it was a 1983 model), and 1980 models (the car's real year) in a similar condition were selling for $3,000, you'd be entitled to the difference of $2,000.

When you learn that you are the victim of fraud or misrepresentation involving a contract, you must take prompt action to cancel the contract, or you may lose your right to do so. For instance, if, after you discover that the car is three years older than the seller represented, you drive it for another six months, putting 10,000 miles on it, you can't expect to cancel the contract and get all of your money back. But you could still sue the seller for the difference in the car's value. If you want to cancel a contract, see a lawyer as soon as you can.

Illegal Contracts

Contracts involving illegal acts or things (for example, contracts to kill someone or contracts to purchase illicit drugs or stolen property) are usually void and cannot be enforced in court. If a hired assassin fails to kill the targeted person, the person who hired him or her cannot sue in court to enforce the agreement or to recover damages because the assassin breached the contract. Conversely, if the assassin does the job but the employer refuses to pay, the assassin will not be able to get a court judgment.

Knowingly selling, buying, or receiving stolen property is illegal, and contracts involving stolen property are usually unenforceable in court unless you didn't know the property was stolen. Suppose Ted offers to sell you a Brand X car stereo worth $250 for $175. Ted tells you that he has a brother in the wholesale business, but in fact, Ted stole it from a stereo store. You have no reason to suspect that the stereo is stolen, and you buy it. A week later, the police confiscate your stereo, or the stereo stops working. Can you sue Ted to get your money back? Yes. Because you had no reason to suspect that the stereo was stolen, you can recover your $175 from Ted. But if you knew or suspected that the stereo was stolen, the court would not let you recover your money, since you were a party to an illegal act.

What about gambling debts? If someone owes you money, can you sue in court to collect it? Except for a few areas in the United States, notably Las Vegas and Atlantic City, contracts involving gambling debts are usually void and unenforceable.

Lending money at a rate above the lawful interest rate is usury. If you quit paying the excessive interest, and the lender sues you, the court will not order you to pay the illegal interest charges just because the contract requires it; the lender can sue you only for interest up to the legal rate. And in some states, the lender forfeits *all* interest and can collect only the amount that was lent.

Special Types of Contracts

Mail-Order Contracts

Countless products are sold each year by mail-order companies that advertise their wares on television, in just about every magazine, newspaper, and other publication imaginable, and through letters and catalogs sent directly to prospective buyers' homes and offices. Some mail-order companies have been in business for decades and enjoy solid reputations. Others seem to come and go every month.

Like any other big business, mail order has its share of customer grievances. Of the millions of complaints the Better Business Bureau receives each year, about 20 percent concern products ordered through the mail. The most common complaints are slow delivery, delivery of damaged goods, and problems with credit or billing. (Problems with credit or billing are treated in chapter 14.)

When you order something by mail, the seller must ship it to you by the date promised, or you can cancel the order for a full refund. How soon must something be shipped to you? If the ad or catalog doesn't specify when to expect the product, you must receive it no more than 30 days after your order and payment have been received by the company or 30 days after your credit account has been charged for a credit purchase.

If the company can't ship the product on time, it must notify you of the new delivery date. If that date is more than 30 days after the old date, the company must send you a prepaid postcard or envelope so you can let it know whether you wish to cancel the order. If the shipping delay will be less than 30 days, you can cancel your order only by sending the company a letter to that effect.

Anytime you wish to cancel an order, do so in writing, and keep a copy for your records. If you do it by telephone, follow up with a letter confirming the cancellation. Keep a copy of the letter in case a dispute arises as to whether or not you notified the company. When you cancel an order, the mail-order company must refund your money in full within seven working days after it receives your letter. If you paid for the merchandise with a credit card, it must credit your account within one billing cycle after it receives your cancellation.

Suppose something comes in the mail that you didn't order. Do you have to pay for it or send it back? No. You can treat unordered merchandise as a gift and keep it without any obligation. (But first make sure that neither you nor anyone else in your family ordered it.) The mail-order company cannot force you to pay for something you didn't order. If you want, you can offer to return the product unused—but only if the company pays the postage.

What should you do if the mailman or delivery service rings your doorbell and tries to hand you a package that is badly torn, crushed, or otherwise damaged? If a package is obviously dam-

aged, you should simply refuse to accept it and send a letter to
the mail-order company informing it of what you did and asking
for another shipment. If you weren't home at the time, and the
damaged package was left on your doorstep or with a neighbor,
return it to the mail or delivery service unopened. Tell them that
you were not home when the package was delivered and that you
refuse to accept the package in a damaged condition.

Now suppose that the package looks fine on the outside and
you accept it, but when you open it, you discover the product in
a thousand pieces. If that happens, immediately return the product to the company with a letter stating why you are returning it.
You will ordinarily have to pay the postage—but reputable companies may let you charge the postage to its account, so call first.

Let's say that you open the package, and the product is fine
except for one thing—it's not what you ordered or what you
expected. Perhaps a mistake was made in the shipping department; perhaps the product you ordered was out of stock so another one was substituted; or perhaps the catalog or advertisement
misrepresented the product. What are your rights in this situation?
You can return the merchandise to the seller, and the seller must
give you a full refund and reimburse you for the postage. If you
suspect that you are the victim of mail fraud or misrepresentation,
send a letter explaining the situation to the U.S. Postal Inspection
Service, Room 3517, Washington, D.C. 20260-2100 or contact
your local post office.

You should be aware that the foregoing rules apply only to
orders made through the mail and not to orders made over the
telephone. Because you have more rights when you order by mail
than if you place the identical order by phone, whenever possible,
you should order through the mail.

Advertisements

An advertisement, whether appearing in a newspaper, in a
catalog, on television or the radio, or in a circular delivered to
your home or business, is usually not deemed to be an offer, but

merely an invitation for offers. By advertising, the retailer is just informing the general public that it has certain items for sale and is asking the customer to come in and make an offer. If a store advertises a 15-inch color television set for $250, the legal effect of the advertisement is to notify potential customers that it has the television set for sale and that it requests an offer of $250. When the customer takes the television set to the check-out stand and hands over a check for $250, the store then accepts the customer's offer.

Does this mean that a store can advertise a television for $250, then raise its price to $500 when you're in the store? Not at all. Although an advertisement legally is not an offer, many laws protect consumers from unfair, misleading, and outright fraudulent advertising practices. For instance, a store can't advertise a product at one price, then charge more for it (unless the mistake was an innocent typographical error). Stores cannot advertise one item for sale and then substitute one of inferior quality at the same price or another one at a higher price ("bait and switch"). Unless the ad states that only a limited number of items are available at a sale price, the store must have a reasonable supply of that item to satisfy expected demand. If you feel a company's advertisement is deceptive or misleading, you can complain to your local office of the Federal Trade Commission and your state's attorney general's office.

Auctions

When you make a bid at an auction, you are offering to buy the item for a certain price. Someone else may bid a higher amount, which is a new offer to the auctioneer. In some cases, a minimum bid may be required. If no bid reaches this minimum, the item can be withdrawn from the auction. An auction can be held "with reserve" or "without reserve." "With reserve" means that the person selling the item reserves the right to refuse all bids, including the highest. When an auction is "without reserve," the seller must sell to the highest bidder.

Suppose you make a bid but then change your mind. Can you withdraw the offer? You can if the auctioneer hasn't yet accepted it. If, for instance, as the auctioneer shouts, "Going once, going twice . . . ," you yell something like, "I've changed my mind; I don't want it," before the auctioneer's gavel comes down a third and final time, the offer is withdrawn. But if you change your mind after the auctioneer has called, "Sold," you are generally obligated to buy the item.

14

Consumer Credit, Debt Collection, and Bankruptcy

AMERICANS LIVE on the "buy now, pay later" plan. In fact, living beyond one's means has become an accepted way of life. The federal government leads the way with deficit spending, so it is no surprise that the average citizen is doing the same thing. But with credit come a number of potential legal problems. Laws have been passed to protect you when you are applying for or have credit. Laws protect you from creditor harassment if you fall behind on your payments. And if you find yourself so deeply in debt that you can't see a way out, you can use bankruptcy laws to get a new start in life.

Good credit is a necessity in today's society. It takes years to build up good credit but only a couple of missed payments to destroy your credit rating. Reestablishing your credit can be a long, difficult process. Because of this, if you ever find yourself facing a problem with getting credit, you should take action immediately. There are a number of steps that you can take yourself, and these are discussed in this chapter. But if you find that you're not making any progress toward resolving the problem on your own, get to a good lawyer immediately. A lawyer can often help save your credit rating or at least minimize any damage.

Consumer Credit and Your Rights

If a Lender Discriminates against You

Lenders mainly look at three things in deciding whether or not to grant you credit: (1) your ability to repay the loan, based on how long you have been working for your present employer, how much you make, whether you have other sources of income, and the amount of your outstanding obligations (including alimony and child support); (2) your reputation for paying loans back—your "credit history"; and (3) your ability to pledge sufficient collateral as security for the loan so the lender can get paid if you default.

Sometimes, however, a lender makes the decision to deny or limit credit based on something that has nothing at all to do with your ability and likeliness to repay the loan. The Equal Credit Opportunity Act prohibits lenders from discriminating against you on the basis of your race, national origin, color, sex, marital status, religion, and age. It also prohibits discrimination against you if you receive public assistance such as Social Security, veteran's benefits, or welfare. If you meet the particular lender's basic standards for creditworthiness, your credit application ordinarily must be approved.

Discrimination often manifests itself as a refusal to loan you money even though you meet all the objective standards; discouraging you from applying for a loan; or lending you money on terms different from those given to other persons with similar qualifications—lending you money at a higher interest rate or for a shorter period of time, for instance, or requiring a larger down payment.

Much credit discrimination is directed against women. If you are a woman, you cannot be denied credit or otherwise be discriminated against because you are single or divorced, nor can the lender ask you whether you plan on having any children. In fact, the lender cannot deny you credit on the assumption that you may have children in the future.

If you are a married woman, you can apply for credit in your own name—either your married or your maiden name—and the lender cannot turn you down because of your sex or marital status. Your husband usually cannot be required to sign the loan application if your income and assets alone meet the lender's standards for creditworthiness. You also cannot be denied credit because your husband declared bankruptcy, nor can your credit cards be immediately and arbitrarily canceled when your husband dies— even if your husband was listed as the "basic" card holder, and you are named as a "supplementary" account holder. You are entitled to have alimony and child support that you receive counted as part of your income, if you want.

Another group that has been the target of credit discrimination is the elderly. Lenders had a history of cutting off or reducing a person's credit as soon as he or she reached a certain age, often 60. The Equal Credit Opportunity Act prohibits a lender from discriminating against you because of your age. A lender cannot refuse you credit or charge you more than others because of your age, nor can the lender close your account or require you to reapply for credit because of your age. The lender can, however, take your age into consideration in determining how much longer your income will continue at its present rate and what your sources and amount of income will be after you retire. Like anyone else, you have to demonstrate that you will have the financial wherewithal to make the payments for the term of the loan.

Your Credit History: The Fair Credit Reporting Act

When you apply for a loan (or an apartment, insurance, or some jobs), your credit history will be checked to determine whether you are "creditworthy." A credit bureau compiles information from various sources—stores where you have charge accounts, the bank where you have your car loan or bank charge cards, and the like—and puts together a credit report on you. A credit report essentially is a list of your current and previous loans and your record of paying them. The date each loan was made or each charge account opened is listed, as are the initial loan amounts or credit limits and the current balances of each. The amount of the monthly payment and other terms are also shown. Most important to the prospective lender and your credit rating are any delinquencies, including missed payments, past due accounts, whether a company has ever written off your loan, whether you have been arrested or sued, and whether you have filed for bankruptcy.

What rights do you have if your application is denied because your file at the credit bureau is incomplete or contains inaccurate information that indicates that you are a bad credit risk? In April 1971, the Fair Credit Reporting Act took effect to protect consumers from having inaccurate, incomplete, and obsolete information about their credit histories circulated. (Under the Fair Credit Act, a credit report is called a "Consumer Report," and the credit agency that furnishes the report is a "Consumer Reporting Agency.") The Fair Credit Reporting Act mandates that bad credit marks—"negative information"—can be kept on file for no more than seven years, except bankruptcy, which can be reported for up to ten years. It also requires credit reporting agencies to adopt fair standards for gathering, maintaining, and reporting information concerning your credit. The Fair Credit Reporting Act applies only to consumer credit and insurance and does not cover commercial credit or business insurance.

Credit reports are not available to everyone. Only people or companies with a legitimate business reason are entitled to see your credit report. This protects your privacy from being invaded by people who have no real need for the information. And credit reports must be obtained with your knowledge—although they need not be obtained with your consent. Someone who obtains your credit report under false pretenses or who uses it for an improper purpose may be subject to criminal penalties. You may also be able to sue that person for an invasion of your privacy.

If you are denied credit or your terms are more onerous than those that others are offered, have the lender put in writing the reason why you were denied credit or why the terms are different. If the reason is that your credit history makes you a bad risk (or more of a risk than other people), ask the lender for the name, address, and telephone number of the credit reporting agency that prepared the report. Call the credit bureau and set up an appointment to discuss why the report is unfavorable. Or you can simply ask the credit agency to send you a letter informing you of the nature, substance, and sources of all information collected about you. If you go down to the credit reporting agency to check your file, you have the right to be accompanied by the person of your choice, such as your attorney, a relative, or a friend whose judgment you respect.

Under the federal Fair Credit Reporting Act, the credit bureau is not required to give you a copy of your file, although it may voluntarily do so if you ask for one. The Fair Credit Reporting Act requires only that the credit agency give you the nature, substance, and sources of the information it has, except for medical information and the names of people (or other sources) who provided information in an investigative report (see discussion below). Some states have passed laws that give you the right to inspect and copy your credit history report anytime you want from any credit bureau for a nominal fee. (Many credit bureaus are listed in the Yellow Pages under the heading "Credit Reporting Agencies.")

The Fair Credit Reporting Act requires the credit bureau to give you the information without charge if you ask for it within 30 days after your application for credit is denied. If you wait more than 30 days to ask for it, the credit bureau can charge you a reasonable fee for providing the information.

If your credit report contains incomplete or inaccurate information, you should request in writing that the credit reporting bureau reinvestigate its information. (If the information is more than seven years old—ten years if it's a bankruptcy—demand that the credit bureau immediately remove it from your file.) Also inform the credit bureau why you feel the information is incomplete or inaccurate. Once you have asked to have the information reinvestigated, the credit bureau must do so, unless the dispute is frivolous or not relevant to the report. If you do not hear back from the credit bureau within two weeks to a month, call it to find out what the results of its reinvestigation are.

If the information is found to be incorrect or cannot be verified, ask that it immediately be removed from your file. Also ask the credit agency to notify everyone who has received a credit report on you within the last six months that certain information has been deleted or corrected, which the credit agency must do at no cost to you. After a few weeks have passed, you should contact those people or companies to determine whether they have in fact received the new information. If they have not, get back in touch with the credit agency and remind it of its obligation to furnish this updated information to those companies.

As long as your request for a reinvestigation is not frivolous, you can sue a credit bureau that refuses or fails to reinvestigate your credit history. You can also sue if the credit bureau fails to correct the information and forward it to companies that have refused you credit within the past six months.

Traditionally, credit bureaus have not been required to verify information before including it in their reports. They have been allowed to rely on the integrity of the company or store that reports the information. All this may be changing, however. Some courts have begun to recognize that a credit bureau cannot simply report any and all information without making some effort to determine its accuracy. Credit bureaus now have a duty to follow reasonable procedures to assure the accuracy of all credit information they report.

What can you do if the credit bureau reinvestigates your complaint but refuses to change its records because it believes the information is correct? You can write a short statement spelling out your side of the disagreement and have it placed in your file. This statement must then be included in future credit reports. You can also demand that the credit bureau send your statement to companies that have requested a report within the previous six months. The credit bureau must send a copy of your statement without charge to companies that turned you down if you make your request within 30 days of the adverse action. Otherwise you may have to pay the credit bureau a reasonable fee to send your statement.

The typical credit report contains only information reported by, say, department stores, banks, and the like. A report that includes interviews with third persons concerning your character, reputation, or manner of living is called an "Investigative Consumer Report." You have the right to be notified anytime a business makes an investigative report on your background, and the business must give you information about the nature and scope of the investigation if you ask for it. You also have the right to learn the substance of the information gathered for the investigative report, although the names of the sources of that information are considered confidential and need not be disclosed to you.

If a credit bureau negligently or intentionally violates a provision of the Fair Credit Reporting Act, you have the right to sue the agency and collect damages, including punitive damages for a willful violation. If you win the case, you are entitled to have the credit agency pay your attorney's fees and court costs as well.

The Truth in Lending Act

The Truth in Lending Act—part of the Consumer Credit Protection Act of 1968—was designed primarily to let you know exactly how much a loan is going to cost. It requires the lender to tell you the amount being financed, the finance charge, the annual percentage rate, and the total of the payments. This information must be disclosed to you before you sign the credit contract.

The finance charge includes the total amount of the interest charges you will pay, any service charges, and other costs. The annual percentage rate is the most important rate in determining what the true interest rate of the loan is. Suppose, for example, you are borrowing $500 at 10 percent interest for one year, and the lender requires you to pay all of the interest ($50) up front. Your net proceeds from the loan then amount to just $450. So you're really paying $50 interest on $450—an annual percentage rate of almost 11.2 percent.

The length of the loan will determine how much interest you eventually pay, as well as the amount of your monthly payments. The shorter the term of the loan, the less you will pay in the long run in interest, but your monthly payments will be more than if you spread the loan out over a longer period of time. How long the loan should be depends in part on the size of the monthly payment you can afford.

Ordinarily, you are not required to purchase disability or accident or life insurance to pay off the loan in the event you are injured or killed and unable to meet your obligations. That insurance is usually optional and is more for the lender's protection than it is for yours. Before signing a loan application, make sure that the lender hasn't included an insurance premium if you don't want it.

Under the Truth in Lending law, if a company advertises some of the terms of a loan, it must advertise all important terms. For instance, if a car dealer advertises a car for $150 a month, it must also tell you how much the down payment is, what the annual percentage rate is, the length of the loan, the total payments, and the cash price of the car.

If a company violates the Truth in Lending Act, you can sue it for damages—including, in many cases, double the amount of the finance charges—and for your attorney's fees as well. Criminal action can also be taken against companies in appropriate cases. Your local office of the Federal Trade Commission can direct you to the proper authorities if you suspect a criminal violation.

The Truth in Leasing Act

As an alternative to purchasing major items—automobiles, appliances, televisions, furniture, and so on—many people are deciding to lease. The Truth in Leasing Act requires the lessor (the company that leases you the product) to tell you basic facts about the terms and cost of the lease, in order to help you decide whether leasing is as attractive as it appears.

Before you sign the lease, the lessor must give you a written statement of the costs involved. This must include the amount of the security deposit required, your monthly payments, and the total amount of any fees you must pay for license, registration, taxes, and upkeep. You must also be given a written statement of the terms of the lease: who is responsible for repairing and maintaining the property; the insurance you are required to maintain on it; any warranties that come with it; and whether you have an option to purchase the property when the lease is over. Standards for determining what wear and tear on the product is reasonable must also be included.

The Truth in Leasing Act applies only to products leased for more than four months and that are used for personal, family, or household purposes. It does not apply to real estate (apartment leases and hotel rooms, for example), nor does it apply to daily rentals of cars and other things.

There are two types of leases: "open-end" leases and "closed-end" leases. A closed-end lease usually costs more each month than an open-end lease, but at the end of a closed-end lease, you simply give the property back and walk away. (If there was an option to purchase the property, you have the right to buy it at the agreed price.)

An open-end lease may cost less each month, but at the end of the lease, you may have to make an additional payment (a "balloon payment") when you return the property. The balloon payment usually cannot be greater than three times the amount of the average monthly payment, unless there is excessive wear and tear on the property. In the lease, the lessor will estimate how much the property will be worth when the lease is over. If, when you return it, the thing is worth less than the lessor had estimated, you will have to make up the difference. If you disagree with the lessor's valuation of the property at the end of the lease, you have the right to have an independent appraiser value the property—at your cost.

Errors on Your Credit Card Statement

Sometimes an item that you never bought appears on your credit card statement. Or the price billed is more than what the price tag or sales advertisement said. There are other types of billing errors: the statement may show a wrong date of purchase (so you may wind up paying more in interest), errors in computation, purchases made by someone not authorized to use your account, and failure to credit your account properly. Your rights when faced with a billing error are covered by the Fair Credit Billing Act.

If you suspect that your bill contains an error, you must give the creditor written notice within 60 days after the bill was mailed to you. You can telephone the creditor to discuss the problem, but doing so will not preserve your rights under the Fair Credit Billing Act. Only a letter containing your name, address, account number, the dollar amount of the suspected error, a description of the error, and why you believe there is an error will preserve your rights. Keep a copy of this letter for future reference.

The creditor must acknowledge receipt of your letter within 30 days, unless the problem is resolved by then. Meanwhile, you do not have to make any payments on the disputed charge. But you still have to pay any charges that you don't dispute. Interest on the disputed amount will continue to accrue until the matter is settled. If you win, you won't have to pay either the charge or any of the interest attributed to it. If you lose, you'll have to pay both.

While your complaint is being investigated, the creditor may not report you as delinquent to a credit bureau, nor may it take any action to collect the disputed charge. It can, however, apply the disputed amount against your credit limit. For example, if your credit limit is $1,000, and you already have $250 in charges, and another $250 is in dispute, the creditor can apply this amount against your credit limit so that you have only $500 credit available. The creditor is also prohibited from making any threats to damage your credit rating unless you pay the disputed amount. It can, however, report you to the credit bureau for failing to pay an undisputed charge and can even take steps to collect that amount.

Within two billing periods, but never more than 90 days, the creditor must either correct the error or give you a written explanation telling why it believes the bill is correct. If the creditor made a mistake and admits to it, you do not have to pay any charges, including any finance charges, on the disputed amount. If the creditor feels that the bill is not in error, it must promptly send you an explanation of its reasons for thinking the charge is correct and a statement of the amount you still owe. You are then obligated to pay the disputed amount, as well as any finance charges that may have accumulated from the date when the item was first charged to your account.

Once the creditor gives you a written explanation of the charge, it has met all of its legal obligations under the Fair Credit Billing Act and can treat the charge as correct. If you still believe the charge is wrong, you should pay the amount in question and write a short letter to the creditor, explaining your position. Ask that a copy of this letter be included in your file at the credit bureau and that copies be sent to those persons or companies whom the creditor notified of the delinquency. If you continue refusing to pay, your credit history may be damaged. The creditor can report you to a credit bureau as being delinquent and can take action to collect the debt. The creditor must also report that the bill is being challenged, however, and must give you a list of the names and addresses of all persons or companies to whom it gave credit information on you. The creditor must notify these same people of the outcome when the dispute is finally resolved. If you want, you can file a lawsuit in small claims court to have a judge settle the controversy, or you can seek the advice of a lawyer.

Your Rights If You Buy Defective Merchandise with a Credit Card

Let's say that Helen uses her A. B. Nickel department store credit card to buy a toaster for $30 from her nearby A. B. Nickel store. When she gets home and plugs the toaster in, it explodes. Helen takes the toaster back to the store, but they refuse to replace it or refund her money. Can Helen refuse to pay the bill for the toaster when it comes? Yes.

Under the Fair Credit Billing Act, if you buy defective merchandise with the store's own credit card, you do not have to pay the balance due. Before you can do this, though, you must make an honest, good-faith attempt to return the product or to settle the dispute with the merchant who sold it to you.

If Helen had bought the toaster with, say, her MasterCard or Visa, the outcome would have been different. When you use a credit card other than one issued by the store, you are not required to pay for a defective product only if the product cost more than $50 and the sale took place in the state in which you live or within 100 miles of your home if the store is in another state.

Harassment, Repossession, and Other Debt Collection Practices

Creditors expect debts to be paid in full and on time. If you miss a payment or two, you can bet that the creditor will take steps to collect it. First you'll get a polite letter reminding you that your payment is past due. If you don't respond with a check, other letters will follow, each firmer in tone than the last. The second or third letter may threaten to turn the matter over to a collection agency or to the creditor's lawyer. If you ignore these letters, you'll soon receive a letter or call from a lawyer or a collection agency. And if that doesn't prompt you to pay up, you may find yourself being sued by the creditor. But there are limits to how far a creditor or collection agency can go to collect a debt.

Let's say that your debt has been turned over to a collection agency, and the collection agency starts calling you at all hours of the day and night, at home and at work. The debt collector calls you names and even goes so far as to threaten to call your boss and get you fired if you don't pay up immediately. Can you do anything to stop this harassment? Yes. A number of laws now protect you from creditor harassment and other strong-arm tactics. The most important of these is the federal Fair Debt Collection Practices Act, passed by Congress in 1978, which protects you against "debt collectors"—persons who regularly collect debts for others. The creditor and his or her attorney are not covered by this act, but state laws usually prohibit them from harassment and other excessive collection tactics.

One thing that is quite common when you fall behind in your payments is a letter from your creditor asking for the full balance of the loan, even though there may be, say, two more years to go. Suppose, for example, that your loan calls for you to make 24 monthly payments of $100. After making six payments, you miss two. The creditor sends you a letter stating that you are in default of the loan and that it is accelerating all of the future payments, so that the entire balance of the loan—$1,800, plus interest—is immediately due and payable. Can the creditor do this? Yes—if the loan agreement contains an "acceleration clause" (which written loan agreements ordinarily do have). Usually, though, if you bring the payments up to date, the creditor won't make you pay the rest at once. But if you don't make up the back payments, the creditor will most likely accelerate the payments and demand the entire amount.

What a Debt Collector Can and Can't Do

A debt collector can contact you in person, by telephone, or by mail. If he or she contacts you in person or by telephone, it must not be at unusual or inconvenient times or places. For

instance, a debt collector can't knock on your door in the middle
of the night. You cannot be contacted at work if your employer
objects, and many state laws prohibit a debt collector from contacting you at work unless you permit it.

A debt collector must tell you his or her name and cannot
lie and say that he or she is from a credit reporting agency or is
an attorney or government representative. Within five days after
the debt collector contacts you, he or she must send you a written
statement showing how much you owe and to whom. The debt
collector must also tell you what to do if you don't think you owe
the money. If within 30 days you send the debt collector a letter
stating that you do not owe the money, the debt collector can
contact you again and resume trying to collect the debt only if he
or she sends you proof of the debt, such as a copy of the bill or
your returned check.

A debt collector is prohibited from harassing you or embarrassing you in front of others. For example, he or she can't
keep calling you ten times a day, use profanity in talking with
you, or threaten you with physical harm if you don't pay up. A
debt collector can't call you a deadbeat in front of your friends
or coworkers. The debt collector also cannot tell you that he or
she will ruin your reputation if you don't pay up immediately.
The debt collector can't threaten to call the police and accuse you
of a crime if no crime has been committed. Nor can a debt collector threaten to take any other kind of legal action against you
unless the legal action is permitted and the debt collector intends
to take it.

A debt collector cannot use any threats, deception, or lies
to make you accept a collect long-distance telephone call or pay
for a telegram. For example, the debt collector can't pretend to
have some distressing news about a relative so you'll accept a
collect call.

The fact that you owe somebody money is usually only a
matter between you and the person or company to whom who
owe the money. A debt collector cannot tell your friends or coworkers that he or she is a debt collector and is looking for you

to discuss a delinquent debt. A collection agency can't even send you a letter that notes on the envelope that the sender is a collection agency. Your creditor may be liable for invading your privacy if he or she tells others of your debt (see chapter 8).

Sometimes a creditor will sell a delinquent debt to another company for less than the amount of the outstanding balance. The creditor is relieved of the burden of trying to collect the debt, and the company that buys it will make a vigorous attempt to collect the full debt. Suppose that you buy a used car from Swift Jim's Used Car Company for $2,000. You pay $500 down, and Swift Jim's finances the rest. Soon after you get the car home, you discover that the salesman grossly misrepresented the car: it's three years older than the salesman said, the odometer was turned back 20,000 miles, and so on. After you unsuccessfully try to return the car to Swift Jim's, you quit making the payments. Swift Jim's sells the debt to Speedy Collection Services, and one of Speedy's employees—we'll call him Gus—contacts you. You tell Gus that you're not going to pay Speedy a dime because Swift Jim's committed fraud. Gus tells you that that is a matter between you and Swift Jim's, not you and Speedy, and since Speedy is the legal owner of your debt, you'd better pay up immediately or face a lawsuit. Is this permissible? No. Although your debt can be sold to another company, you are still free to assert any legal defenses you have against the original creditor. So anything you could prove against Swift Jim's to get you off the hook can be used against Speedy. Speedy is guilty of an unfair debt collection practice by telling you otherwise.

How to Stop Creditor Harassment

How can you stop a collection agency from bothering you? Simply by writing a letter to the collection agency, telling it that you won't or can't pay the debt and to leave you alone. This bars the collection agency from contacting you again, except to say that there will be no further contact or that some specific action— a lawsuit, for instance—will be taken against you (but only if the collection agency intends to do so). This rule usually applies only to collection agencies. The creditor (or its attorney) can continue contacting you, as long as it does not harass you.

If a debt collector continues to harass you even though you've sent a letter asking it to stop, or uses any unlawful tactics, you should contact an attorney immediately to get the debt collector off your back. One added advantage to hiring an attorney is that once your attorney notifies your creditors and the collection agencies that he or she represents you, your creditors and the collection agencies must deal with your attorney, not you. Another thing you can do is to file a complaint with the Federal Trade Commission and your state attorney general's office.

Repossession: Here Today, Gone Tonight

Can a creditor repossess the merchandise you bought with the loan if you fall behind on the payments? That depends on the nature of your loan. There are two types of loans: secured and unsecured. A secured loan is one that requires you to pledge something as collateral. For instance, if you buy a car with the loan, the creditor will usually require you to put up the car as collateral. The creditor takes a "security interest" in the car. An unsecured loan, on the other hand, does not require any collateral. When you buy something with a bank charge card, that is usually an unsecured loan.

If you default on an unsecured loan, the creditor's only recourse (after letters and collection agency efforts fail) is to sue you, get a judgment, then collect from any assets or money you may have. But if you default on a secured loan, the creditor can repossess the collateral you pledged and sell it to pay off the outstanding balance. If the money from the sale isn't enough to pay the loan off in full, the creditor can sue you for the rest. Conversely, if there's any money left over from the sale after the loan is paid off—a rare situation—it must be returned to you. When, for example, you buy a television set from an appliance store on an "installment contract," the appliance store often retains ownership of the set until you make the final payment. Although this is a little different from a secured loan, the rules regarding repossession are the same.

Before your creditor can repossess the collateral, you must be in default of the loan. What constitutes a default is usually defined in the finance agreement. Failure to make payments is the obvious default. But depending on the terms of the loan, you can be in default if you don't keep adequate insurance on the collateral at all times (this usually applies only to cars); if the collateral is lost, destroyed, or substantially damaged; if you die or file for bankruptcy; or if you sell the collateral without the creditor's permission.

Once you default on a secured loan, the creditor normally has the right to repossess the collateral. In most states, the creditor usually does not have to go through the courts to repossess collateral, at least not if it can do so without a "breach of the peace" (see discussion below). Some states require the creditor to notify you that you are in default before repossessing the collateral and give you the chance to "cure" the default—make the delinquent payments, get insurance, and so on. Other states allow the creditor to repossess the thing without notifying you that you are in default. (In practice, most reputable creditors will notify you of the default and give you the opportunity to correct it.)

The main restriction on a creditor's right to repossess something is that it must do so without committing a "breach of the peace." This means that the repossessor must avoid the possibility of a physical confrontation with you. If it appears that the repossessor will not be able to take the collateral without a physical confrontation, the repossessor must leave and try again some other time. It is also a breach of the peace for a repossessor to enter your home or garage without your consent. Some states also bar a repossessor from breaking into a locked car to repossess it, even if the car is on a public street. If a repossessor does breach the peace, you can sue for the damages you sustain, including any physical injuries or damage to your property.

All is not necessarily lost after the collateral is repossessed.

Some states give you the right to cure the default by paying all outstanding loan charges—including interest, late charges, and penalties—and reimbursing the creditor for its reasonable attorney's fees and cost of having the collateral repossessed. You may not have much time to cure the default after the collateral is repossessed, so you should act quickly and call the creditor as soon as you can bring the payments current.

Lawsuits: The Ultimate Form of Debt Collection

If you don't respond to collection attempts or can't work out some repayment arrangement with the creditor (see discussion below), the creditor may sue you. Unless you have a good excuse—for instance, the product you bought with the loan fell apart as soon as you got it home—there's not much you can do to defend the lawsuit. If you ignore the lawsuit—and many people do in this type of case—the creditor will ask the court to enter a judgment against you.

After a judgment is entered against you, your creditor (who is now your "judgment creditor") will try to collect the judgment. If you pledged anything as collateral, the judgment creditor will get this if it hasn't already. Up to 25 percent of your wages can be garnished; rather than paying the money to you, your employer pays it directly to your judgment creditor. The judgment creditor can also get at your bank account and other assets. Some property is exempt up to a certain amount: your house, a car, your business tools, personal and household goods, and life insurance and retirement proceeds, among other things.

When You're In over Your Head: Repayment Plans and Bankruptcy

What can you do when your monthly expenses exceed your income, you fall behind on some payments, your creditors are hounding you, and a lawsuit seems inevitable? There are several options, depending on just how deep in debt you are. Running short $50 each month is one thing; being a few thousand behind and adding to this every month is quite another.

How do people fall into a financial abyss? For some, the lure of easy credit is too much to resist, and they soon find themselves overextended. But more often than not, serious financial trouble arises because a worker is laid off or there is a serious illness that drains finances. Whatever the cause of the situation, the thing *not* to do is ignore it. Ignoring the problem won't make it go away; it *will* make it worse.

You need to take stock of the situation. First determine what your monthly after-tax income is: add up your salary, alimony, interest from bank accounts, and other income you regularly receive. How much money do you have in the bank and how much in "liquid assets"—things that can be sold quickly for cash, such as stocks and bonds? Next figure your monthly expenses. Include everything: the mortgage or rent payment; the car loan; food; clothes; utilities and telephone; gas, parking, and other car expenses; credit card payments; all insurance premiums—home, car, medical, and life; medical and dental expenses; and so on. Comparing the totals will give you an idea of where you stand.

Now separate your "necessary" monthly bills—mortgage or rent, food, utilities and telephone, clothes, car expenses, and insurance premiums—and deduct the total from your monthly income. The difference is how much you have left to pay the rest of your bills. If it's just a matter of being a poor manager of money, a call to a credit counselor may be in order. (Look in the Yellow Pages under "Credit and Debt Counseling Services" for credit counselors near you, and check any company out with the Better Business Bureau.) But if you're pretty deep in debt, a call to a lawyer is usually advised.

Voluntary Repayment Plans and Debt Consolidation

If things aren't too far out of hand, or your financial difficulties are only temporary—say, your layoff is expected to last only a few months—you can try to work out a solution with your creditors yourself. You can ask all of your creditors to accept a smaller amount each month for a longer period of time, or you can ask that each creditor agree to reduce the amount of the debt by a certain percentage, or both. All creditors should be asked to accept the same percentage of reduction. If you can only afford to pay 60 percent of the bills each month, then ask each creditor to accept 60 percent. Try to get each creditor to waive late fees and penalties. Sometimes you can persuade a few creditors to give you a reprieve of a couple of months, so you can pay off other creditors and make your overall debt more manageable.

Your chance of working out a voluntary repayment plan with your creditors is best if you contact them as soon as you start receiving past due notices. Speak to the person who has the authority to approve repayment plans, and discuss your situation frankly and sincerely. Tell why you can't keep your payments up to date and exactly what you can pay. You'll need to show each creditor the worksheet with your monthly income and list of expenses, and a schedule showing how much you propose to pay each creditor.

A voluntary repayment plan can work only if all of your creditors agree to it. If a creditor ever balks at your proposal and sues you for the delinquent debt, then you may have to consider filing for bankruptcy. You can sometimes bring a reluctant creditor into line with the others by mentioning that your other creditors have agreed to the plan and that you may have to file for bankruptcy if you can't work things out on your own.

Another thing to consider if you can't quite meet all of your monthly bills is "debt consolidation." Debt consolidation usually consists of exchanging all of your smaller debts for one large debt for a longer period of time. Rather than owing, say, five creditors a total of $5,000, you get one loan so that you owe only one creditor the full amount. The advantage to this is that your monthly payments are reduced over the longer period. Where can you get a debt consolidation loan? Try your bank or credit union; you may not have much luck if you don't have anything to put up as collateral, however. You'll often have a better chance of getting a debt consolidation loan from a finance company, although the interest rate generally is higher.

Bankruptcy

If your creditors don't agree to a voluntary repayment plan or if your financial condition is so bad that there is no other way out, it is time to consider filing for bankruptcy. There are two types of bankruptcy: straight bankruptcy—called "Chapter 7" because it is found in Chapter 7 of the federal Bankruptcy Code—in which your assets are sold and the funds distributed to your creditors, and Chapter 13 repayment plans for individuals. (Businesses in financial difficulty can reorganize under Chapter 11.) Bankruptcy proceedings come under the exclusive jurisdiction of the federal courts; you can't file for bankruptcy in a state court.

Filing for bankruptcy does not carry the stigma it once did. It is an accepted solution to a difficult situation, one that nearly 340,000 individuals took advantage of in 1985 by filing for protection under Chapters 7 and 13 of the bankruptcy laws.

Filing for bankruptcy does not mean that you will lose everything you own. In fact, some people lose little or nothing of what they have and still get all of their debts canceled. This happens because most of their assets are completely or partially exempt from bankruptcy. Your house is exempt up to a certain amount. One car and household items such as furniture, appliances, and clothing are exempt up to a certain amount. Property you use in your business or trade is also partially exempt.

Most people need to hire an attorney to represent them in a bankruptcy, since the forms and procedures are usually too difficult for the average person to handle. A good bankruptcy attorney will see that all of your property which is exempt from bankruptcy is protected, so you don't part with something the law says you can keep. An attorney will also save you from having to talk to your creditors—something you may have been avoiding.

You can't protect an asset from bankruptcy merely by putting it in your parent's or a friend's name. Unless it is a bona fide sale—one for fair value, not a token sum—any such "sale" will usually be voided by the court and the asset treated as though you still own it.

Let's say that you owe your friend Gail $1,000. You know you'll be filing for bankruptcy in a week or two, but you want to make sure Gail gets everything you owe her, so you use your last cash to pay her. Is this fair? No. If your other creditors find out about it, they can require Gail to pay the bankruptcy trustee (discussed below) the amount over what she should have received. For example, if each creditor is only going to get 10 cents for every dollar you owe, Gail must return $900 to the trustee. That $900 will then be divided among the remaining creditors. Money paid to a creditor within 90 days before you file bankruptcy is called a "preference payment," which the creditor may be required to return.

Chapter 13 Repayment Plan

Chapter 13 involves a repayment plan in which you pay your creditors as much as you can. Sometimes this means paying the whole debt in smaller amounts over a longer period of time. It can also mean reducing the size of the debt as well, so instead of having to pay off the full $20,000 you owe (for example), you'll only have to pay $15,000. Can everyone take advantage of the Chapter 13 repayment plan? No. You must have a regular income, unsecured debts (see earlier discussion) of not more than $100,000, and secured debts of not more than $350,000.

A trustee appointed by the bankruptcy court will review your proposed plan to determine whether it is made in good faith and is feasible. Some of the things the trustee (and later the bankruptcy judge) looks at are how much of each debt you plan to pay off, the length of time of the plan, your employment history, whether you have any hardships, how often you file for bankruptcy, and your sincerity and honesty. Most repayment plans must be completed in three years, but the judge can extend your plan to five years if you have a good reason.

Once the bankruptcy judge approves your repayment plan, each month you will send a check to the bankruptcy trustee, who in turn will pay each creditor his or her share. What happens if you can't make the monthly payments as required? You can ask the bankruptcy court to approve a modified repayment plan that is within your financial abilities, or you can consider filing for straight bankruptcy.

Straight Bankruptcy: Chapter 7

Chapter 7 of the Bankruptcy Code lays out the procedure for filing for straight bankruptcy. The purpose of letting you declare bankruptcy is to let you get a fresh economic start in life. In a Chapter 7 proceeding, all of your assets (except for those that are exempt) are gathered up and sold, and your creditors are paid off with the proceeds. Except for a few types of obligations (see discussion below), once the bankruptcy is finished, all of your debts are discharged, even if your creditors get only pennies on the dollar. Most Chapter 7 bankruptcies start when you, the debtor, file for bankruptcy. Sometimes a creditor files an "involuntary petition" to force the debtor into bankruptcy.

What Happens After You File for Bankruptcy

The moment you file for bankruptcy—either type—any lawsuits pending against you for the payment of debts are automatically stopped ("stayed"), and no new actions can be filed against you. Your creditors are also prohibited from contacting you or your employer or trying to make any attempt to collect the debts. You must list all of your creditors on the forms filed with the bankruptcy court. If you don't list a creditor, the debt you owe that creditor is not discharged, and that creditor can sue you for it.

Shortly after you file for bankruptcy, you must appear at a court-scheduled meeting of your creditors. At this meeting, the creditors can ask you questions regarding your assets and how you got so deeply into debt. For the average personal bankruptcy, the creditors' meeting is a mere formality, lasting only a few minutes. Most of the time, no creditors even show up.

When your bankruptcy proceedings are over, all but a few of your outstanding debts are canceled, or "discharged," by order of the bankruptcy court. A few types of debts, however, are not canceled. Suppose you're going to file bankruptcy, but before you do, you've decided to live like royalty for a month, charging everything on your credit card. You even get a loan for $1,000 and blow it on a big party for all of your friends. The next day you file bankruptcy. Do these debts get discharged in bankruptcy? No. If you buy something with a credit card within 20 days of filing for bankruptcy, that debt does not get canceled. Personal loans and installment purchases (such as buying a television set on time) are not discharged if they are made less than 40 days before you file.

If you filed for Chapter 7, any alimony and child support payments you owe are not discharged. Some back taxes owed to the government are not canceled, and there are restrictions on discharging student loans. Money owed to someone because you intentionally hurt him or her is not discharged (but damages resulting from your negligence are). Debts resulting from your fraud also are not canceled.

In Chapter 13 proceedings, all of your debts are discharged except for alimony and child support payments and long-term debts that are not paid off during the term of the repayment plan— for instance, a ten-year loan that still has several years to go on it after you finish the repayment plan.

If you file for bankruptcy under Chapter 7, and the court approves it, you cannot file for bankruptcy again for six years. There is no such waiting period after filing for a Chapter 13 repayment plan. (And remember that, as noted earlier in this chapter, bankruptcy stays on your credit rating for up to ten years.)

15

SUING IN SMALL CLAIMS COURT

SUPPOSE YOU RUN into a minor legal problem and feel that the other person should pay you, say, $250. You don't want to hire a lawyer, but neither do you want to forget the $250. What can you do? You can file a complaint in small claims court and be your own lawyer. Small claims court provides a fast, informal, and inexpensive avenue to the judicial system when the amount of money involved is relatively small. It dispenses with many traditional legal formalities in favor of a simpler process that saves time and money. In small claims court, it may take as little as four weeks from the time you file a claim until the trial is held and the judge makes a decision. Compare this with the several years it often takes to get to trial in "regular" courts.

Some states prohibit lawyers from appearing in small claims court except in a few situations, such as when the lawyer files his or her own claim or is being sued, or represents a corporation that is being sued. But even in states that allow lawyers to represent clients in small claims court, most people represent themselves. The cases are usually too small to justify the expense of hiring a lawyer; it could easily cost you more for the lawyer than you'll get in your judgment.

Here are some definitions of terms we'll be using throughout this chapter: The "plaintiff" is the person who files the lawsuit; the "defendant" is the person being sued. A "complaint," or "claim," is the document the plaintiff files with the court to start the lawsuit. It lays out the basic facts of the case and states how much money the plaintiff is asking for. The "answer," or "response," is the defendant's response to the complaint. A "counterclaim," or "cross-complaint," is a lawsuit the defendant files against the plaintiff. A "judgment" is the judge's decision in the case. (A decision by a jury is a "verdict.")

What to Consider before Filing a Lawsuit

A lawyer considers three things before filing suit for a client: (1) Does the client have a "cause of action" against the defendant? (2) Is the case barred by the "statute of limitations"? and (3) What are the chances of proving the case and collecting from the defendant? Since you will be your own lawyer in small claims court, you'll need to consider these questions before you file suit.

Do You Have a Leg to Stand On?

Whether you have a legal leg to stand on—a "cause of action" against the defendant—is the meat of the lawsuit. If you have a cause of action, it means that the defendant has committed a legal wrong against you for which you can sue. If someone damages your car in an accident, for instance, and the accident was his or her fault, your legal cause of action is for "negligence."

The other chapters in this book can tell you whether or not you have a cause of action in many situations. If, after reading the relevant chapters, you're still unsure about what your rights are, discuss the specific facts of your case with a lawyer first. Some lawyers offer a free initial consultation, and many others charge only $25 to $50 for the first 20- or 30-minute consultation (see chapter 19), which may be all you'll need. Most areas have a legal aid society, which provides low-cost legal advice for people who can't afford a lawyer.

How Long Do You Have to Sue?

You don't have forever to sue someone. Every state has a "statute of limitations" that governs how long you have to sue for various types of cases. In some states, for example, you have only one year to file a suit for personal injuries or damage to your property. If you let more than one year pass before you file your complaint, you'll soon find that your suit is barred. You can go ahead and file the suit, but the judge will see that it is too late and will dismiss it. Generally, you have more time to file a lawsuit based on a contract or damage to real estate than one for personal injuries or property damage.

You can find out how long you have to sue in your own situation by calling the small claims court clerk or going to your local law library and looking it up in the codes or books of statutes (most public libraries also have these books). As a general rule, no matter what type of case you have, you should file your lawsuit as soon as possible after you realize that you won't be able to work things out without a lawsuit.

Special rules apply if you are suing a state or municipal government or one of its agencies or divisions. (Some states do not permit you to sue the government in small claims court.) You must file a "claim" with the proper government body before you can sue in any court, including small claims court. You may have to file the claim within as few as 60 days after the incident, or the claim will be barred unless you can show a good reason for not having filed it on time. (Claims must also be filed if you want to sue the United States, but you can't sue the United States in small claims court. Suits against the United States can be filed only in federal courts, not state courts.)

Where do you file the claim? If it is against the state, call the local office of the state's attorney general. Call the county clerk or district attorney if your claim is against a county, and the city clerk or city attorney if your claim is against a city. They can advise you on how long you have to file your claim and where to file it. Usually they will also send you a standard form for you to fill out. If not, your claim can be a letter. Include your name, address, telephone number, date and place of the incident, a description of your claim, and the amount of money you are requesting. You should usually hear back within 60 days as to whether your claim has been approved or rejected. If rejected, you normally have six months to file your suit.

Can You Win the Case and Collect the Money?

Will you be able to convince the judge that justice is on your side? If it's just your word against the defendant's, your chances of winning are less than if you have an unbiased witness by your side backing you up. Also important: do you have any tangible evidence to show the judge? If you bought a defective product from the defendant, for example, bring the product to court, as well as your canceled check and the receipt for it. Pictures of, say, the damage to your car or bad construction work can be most helpful. Hospital and doctor bills, repair estimates, and other documentation are also important.

One final thing to consider before filing your small claims court suit: how likely is it that you will ever collect a dime from the defendant? Nothing can make a victory as sour and hollow as the frustration of trying to collect from a person who has no money, someone who is "judgment-proof." Consider the wisdom in the saying, "You can't squeeze blood from a turnip," before filing your suit. But even though the defendant can't pay now, you may be able to collect in the future. Judgments are good for at least several years, and you may be able to get the time extended if the defendant still hasn't paid.

Sometimes a defendant will threaten to file bankruptcy if you sue. What should you do? Go ahead and sue. Threatening bankruptcy if a lawsuit is filed is a common ploy of some defendants, from individuals to big corporations alike. It is unlikely that a lawsuit in small claims court would be enough to force a person into bankruptcy. But even if it did, you could still file a claim for your money with the bankruptcy court.

How Much Can You and Should You Sue For?

Generally, you can sue only for money damages in small claims court. The damages can be for just about any type of case: someone dents your car, the dry cleaner ruins your sweater, your neighbor's dog digs up your yard, someone refuses to pay you back a loan, you bought a defective product and the store won't give you your money back, and so on. In most states you cannot bring an action in small claims court to, say, get an injunction to prohibit a person from harassing you or maintaining a nuisance, nor can you evict a tenant through small claims court. Many states do not allow cases for libel or slander in small claims court. If you are suing the defendant for taking property from you, the judge can order the defendant either to return the property or to pay you its full value (to the maximum amount permitted in small claims court).

The maximum amount you can sue for in a single small claims action varies widely from state to state. Here is a state-by-state rundown of the current limits:

Alabama	$1,000
Alaska	$5,000
Arizona	$500
Arkansas	$500
California	$1,500
Colorado	$1,000
Connecticut	$1,500
Delaware	$2,500
District of Columbia	$2,000

Florida	$5,000
Georgia	varies, set by each county
Hawaii	$2,500
Idaho	$2,000
Illinois	$2,500
Indiana	$3,000
Iowa	$2,000
Kansas	$1,000
Kentucky	$1,000
Louisiana	$1,200 in justice of peace courts, $2,000 in city courts ($5,000 in city courts in New Orleans, Ville Platte, Plaquemine, Bossier City, and Lafayette), $10,000 in parish courts
Maine	$1,400
Maryland	$1,000
Massachusetts	$1,500
Michigan	$1,500
Minnesota	$2,000
Mississippi	$1,000
Missouri	$1,000
Montana	$1,500
Nebraska	$1,500
Nevada	$1,500
New Hampshire	$1,500
New Jersey	$2,000
New Mexico	abolished small claims court in 1980; replaced it with magistrate or metropolitan court, can sue for up to $2,000
New York	$1,500
North Carolina	$1,500
North Dakota	$2,000
Ohio	$1,000
Oklahoma	$1,500
Oregon	$1,500
Pennsylvania	$5,000 in Philadelphia Municipal Court, otherwise $4,000
Rhode Island	$1,000
South Carolina	$1,000
South Dakota	$2,000

Tennessee	$10,000 ($15,000 in Shelby County)
Texas	$1,000
Utah	$1,000
Vermont	$2,000
Virginia	$7,000
Washington	$1,000
West Virginia	no small claims court, but you can sue for up to $3,000 in county magistrates' courts
Wisconsin	no small claims court, but small claims procedure available in circuit courts if case does not exceed $1,000
Wyoming	$750

Since these figures can go up every year or two, if your claim exceeds the amount listed above, you should call the clerk of your local small claims court to learn the current limit before you file suit. If it's near the end of the year and you don't have a problem with the statute of limitations (see discussion above), you can ask the clerk whether the limit will be increased on January 1 and, if so, hold off suing until then. In many states, the maximum amount you can sue for is exclusive of interest and your "costs" (such as the cost of filing the complaint and having someone serve it upon the defendant).

Determining How Much to Sue For in Your Case

How much you should sue for depends on what types of damages are recoverable in your particular case. The following discussion enumerates the kinds of damages you can recover in cases that frequently make their way to small claims court: personal injury cases, property damage cases, breach of contract cases, and landlord-tenant disputes. In addition to the specific damages listed below, in every type of case, you can recover certain costs if you win. These include the costs of filing the complaint and having it served on the defendant as well as subpoena costs to compel the attendance of witnesses (see discussion below). Some costs are not recoverable, the main ones being the time you take off work to appear in court and your travel expenses to and from the courthouse.

Personal Injury Cases

If the defendant injured you, you can sue for all of your medical expenses (up to the maximum limit), including doctor and hospital bills, prescription drugs, transportation to and from the doctor or hospital, ambulance costs, and so on. How do you prove your medical expenses? By showing the judge all of your doctor and hospital bills, receipts for prescription drugs, and dates of doctors' appointments and distances traveled to and from the doctors' offices. If a number of receipts are involved, summarize them on one piece of paper, and attach the summary to the stack of receipts and bills, which should be arranged in chronological order.

In personal injury cases, you can also recover damages for your "pain and suffering." This is a rather nebulous term, and pain and suffering are difficult to set a price on. The judge will consider the type and severity of your injury in deciding how much to give you for pain and suffering. Many judges tend to use a set formula, such as two or three times the medical expenses. For example, if your medical bills were $250, the judge would award you another $500 to $750 for pain and suffering.

If you lost money because you couldn't work for a while, then you can recover damages for your "lost wages." You can prove the amount of these damages by your own testimony that you couldn't work on specific dates. Suppose you missed two days of work because of the accident. One simple yet effective way of proving the amount of your lost wages is to bring to court your paycheck stub for that week and for the weeks immediately before and after to show how much you lost. You should back this up with a letter from your boss or personnel director, verifying the dates of your absence and the amount of wages you missed.

In personal injury cases, you also should take into account your property damage, such as the damage to your car or its contents, to your clothing, and so on.

Property Damage

There are several rules for computing damages if you are suing for damage to or destruction of property. If something is damaged, usually you can get back the cost of repairing it; if it costs $100 to fix the damage, for example, that's what you will get. If the repair cost exceeds the value of the property, the judge will give you the smaller amount. For instance, if someone damages your sofa, and it will cost $750 to repair it, but your sofa is old and was worth only $200 before it was damaged, the judge will award you only $200.

If your property was destroyed, lost, or stolen, the judge will make the defendant pay you its reasonable value at the time it was destroyed, lost, or taken. You can't get the amount it costs to replace the item today, however. You won't even get what you paid for the item unless it was almost new and still in excellent shape. Suppose Helen takes her two-year-old stereo to a repair shop for a minor repair, and her stereo is lost. Helen paid $500 for the stereo, and a new one costs $600 today. The question is how much Helen's stereo was worth when it was lost. Invariably, the parties will disagree on the stereo's condition. Helen will likely claim that it was in excellent condition and worth its original $500, while the repair shop will contend that it was worn out and damaged and worth $50 at most.

Sometimes the judge will estimate how long the thing would have lasted, then deduct a certain percentage for each year you had it. For instance, the judge could determine that the stereo would have lasted five years from the date Helen bought it, so its value declines by 20 percent each year. Since Helen had the stereo for two years, the judge would deduct 40 percent ($200) of the original cost ($500) and award Helen $300. (Helen should have the original receipt, canceled check, or other evidence showing how much she paid for the stereo, especially if the defendant disputes what it originally cost her.)

Breach of Contract Cases

How much money you can get in a breach of contract case depends on the situation. For instance, if the defendant breached a contract to sell you his or her car for $1,500 and you paid $2,000 for a similar car, you can collect $500. If a painter walked off the job, and it cost you $300 over and above what you were going to pay the first painter to get the job finished, you can recover $300. If you did some work for the defendant and didn't get paid, you can recover the contract amount. Other ways of determining your damages in contract cases are discussed in chapter 13.

If your case involves a written contract, take a close look at the contract to see what other damages are recoverable. For example, the contract may provide that the defendant has to pay you interest on the money from the day when it should have been paid to you.

Landlord-Tenant Cases

The two kinds of suits filed most frequently by tenants against landlords are for failing to return the tenant's security or cleaning deposit and for the cost of having something repaired that the landlord refused to fix. Chapter 6 discusses the tenant's right to the return of the full security and cleaning deposit, except for a reasonable amount to cover repairing or cleaning the apartment for damage or dirt that exceeds normal wear and tear. The tenant is also entitled to recover interest on the money from the date when the deposit should have been returned. In some states, you can recover two or three times the amount of the deposit if the landlord unjustifiably refuses to return it or if he or she does not send you an itemized expense list within, say, ten days or two weeks. In repair cases, you can recover the cost of having the problem repaired or, if you did it yourself, the cost of the materials and supplies (but not your own labor). You can also ask the judge to order the landlord to refund you part of the rent for the period during which the problem was left unfixed.

What to Consider If Your Damages Are over the Limit

Suppose the small claims limit in your state is $1,000, but the defendant owes you $1,500 from a single loan. Can you file two suits—say, one for $1,000 and the other for $500? No. You cannot split a single claim. But if the defendant owes you $1,500 from two loans of $750 each, then you can file two separate claims for $750.

If the small claims limit is $1,000 and the defendant owes you $1,250, should you file in small claims court for $1,000 and forget about the other $250, or hire a lawyer to sue in regular court for you? In this situation, you're usually better off filing in small claims court yourself. This has a number of advantages. First of all, you will get your trial—and your money—months or years faster than you would if you sued in regular court. Second, it will undoubtedly cost you at least $250 to have a lawyer handle your case. If the lawyer agrees to represent you for 33⅓ percent of the recovery, and he or she recovers the full $1,250, you will receive only about $835 (the other $415 or so goes to your lawyer). If the lawyer charges you only a quarter of the recovery, you'll end up with $937.50 and your lawyer will get $312.50. Nonetheless, if your claim is over the small claims court limit, you should seriously consider talking to a lawyer about representing you and suing in regular court. In some cases, especially those involving personal injuries, the lawyer may feel that the case is worth more than you have estimated. By having the lawyer represent you, your eventual recovery—even after paying the lawyer's fees—might be more than what you could have recovered in small claims court.

Making a Demand for the Money

You've decided how much you're going to sue the defendant for. Is there anything else you need to do before you file your

complaint? Yes. Ordinarily, you must make a "formal demand"
of the defendant to pay the money. Do this by sending the defendant a letter that states how much money you are asking for
and why you believe you are entitled to it. Include the relevant
facts and dates, and send a copy of any documents, such as the
contract, a repair estimate, or a sales receipt, to support the
amount of damages you're claiming. The demand letter should
give the defendant about two weeks to respond. Remember to
keep a copy of all letters to show the judge at the trial.

Do you need to send the letter via certified mail, with a
return receipt requested? Usually not. But how will you know if
the defendant ever received it if you never get a response? The
law presumes that a letter with the correct address and sufficient
postage was delivered to the addressee in due course. Small claims
court judges have heard the excuse, "But Your Honor, I never
received the letter," so many times, they rarely believe it. One
problem with sending a certified letter with a return receipt requested is that the defendant may refuse to accept it. If you want
a record from the post office that you mailed the letter but don't
want to risk having the defendant refuse it, ask the post office
for a "Certificate of Mailing." You'll have proof that you sent
the defendant the letter, and the defendant will be none the wiser.
Here is an example of a demand letter:

Mr. John Doe
9876 First Avenue
Bayside, USA

November 15, 1986

Dear Mr. Doe:

I hereby request you to pay me the sum of $500 for the
damages you did to my car on July 24, 1986.

This claim is based on the fact that while my car was
legally parked in the parking lot of ABC Supermarket on

2nd Street, Hometown, you ran into it while backing out of another parking space. I have three witnesses who saw you hit my car, and all can identify you and your car.

As proof of the amount of the damage, I am enclosing a copy of the estimate I received from Harry's Body Shop. Please send a cashier's check or money order payable to me for the entire $500 at 1234 Coast Highway, Oceanview, USA, no later than December 1, 1986.

Sincerely,

Martha J. Smith

Try to Settle Out of Court

The defendant's response to your demand letter will determine your next step. If you don't receive a response or if the defendant replies that he or she will not pay you anything, then you have no choice but to file in small claims court or forget the whole thing, or perhaps have a lawyer write a letter on your behalf.

What if the defendant expresses an interest in settling the matter but doesn't want to pay you the full amount? If, for instance, the damage to your car is $600, and the defendant offers you $500, should you take it? Probably. You'll have a much better chance of settling the case if you are flexible and willing to compromise some. It's usually worth it to settle the case and get the $500 in your hands today. How low you should be willing to go in order to settle depends on the facts of your case, especially on how clear the defendant's fault is. Unless the question of who is at fault is "iffy," you normally shouldn't settle for less than 75 or 80 percent of what the fair damages are.

Sometimes the defendant doesn't dispute the fact that he or she owes the money but claims that he or she can't pay you right now. In this case, offer to let the defendant pay you, say, 25 percent or more now (as much as he or she can) and then make monthly payments for the balance. For instance, suppose the defendant owes you $1,000, but doesn't have the money to pay right now. Have him or her pay, say, $400 down and make six monthly payments of $100. If the defendant agrees to this, put it in writing, and have him or her sign the agreement. Include a clause stating that if a monthly payment is more than ten days late, the entire balance becomes due immediately. That way, if the defendant doesn't make a payment or two, you can go into court and sue for the full unpaid balance.

Filling Out, Filing, and Serving the Complaint

You can get the proper forms to file the summons and complaint ("claim" or "petition" in some states) from the small claims court clerk. (You should also ask the clerk for a pamphlet on small claims court. This contains important procedural information, such as how much you can sue for, how soon before the court hearing you must serve the defendant, and the like so you won't have to call the clerk every time you have a question.) The forms are usually brief and easy to fill out. The information asked for is the bare minimum: your name, address, and telephone number; the defendant's name and address; a brief summary of the case (usually just a couple of sentences); and how much money you're asking for. If a written contract is involved, attach a copy of it to the complaint. You may also want to attach a copy of estimates, invoices, medical bills, photographs, or anything else that shows your right to recover the amount requested.

Whom Should You Sue?

One problem you may face is whom to sue. If more than one person is involved, consider suing all of them. (Some states, however, prohibit you from suing in small claims court someone who lives in another state.) If you were injured in an automobile accident, for instance, and the person driving the car was not the owner, consider suing both the owner and the driver (see chapter 2). If at the time of the accident you didn't ask the driver to show you the registration form, and he or she refuses to send you a copy, you can find out who the owner is by contacting the department of motor vehicles.

If you are suing a business, you will want to find out who the owner is. For example, "Speedy Cleaners" may be owned by Cindy Edwards. You should state the owner's name and the business's name on your complaint this way: "Cindy Edwards, doing business as (or dba) Speedy Cleaners." If the business is operated by a partnership, you should name each partner as a defendant, as well as the partnership itself: "Acme Repair Shop, a partnership, and Joe Brown and Sue Green, individually and as partners." You can find out the names and addresses of the owners of a business by checking the "fictitious business statement" records of the county clerk in the county where the business is located.

If the business is a corporation, you normally must sue the corporation in its name alone because it is deemed a separate, "living" legal entity. Call the corporations department of the secretary of state for your particular state, and ask for the name and address of the corporation's "agent for service of process" (the person who is authorized to accept complaints filed against the corporation).

Where to File the Complaint

Once you've filled out the complaint, you'll have to file it with the small claims court clerk. But which court should you file in, the one closest to you or the one closest to the defendant? Where you can or must file your complaint depends on the type of case. If you're suing the defendant for personal injuries or property damage, you can file your complaint in the court in the county or judicial district (see discussion below) where the defendant lives or has his or her business, or where the accident occurred. For example, suppose that your car is hit in Orange County by the defendant, who lives in Lincoln County. You can sue in either county. You usually cannot sue in a county just because you live there.

For cases based on a contract, you can file suit in the county or judicial district where the defendant lives or has his or her business, where the defendant signed the contract, or where the work was to be done. For example, if you had some construction work done on your summer cottage in Zebra County, and the defendant signed the contract at his office in Washington County (where he also lives), you could file the suit in either Zebra or Washington county. If the contract involves something bought on time—for instance, a car or appliance—the suit can be brought in the county or judicial district where you currently live, where you lived when the contract was signed, where the contract was signed, or where the car (appliance, etc.) is kept.

Larger counties often have two or more judicial districts within them. In that case, you must file in the appropriate district, usually the one closest to where the defendant lives or has his or her business, to where the accident happened, or to where the contract was signed. If you're not sure which court to sue in, call the clerk of any small claims court in that county, and ask him or her.

To file the completed and signed forms, take them to the clerk. If the forms are properly filled in, the clerk will ask you to pay the filing fee (currently running from $5 to $20, depending on the state) and will then stamp your complaint as filed. At this time, ask the clerk to set a date for the trial. The clerk will give you a choice of dates, so pick the one most convenient to you.

Serving the Defendant with the Complaint

You are now ready to "serve" the defendant with the summons and complaint. The defendant must be served with the summons and complaint a specified number of days before the trial, usually 20 to 30 days. This amount of time varies from state to state and can also vary within a state, depending on whether the defendant lives in the same county where the courthouse is. The small claims court clerk can tell you how soon before the hearing the defendant must be served with the summons and complaint. If you don't serve the defendant in time, call the court clerk and ask to have a new date assigned for the hearing.

There are two convenient and common ways of serving a defendant. In most states, you can ask the small claims court clerk to serve the defendant through the mail. This usually costs only a few dollars. If you opt for this route, check back with the clerk a week or two later to see whether the defendant received the letter. If not, you may have to ask for a continuance and try to serve the defendant another way.

The second common way of serving the defendant in a small claims court action is to have the marshal's office do it. The small claims court clerk has the forms or can otherwise tell you how to get the marshal to serve the defendant and how much it will cost. If you win the case, the defendant must reimburse you for your costs of serving the summons and complaint. After the marshal serves the defendant, he or she will file a "Proof of Service" with the court. A Proof of Service is a legal document signed under oath stating that the marshal served the defendant with the summons and complaint on a certain date at a certain place and time.

In most states, the summons and complaint can be served on the defendant by anyone who is over 18 and not a party to the action—a licensed professional process server, even a friend. Make sure that the person who serves the defendant properly fills out and signs the Proof of Service (which you can get from the small claims court clerk when you file the complaint) and that it is filed with the small claims court clerk.

What to Do If You Are the Defendant

Let's suppose for a while that you are a defendant and have just been served with a summons and complaint for a small claims court action. What should you do? If the plaintiff never contacted you, call or write him or her, and see if you can't settle the case. If you can't reach a compromise, you may want to file a response to the complaint, stating why you believe you don't owe any money or as much money as the plaintiff is asking for. The summons usually shows how much time you have to file a response, often 15 to 20 days. If you plan on filing a response, call the small claims court clerk to see how soon before the trial you must file it. In most states, you don't have to file any response and can just show up at the hearing and present your side of the case. It is better to file a response, though, so the judge can read it before hearing the trial.

If you believe that you are entitled to damages from the same transaction or accident as the plaintiff is suing you on, you must file a "counterclaim" against the plaintiff. If you don't, you will lose your right to sue the plaintiff for those damages later on. Suppose, for example, the plaintiff is suing you for $500 in damages that his or her car suffered in a "fender bender" between the two of you. Your car was damaged to the extent of $350 in the same accident, and you feel that the plaintiff, not you, caused the accident. You must file a counterclaim for $350 with your response to the complaint, or you will lose your right to assert it later.

How to Get the Winning Edge

Preparing Your Case: The Key to Success

Regardless of how clear-cut you feel your case is, you may not win unless you prepare your case thoroughly before the trial. You'll only have a few minutes to persuade the judge of your cause, so you must make your presentation as effective as possible. Know what you're going to say before you walk into the courtroom. Most presentations should be in chronological order, since this is how the law—and the judge—generally views things. Stick to the heart of the matter, and leave side issues alone. Do you have a "smoking gun"—one piece of evidence that especially proves that justice is on your side? If so, then concentrate on it.

Practice your testimony in front of a mirror a few times, then do it in front of family and friends. Ask if they understood it easily, if any part left them confused, and if anything is missing. If you're shy in front of family and friends, imagine how difficult it will be to present your case in front of a judge and a number of spectators without practice.

Get all of your exhibits—the canceled check, invoice, receipt, written contract, medical bills, pictures, and so on—ready so they'll be handy when you need them. Make at least three copies of every document. You will hand the original to the judge at the trial. Attach one copy to your complaint, have one copy ready to hand the defendant at the trial, and keep one copy with you throughout the trial. If you have photographs, number each one on the back in the sequence in which you plan to use it, along with the date when it was taken. If a couple of photographs particularly support your position, think of having them enlarged to 8" x 10". Keep all of your exhibits in the order in which you intend to introduce them at the trial so you don't get flustered by having to shuffle through them under the judge's increasingly impatient glare.

A week or two before your trial, go to the small claims court to watch the proceedings. Small claims court proceedings are open to the general public, and all you have to do is walk through the door and take an empty seat. By visiting small claims court before your own hearing, you will become familiar with the surroundings and know what to expect when you get there. The last thing you need to worry about at your own trial is where the courthouse is, which courtroom to go to, where to check in, which table to sit at when you present your case, and so on. You will have an immediate advantage over someone who has never been in small claims court before.

Sit through at least three or four cases, preferably in front of the same judge who will be presiding over your case. Soon you will be able to see which side is better prepared and who presents his or her case with more confidence. Notice how the judge conducts the proceedings. Are the parties permitted to ramble on, or is the judge a no-nonsense type who wants "just the facts"?

You will probably immediately notice two differences between real small claims court and its television counterparts. First, each case lasts only about five minutes, not the fifteen or so minutes you usually see on television. Also, the judge does not go back into chambers to decide each case, as television portrays. (In television court, this is just an excuse for a commercial break.) Participants in real small claims court do not get away with interrupting the other party or arguing with the judge, as their television counterparts seem to do. Judges do not tolerate this in the courtroom and will quickly admonish anyone who disrupts the proceedings. Persons who continue to be unruly may find themselves being escorted out of the courtroom or even taken into custody for contempt of court.

You'll also notice that the judge does not let the parties read from prepared statements. Often when the judge tells a person to explain the situation in his or her own words, the person is totally lost; this is another reason why you should practice your presentation beforehand. But while the judge won't let you read a prepared statement, you should have a sheet of paper with some critical notes—things you want to emphasize to the judge. A lawyer wouldn't try a case without an outline or a few notes, and neither should you.

Support Your Testimony with Witnesses

As in any court, you have the right to subpoena witnesses, including police officers, to compel their appearance in court. If a witness (or even the opposing party) has documents or pictures that you want him or her to bring to court, you can serve that person with a "subpoena duces tecum," available from the small claims court clerk. Subpoenas, however, are rarely used in small claims court, since the witnesses are often friends, family, or neighbors. A word of caution—never force a witness to appear against his or her will. An unwilling witness might "forget" key facts, claim not to have seen anything, or even testify out of spite that the situation is all your fault.

Never ask a witness to testify unless you have an idea of what he or she is going to say. Nothing is as dangerous as calling a witness without knowing what he or she saw. Never assume that the witness agrees with your version of the facts. Everyone's perception of an event can be different, so talk to the person before asking him or her to appear at the trial.

How important is it for a witness to appear? It can be extremely important. The judge won't simply take your word that you heard the witness say that he or she saw or heard something. This is "hearsay"—saying as true something that someone else said, a second- or third-hand statement. If, for instance, a person heard the defendant say that she was speeding at the time of the accident and tells this to you, you can't tell the judge that that person told you the defendant was speeding. Only the witness himself or herself can testify to this, because the witness heard it firsthand.

What can you do if a key witness won't be around for the trial? Perhaps he or she lives in another state, is ill, or otherwise can't make it. If the witness is only temporarily unavailable—out of town on a business trip, for instance—ask the clerk or judge to continue the case for a week or two until the witness gets back. But if the witness won't be able to make it to the trial at all, you should have the witness sign an affidavit telling what he or she saw. Blank affidavit forms are available at many stationery stores. (An affidavit is the witness's statement, signed under oath.) The witness must usually sign the affidavit in front of a notary public, who then affixes his or her seal and signature. If you can't get an affidavit from the witness, at least have the witness give you a written, signed, and dated statement, including his or her address and telephone number.

When a witness can't appear at the trial, some judges will

let him or her testify by telephone. The small claims court clerk or the judge's own clerk can advise you on this practice in your area. It is your responsibility to make sure that the witness knows the day and time of the trial and is available at a certain telephone number if the judge decides to call.

The Trial: Time for Your Hard Work to Pay Off

Before the trial, the judge may order you and the defendant to go into the hall for a few minutes to try to settle the case. If you manage to reach a settlement, put it in writing, and both of you sign it. Then tell the judge or his or her clerk that you have settled the case, and ask if it's okay to go home.

As the plaintiff, you present your case first. The burden is on you to prove your case to a "preponderance of the evidence." You must convince the judge that your version of the facts is more likely to be true than the defendant's version. All you have to do is tip the scales of justice ever so slightly in your favor, and you've won. You can do this with witnesses, pictures, canceled checks, copies of the contract, the damaged article, or any other tangible evidence. You really have *two* things to prove: liability (that the defendant committed a legal wrong) and damages (how much money you should get). Proving one without the other won't do you any good. All the liability in the world means nothing if you don't demonstrate any damages. Likewise, the most severe damages will get you no award if you don't prove that the defendant is legally responsible for them.

The judge may have read your complaint before the hearing, but don't count on it. Besides, the complaint often gives room for only a sentence or two, so it doesn't say much anyway. Give the judge a one- or two-sentence introduction as to what the case involves, then get on with your story. For example: "Good afternoon, Your Honor. My name is Beth Williams. I'm suing the defendant, Honest Car Repair Company, for not repairing the transmission on my car correctly. I took the car in to Honest Car

Repair on June 1 because the transmission was slipping. They told me it would cost $250 to fix . . ."

There isn't much time, so stick to the relevant facts, and get to the heart of the matter right away. If you have prepared your case as suggested earlier, you'll have a concise and organized presentation. Exude confidence and show courtesy to the other side. Remember to conduct yourself properly in court, and instruct your witnesses to do the same.

Show the judge your exhibits, and explain each of them. Go through receipts and records. Never hand an exhibit or receipt to the judge without asking his or her permission first. Usually you will hand the exhibit to the bailiff, who will take it to the judge. Then have your witnesses testify. Although both parties and their witnesses will be sworn to tell the truth under penalty of perjury, rarely will the judge ask anyone to take the witness stand. You and your witnesses will tell your story from the counsel table, usually standing up. Introduce each witness to the judge like this: "Your Honor, I would like to introduce my witness, Gloria Jones."

When you and your witnesses are done testifying, the judge will ask the defendant to present his or her case. Sometimes, when the plaintiff's right to recover damages seems obvious from the complaint, the judge will simply skip the plaintiff's testimony and ask the defendant to present his or her case first. If the defendant has nothing substantial to say, the judge may find in the plaintiff's favor. If the defendant does raise a defense, the judge will then give you the opportunity to present your case. After the defendant is finished, you will get a chance to respond to ("rebut") the defendant's assertions.

What Happens If You Don't Appear at the Trial?

What happens if the defendant doesn't show up at the trial? The judge will probably enter a "default judgment" against him or her. Before doing so, the judge will look at the file for your case to see whether the defendant was properly served with the summons and complaint and notified of the correct time, date, and place of the trial. If the file doesn't show that the defendant was properly served (if, for instance, you forgot to file the Proof of Service or it isn't signed by the person who served the defendant), the judge will not enter the default judgment. Ask the judge for a continuance to give you time to serve the defendant or file the Proof of Service.

If the defendant was properly served, the judge may ask you to summarize your case and justify the amount of damages you are claiming. Once the judge enters the default judgment against the defendant, you can collect from the defendant the same as if he or she had appeared and fought the case and lost.

Sometimes the defendant can convince the judge to vacate, or "set aside," the default judgment so that he or she can defend the case. For example, if the defendant could show that he or she was involved in an automobile accident on the way to the hearing and was unable to call the court or the opposing party of the predicament, the judge would probably set aside the default. But the excuse must be sufficient in the eyes of the law to justify a failure to appear—forgetting to mark the date on the calendar is normally not enough. And the defendant must act promptly after receiving notice that a default judgment was entered against him or her. The longer the defendant waits, the more reluctant the judge will be to vacate the judgment.

Suppose you, the plaintiff, fails to show up at the hearing without calling the small claims court clerk. If the defendant appears, the judge will normally enter a judgment against you, and you'll have a harder time getting excused from not appearing than a defendant would. If neither side shows up, the judge may take the case "off calendar." You will then have to call the clerk and ask for a new trial date.

If you find that you are going to be unable to appear at the hearing because of, say, illness or a business trip, call the opposing party, explain your situation, and ask for a continuance of a week or two. If the other side agrees, call the small claims court clerk to get the date changed. If the other party does not agree to your request for a continuance, you should still call the small claims court clerk and explain the situation. You can generally get one continuance even though the other party objects. But don't expect to get one continuance after another. The judge usually will not tolerate more than one or two continuances.

The Judgment

After both parties have presented their cases, the judge will make a decision. Judges usually don't announce small claims court judgments from the bench but mail them in the next day or two. This is mainly to prevent a disappointed party from taking up everyone's time by complaining to the judge.

What can you do if you don't agree with the judge's decision? If you're the plaintiff, usually nothing, since you ordinarily have no right to appeal a small claims decision. But if the judge rules in favor of the plaintiff, the defendant has the right to appeal the decision. In most states, the appeal is heard by one to three judges and basically consists of starting all over again from scratch. There is no court recorder in small claims court, so the appellate judges don't have a transcript of the earlier proceedings to review. You can have a lawyer represent you at the appeal even if your state doesn't permit a lawyer in small claims court, but before you hire one, consider the cost.

Examples of Small Claims Court Trials

Here are three sample trials involving disputes that frequently wind up in small claims court.

Example #1: Parking Lot Collision

In the following example, the plaintiff's (Ms. Johnson's) car was damaged in a supermarket parking lot when the defendant

(Mr. Stanton) struck it while backing out of an adjacent parking space. Ms. Johnson was in the store and did not see the accident happen. But an eyewitness, Larry Davis, a box boy at the supermarket, saw the collision and managed to write down the license number of Mr. Stanton's car. Ms. Johnson tracked down Mr. Stanton through the department of motor vehicles. The damage to Ms. Johnson's car is estimated at about $650.

Judge: Are both parties in the case of *Johnson v. Stanton* here?

Plaintiff (Ms. Johnson): I am Ms. Johnson, Your Honor.

Defendant (Mr. Stanton): I am the defendant, Mr. Stanton.

Judge: Fine. Would you please proceed, Ms. Johnson.

Plaintiff: Thank you, Your Honor. I am suing Mr. Stanton for $650 for the damage he did to my car when he backed into it while it was parked in the parking lot of ABC Supermarket on October 1, 1986, at about 2:00 P.M. I had parked my car and gone into the store to do my shopping. I did not see the accident happen, but I have a witness who did. I would like to introduce Larry Davis, a box boy at ABC Supermarket, and have him explain what he saw.

Judge: Please tell me what you saw, Mr. Davis.

Mr. Davis: I had just finished helping another customer to his car, when I heard a loud "thud" sound come from the next row. I looked over and saw the rear bumper of Mr. Stanton's car wedged into the rear fender of Ms. Johnson's car, which was parked. Mr. Stanton then put his car into forward and drove away. He did not stop to look and see if he had caused any damage to Ms. Johnson's car, but I'm sure he knew he had hit Ms. Johnson's car, because the thud was pretty loud. I managed to get Mr. Stanton's license plate number before he drove away. I then went to look at Ms. Johnson's car and saw that it had been hit fairly hard. I went into the store and used the public address system to see who owned a blue 1982 Ford Mustang. Ms. Johnson responded, and we went back outside to see her car.

Judge: Did you see the person who was driving the car that hit Ms. Johnson's car?

Mr. Davis: I only caught a glimpse of him, but I am sure that it was the defendant, Mr. Stanton, who was driving. He had dark hair and was wearing the same type of glasses he has on now.

Judge: Thank you. Ms. Johnson, would you like to continue?

Ms. Johnson: Thank you, Your Honor. When I came out to the car, I found that the fender had been damaged quite a bit. I would like to show you this picture of the fender, which was taken when I got home. It shows the extent of the damage. I have another picture I would like to show you that is a close-up of the fender and shows yellow paint on my blue paint. Mr. Stanton's car is yellow. I also have two estimates I would like you to see. One is from Tony's Body Shop; the other is from Harry's Ford. The estimate from Tony's is for $635, and the estimate from Harry's is for $660. Before I filed this claim, I wrote a letter to Mr. Stanton, asking him to pay the damages. I included a picture of the damage, as well as copies of the estimates. He did not reply to that letter. Here is a copy of that letter for you to look at. That is all I have to say, Your Honor.

Judge: Thank you, Ms. Johnson. Mr. Stanton, what do you have to say?

Mr. Stanton: The only thing I have to say is that it wasn't my car that hit Ms. Johnson's car. I didn't even go near the supermarket that day. I was really surprised when I got a letter from her asking me to pay for the damage to her car.

Judge: Are there any other drivers in your family, Mr. Stanton?

Mr. Stanton: There is my wife.

Judge: Do you know where she was that day?

Mr. Stanton: I assume she was at work.

Judge: Does she drive her own car?

Mr. Stanton: Yes. She has a blue two-door sedan that she uses.

Judge: Mr. Davis, can you describe the car you saw hit Ms. Johnson's car?

Mr. Davis: Yes, Your Honor. It was a yellow station wagon. I believe it was a Chevrolet. It looked like it was a couple of years old.

Judge: Do you remember what the license plate number was?

Mr. Davis: Yes. I wrote it down. It is 123 ABC.

Judge: Are you sure of that?

Mr. Davis: Yes. I got a good look at it when Mr. Stanton was leaving.

Judge: Mr. Stanton, do you own a yellow Chevrolet station wagon?

Mr. Stanton: Yes, I do.

Judge: What year is it?

Mr. Stanton: It is a 1983.

Judge: What is its license plate number?

Mr. Stanton: 123 ABC.

Judge: Can you explain how Mr. Davis happened to see your car if you weren't at the supermarket that day as you claim?

Mr. Stanton: No, Your Honor. I only know that I didn't go to the supermarket that day.

Judge: Thank you. That is all. You should receive my judgment in the mail in two or three days.

The judge would most likely find in Ms. Johnson's favor and award her at least $635 to get her car fixed. Ms. Johnson meticulously prepared her case, including taking pictures of the damage to her car and showing paint on her fender matching the color of the defendant's car. The independent, unbiased eyewitness who saw Mr. Stanton hit her car would certainly impress the judge. One thing that Ms. Johnson could have done to disprove Mr. Stanton's contention that he didn't go to the store that day was to talk with the clerks and other employees at the supermarket to see if they remembered whether or not Mr. Stanton was in the store on the day in question. In this case, that wasn't critical, since the eyewitness proved that Mr. Stanton was in the parking lot.

Example #2: Dry Cleaners Ruined Dress

In this example, the plaintiff took her dress to the dry cleaners to have it cleaned, but when she took it out of the plastic bag three days later, she discovered a hole in the back.

Plaintiff (Ms. Laird): Your Honor, on September 12, 1986, I took a white dress to the defendant's dry cleaning store to have it cleaned. It was in excellent condition when I took it in. There were no rips, tears, or holes. I picked the dress up three days later—that would be September 15—and paid $5. I didn't take it out of the plastic bag until three days later, when I was going to wear it, and I found a large hole in the back. I have the dress here, and you can plainly see the big hole here. As soon as I discovered the hole, I called the dry cleaners and told them what I had found. They said they were sorry for putting the hole in the dress and would dry clean another dress for me without charge. I told them that wouldn't do, because the dress cost me $75, it was only a month old, and I had worn it only twice. I told them I wanted $75. They refused. I then wrote a letter to the dry cleaners, stating what I had found and requesting a check for $75. I never received an answer to that letter. I have a copy of the letter here, if you care to see it, Your Honor.

Judge: Do you have anything more to say, Ms. Laird?

Ms. Laird: Yes, Your Honor. Although I don't have the receipt for my dress, I do have a letter here from the manager of Cindy's Fashions, the clothing store where I bought the dress. [The letter should be on company stationery.] As you can see, the manager states that the current price of the dress is $75 and that it has been $75 for at least six months. She also remembers selling a dress of that style to me about a month before the defendant ruined it.

Judge: Thank you. Do you have anything to say, Mr. Harper?

Defendant [Harry Harper, owner of Harper's Dry Cleaners]: Your Honor, I would like to say two things. First, I don't believe that we caused the hole in the dress. There is simply no way we could have done that. I think that she probably ripped the dress after she got it back from us and is just trying to figure out some way of getting a new dress without paying for it. Second, the dress she has there is not worth $75, even if there was no hole. If I could see the dress for a minute . . . thank you. As you can see, Your Honor, there is a stain on the front that can't be taken out. You can also tell by looking at the dress that it has been worn more than twice.

Judge: Ms. Laird, when you called the dry cleaners to tell them you had discovered the hole, do you remember who you talked to?

Ms. Laird: Yes, I believe it was Mrs. Harper that I spoke with.

Judge [to the defendant, Mr. Harper]: I presume Mrs. Harper is your wife?

Mr. Harper: Yes.

Judge: Is she here today?

Mr. Harper: No, Your Honor. Someone had to stay at the shop.

Judge: Does either side have anything to add? If not, thank you, and you'll receive a decision in the mail in several days.

In this case, the judge would probably find in favor of the plaintiff, but might award only $45 or $50 depending on the condition of the dress. The defendant should have presented the testimony of Mrs. Harper to the effect that she never told the plaintiff that they had caused the hole. Without that testimony, the judge would probably accept the plaintiff's version as true.

Example #3: A Landlord's Failure to Return a Tenant's Security Deposit

The following case involves a landlord's failure to return a tenant's security deposit of $500. The tenant claims he left the apartment in better condition when he moved out than it was in when he moved in.

Plaintiff [Bill Butler]: Your Honor, on August 1, 1984, I rented the apartment in question from the defendant, Mr. Turnball. I had to pay $500 as a security deposit. I have here a copy of the lease signed by myself and Mr. Turnball, which shows that I paid $500 as a security deposit and acknowledges its receipt by Mr. Turnball. On July 31, 1986, I gave Mr. Turnball written notice that I would be moving out in 30 days. I managed to get all of my furniture and belongings out of the apartment by August 25. I had the carpets cleaned by a commercial establishment, Sonny's Carpet Cleaning, on August 27. Here is the receipt from Sonny's for the work. I used Sonny's on the recommendation of Mr. Turnball, who told me that he regularly used Sonny's and was always pleased with their work.

I also thoroughly cleaned out the oven, refrigerator, bathrooms, and all other rooms. When I originally moved into the unit, the place was a mess, and it took me a week to clean it up. I feel that I left the apartment in a very clean condition—certainly much cleaner than it was when I moved in. Unfortunately, I don't have any pictures of the apartment, but I do have a witness who can support my testimony that the apartment was clean when I left it. I would like to introduce Valerie Lopez.

Ms. Lopez: Your Honor, I helped Bill clean out the apartment, and I can assure you that it was very clean when we were done. It took us two days, and we mopped the floors, cleaned all of the windows, cleaned the oven, and had that place looking spotless. I couldn't believe it when Bill told me that Mr. Turnball refused to return any part of the deposit.

Mr. Butler: Your Honor, after a few weeks, I called Mr. Turnball because I hadn't received my deposit back, nor had he sent me a statement showing how the money was used. He laughed at me and said it would be a cold day in July before he'd send me any money. I wrote a letter demanding the return of my security deposit—here is a copy for you to see—but he never answered.

Judge: Thank you, Mr. Butler. What do you have to say, Mr. Turnball?

Mr. Turnball: Your Honor, when I walked into that apartment after Mr. Butler left, I was shocked to see how dirty it was. The carpet was filthy, the bathrooms hadn't been cleaned, the oven was dirty, the walls were all banged up. I had to hire carpet cleaners and a cleaning service to get the place back into good order. It cost me more than $500 to clean it up. I couldn't believe Mr. Butler had the nerve to ask for the deposit back.

Judge: Do you have any receipts showing your costs?

Mr. Turnball: No, Your Honor, I didn't think it would be necessary for me to bring them.

Judge: Do you have any pictures showing the condition of the apartment after Mr. Butler moved out but before you cleaned it?

Mr. Turnball: No, Your Honor, I never thought to take any.

Judge: Mr. Turnball, did you ever send the plaintiff an itemized list showing how the cleaning deposit was spent?

Mr. Turnball: No, sir.

Judge: Are you aware that in this state a landlord is required to send a statement to the tenant 14 days after the lease is terminated, showing exactly how the cleaning deposit was spent, and returning the remaining amount?

Mr. Turnball: I am aware of that, yes.

Judge: Why didn't you send Mr. Butler a statement?

Mr. Turnball: I guess I just forgot.

Judge: Mr. Butler, did you see the carpet after Sonny's had cleaned it?

Mr. Butler: Yes, I saw it the next day when Ms. Lopez and I went to finish the other cleaning.

Judge: How did it look?

Plaintiff: It was spotless. It was much cleaner than when I had moved in.

Judge: I'm going to break with my usual procedure and an-

nounce my judgment right now. Mr. Butler, I am awarding you
$1,500, which is the most money I can award in small claims court.
From the evidence presented, I find that you left the apartment
in a clean condition. I have your receipt from Sonny's Carpet
Cleaning Service for $75 to have the carpets cleaned, so I certainly
can't believe Mr. Turnball's testimony that the carpet was filthy.
This is especially true since Mr. Turnball himself recommended
that particular company. I am inclined to believe everything Mr.
Butler said and to take everything Mr. Turnball said with a grain
of salt. Mr. Turnball claims to have spent $500 to clean the apart-
ment but has no receipts to prove it, nor does he have any pictures
supporting his claim that the apartment was filthy. Mr. Turnball
also knew that the law required him to send Mr. Butler an itemized statement of expenses within 14 days but did not do so. I
am therefore awarding the plaintiff his full $500 and am tripling
that amount as permitted by law.

Turning Your Judgment into Cash

The final step is to collect the judgment from the defendant.
In many cases, the defendant, now the "judgment debtor," will
pay the judgment, albeit grudgingly, but maybe not right away.
Expect to wait at least a week or two after the defendant receives
the judgment before you get a check. If you don't get the money
after a month goes by, write the defendant a brief and polite—
yet firm—note asking for payment of the award in the next two
weeks.

If that doesn't do the trick, follow up with a letter telling
the defendant that if you do not receive payment in full in seven
days, you will go back to court to enforce the judgment. Advise
the defendant that in addition to the amount the judge awarded,
the law entitles you to be reimbursed by the defendant for your
costs of collecting the judgment. This is enough to persuade many

defendants to pay, at least if they have the money. If the defendant can't pay you in full, consider having him or her pay as much as he or she can now and working out some monthly terms. Put the payment agreement in writing, have the defendant sign it, give him or her a copy, and keep the original.

If you are the defendant, before paying the plaintiff the full amount, obtain a "Satisfaction of Judgment" form from the small claims court clerk's office, and have the plaintiff sign it when you give him or her the money. If you mail the plaintiff a check, send the form with it, along with a self-addressed, stamped envelope for him or her to return the form to you. (If you are the plaintiff, insist upon payment in cash or by cashier's check or money order. If the defendant convinces you to accept a personal check, do not sign this form until the check clears the bank. Otherwise, you may end up with nothing if the check bounces.) Once the plaintiff signs the Satisfaction of Judgment, the defendant should make a copy and file the original with the small claims court clerk.

Suppose your letters to the defendant prove futile. What next? You'll need to find out what assets or sources of income the defendant has that you can reach ("levy on") to pay ("satisfy") the judgment. The two best ways to collect your money are from the defendant's bank account and by garnishing his or her wages (see discussion below). Some property is partially or totally exempt from judgments: the equity in a house and a car up to a certain amount, and clothes, furnishings, and personal effects. The defendant's wages are also partially exempt. The amount of the exemption for the different assets varies from state to state, and the small claims court clerk may have a schedule for your state.

You'll need to find out where the defendant works or has his or her bank accounts if you don't already know this information. In some states, when the judgment is against the defendant, the clerk automatically sends a "Judgment Debtor's Statement of Assets" form with the judgment. The defendant must fill out and return this form to you if he or she doesn't pay the full judgment by the prescribed time, usually 30 to 45 days.

The defendant must state on the form where he or she works and list bank accounts, cars, real estate, stocks and bonds, and other assets he or she has. If the clerk in your area doesn't send out the form, ask for the form, and send it yourself. The clerk can also instruct you on what other procedures are available in your state to find out what the defendant owns.

Now that you know where the defendant's bank account is or where he or she works, you will need to fill out a "Writ of Execution" form (available from the small claims court clerk) and file it with the court. Ask the clerk how many copies you will need, and make an extra one for your records.

Take the Writ of Execution to the marshal's (or sheriff's) office in the county where the bank account is located. The marshal will serve the bank with the Writ of Execution, and the bank must give the marshal all money in the account over the exemption amount, if any (up to the amount of your judgment plus the marshal's fee). If you are garnishing the defendant's wages, the marshal will serve the employer with the Writ of Execution. The employer then withholds the prescribed amount from the defendant's regular paycheck (usually up to 25 percent at most, depending on how much the defendant earns) and pays it to the marshal, who in turn gives it to you. This continues until the judgment is paid off.

If the defendant owns a business, you can have the marshal do a "till tap," in which the marshal goes to the business and takes all of the money out of the cash register, up to the amount of the judgment and the marshal's fee. Another possibility is a "keeper"—the marshal stays for a few hours or a few days and collects all the money the business takes in.

Keep track of all the expenses you incur in collecting the judgment, including the marshal's fees and the costs of filing various forms with the clerk, and add these to the judgment. Don't overlook the fact that you are entitled to interest at the legal rate (which varies from state to state) from the date the judgment is rendered.

16

CIVIL RIGHTS AND LIBERTIES

THE UNITED STATES CONSTITUTION gives us many fundamental and inalienable rights: among them, the right to practice the religion of our choosing, the freedoms of speech and peaceable assembly, the right to bear arms, the right to be free from discrimination, the right to travel freely, and the right to protect our writings, creations, and inventions. This chapter is concerned not only with what these rights are, but also with when and how far the government can restrict them. (Constitutional rights related to criminal proceedings—the right against self-incrimination, for example, or the right to be free from unwarranted searches and seizures—are discussed in chapter 18.)

One thing to keep in mind throughout this chapter is that few of our constitutional rights are absolute. As the examples in this chapter will demonstrate, it essentially boils down to balancing the competing interests of the individual's rights against the government's rights. The government can limit your rights only when its own interest is so strong and compelling that it is justified in doing so.

The last section of this chapter concerns your right to sue the government for damages when you are injured by a government employee or by a dangerous condition on government land. Although most people would not consider this a civil right or liberty in the strictest sense (and indeed nothing in the Constitution gives you the right to sue the government), on the other hand, what could be a more fundamental right than holding the government liable for the injuries it causes you? The Constitution requires the government to compensate you fairly when it takes your property (see chapter 5). Nothing less should be required of the government when it takes, say, your arm or your life.

Your Right to Freedom of Religion

The First Amendment to the United States Constitution begins, "Congress shall make no law respecting an establishment of religion, or prohibiting the free exercise thereof." The first part of this provision is known as the "establishment clause"; the second part, the "free exercise clause."

The Establishment Clause

The establishment clause prohibits Congress from establishing a national religion. But it goes much farther than that. The government cannot favor one religion over others, nor can it hinder or forbid a religion. Essentially, the establishment clause requires that the government not interfere in religion, that there be a "wall of separation" between the two. Is every law that affects religion unconstitutional? No. Many laws passed by Congress and state legislatures directly or indirectly affect religion but are nonetheless constitutional.

As the U.S. Supreme Court has acknowleged, the total separation of church and state is not truly possible. Given that admission, the question becomes how much association between church and state is permissible. In 1971, the U.S. Supreme Court declared that a law that affects religion does not violate the establishment clause if the law has a secular purpose, if its primary effect neither advances nor inhibits religion, and if it does not foster an excessive government entanglement with religion. This test (known as the *Lemon v. Kurtzman* test) has been used ever since to determine if a law unconstitutionally intrudes upon religion.

The government attempts a "benevolent neutrality" toward religion, aiming neither to promote nor inhibit religion, but to reasonably accommodate it if that can be done without too much government involvement. This explains the tax-exempt status afforded religious organizations. Another example of the government's "hands-off" approach: disputes in internal religious matters must be resolved within the confines of the religious organization. For instance, if there is a disagreement on how a particular passage from a religious writing should be interpreted, the courts will not decide which of the interpretations is correct or more acceptable.

Every winter come the challenges to city or county Christmas displays, such as the nativity scene on the lawn in front of city hall or the cross atop it. Generally, the courts hold that such displays violate the First Amendment, since they amount to government support of a religion. But in 1984, the U.S. Supreme Court held that a nativity scene set up by the city of Pawtucket, Rhode Island, was permissible because it was included with a reindeer and other secular objects. The Court concluded that the complete display symbolized a secular American holiday rather than a religious one. Christmas trees put up by a government body are generally permitted on the basis that they do not symbolize any religious holiday. But whether children in public schools can sing Christmas carols depends on the carols. Students in public schools are ordinarily prohibited from singing religious carols, such as "Joy to the World." But secular carols—"Jingle Bells," for instance—are usually allowed.

Your Right to Practice Your Religious Beliefs

The "free exercise clause" of the First Amendment guarantees you the right to practice your religious beliefs without government interference. Does this mean that the government cannot place any restrictions on religious practices? No. The government need not always yield to religious beliefs when laws and religious tenets clash. Some acts can be prohibited when the government has a "compelling interest" that supersedes an individual's right to free exercise of religion. Human sacrifice can be banned, for example, as can bigamy or polygamy, even if they are sanctioned by a person's religion. The government can't, however, restrict your right to *believe* in any aspect of your religion.

Does the free exercise clause include the freedom to use illegal drugs for religious purposes? Yes, if the use is a legitimate part of a religious service. For instance, members of the Native American Church are allowed to use peyote (a hallucinogen) during religious services. The use of the drug must be in strict accordance with the church's tenets, which otherwise prohibit the drug's use. But you can't set up a phony religion advocating that an illegal drug—say, cocaine—must be used daily for spiritual enlightenment and expect to be immune from criminal prosecution for violating drug laws.

Another time religion comes into conflict with government authority is when a child is badly in need of medical treatment or requires a lifesaving blood transfusion, but the parents object on religious grounds. Whose will prevails, the parents' or the government's? In questions involving the life or death of a child, the government usually wins. Parents who, on religious principles, have deliberately withheld medical treatment from a seriously ill child have been successfully prosecuted for such crimes as child abuse and endangering the child's life—even involuntary manslaughter when the child has died from the lack of medical care.

The federal government has laws regulating who can immigrate into the United States. There are formal procedures to comply with and quotas specifying how many people from a given country can move here each year. Suppose a church proclaims itself a sanctuary for refugees from countries with rampant political strife. Some church members, acting in accordance with their religious beliefs and the church's declaration, help refugees from those countries unlawfully enter the United States. Can those church members be convicted of breaking the law, even though they were following their religious principles? Yes; the government's interest in regulating immigration is superior to the individual's religious practices in this situation.

Another example of permissible government intrusion upon religious practices: in 1986, the U.S. Supreme Court held that the Air Force could prohibit a commissioned officer who was an orthodox Jew and ordained rabbi from wearing a yarmulke while on duty. The Court deferred to the judgment of the Air Force that the tradition of outfitting military personnel in standardized uniforms encouraged the subordination of personal preferences and identities in favor of the overall group mission. Wearing of the yarmulke detracted from the uniformity sought by dress regulations. The effect of the Court's decision was to uphold the Air Force's distinction of banning visible religious apparel or symbols but allowing those that are hidden from view.

Whenever a person claims to be exempt from a law because of his or her religious convictions, the judge can inquire into the sincerity of the person's beliefs. The judge cannot, however, make a determination of whether a particular religious belief is acceptable, logical, consistent, or even comprehensible. But the judge can decide whether a belief properly comes under the heading of religion. For instance, one court held that whether a person is pro- or antinuclear is a political issue, not a religious one. The religion does not have to be a traditional one, nor is belief in a Supreme Being required. But protection is not given to "religions" that are obviously shams and whose members have no religious sincerity. "Religions" that are set up solely to get around drug laws or taxes and that lack true religious foundation are not protected by the First Amendment.

Religion and Public Schools

Much of the controversy regarding the separation of church and state involves religion's role in public schools. And in this

area, nothing engenders as much dispute as whether prayer—
forced or voluntary—should be allowed in public primary and
secondary schools. To date, the U.S. Supreme Court has ruled
that laws requiring or permitting prayer in public schools are
unconstitutional. For example, in 1985, the Supreme Court held
that an Alabama law prescribing a one-minute period of silence
in all public schools for "meditation or voluntary prayer" was
unconstitutional because the law was designed solely to return
prayer to public schools. Reading passages from the Bible or other
religious writings is also prohibited.

The U.S. Supreme Court has ruled that public primary and
secondary schools cannot permit student religious groups to use
school facilities for meetings. But in 1984, President Reagan signed
a bill that bars public high schools from prohibiting students from
voluntary religious meetings before and after school.

Can parents refuse on religious grounds to send their children
to public schools? Yes, but the state can require that the children
receive equivalent instruction in a private school. The children
must attend a parochial or other private school that meets the
state standards of education, or the children can be compelled to
attend public school. Parents who refuse to comply with the
compulsory education law can be prosecuted and punished.

One interesting case in which the parents could not be punished for violating compulsory education laws involved a Wisconsin law that required all children to attend school until they
reach 16. Amish parents, however, refused to let their children
attend school beyond the eighth grade for fear that secondary
education would expose them to outside worldly influences that
conflicted with Amish tenets. The U.S. Supreme Court declared
the Wisconsin law unconstitutional because, if enforced, it would
do more harm to the Amish religion than it would do good for
the children.

Can a child in a public school be forced to salute the flag
and recite the Pledge of Allegiance? Not if doing so would violate
his or her religious beliefs. But the government can require children to be vaccinated over their religious objections (or the ob-

jections of their parents) before attending public school, because of the state's compelling interest in preventing the spread of childhood diseases.

The government generally cannot give money to parochial schools, nor can it pay the salaries of public school teachers who teach classes in church-affiliated schools, even if they teach secular subjects only. Some assistance can, however, be given directly to the students, such as lunches or street crossing guards. And public schools can lend textbooks to parochial schools, since that promotes the state's legitimate interest in the students' secular education. The U.S. Supreme Court has also ruled that the federal government can give money to parochial colleges and universities to construct buildings and facilities that can be used only for secular educational purposes. The government cannot, however, give construction money to a parochial primary or secondary school, even if the school promises to use the proposed building solely for secular education. Why? Because the curriculum in parochial elementary and secondary schools includes substantial religious indoctrination, while church-related colleges and universities do not.

Religion and Your Job

Can an employee who refuses to work on his or her sabbath be fired, demoted, transferred, or subject to other disciplinary action? In some situations, yes. A Connecticut law prohibited employers from firing employees who refused to work on their sabbath. The U.S. Supreme Court ruled that this law was unconstitutional because it forced employers to conform their business practices to the particular religious practices of the employee. Sabbath religious concerns automatically prevailed over all secular interests at the workplace, and the law did not take into account the interests of the employer or of other employees who did not observe a sabbath. This Court decision does not, however, prevent a state from requiring employers to accommodate their employees' religious practices to the extent that it can be done without excessive disruption to the business or inconvenience to the other employees.

Some states still have "Sunday closing laws" that prohibit many types of businesses from operating on Sundays. Although such laws may have some religious undercurrents, the U.S. Supreme Court has consistently held that these laws are constitutional because they give the workers a needed day of rest and promote community welfare and order.

Your Right to Freedom of Speech

Freedom of speech, guaranteed by the First Amendment, lets us speak our minds without fear of government recrimination. We can give speeches, write articles, or hold rallies criticizing the government, advocating other political systems, or generally saying whatever we want without risking imprisonment or other punishment. And speech isn't limited to the spoken or written word. It can be symbolic, such as dancing or wearing clothing; even burning a book is a form of symbolic speech.

Like most other constitutional rights, the right to freedom of speech is not absolute. Limitations can be placed on our speech when the government has an overriding interest. The classic example of speech that is not protected by the First Amendment is running into a crowded theater and falsely yelling "Fire!" Preventing the high potential for injuries caused in the ensuing panic greatly outweighs the person's right to that kind of speech.

The right to free speech also does not include the liberty to slander or libel someone else (see chapter 8). If you defame someone, you cannot escape paying the damages you caused that person by claiming that you have the right of free speech. You can be prosecuted for burning or otherwise desecrating the American flag, even though that is a type of symbolic speech. The First Amendment also doesn't give you the right to ask someone else to commit a crime for you. (If you do, you are guilty of the crime of solicitation; see chapter 18.) The government can prohibit you from standing on the sidewalk outside a jail and talking to the prisoners inside without permission. The courts have held that all of these are valid restrictions on your right to free speech.

Obscenity

The First Amendment does not protect obscenity. The U.S. Supreme Court has defined obscenity as material that, taken as a whole by the average person applying contemporary community standards, "appeals to the prurient interest in sex, portrays sexual conduct in a patently offensive way, and does not have serious literary, artistic, political or scientific value." "Community standards" refers to the entire state, not each community within the state. And the standard used is that of the reasonable adult, exclusive of children. (But a state can forbid the sale of adult-oriented material to minors.) Deciding what is obscene and what is not is admittedly a difficult task, one that is done on a case-by-case basis by the judge and jury.

Although the government can prevent the sale or distribution of obscenity, it is not a crime to keep obscene material in your own home. An individual's right to privacy outweighs the government's interest in protecting society from obscenity.

Speech That Presents a "Clear and Present Danger"

The fact that speech is offensive or annoying to some—or even to many—generally is not sufficient cause to prohibit it. In one decision of the U.S. Supreme Court, Justice William O. Douglas stated: "A function of free speech under our system of government is to invite dispute. It may indeed serve its high purpose when it induces a condition of unrest, creates dissatisfaction with conditions as they are, or even stirs people to anger. Speech is often provocative and challenging. It may strike at prejudices and preconceptions and have profound unsettling effects as it presses for acceptance of an idea. That is why freedom of speech [is] protected against censorship or punishment. . . ."

Suppose a communist group is holding a meeting in a park near city hall. The speaker is advocating the immediate overthrow of the government by any means possible, including force. The crowd becomes unruly, the speaker's harangue continues, and it appears that some type of illegal action is imminent. Can the police step in and break up the meeting and arrest the speaker and others for breach of the peace without violating the First Amendment guarantee of free speech? Yes. In this case, there is a "clear and present danger" of immediate unlawful action, a "call to arms," which goes beyond merely making some people angry.

On the other hand, if the speaker had merely been explaining his or her philosophical view that the forcible overthrow of the government is proper and was not advocating any specific plan, and if the crowd was not stirred to action, the police would have to let the meeting proceed. This is because the First Amendment guarantees you the right to express your belief in any political theory in the abstract. But when you go beyond merely explaining your convictions and start advocating that something be done now to overthrow the government, your speech is no longer protected by the First Amendment.

Your Right to Peaceably Assemble

Closely allied with freedom of speech is the freedom of peaceable assembly, also guaranteed by the First Amendment. A city or county government can require you to obtain a permit or license to hold a meeting, rally, or demonstration, and it can charge you a fee to help cover the costs of police protection and the like. The permit can even impose reasonable regulations as to the time, place, and duration of the meeting, but it cannot regulate its content; in other words, the government can't censor what you say at the meeting.

A city cannot deny a group a permit to meet in a public place (such as a park) or march in the streets just because the group's views are unpopular. This was made clear by a case in the late 1970s involving a Nazi group that wanted to hold a demonstration in front of the town hall in Skokie, Illinois, a predominantly Jewish community. The city denied the group's request for a permit to hold a rally during which the members would be wearing uniforms with swastikas and holding signs advocating white rights. The city's denial of the permit was overturned by the courts, and eventually the group was permitted to demonstrate as originally planned.

Your Right to Bear Arms

The Second Amendment to the Constitution reads: "A well regulated militia, being necessary to the security of a free State, the right of the people to keep and bear arms, shall not be infringed." America would not have gained independence from Britain without the Minutemen and others who were ready to pick up their guns on a moment's notice and fight for their new country. This is what the writers of the Second Amendment primarily had in mind: arms as necessary to protect the country, rather than an individual's right to own a gun for private (nonmilitary) use.

The government has the power to regulate many aspects of gun ownership and possession, and there are a number of restrictions on your right to keep and bear arms. You can't, for example, carry a concealed gun or knife with you in public without a permit. Many states require you to wait a few days between the time you apply to purchase a gun and the time you can actually buy it. State laws often require handguns and other types of weapons to be licensed. Some states require a gun dealer to fingerprint and

investigate a purchaser before selling a weapon to him or her.
The sale of certain types of weapons is often banned outright,
such as automatic rifles, submachine guns, hand grenades, and
other military-type weapons. Convicted felons are usually barred
from owning or possessing weapons for a certain period.

Your Right to Be Free from Discrimination

A number of laws—the most important of which are the
Civil Rights Acts of 1964 and 1968—prevent you from being sin-
gled out and discriminated against in various situations because
of your race, color, national origin, religion, sex, age, or handicap.
Other chapters in this book discuss discrimination in particular
situations: your right to be free from discrimination and harassment in employment (chapter 11) or when applying for credit
(chapter 14), for instance, or from being discriminated against
when you want to buy a house (chapter 5) or rent an apartment
(chapter 6).

The government or a government agency is barred from
discriminating against you on the grounds of race, color, national
origin, religion, or sex because of the Fourteenth Amendment
guarantee of "equal protection of the laws." Discrimination by a
business that is "engaged in or affects interstate commerce" is
prohibited by the Civil Rights Act of 1964 and other laws. For
instance, a restaurant that serves people regardless of where they
live (that is, in state or out of state) cannot refuse to serve blacks
or other minorities. Purely private and individual discrimination,
however, is not prohibited. For instance, a private men's club
that is supported solely by its membership dues can prohibit women
and even blacks from membership. The club generally can't, however, discriminate if persons out of state belong as members or
even if, for example, a private tennis club has a regular annual
match with a private club from another state. In that situation,

the club would be involved in interstate commerce and therefore subject to the Civil Rights Act and other laws relating to discrimination.

To compensate for years of discrimination by some companies and educational institutions against blacks and other minorities, the federal government has required them to create "affirmative action" programs to increase the opportunities for minorities. Other employers and schools have voluntarily set up affirmative action programs to aid minorities. These programs have resulted in lawsuits by white workers and white students for "reverse discrimination." The gist of these lawsuits is that it is unconstitutional to give anyone better or different treatment solely because of his or her race; discrimination in any form is wrong, even if it is designed to make up for past discrimination.

The most widely known reverse discrimination lawsuit was Allen Bakke's seminal case in the 1970s against the Regents of the University of California for refusing him entrance to the U.C. Davis medical school while admitting minorities whose grade point averages and entrance examination scores were significantly lower. Bakke challenged the special admissions program that reserved 16 of the 100 positions for blacks and other specified minorities, leaving white students to compete with all other students, including blacks and the other minorities, for the remaining 84 positions. In 1978, the U.S. Supreme Court held that the medical school should have admitted Bakke because his race was the only reason for his rejection. But the Court also ruled that as part of an overall admissions program, the university could consider an applicant's race to promote ethnic diversity among its student body.

Another reverse discrimination case was filed by Brian Weber against his employer, Kaiser Aluminum and Chemical Corporation, and his union, United Steelworkers of America. For years, Kaiser's craft forces consisted almost exclusively of whites, although the labor force from which it drew employees was about 40 percent black. To make up for this past imbalance, a collective bargaining agreement between Kaiser and United Steelworkers gave a promotion edge to blacks over whites with seniority. Weber contended that he was discriminated against because a black with less seniority was selected for a training program instead of him, solely because of race. The U.S. Supreme Court rejected Weber's argument and ruled that the program was necessary to accomplish the racial balance and integration sought by the Civil Rights Act of 1964. In another case, however, the U.S. Supreme Court ruled that an established seniority program that tended to favor whites over minorities by protecting them from layoffs did not violate the Civil Rights Act.

Although the proposed Equal Rights Amendment to the Constitution—which would have banned discrimination on account of sex—was defeated, women's rights have increased greatly in the last two decades. Women generally cannot be discriminated against, except by private clubs or when being male is a bona fide job requirement. A number of state constitutions expressly forbid discrimination on the basis of sex. This brings up another important question: do gays have a right not to be discriminated against because of their sexual preference? Laws that prohibit discrimination against a person because of his or her sex are to be distinguished from laws that prohibit discrimination on the basis of a person's sexual preference. Although some states and cities have laws prohibiting discrimination against a person because of his or her sexual orientation, gays generally do not enjoy the same protection from discrimination as do minorities and women.

Your Right to Travel Freely

The Constitution protects your right to travel freely about the country. The government cannot restrict a person's right to travel within the United States except under extraordinary circumstances; a suspect out on bail, for instance, or a convicted felon on parole or probation may be prohibited from leaving the county or state without the permission of the court or the parole or probation officer. If you're divorced and have custody of the children, you may need court approval to take them with you if you want to move to another state.

The federal government can restrict your travel to "enemy" countries—countries we are at war with, for example, or with which we have no official diplomatic relations. You can't, for example, visit Cuba, North Korea, or Vietnam except under rare circumstances. And if you receive Social Security benefits, they may be affected while you are in certain "unfriendly" nations (see chapter 12).

When you travel by air, you may encounter some common problems that are appropriate to discuss here. What, for instance, are your rights if your luggage is lost, destroyed, or damaged by the airline company? For domestic flights—flights originating and ending in the United States—the current limitation on the airline's liability is $750. For international flights, the limit is 250 francs per kilo (about 2.2 pounds) of checked baggage, up to 20 kilos. The conversion rate is based on the value of the franc at the time the luggage is lost, destroyed, or damaged. If your luggage is worth more, you will have to declare the higher value and pay an extra charge to get additional coverage. These limitations may not apply if you can prove that the airline company deliberately lost, destroyed, or damaged your luggage.

You are entitled only to the value of your luggage and the contents as of the date when they were lost, destroyed, or damaged. For instance, if your suitcase cost $100 but was four years old, the most you'll get for it is about $50 unless you can show that it was in exceptionally good shape. You won't get the amount it cost (unless it was new) or what it will cost to replace it with a comparable new one.

Suppose you buy $1,000 worth of baggage insurance, but your baggage and the contents are only worth $500. If everything is lost or destroyed, how much do you get, the full $1,000 or only $500? Just $500. It doesn't matter how much you insure it for; you still get only the actual value of the property that was lost or destroyed.

What are your rights when you are bumped from an overbooked flight? At the very least, you are entitled to a seat on the next flight out or a refund of your money. If you're required to spend an extra night at a hotel or to make a second trip to the airport, write a letter to the airline company asking for reimbursement of those costs. Include copies of all receipts (such as the hotel bill and restaurant check), and remember to keep a copy of everything for your records. The airline probably attempted to limit its liability with a disclaimer on the ticket or elsewhere limiting it to providing you with a seat on the next available flight out or refunding your money. In some cases, the courts will not enforce the airline's disclaimer, freeing the passenger to recover as much damages as he or she can prove. If your damages are substantial—you were stranded for a week, for example, or you missed an important business meeting and lost a big sale—you should contact a lawyer to see what action, if any, would be appropriate against the airline.

Another thing worth noting here about air travel is that if a passenger is injured or killed in an accident on an international flight originating, ending, or having a stopping point in the United States, the damages are limited by the Warsaw Convention to $75,000. Let's say that Joe Banes and Janet Smith board an airliner at Los Angeles International Airport. The plane's ultimate destination is London, where Joe is headed, with a stop in New York, Janet's final destination. The plane crashes on the way to New York, and both Joe and Janet are killed. Because Joe was on an international flight—Los Angeles to London—his survivors (his next of kin, such as his wife and children; see chapter 3) are subject to the limitations of the Warsaw Convention and can recover no more than $75,000. Janet's survivors, on the other hand, are not subject to any limitations because Janet was on a purely domestic flight—Los Angeles to New York. One important restriction on the Warsaw Convention limitation on damages: the limitation must appear on the passenger's ticket, and the language must be printed in type large enough to catch your attention. A limitation in fine print is not effective to notify the passenger of the Warsaw Convention limitation.

Your Right to Copyright Protection

When you write, for instance, an article, a book, or a screenplay, do you have any protection against someone else using all or part of your work in his or her own article, book, or screenplay? You are protected by the Copyright Act of 1976, which applies to "works" made after December 31, 1977. The Copyright Act protects you from others infringing upon your work by using it for their own gain, such as plagiarizing it, quoting it, adapting it (using your book as the basis of a movie, for instance), or reproducing it (record or videotape piracy or "bootlegging").

What types of works can be copyrighted? Books, articles, poems, screenplays, theatrical plays, song lyrics, musical compositions, computer software programs, video games, motion pictures, videotapes, television programs, phonograph records, cassette tapes, photographs, paintings, drawings, catalogs, maps, compilations of information (such as telephone directories), instruction manuals, choreographed dances, and others. But only original "expressions of ideas" can be copyrighted. Ideas, titles, and general plot themes are not protected by the copyright laws.

How to Copyright Your Work

Only the author or the person to whom the author has transferred the copyright can copyright a work. In a "work for hire" (see chapter 11), the employer (the person who commissions the work) is considered the author of the work. A work is copyrighted only if all copies that are distributed to the public contain a proper notice of copyright. This is done by writing "copyright" or "copr." or simply "©," followed by the year the work was finished or first published, and your name: "Copyright 1986 Denise Williams," for example, or "© 1986 Randy Barnes." If your work reaches the public without a copyright notice, it could enter the "public domain," which means that anyone is free to use all or any part of it.

You don't need to register your work with the Copyright Office in order for it to be copyrighted, but you do need to register it to recover damages if someone infringes upon your copyright (see discussion below). To register your work, write to the Copyright Office, Library of Congress, Washington, D.C. 20559, state the type of work you want to register, and request the form for it. After you have completed the form, return it with your check for $10 and two copies of the work, if published (one if unpublished).

Your best copyright protection is to register your work with the Copyright Office as soon as you complete it and to put the proper copyright notice on the title page of every copy you send out. If you will be submitting your unpublished work to others—for instance, to a magazine, a book publisher, a movie or television production company, or a music company—keep a record of those submissions. It may well be worth the extra money to send your work via certified mail, return receipt requested. This way, if you suspect someone of using your work without your consent, you will be able to prove without a doubt that the alleged infringer at least had possession of your work at a certain time. Many cases of copyright infringement—particularly those involving musical compositions and screenplays—are won or lost on the ability to prove if and when the alleged infringer received the work.

How Long a Copyright Lasts and Transferring Your Rights

How long does a copyright last? If the author owns the copyright, it lasts for the author's life plus 50 years. The author can specify in his or her will who owns the copyright after he or she dies. If the author dies without a will, his or her next of kin becomes the owner of the copyright. In a "work for hire," the copyright lasts for 100 years after the work is finished or 75 years after it is first published, whichever is sooner.

You can transfer all or part of a copyright you own to another person unless you have already assigned the copyright to someone else. Transfers of exclusive rights—such as giving a magazine the right to be the first to publish your article ("first serial rights")—are required to be in writing. But even if you're giving someone a nonexclusive right to use your work, get the agreement in writing and read it carefully. Know exactly what rights you're giving up before signing the agreement. If there's any part of the agreement that you don't understand, consider talking to an experienced copyright lawyer.

What Constitutes a Copyright Infringement

If you claim that your copyrighted work has been infringed upon, you must prove three things: (1) that you own a valid copyright to the work; (2) that the infringer—the person who used your work without permission—had access to your copyrighted work (there is no copyright violation if someone else creates a similar work without knowing about yours); and (3) that when considered in their entirety and final form (that is, the form in which the public sees them) the two works are "substantially similar."

In determining whether two works are substantially similar, the judge considers specific similarities between the plot, theme, dialogue, mood, setting, pace, characters, and sequence of events. As noted above, the mere fact that someone used your idea or plot theme as the basis for a work is not enough for a case of copyright infringement. Each case is determined on its own merits, by comparing the total concept and feel of the allegedly infringing work with the copyrighted work. Random and insignificant similarities between two works are not enough. But determining whether the infringement is "substantial" can be a difficult question.

Let's say you write an article revolving around a wealthy

person living in a large mansion, who is attended to by several servants, gets around town in a chauffeur-driven limousine, eats at the best restaurants, and so on. Your article is published in a magazine, and a few months later you see an article in another magazine involving a wealthy person with similar attributes, but the plot is considerably different. Assuming you can prove that the alleged infringer read your story, if you sue for copyright infringement based on the similarities in the lifestyles of the two characters, will you win? Probably not. That a rich person lives a certain lifestyle comes under the heading of "scènes à faire": incidents, characters, or settings that are standard to certain ideas and themes and therefore not protected by the copyright laws. Some other examples of scènes à faire include a church wedding, a barroom brawl, a high-speed police pursuit, and a formal cocktail party.

"Fair Use" of a Copyrighted Work

Not all use of a copyrighted work without the copyright owner's permission is prohibited. "Fair use" is permitted. Fair use is "a privilege in others than the owner of the copyright to use the copyrighted material in a reasonable manner without the consent of the copyright owner." In determining whether the use of a copyrighted work comes under the heading of fair use, a judge considers the following factors:

• The purpose and character of the use, including whether the use is a commercial one or is for nonprofit educational purposes. Uses which are generally permissible include using the copyrighted material for criticism, comment, news reporting, teaching (including photocopying the material for classroom use), and research. Book reviewers, for instance, generally can quote copyrighted material without violating the Copyright Act.

Not all use for criticism, news reporting, and the like is considered fair use. An example: former President Gerald Ford had a contract with Harper and Row Publishers and *Reader's*

Digest to publish his memoirs. *Time* magazine agreed to pay $25,000 for the exclusive right to excerpt 7,500 words from the memoirs, which *Time* planned to publish the week before the book was shipped to bookstores. But before it did, *The Nation*, a political commentary magazine, obtained an unauthorized copy of the manuscript and used it to scoop *Time* by publishing a 2,250 word article on Ford's pardon of former President Richard Nixon. *The Nation*'s article included a number of direct quotes from the book, most of which concerned Ford's pardon of Richard Nixon. Although *The Nation* quoted a total of only 300 words from the book, the U.S. Supreme Court found that it was guilty of copyright infringement, because the quoted material was "essentially the heart of the book."

• The nature of the copyrighted work. Works that are factual in nature can be used a little more freely than original works of fiction and fantasy, for instance.

• The amount and substantiality of the copyrighted work used in relation to the copyrighted work as a whole. There are no hard and fast rules on just how much of a copyrighted work can be used without infringing on the copyright. Each case is decided on its own facts, with the judge taking into consideration the amount of copyrighted material that was used and the length of the entire copyrighted work. For example, quoting a 100-word paragraph from a six-volume historical work might not be considered a substantial infringement, but quoting 25 words from a 50-word poem could be.

• The effect the use has upon the potential market for or value of the copyrighted work. This is generally considered to be the single most important element of fair use. The focus here is on whether the use materially impaired the marketability of the copyrighted work. If the use resulted in a significant reduction in the value of the copyrighted work, the copyright owner has a much better chance of winning a lawsuit for copyright infringement.

Your Rights When Someone Infringes upon Your Copyright

When someone unlawfully infringes upon your copyrighted work, you usually need to be represented by an experienced copyright lawyer in order to enforce your rights. Depending on when you copyrighted your work (see discussion below), you are entitled to recover the following types of damages in a copyright infringement case:

1. You can ask the judge for an "injunction" to stop any further infringement of your copyright.

2. You can also recover money damages based on one of the following:

(a) The "actual damages" the infringement caused you. Actual damages compensate the copyright owner for the extent that the work's market value was injured or destroyed by the infringement. If, for instance, before the infringement you could have sold the work for $5,000, but now it is worth only $1,000, your actual damages are $4,000.

(b) The profit made by the infringer. This is the amount of the infringer's gross sales minus any costs—such as printing, promoting, and distributing the work—and overhead. (In one case, a magazine used a copyrighted photograph of Raquel Welch without permission on the cover of its February 1983 issue of *High Society's Celebrity Skin*. The judge awarded 75 percent of the magazine's profit from that issue to the photograph's copyright owner because of the cover picture's importance in attracting the customer's attention.)

(c) "Statutory damages" set by federal law. Statutory damages are used when neither your actual damages nor the infringer's profits can be ascertained with a reasonable degree of certainty. At his or her discretion, the judge can also award statutory damages instead of actual damages or the infringer's profits, even if actual damages or the infringer's profits are ascertainable. (This is usually done when the actual damages and infringer's profits are relatively small.) Statutory damages generally range from $250 to $10,000 for each infringement. If the judge finds that the infringement was "willful," he or she can award up to $50,000.

3. In many cases, you can also recover your attorney's fees from the infringer if you win the case.

Before you can recover damages in court for an infringement, you must register your work with the United States Copyright Office. If you want to recover statutory damages and attorney's fees, you must register your work with the Copyright Office *before* the infringement of an unpublished work, or within three months after the first publication of a published work. If you wait until after the infringement to register your work, you will only be permitted to recover your actual damages or the infringer's profit from the infringement.

Your Right to Patent
Your Inventions

If you invent something, you should think about protecting yourself with the rights afforded you by the law—most importantly, the right to patent your invention. Many types of inventions and discoveries can be patented: a new product or machine, a novel manufacturing process, compositions of matter (combining two or more ingredients to form a new compound with different or additional properties), even original designs for an "article of manufacture," to name some. Improvements to existing products, machines, processes, and designs can be patented in many cases. You generally cannot patent an idea, however, if you do not have the means to carry it out. Another major limitation is that an invention can be patented only if it has some "utility." You can't get a patent if your invention is useless or trivial. (This requirement of utility does not apply to patents for designs.)

A patent gives you the exclusive right to your invention for seventeen years (ten years for a design patent). You can retain all rights to use, make, and market your invention yourself during that time, or you can give or sell some or all of these rights to others. If someone infringes upon your patent (copies or uses your invention without your consent), you can sue to stop the infringement and to recover the monetary damages the infringement caused you.

You must be the original inventor to obtain the patent; if someone else has invented something but has not applied for a patent, you cannot apply to patent it. Your employer may have some or all rights to the patent if you developed it on company time, however (see discussion in chapter 11). Falsely claiming on a patent application that you are the original inventor can be a serious matter.

You may lose your rights to patent your invention if you don't protect yourself properly. For example, you can't patent your invention if it has already been available to the public for a year and you haven't applied for a patent. Putting "patent pending" on the invention won't help you if in fact no patent is pending; doing so may even subject you to criminal penalties. (You generally cannot put "patent pending" on your invention until you have filed an application for a patent with the United States Patent and Trademark Office.)

The best thing to do if you have a finished invention—or even just an idea in mind that you plan to pursue—is to talk to a patent lawyer. Since patent law is a very complex area, lawyers who deal in this field tend to be specialists; many of them have engineering degrees as well as degrees in law. Before filing an application for a patent, a patent lawyer will search the patent office records to see whether someone else has already obtained a patent for a similar invention. (If you're still in the idea stage, a patent search now could save you considerable time and money by preventing you from putting a lot of effort and expense into developing your invention, only to discover later that someone else already has a patent on it.)

Be careful in selecting a company that promises to help you develop and market your ideas and inventions. Hiring a company that is not fully established or experienced in this area could result in your spending thousands of dollars and getting nothing in return, or worse. You should consult a patent lawyer before making any commitment to one of these companies. An experienced patent lawyer can give you some advice on marketing your invention, including telling you which companies live up to their promises and which companies to avoid. At the very least, check the company out with the Better Business Bureau. Ask the company for references, including the names and addresses of others whose inventions it has marketed; contact those people and ask how much the company's services cost them, what the company did, and whether they were pleased with the company's efforts. Don't sign a contract with a development and marketing company until you've read it carefully, and pay special attention to just what the contract requires the company to do. If there's anything you don't understand, or if it appears that the company really isn't obligated to do anything, talk to a lawyer before signing the contract.

Your Right to Know What the Government Knows

The Freedom of Information Act, signed into law in 1966, gives you access to information the government has in its files. The information need not mention or even pertain to you. The idea behind the Freedom of Information Act is this: the government is "we the people," and we the people have the right to know what the government knows.

Generally, the government can withhold requested information only when a sufficient reason exists. Many refusals, for example, are based on the assertion that to disclose the information would compromise national security. The government also won't give out information that constitutes a company's trade secrets (see discussion in chapter 11). If you don't agree with the government's refusal to furnish the information to you, you can sue in court to have a judge decide whether the government's refusal is justified.

To obtain the information, you must request it either in person or by mail directly from the appropriate government agency. Your request must identify the information as precisely as possible. Which agency you should contact depends on the type of information you're seeking. If, for example, you want to learn what the F.B.I. knows about you, you must direct your request to it. The names and addresses of the agencies where various information is kept are published in the Federal Register, which is available in many large libraries. When you request information from the government, you will have to pay a "search and copy" fee, the amount of which depends on how difficult the information is to find and how many pages there are to copy.

Critics of the Freedom of Information Act contend that it doesn't go far enough, that the information should be more readily available, and that requests should be fulfilled cheaper and faster (it often takes several months or more from the time you ask for the information until the agency sends it to you). The government contends that the fees and procedures are necessary to protect its agencies from people who would otherwise harass them with a flood of burdensome and insincere requests.

Another law to be aware of is the Privacy Act of 1974, which regulates the government's use of information a government agency obtains on you. The Privacy Act gives you the right to demand that information important to you be used only for the purpose for which it was originally gathered. The Privacy Act also gives you the right to obtain copies of the information, correct errors in it, and make additions to it.

Your Right to Sue the Government for Personal Injuries

Suppose you're injured by the negligence of a government employee—federal, state, county, or city—or you are hurt on government property because of a dangerous condition. Do you have a legal right to make the government pay for your injuries and associated damages, such as your medical bills, the damage to your car, the wages you lost while you were out of work, and your pain and suffering?

Historically, if you were injured by a government employee or on government property, you could not sue the government. This rule originated in England, when the king had the ultimate authority regarding who could sue whom. Since the courts were in fact the king's courts, he naturally ordained that no one could sue the government (which was, of course, the king).

This rule of "sovereign immunity" made its way to the United States, and as a result, neither the federal government nor a state or local government can be sued without its permission. Generally speaking, today laws permit suits against them for personal injuries in some situations. If a government employee on duty causes injuries through his or her careless driving, for instance, the government is usually liable to the injured person.

If you want to sue the United States government, your injury must fall within the provisions of the Federal Tort Claims Act. State and local governments generally have laws regulating personal injury suits against them. Some states, for example, still do not permit a suit against them for medical malpractice in a public hospital.

Examples of Injuries Caused by Government Employees or Public Property

The most common injuries caused by a government employee are traffic accidents traceable to the negligence of the driver of a government-owned vehicle, such as a city or county bus, a police car or fire truck, a city landscaping truck, or even an army truck. Brutality and false imprisonment by police officers are other examples of injuries caused by government employees. One important limitation on the government's liability is that generally the employee must be on the job when he or she hurts you. Let's say you're injured in a car accident caused by the careless driving of a city police officer. If the accident happened while the officer was on duty, the city is liable. But if it happened, say, on the officer's day off while the officer was driving his or her own car, the city is not liable. The government also is usually not liable if a person is hit by a police car or fire truck that is responding to an emergency call.

Governments generally have the obligation to maintain their property in a reasonably safe condition, and if they fail to do so, you can sue for your resulting injuries. For instance, if you slip on a loose tile at the department of motor vehicles, if your heel catches a piece of loose carpet at the Social Security office, or if you fall on a freshly waxed floor at the county courthouse, the government is liable for your injuries. Defects in the design of highways or other roads have also been the basis of many lawsuits against the government. If, for instance, a corner is too sharp for the speed limit, a car may veer off the road while trying to negotiate it at the posted speed limit and crash into a tree or a ditch. Failure to maintain landscaping on public property is another source of lawsuits against a government for personal injuries. For example, the city may permit a hedge at a busy intersection to grow too dense, making it dangerously difficult for approaching drivers to watch for cross-traffic.

Suppose you're driving down a city street, and your car hits a pothole, which causes several hundred dollars' worth of damage to your car. Is the city liable for your damages? That depends on whether the city had "notice" of the pothole. If the pothole was new, and the city didn't know about it, then the city is probably not liable. But if the pothole has been there for quite some time, the city ought to have known it was there and should have either repaired it or placed a barrier around it. Some cities have laws that make the city liable for damages caused by potholes only if the proper department had received a written notice from someone informing it of the pothole and its location.

Filing a Claim with the Government

Before you can file a lawsuit in court against the government, you must first file a "claim" with the proper administrative body, such as the city or county clerk, or the appropriate state or federal agency. The time you have to file a claim against the government is considerably shorter than the time (the "statute of limitations") you have to sue a private individual. You may be required to file your claim with the government within as few as 60 days of the accident. If the government rejects your claim, you then have a specific amount of time, which varies from state to state, from that date to file your lawsuit in court.

If you file the claim late, you can be excused from the time requirement if you have a valid legal reason—if you were unconscious, for example, or in the hospital or otherwise unable to file a claim on time. But mere ignorance of the fact that you had to file the claim is generally no excuse for not filing it or for filing it late. A claim that is filed late is usually denied without the merits of the claim even being considered, unless you show a valid legal reason why it was not filed on time. If the government agency refuses to consider your claim because it was filed late and rules that you don't have a sufficient legal reason for being excused from the time requirement, you can file a petition in court asking for relief from the time requirement.

If you suspect that a government employee or that government property is partly to blame for your injuries, you should promptly consult an experienced personal injury lawyer to determine what rights you have against the government. Suits against governments tend to be more complex and must comply with many technical formal procedures. For these reasons, a lawyer's help is warranted for most claims against a government.

If your claim is a small one—say, $200 or $300—and is against the city or county, you may be able to handle the claim yourself. You can get information about filing a claim against a city or county by calling the city clerk or city attorney's office or the county clerk or district attorney's office—whichever is appropriate. Ask how much time you have for filing the claim from the date of the accident, and ask whether there is a specific form the city or county can send you to fill out. If the claim can simply be a letter from you, include your name, address, and telephone number; the date and place of the accident; a complete description of the accident (for instance, on August 23, 1986, you were stopped at a red light on Madison Avenue, when a city maintenance truck, license number 876 DVE, driven by James Smith, rear-ended you); proof of your damages (such as a repair estimate or doctor's bills); and ask for a specific amount of money (the total of your medical bills, property damage, lost wages, pain and suffering, and any other damages you suffered from the injury). If your claim is rejected, you may be able to sue the city or county in small claims court (see chapter 15).

17

ANATOMY OF A
CIVIL LAWSUIT

IN 1984, one civil lawsuit was filed for every 15 Americans, and some 16,750,000 civil trials took place—about 150,000 trials in the federal courts, the rest in state courts. Some have criticized America as a litigious, even sue-happy society, with people ready to file a lawsuit at the slightest provocation. Is this true? In the sense that we have chosen to settle our disputes in a civilized manner in the courtroom, rather than in the middle of a dusty street at high noon, perhaps it is. Those who founded this country recognized that might does not mean right, and that unless given an opportunity to be heard in a fair and impartial setting, the meek would be subject to the tyranny of the more powerful. The activity in our courts is really the modern incarnation of the colonial spirit, which declared, "Don't tread on me." When an American feels trod upon, he or she can seek justice in a fair and impartial court of law.

When you add to the number of lawsuits filed each year the number of witnesses and jurors who can be involved in a case, it becomes clear that sooner or later you are likely to participate in a lawsuit—if you haven't already or aren't now involved in one. To help you understand how a case proceeds through the legal system, this chapter traces the course of a civil lawsuit, from the time the complaint is filed until the jury's verdict is announced. (A criminal trial generally follows the same format, but with emphasis on the defendant's constitutional rights and due process; see chapter 18.)

For this chapter, let's assume that you were injured in an automobile accident: you were making a left turn when the defendant—Bob Jones—who was doing 50 in a 35-mile-per-hour zone, ran into you. We'll also assume that you're being represented by an attorney, since, as noted in chapter 19, it's not a good idea to act as your own lawyer in court except in small claims court or traffic court.

Starting a Lawsuit

How Long Do You Have to Sue?
The Statute of Limitations

The first thing you need to be aware of is that you don't have forever to file a lawsuit. Every case—civil and criminal (except murder)—is subject to a "statute of limitations," a time limit on when you can file your lawsuit in court. If you do not file it within the prescribed time, you lose the right to sue the other person. The time you have to file a lawsuit varies depending on the nature of the case and from state to state. For example, depending on the state, you have from two to ten years to file a suit for breach of an oral contract and three to fifteen years if the contract was written. The statute of limitations for personal injury cases ranges from one year to six years. (If you've been injured by a government employee, you normally must file a claim with the appropriate government body within as few as 60 days—see chapter 16.)

Let's say that the statute of limitations for personal injury cases in your state is two years. Suppose your nine-year-old daughter is also hurt in the accident. Do you have to file suit by the time she is eleven? Generally not. In the case of a minor, the statute of limitations is usually suspended ("tolled") until the child reaches the age of majority. If the age of majority in your state is eighteen, then your daughter has two years from her eighteenth birthday to file her lawsuit against the person who hit her. (Other times when the statute of limitations is suspended include while a person is insane, or is hospitalized because of the accident.) If you want to file a lawsuit for your daughter while she is a minor, your attorney will have to get a court order naming you your daughter's "guardian ad litem"—literally, guardian for the lawsuit.

Filing the Complaint

The first step in every lawsuit is the filing of a "complaint" in court. Because you are filing the complaint, you are the "plaintiff"; the person you are suing is the "defendant." The complaint tells why you feel the defendant is responsible for your damages. It lays out the legal grounds for the suit, the "cause of action"—for instance, breach of contract, divorce, false imprisonment, or, in our sample case, negligence. In a breach of contract action, for example, your lawyer would allege in the complaint that you had a contract with the defendant (and spell out what the basic terms of the contract were), that you did everything the contract required you to do, that the defendant breached the contract by not doing something as required by the contract, and that you suffered damages because of the defendant's breach of contract.

Before filing the complaint, your lawyer will usually first conduct a preliminary investigation to determine if there appear to be grounds for the suit. A lawyer who doesn't investigate the facts before filing what turns out to be an unfounded lawsuit may be liable to the defendant for the tort of malicious prosecution (see chapter 8). The person who told the lawyer to file the suit may also be liable for malicious prosecution.

Where is the complaint filed? That initially depends on the nature of your case. If you're filing for bankruptcy, you can only file it in the bankruptcy division of the United States District Court. Such things as divorce and probate can be filed only in a state court, and usually there are courts specifically designated for these proceedings—family, or domestic, court for divorces and surrogate, or probate, court for will probates (see chapter 20) Automobile accidents, medical malpractice actions, and other cases for personal injuries are ordinarily filed in a state court of general jurisdiction, such as superior, or district, court.

When your lawyer files the complaint with the court, the clerk issues a "summons," which signals the official start of the lawsuit. The summons notifies the defendant that a lawsuit has been filed by you and that he or she must answer it within a certain time.

The summons and complaint must now be formally delivered to ("served on") the defendant. Your lawyer will probably have this done by the marshal's office, a professional process server, or a member of the lawyer's staff. Sometimes the complaint can be served on the defendant by mail, but this is usually done only when the defendant is already represented by a lawyer, and the lawyer agrees to accept service of the summons and complaint on behalf of his or her client. (Service by mail is routinely done in small claims court actions; see chapter 15.)

The Defendant's Response to the Complaint

The defendant (through his or her attorney) must file a response to the complaint with the court within a specified time, usually 20 or 30 days. The most frequent response the defendant's attorney files is an "answer" that generally denies all of the complaint's allegations. In essence, a general denial states: "I deny everything; I didn't do anything wrong." The answer may contain an "affirmative defense" that something bars or limits the plaintiff's claim. The fact that the statute of limitations expired before the complaint was filed is an affirmative defense. In our sample case, the defendant's affirmative defense will be that you were comparatively negligent (see chapter 8) for making the left turn before it was safe. Occasionally the defendant admits doing the wrongful acts but claims that the amount of damages the plaintiff is asking for is too high. The case then proceeds to trial solely on the issue of damages—how much the plaintiff should get. With the answer, the defendant can also file a countersuit, or cross-complaint, against you.

Sometimes instead of filing an answer, the defendant will file a "demurrer" (in federal court, a "motion to dismiss") to the complaint. A demurrer is designed to get a complaint thrown out of court if the complaint doesn't contain enough facts to show that the defendant did anything legally wrong—if it doesn't state a "cause of action" against the defendant. Suppose the main facts alleged in your complaint are these: "On September 15, 1986, the defendant was driving his car down Main Street and struck the plaintiff, thereby injuring her." If the defendant files a demurrer to the complaint, will the demurrer be sustained? Yes. Your lawyer has not alleged any facts in the complaint that indicate that the defendant was at fault. It is not against the law to drive down Main Street, and the complaint doesn't tell how the plaintiff was injured. It may be that the defendant wasn't paying attention, but it could just as well be the plaintiff who caused the accident. Neither the defendant nor the judge should have to guess at what you're claiming the wrongful conduct to be.

The first time a demurrer to a complaint is sustained, the judge will normally give your lawyer a chance to "amend" the complaint to allege the necessary facts. For instance, your attorney could change the complaint as follows: "On September 15, 1986, the defendant was driving his car down Main Street at 50 miles per hour in a 35-mile-per-hour zone, and, because of this unlawful act, struck the plaintiff, who was lawfully making a left turn." The complaint now alleges that the defendant was doing something wrong that resulted in your being injured.

The amended complaint must be served on the defendant. If the defendant files a demurrer to your new complaint, the judge should overrule it, and the defendant will then have 20 or 30 days to file an answer. Let's say the judge sustains the defendant's demurrer and won't let your lawyer amend the complaint again. What then? The complaint is thrown out of court completely.

The only way you can get another chance is to appeal the judge's ruling to a higher court and try to convince the appellate court that the ruling was wrong.

What happens if the defendant simply ignores the complaint and doesn't do anything about it? When the time that the defendant has for responding to the complaint expires, your attorney can file for a "default." The judge will grant the default if the defendant was properly served with the summons and complaint, if the time for answering the complaint has run out, and if the defendant was notified of the default hearing. Can a defendant get a default set aside so he or she can answer the complaint? Yes, but usually only if the defendant acts quickly after learning that the default was entered against him or her and can show some valid reason for not responding to the complaint: if, for example, the defendant was ill when he or she was served with the complaint and was unable to do anything about it, or the process server lied about serving the defendant and threw the summons and complaint into the trash instead of giving them to the defendant.

What Happens before the Trial

Pretrial Investigation

After the complaint and answer have been filed and served, the formal and intensive investigation process—called "discovery"—begins. During this stage, each side gathers evidence and prepares his or her case. Your attorney will want to find out as much about the case as possible, both yours and the defendant's.

In our sample case, if he or she hasn't already done so, your lawyer or an investigator may go to the accident scene to take pictures and measurements. Witnesses will be interviewed and accident reports and medical records reviewed. If there is any indication that a defective condition in either car contributed to the accident or made your injuries worse than they would have been otherwise, various experts in automobile design or manufacture may be retained to study the problem for a possible lawsuit against the car's manufacturer. If you have been seriously injured, you will be evaluated by medical specialists to determine the extent of any permanent disability and the cost of medical care to treat you.

The formal discovery process also gives your lawyer the chance to find out what evidence the other side will be presenting at the trial. There are several ways of doing this. One is through "written interrogatories"—a list of questions asking the defendant, under oath, for information about the case: How fast were you driving? Where were you coming from? Where were you going? Did you have anything to drink that day? Did you take any drugs or medications that day? Who was in the car with you? What are the names and addresses of the witnesses you plan to call at trial?

The most important—and enlightening—part of discovery in many cases is the "deposition" (in some parts of the country, "examination before trial," or simply "EBT"). In the deposition, a lawyer asks questions of the opposing party or a witness for the other side. A deposition is testimony taken outside of court, and you are sworn in and give your testimony under oath, just as you are when you testify in court. You can be held guilty of the crime of perjury if you lie at a deposition.

Your lawyer will "depose" the defendant, and the defendant's lawyer will "depose" you. If either side will be calling other witnesses to testify, the opposing lawyer may want to depose them as well. The deposition is usually held in the office of the lawyer taking the deposition, with lawyers for both sides present. The deposition proceedings are taken down by a court reporter and can be used at the trail. Some depositions are videotaped, particularly when there is a strong chance that the witness will be unable to testify at the trial because of, say, age, illness, or a move out of state.

After the court reporter has transcribed your deposition testimony, you are given the chance to review it to see if your answers were recorded accurately. You can make changes on the record but may be asked to explain those changes later at the trial: it's one thing to explain correcting a mistake that the reporter made; it's quite another to explain why you changed your answer. Similarly, if you say one thing at the deposition but another at the trial, your veracity will be questioned at the trial. Unless you can explain the discrepancy to the satisfaction of the jury, the jury may find it hard to believe anything you say. Because of this, you should answer deposition questions with as much care and thought as if you were sitting before a jury at a trial.

The discovery stage of a trial is crucial in preventing either side from being unduly surprised by the other at trial. It is designed to provide a fair and faster trial. Unfortunately, some lawyers have gotten into the habit of using the discovery process as a means for harassing the other side rather than as a part of a good faith effort in preparing their cases. When a lawyer abuses the discovery process, many judges will impose penalties ("sanctions") ranging from monetary fines to throwing the case out of court.

Out-of-Court Settlements

The vast majority of legal disputes—more than 90 percent—are settled out of court. Some are settled before the complaint is even filed; others are settled after the complaint is filed but before the trial has commenced; some are settled during the trial; and still others are settled after the trial, while the case is on appeal to a higher court.

Why are so many cases settled out of court? The main reason is that plaintiffs and defendants alike often want to avoid the *risk* each side faces in going to trial. No matter how strongly justice appears to be on your side, if you are the plaintiff, there is always the chance that you might lose the case or that the jury will be stingy with its award. For the defendant, there is the risk that the jury will base its decision on sympathy rather than the facts and will find liability where there is none or will be too liberal in its award. Because of the uncertainties, the plaintiff may accept a sum smaller than the one he or she originally hoped for, and the defendant may pay an amount higher than he or she would like.

Pretrial Motions

Before a trial begins, any number of motions may be made by either side. Three of the more frequent and important pretrial motions are motions for summary judgment, for judgment on the pleadings, and to exclude evidence at the trial.

A motion for "summary judgment" is an attempt by one side to have the case decided by the judge before the trial. Let's say that your attorney feels that there are no facts in dispute and that no one could reasonably dispute your right to win and files a motion for summary judgment against the defendant. Your attorney submits a legal brief outlining your position, which must be supported by evidence, such as depositions and sworn affidavits (witnesses' statements, signed under oath). If the defendant can't present any evidence to contradict your evidence and show the disputed facts, the judge will grant your motion for summary judgment. Why? Because no dispute of fact exists. In other words, the evidence presented to the judge shows that you are clearly entitled to win. But if the defendant can present any evidence that contradicts your assertions, the judge will deny the motion for summary judgment. The judge does not make a determination at this point as to who is more likely to be telling the truth—that is left for the jury to decide at the trial. The judge only decides if there is in fact a dispute.

A motion for summary judgment may be preceded by a motion for "judgment on the pleadings." This motion is made after the complaint and answer have been filed. Let's say that your complaint alleges that the defendant breached a contract, and the defendant's answer admits this and doesn't contain any affirmative defenses that would bar your suit. It is clear from the complaint and answer (the "pleadings") that you are entitled to recover your damages from the defendant. Your attorney would therefore file a motion for judgment on the pleadings, which would be successful. The major difference between a motion for judgment on the pleadings and a motion for summary judgment is this: in a motion for judgment on the pleadings, the judge can look only at the pleadings themselves and the allegations they contain, while in a motion for summary judgment, the judge can look at affidavits, depositions, and other evidence in addition to the pleadings.

Before the trial, motions may be made to exclude evidence from being presented at the trial for one reason or another. These are called "motions in limine." Suppose the defendant had caused an accident a year or so before the one in which you were hurt. Your lawyer normally is not allowed to bring this up at your trial. The question is whether the defendant was negligent when he hit you, not when he hit someone else a year earlier. (The danger in permitting evidence of an earlier accident is that the jury will find the defendant liable because of that accident or because he generally may be a poor driver, and not because he necessarily did anything wrong at the time in question.) To prevent your attorney from making any reference to the earlier accident at the trial, the defendant's attorney may ask the judge for a pretrial ruling that your attorney cannot mention it to the jury.

The Trial

Jury Selection

The selection of jurors who will hear the facts and decide the case can be the most decisive part of the trial. (What to expect when you are summoned for jury duty is discussed in chapter 20.) One juror hostile to your case can influence others to vote his or her way or may simply hold out so that the jury is unable to reach a decision, resulting in a hung jury. (In civil cases, the lone holdout juror is not as important as in criminal trials, as most civil cases need not be decided by a unanimous jury. For example, if there are twelve jurors, in some states, only nine or ten jurors need to be in accord; if six jurors are permitted, only five must agree.)

Prospective jurors are initially chosen from the surrounding community. At one time, their names were taken from the voter registration rolls. Today, a much broader base is used, including registration information from the department of motor vehicles. From this group, a panel will be sent for questioning to the courtroom where your case will be tried.

Most of the time, the lawyers for the parties question ("voir dire") the prospective jurors for possible prejudice and bias. Some judges (especially federal judges) prefer to question prospective jurors themselves. Your lawyer will try to select jurors who are most likely to be favorable to your cause, and to keep off those who may side with the opposition. The defendant's lawyer will do likewise.

Suppose your lawyer feels that a prospective juror—let's say, a woman—is prejudiced against your case, and doesn't want her to decide your fate. How can your lawyer keep her from being a juror? By "challenging" her. There are two types of challenges used to exclude a prospective juror from hearing a case: challenges for cause and peremptory challenges. A "challenge for cause" is allowed when a prospective juror is clearly biased for or against one side or has an interest in the outcome. The juror may be a friend or relative of the defendant or the defendant's attorney, or may be prejudiced against you because of your race or religion. Or the juror may have a preformed opinion on the case and can't objectively weigh the facts presented in the courtroom.

If the judge doesn't feel that there is sufficient cause to excuse the juror, your lawyer can still get her removed by using a "peremptory challenge." A peremptory challenge can be used to exclude a juror for any reason or for no reason. Your lawyer may feel that because the woman is a redhead or thin or black that she may not be sympathetic to your case. Or your lawyer may have noticed that the woman gave the defendant's lawyer a smile or nod, but when your lawyer looked at her, she had an icy glare.

These things are not enough for a judge to excuse a juror for cause, but they may be enough to give your lawyer reason to excuse the person. Why is it important to distinguish between challenges for cause and peremptory challenges? Because your lawyer gets an infinite number of challenges for cause, but only a limited number of peremptory challenges, such as six or ten, depending on the state. Once the peremptory challenges are used up, a juror can be challenged only for cause. If the judge doesn't think the person is prejudiced, that person sits as a juror in your case.

Opening Statements

When the last juror has been selected, the trial starts. The first thing that happens is that your attorney gives an "opening statement" to the jury, summarizing what he or she is going to prove. An opening statement is just that: a statement of the evidence your attorney intends to present. Your attorney is not allowed to argue against the defendant's version of the facts; that is reserved for the summation at the end of the trial (see discussion below). After your attorney is finished, the defendant's attorney can make an opening statement. Or the defendant's attorney can wait and make his or her opening statement after your attorney has rested your case. Most of the time, the defendant's attorney will make an opening statement right after the plaintiff's attorney's opening statement, if only to remind the jurors that there is another side to the story and that they should keep an open mind.

Suppose your attorney forgets to state some important facts during the opening statement—that the defendant was speeding when his car hit you, for instance. When your attorney sits down, the defendant's attorney may move for a "nonsuit." This motion asks the judge to throw your case out of court because your attorney hasn't alleged the basic facts to show that the defendant committed a legal wrong. The judge will give your attorney the chance to amend the opening statement to allege the missing facts. But if it is clear to the judge that your attorney will not be able to add anything new to the opening statement even if given the chance, the judge will grant the defendant's motion for nonsuit.

The Cases in Chief

After the opening statements, your lawyer presents your "case in chief." As this is a civil case, your lawyer has the burden of proving your case to the jury by a "preponderance of the evidence"—a "probability" that the defendant is liable for your damages. During the case in chief, your lawyer will call witnesses and present evidence demonstrating your right to recover damages. Expert witnesses are frequently used by both sides to support their positions. In a traffic accident, an expert in accident reconstruction may be called to give an opinion on the cause of the accident. Doctors may be called to the stand to describe the nature and permanency of your physical and emotional injuries.

Your lawyer calls the first witness to the stand (it may well be you), the clerk swears the witness in, and your lawyer proceeds with "direct examination." When your lawyer is finished questioning a witness, the defendant's lawyer has the chance to "cross-examine" the witness. More leeway is given to the lawyer while cross-examining a witness. For instance, leading questions—questions that suggest an answer—aren't allowed on direct examination but are permitted during cross-examination. It would be a leading question and therefore improper for your lawyer to ask you on direct examination, "You looked far down the road in front of you before making your turn and didn't see any cars, didn't you?" That is leading because it suggests an affirmative answer. But it would be proper for the defendant's lawyer to say something like, "Isn't it true that you were in a hurry to get home that day?" This question also suggests an answer—again in the affirmative—but because it is on cross-examination, the question is proper. Why permit leading questions on cross-examination but not on direct examination? Because there is a much greater danger that you will be led to an answer by your own lawyer than by the other party's lawyer.

Neither lawyer can badger or intimidate a witness. Television lawyers notwithstanding, lawyers are not permitted to walk up to a witness and browbeat him or her. The lawyers usually must remain at the counsel table or stand at the lectern beside it. About the only time a lawyer is allowed to approach a witness is to hand him or her a document or picture to look at, and then only if the lawyer first asks the judge for permission to do so. Failure to follow court etiquette can get the lawyer a terse admonishment from the judge, and even a contempt citation if he or she continues to ignore courtroom decorum.

When your lawyer is finished representing all of the witnesses and evidence to prove your case, he or she officially concludes ("rests") the case in chief. If your lawyer neglected to present some crucial testimony, the defendant's lawyer can make a motion for nonsuit at this point.

The defendant's attorney now proceeds with the defendant's case in chief and calls witnesses for the defense. (Sometimes the defendant's attorney will rest the case without calling any witnesses or presenting any evidence.) Just as the defendant's attorney has the right to cross-examine your witnesses, your attorney can cross-examine each defense witness. When the defendant's attorney rests the case, your attorney has the opportunity for "rebuttal"—to present additional evidence that contradicts or explains the evidence presented by the defendant's attorney.

When the defense has rested its case, your lawyers may ask the judge to grant you a "directed verdict." This is a request that the judge take the case out of the jury's hands and decide in your favor because no reasonable person could dispute your right to recover damages. The judge will grant this motion only if there is no doubt as to how the jury will decide.

Closing Arguments and Jury Deliberations

Now that both sides have rested their cases, each attorney is allowed to make a summation, or "closing argument," to the jury. In some states, the defendant's attorney goes first, then your attorney. In other states, your attorney goes first, then the defendant's attorney, and then your attorney gets a chance to say a few final words. Regardless of the procedure, your attorney gets the last word. Why? Because the burden of proving the case is on your attorney.

After the closing arguments, the judge instructs the jury on the burden of proof, the law that applies to the case, and how the jury must apply the law to the facts of the case. Jury instructions can be very lengthy, convoluted, and difficult for the average juror to understand. The danger here is that the jurors may disregard the instructions and decide the case on what they feel the law ought to be, not what it is.

One of the jurors is appointed foreman. In some states, the jurors themselves select the foreman as the first order of business when they begin deliberations. Other states call for the judge to name the foreman. Still others have a simpler system: the first person chosen for the jury is automatically the foreman.

Back in the jury room, the jurors begin their deliberations. They weigh the evidence, decide which witnesses were telling the truth, and reach a verdict in favor of one party. Or they reach the conclusion that they are hopelessly deadlocked. During the deliberations, the jury may ask to see some of the exhibits again, have trial testimony reread, or have the judge give a further explanation of jury instructions. Jurors in civil trials are almost never isolated ("sequestered") from the public and the media during the course of the trial and deliberations. (In criminal trials involving controversial cases, juries are routinely sequestered.)

When a verdict is reached, the jury files back into the courtroom. The judge asks the foreman whether the jury has come to a verdict, the foreman replies affirmatively, and the judge instructs the foreman to hand the verdict to the bailiff or court clerk. The clerk then announces the verdict in open court.

Suppose that the jury returns a verdict for the defendant. What can your lawyer do? The first thing is to ask the judge to disregard the jury's verdict and instead enter a judgment in your favor. This is called a motion for a "judgment notwithstanding the verdict." The judge will grant the motion only when it is obvious that the jury's verdict is wrong—a rare event. If the judge denies your lawyer's motion for a judgment notwithstanding the verdict, you can appeal your case to a higher court (see chapter 20).

Court Congestion and Trial Delays

The American legal system is threatened by a judicial logjam. In some major metropolitan areas, it takes as long as five years to get a civil case to trial from the time the complaint is filed. Although some progress has been made, the problem continues; in some areas, it grows worse each day. The main solution is obvious: we need to build courtrooms, appoint more judges, and hire more court personnel. But this solution would cost money— much more money than anyone is willing to spend. We must realize that unless money is spent to eradicate the court congestion, the judicial system inevitably will collapse. And then what could we do if someone trod on us?

Part of the blame for trial delays goes to the lawyers themselves. Some lawyers routinely ask for delays and put off cases as long as possible because they try to handle too many cases at one time, or they simply don't take enough interest in office management and the orderly flow of cases. Other lawyers file every kind of motion they can think of to increase their fees or to harass the other side, and in so doing, they add to the congestion in court. Many states have taken steps to eliminate these tactics. Now when a motion is filed without reasonable grounds and in bad faith, the judge can order the offender to pay the other party the cost of opposing it.

One thing that causes unnecessary delays in many civil cases is the practice of insurance companies to delay settlement in order to reduce their costs. For example, suppose that Helen is injured on August 1, 1986. Her damages—including medical expenses, lost wages, and pain and suffering—total $50,000. As soon as it is notified of the claim, Helen's insurance company puts $50,000 aside, and invests it at 10 percent interest. The insurance company stalls and finally settles the case five years later for $50,000. In the meantime, the $50,000 it originally set aside has grown to more than $80,000. By delaying the settlement, the insurance company is tens of thousands of dollars ahead of where it would have been had it paid the money when the claim was first made.

Arbitration as an Alternative to the Courtroom

Rather than having their disputes decided in court, many people are choosing to settle them in "arbitration." Arbitration is generally a faster, less costly procedure than going through the legal system. Instead of a judge presiding over the case, in arbitration the controversy is heard by an "arbitrator" who is chosen by mutual agreement of the parties. The arbitration usually is not held at the courthouse but in a hearing or conference room, often in the arbitrator's office. Arbitration proceedings are similar in structure to trial proceedings—with opening statements, cases in chief, rebuttals, and closing arguments—but more informal. The rules of evidence are relaxed somewhat, but just as in a trial, each witness is sworn in and testifies under oath and can be cross-examined by the opposing party's attorney. There is no jury; the arbitrator decides the case.

When does a case go to arbitration rather than through the traditional legal system? Most of the time, a dispute goes to arbitration because you signed a contract providing that any disagreements be arbitrated. When a contract calls for arbitration of disputes, the decision of the arbitrator is final. If you don't agree with it, you can't sue in court and ask for a jury trial. You can, however, ask a court to invalidate the arbitrator's decision if the dispute was outside the arbitration agreement or if there was some impropriety in the arbitration proceedings that may have affected the outcome.

Occasionally in a court proceeding, the judge will order the parties in a civil dispute to arbitration. When this happens, the arbitrator's decision usually is not binding; if you don't like it, you can still proceed to trial with the case. Why, then, does the judge bother sending the case to arbitration? Because many cases are settled through arbitration, thereby reducing the court's backlog.

Should you be represented by a lawyer at an arbitration hearing? If the dispute could otherwise normally be heard in a small claims court, there's probably no reason why you can't be your own lawyer. But if the stakes are any higher, you should seriously think about hiring a lawyer to represent you.

18

CRIMES AND CRIMINAL JUSTICE

CRIMINAL LAW prescribes the rules that we as civilized people must respect and live by in order to keep our society from collapsing into chaos. Without a set body of criminal rules, administered by an impartial justice system, the law would be whatever the richest person or fastest gun in the territory said it was. American history—particularly settlement of the open West—proved that while vigilante justice is swift, it is often wrong, and the punishment is frequently far worse than the crime justifies.

Criminal law in the United States really encompasses two distinct areas. The first of these includes the rules defining what is a crime. The second includes the rules that the police, prosecuting attorneys, and courts must obey before a person can be convicted of and punished for a crime. The first half or so of this chapter discusses the elements of many of the more common crimes and the defenses often raised by criminal defendants. The second half deals with a person's rights when he or she is suspected of committing a crime.

This chapter is not designed as an aid to help you defend yourself against a crime. When you're charged with a crime more serious than a routine traffic violation (see chapter 2) or a very minor offense (drinking a beer in a public park, for instance), you'll usually want to be represented by a good criminal lawyer because of the potential consequences. What this chapter will do is give you a close look at the criminal justice system to help you understand how it works.

CRIMES

Just what is it that makes an act a crime? Some acts are crimes because they are inherently evil ("malum in se"), such as murder, rape, robbery, or arson. Other acts are crimes not because they are necessarily evil, but because they are contrary to an important social objective. Such a crime is referred to as a "malum prohibitum." For instance, fishing without a license or catching more than the limit is not wicked in itself. Laws prohibit this type of thing to preserve natural resources. Other acts—speeding, for instance—are prohibited to protect the safety and welfare of the public.

Crimes are generally categorized as either felonies or misdemeanors, although some are treated only as infractions or minor offenses. Felonies are the most serious types of crimes. Originally, only nine crimes were felonies: murder, manslaughter, burglary, robbery, larceny, rape, sodomy, arson, and mayhem (maiming or permanently disfiguring someone). Today, many other crimes are also felonies. The punishment for a felony is stiffer than it is for a misdemeanor. In many states, the punishment for a felony is imprisonment for *at least* one year (or death in some limited cases), while for a misdemeanor it is *no more* than one year in jail.

Two things must be present in order for a crime to be committed: an act (the physical element) and a particular state of mind (the mental element). The act is the body of the crime—the corpus delicti. In a murder, for example, it is the killing of a human being by another human. In arson it is the burning of a structure. Sometimes the act can consist solely of words, as in solicitation (see discussion below).

The mental element is the person's intent to do the illegal

act. In law it is frequently said that an act is not a crime if done without a guilty mind. Killing someone, for instance, is not a crime if it was purely accidental or justified self-defense, because there was no wrongful intent. And just as the act needs the intent to be a crime, the intent needs an act to be a crime. Merely thinking about doing something illegal is not a crime, regardless of how evil the thoughts are.

Preliminary Crimes

The crimes of solicitation, conspiracy, and attempt are known in law as "preliminary crimes," since they occur before the intended crime. Preliminary crimes are punishable because they go far beyond merely thinking about committing an illegal act.

Solicitation

You are guilty of solicitation when you ask someone to commit a crime for you or to help you commit a crime, or when you advise someone on how to commit a crime. The only act required for the crime of solicitation is that of asking or advising the other person. Although solicitation is usually associated with prostitution, you are guilty of solicitation anytime you ask someone to commit any crime for you, or advise on how it should be done. For example, it is solicitation to ask a person to kill someone or to commit a burglary for you, or to tell him or her how to do it.

Conspiracy

A "conspiracy" is an agreement between two or more persons to commit a crime. A married man and his mistress, for example, may plot to kill his wife and collect the insurance money. But in order for the crime to be committed, more is required than a mere agreement. One of the conspirators must do an "overt act" that furthers the conspiracy. Suppose after making the agreement with his mistress, the man buys a gun to kill his wife with. The husband and mistress are guilty of conspiracy because buying the gun to achieve the goal of the conspiracy—killing the wife— was the necessary overt act. If the two now decide to forget the whole thing, they are still guilty of conspiracy. The underlying crime—here, murder—does not actually have to be achieved.

Suppose Joe asks you to help steal a car. You think he is joking and say yes, but you don't really intend to assist with a theft. Joe then goes to the hardware store and buys some tools to use to steal the car (the "overt act"). Are you guilty of conspiracy because you apparently agreed to help? No. You are guilty of conspiracy only if, when you agree to assist with the crime, you actually intend to help.

Attempt

An "attempted crime" takes place when you intend to commit a particular crime and come dangerously close to completing it. This occurs when you enter the "zone of perpetration"—you are close enough to the victim that you could actually commit the crime. For example, a man jumps out of the bushes at night and grabs a passing woman, intending to rape her. At that point, he has committed the crime of attempted rape. Suppose the assailant changes his mind after grabbing the woman and does nothing more, or the victim manages to escape unharmed. Does that relieve him of criminal responsibility for the attempted rape? No. The crime of attempted rape was complete when, intent on raping the woman, he grabbed her.

The following example shows how solicitation can escalate to a conspiracy and then to an attempt. Say that Joe decides to rob a liquor store and asks Bud to help him. Joe is guilty of solicitation at this point, since he has asked someone else (Bud) to help him commit a crime. Bud agrees to help, then borrows a gun to use during the robbery. Bud and Joe are now both guilty of conspiracy: by borrowing the gun, Bud has committed the necessary overt act that furthers their agreement to rob the liquor store. On the night of the planned robbery, the two men drive to the liquor store and walk in. But once inside, they see a police officer, call the whole thing off, and leave. Both are guilty of attempted robbery because they were close enough to commit the crime.

Accomplices and Accessories

A person who guns down another in cold blood without a valid legal excuse is guilty of the crime of murder. But what of someone who helps the killer before, during, or after the murder or who helps anyone with any other crime? Is he or she guilty of the same crime as, well, some other crime, or no crime at all?

Anyone who participates in any way in the actual crime— an accomplice—is generally as guilty as if he or she actually commits the crime. For example, if one member of a gang goes inside the bank while another waits in the car with the motor running, and a third is up the street as a lookout, the driver of the getaway car and the lookout are just as guilty as the gang member who goes inside the bank and does the dirty work.

You are an "accessory before the fact" if you incite, aid, or abet someone in the commission of a crime. For instance, if you obtain firearms or ammunition for someone else, knowing that he or she intends to use them to commit a crime, you are an accessory before the fact. Stealing a bank's blueprints to facilitate another person's burglary is another example of an accessory before the fact. An accessory before the fact is generally as guilty as the person who actually commits the crime.

An "accessory after the fact" is someone who knowingly conceals a criminal, helps a criminal escape, or otherwise deliberately acts to prevent a criminal's capture. An accessory after the fact is not guilty of the main crime (unless he or she had a hand in it) but is criminally responsible for harboring or concealing the fugitive. Someone who deliberately conceals another person's felony is guilty of the crime of "misprision of felony." If you accept money or property from a person in exchange for agreeing not to report or prosecute his or her crime, you commit the crime of "compounding."

Crimes of Theft

Larceny

Larceny (theft) is the "unlawful taking and carrying away of another person's personal property, with the intent to permanently deprive the owner thereof." Stealing someone else's stereo system either for your own use or to sell is larceny, for example: you took the stereo without the owner's consent, and you did not intend to return it.

Taking a car for a joyride usually isn't larceny (although it is its own separate crime), since there is no intent to permanently deprive the owner of the car. But if the car is destroyed or damaged in an accident during the joyride, it then becomes larceny, even if the accident wasn't the fault of the joyrider. The "borrowed" property must be returned in the same condition it was in when it was taken, otherwise a larceny is committed. Suppose the joyride begins in Detroit, and the car is abandoned undamaged in New Orleans. Is it larceny? Yes. The car must be returned at or near the spot where it was taken; otherwise it is larceny.

The difference between grand larceny (a felony) and petit larceny (a misdemeanor) is determined by the value of the property taken. In some states, for example, it is grand larceny if the property stolen is worth $200 or more and petit larceny if it is worth less than $200.

Embezzlement

You commit the crime of embezzlement when you wrongfully take something that someone else has entrusted to you. The main difference between larceny and embezzlement is that in embezzlement, you start off with lawful possession of the property. For example, the corporate accountant who juggles the books and skims 10 percent off the top is guilty of embezzlement, since he or she was lawfully entrusted with the money in the first place. But if a cleaning woman sees the money in an open safe and takes it, she is guilty of larceny, because the company never entrusted the money to her.

Forgery

You are guilty of forgery when you make or alter a writing that has some legal significance. It is forgery to sign a person's name to a check without his or her consent. It is also forgery to change the amount on the check without the person's permission. If you pretend to be someone else and sign his or her name to a contract without the person's consent, that, too, is forgery. A contract has legal significance because it obligates a person to do certain things.

Burglary

Burglary was originally defined as the "unlawful breaking and entering into the dwelling house of another in the nighttime, with the intent to commit a felony therein." Breaking into someone's house during the day was not a burglary, nor was it a burglary to break into a commercial building, a barn, or an unattached garage. Today burglary is usually defined as entering a structure at any time with the intent to commit any felony or misdemeanor larceny. (Breaking into a car or other motor vehicle in order to steal something is auto burglary.)

While we usually think of burglary as stealing money or

property from a house or business, it is also burglary to enter a structure to commit a murder, rape, arson, or any other felony. The crime of burglary is complete when the felon enters the structure, regardless of whether the intended felony is accomplished. Suppose, for example, Fred decides to break into a house to steal the jewelry and cash. He pries open a window and crawls through, but when he is confronted by a large barking dog, he leaves without taking anything. Fred is still guilty of burglary, since he entered the house intending to commit a felony (larceny).

Suppose Betty breaks into a house seeking shelter from a storm, and once inside decides to steal some money or property. Is that a burglary? No. When Betty entered the house, she did not intend to commit a felony inside. She decided to steal only after entering the house. She would, however, still be guilty of breaking and entering (using force to enter a house or other structure without permission), as well as larceny.

Robbery

Robbery is the use of force, or the threat of immediately using force, to take money or property from a person. Shoving a gun into someone's ribs and demanding all of his or her money is an obvious example of robbery. The force can be directed against either the victim or a member of his or her family. For example, a father and daughter are walking down a street one night and are accosted by a robber. The robber threatens to hurt the daughter if the father doesn't hand over his wallet. This is a robbery, although the force is not directed at the father.

Stealing a wallet from an unconscious person generally isn't considered robbery (unless the thief knocked the person out), since the victim doesn't surrender his or her money in the face of any force or threats. This doesn't mean that it's not a crime to take things from an unconscious person; it is larceny.

Extortion

"Extortion" (blackmail) takes place when someone forces you to pay money or to hand over something by threatening to hurt you (or a member of your family) or to destroy your reputation sometime in the future. If, for example, someone threatens to break your arm next Friday unless you pay him or her $750, that is extortion. Extortion differs from robbery in that it involves a threat of future harm, while robbery entails a threat of immediate force if you don't comply with the robber's demands.

The crime of extortion often involves a threat to release information that could damage a person's profession or marriage. For instance, a person may threaten to expose a woman's extramarital affair to her husband if she doesn't pay a certain sum. Or a person may threaten to expose a politician's shady dealings with a real estate developer before an election, unless the politician pays $10,000.

Crimes Involving Property

Receiving Stolen Property

The crime of receiving stolen property consists of taking possession of property you know to be stolen. You can intend to keep it yourself, sell it to someone else, or even store it temporarily for the person who stole it. Can you get yourself off the hook by proving that you paid the thief or fence fair value for the property? Not if you knew it was stolen when you bought it.

Suppose you buy a a new automobile stereo cassette system from Jim, who, as you know, has a history of arrests for stealing property. The stereo is worth $350, but Jim sells it to you for only $50. You realize that the stereo is probably "hot" but decide that the risk is worth taking. Are you guilty of receiving stolen property? Yes. In this case, the circumstantial evidence is probably enough to prove that you knew the stereo was stolen. You don't have to know who stole the property or from whom it was stolen, only that it was wrongfully taken from its rightful owner.

Arson

Arson was initially defined as the deliberate burning of another's house. If you burned a commercial building or your neighbor's barn, you weren't guilty of arson (although you were guilty of other crimes). Today arson is usually defined as the deliberate burning of *any* structure owned by another person. Is it arson to torch your own house? At one time it wasn't, unless you did it for an unlawful purpose, such as to collect the insurance money. Many urban areas, however, now make it illegal to burn your own house for any reason, because of the danger to nearby structures.

Suppose Ellen sets your house on fire, but you quickly see the flames and manage to put them out before any real damage is done. Is Ellen guilty of arson? Probably. The house need not be demolished or even substantially damaged by fire. All that is required is any burn damage, even if it is mere charring. But if the only harm is smoke damage, such as blackening of the walls, the damage is not enough for arson. Ellen would be guilty of attempted arson, however.

Possession of Drugs

To establish the crime of unlawful possession of a drug, the prosecution must prove, first of all, that the drug is in fact what it purports to be (that is, it is cocaine and not, say, flour) and, second, that you knew you had this drug on your person, in your car, or in your house. You are not guilty if you did not know that what you had was a drug. Suppose, for example, your friend Faye tells you that she grows her own oregano and gives you a plastic bag containing some of the leaves; you do not realize that Faye has actually given you marijuana as a joke. In this instance, you are not guilty of drug possession, because you honestly believe that the leaves are a harmless spice. By the same token, if someone borrows your car and leaves a packet of drugs inside that a police officer later discovers, you can get out of any charges filed against you by proving that you knew nothing about it. But be aware that such claims are viewed with great skepticism, and you will have to clearly prove your ignorance of the drugs' presence.

Growing marijuana plants is a crime, the severity of which often depends on how many plants are growing. If, for instance, there is only one plant, which the person grows for personal use, it is often a misdemeanor. But if there are a number of plants, the assumption made is that the person is selling to others, and therefore he or she may be charged with a felony.

Crimes against a Person

Assault

There are several definitions of a criminal assault. In some states, an assault is defined as attempted battery (see discussion below), plus the ability to actually carry out that battery. Other states define assault as a deliberate threat to commit battery, even though the person doesn't intend to carry out the battery. Suppose Jack intends to scare Rodney by jumping out of the bushes at him as though he were going to hit him. Jack does not intend to hit Rodney, nor does he touch Rodney at all. In states that define assault as attempted battery, Jack is not guilty of assault, since he never intended to touch Rodney—that is, he never intended to commit battery on Rodney. But in those states that apply the second definition, Jack is guilty of assault because he deliberately threatened to commit battery on Rodney.

Battery

The crime of battery is defined as a deliberate harmful or offensive touching of someone else without his or her consent.

Although we tend to think of battery as a violent act, such as a punch in the nose or a kick to the stomach, a light brush of the hand can be battery in some cases. A man who deliberately rubs his hand across a woman's breast without her consent, for example, commits battery, even if the woman isn't injured.

False Imprisonment

False imprisonment is the deliberate confinement of a person without his or her consent or without legal justification (a lawful arrest, for instance). The confinement can be physical, such as putting the victim into a room or cell and locking the door. Or it can be psychological—threatening to break the victim's arm if he or she tries to leave.

Kidnapping

A person is kidnapped when he or she is moved from one place to another against his or her will. In some states, it is also kidnapping to secretly confine the victim, even though the victim isn't taken anywhere. A kidnapping can be accomplished through force, such as knocking the victim unconscious. Or it can consist of threatening to harm the victim or members of his or her family if the victim doesn't accompany the kidnappers. Does the kidnapper have to make a demand for ransom in order for the crime of kidnapping to be committed? No; but if such a demand is made, the punishment is usually increased.

Rape

Rape—"unlawful carnal knowledge"—is sexual intercourse with a woman without her consent. (As far as the law in most states is concerned, a man cannot be "raped," though he can be sodomized.) The rapist does not have to use physical force; threats of harm are sufficient. The victim does not have to resist the rapist physically, at least not if any resistance would be futile and would subject her to more danger. If, for example, a rapist wields a knife in front of his victim, telling her that he will slit her throat if she does not cooperate, the woman does not have to attempt to struggle with the rapist. To do so could well mean her death.

Is it rape even if the assailant does not reach climax? Yes. The crime of rape is committed as soon as there is any penetration of the woman's vagina by the man's penis. (Inserting a foreign object into the woman's vagina is "rape by artifice." "Sodomy" is a broad crime covering any forced sexual act that is deemed unnatural, including anal or oral copulation. About one-third of the states make sodomy a crime even if it is done in private between consenting adults.)

Suppose an impotent man is accused of rape. Can he be convicted? Not if he can prove his impotency; he would be physically incapable of rape. But depending on the state's definition of attempt, he could be found guilty of attempted rape. If the state where the act took place requires the person to have the ability to commit the crime, then he would not be guilty of attempted rape. But he would be guilty of assault, battery, and false imprisonment.

Traditionally, a married man could not be guilty of raping his wife, although he could be guilty of some other crime, such as assault or battery. Today many states have laws that make it rape for a married man to force himself upon his wife when she refuses to engage in sexual relations.

"Statutory rape" is sexual intercourse with a female under a certain age, usually 14 to 18 years old, depending on the state. A girl under the statutory age is legally incapable of consenting to sexual intercourse. It therefore won't help the man to claim that the girl consented to the act. Suppose a man sees a young woman drinking in a bar and naturally assumes that she is at least 21 (the state's legal drinking age). If the two of them have intercourse, but it turns out that the girl is only 16 (and in that state, the age for statutory rape is under 18), and the man is later prosecuted for statutory rape, can he claim that he was honestly mistaken about the girl's age? At one time, the only defense permitted was that the man was married to the girl at the time of the intercourse. Mistakes—even honest and sincere ones—were not taken into consideration. Today, however, some states do permit the man to prove that he was mistaken about the girl's age if the girl intentionally misled him or if his mistake was reasonable under the circumstances.

Mayhem

Mayhem is the deliberate act of maiming a person or causing permanent disfigurement. Years ago, mayhem was defined as cutting off the victim's limb, leaving the victim less able to protect himself or herself against adversaries. Today the crime of mayhem includes acts that cause someone to lose a limb, finger, eye, or any other part of the body, or acts that result in significant scarring or other permanent disfigurement, such as throwing acid into a person's face.

Homicide, Murder, and Manslaughter

A common misconception about homicide is that it is a crime, that it is in fact synonymous with murder. But homicide itself is not a crime. *Homicide* means only the killing of one human being by another human being. Some killings are not criminal: accidental killings or killings in self-defense, for example, or the executioner's act of releasing the gas into the gas chamber to carry out a convicted felon's death sentence. The types of homicide that are crimes are murder, voluntary manslaughter, and involuntary manslaughter.

Does the body of the victim have to be found in order to get a verdict of murder or manslaughter? No. The fact of death can be proved by circumstantial evidence, such as that when the victim suddenly and inexplicably disappeared and the suspect had traces of the victim's blood on his or her clothes.

Murder

Murder is the unlawful killing of one human being by another with malice aforethought. *Malice aforethought* means in a particularly evil or heinous state of mind. Malice aforethought does not mean only that the murderer thought about killing the victim beforehand or even meant to kill him or her. Rather, malice aforethought includes all the following situations:

1. *Intentionally killing the victim.* One person deliberately, and without legal justification, takes the life of another person— a murder in "cold blood."

2. *Intending to seriously harm the victim.* Doug beats Jerry over the head with a lead pipe, for example, intending only to hurt Jerry seriously, not kill him. But if Jerry dies of the injuries inflicted by Doug, Doug is guilty of murder. This is because of the likelihood that death can result from a serious injury.

3. *Killing someone during the course of a dangerous felony, such as a burglary, robbery, rape, or arson.* For example, during a bank robbery, the bank guard draws his gun and is shot and killed by one of the felons. Even though the felon acted to protect his own life, he is guilty of murder. The felon was committing a dangerous felony and in effect invited this type of reaction from the guard. This is known as the "felony-murder rule."

4. *Doing something that has a high risk of death or serious injury, in disregard of the consequences.* Suppose Ben shoots into a crowd but doesn't intend to shoot anyone in particular; indeed, he may not intend to shoot anyone at all. The bullet strikes a young girl and kills her. Or suppose Ben shoots at a passing train and kills someone he never even saw. In both examples, Ben is guilty of murder because of the strong probability that his act would kill or seriously hurt someone. This type of murder is called a "depraved heart" killing.

5. *Killing a police officer while resisting arrest.* A person who kills a police officer while resisting a lawful arrest is guilty of murder, even if the person didn't intend to kill the officer.

Degrees of Murder. Most states break murder down into two degrees: first and second. The difference is based on the suspect's intent in committing the crime or the manner in which he or she carried it out. The severity of the punishment also varies, with first-degree murder being subject to more severe penalties, including death in certain circumstances.

First-degree murder is usually defined as any one of the following:

1. A murder that was willful, deliberate, and premeditated. This is often called murder in cold blood.

2. A murder caused by the use of poison, torture, explosives, or ambush ("lying in wait").

3. Killings committed in the course of certain felonies—usually arson, burglary, robbery, rape, and mayhem. If, for example, during the course of a rape, the rapist strikes his victim with a blunt object, killing her, he is guilty of murder, even if he did not intend to kill the woman.

Second-degree murder usually comprises the following:

1. A murder in which the suspect intended to kill the victim, but the killing was not premeditated—a "spur-of-the-moment" killing.

2. A murder in which the suspect intended to seriously harm—but not kill—the victim.

3. A "depraved heart" killing.

4. Killings committed in the course of a felony, other than those listed under first-degree murder.

Manslaughter

Manslaughter is the unlawful killing of a human being by another human being, but without malice aforethought. There are two types of manslaughter: voluntary and involuntary. Voluntary manslaughter is more serious than involuntary manslaughter, and the punishment is accordingly stiffer.

Voluntary Manslaughter. Voluntary manslaughter is an *intentional* killing without malice aforethought. Usually there are some mitigating circumstances that justify reducing a murder charge to the lesser offense of manslaughter. A common example of voluntary manslaughter is a killing committed in the "heat of passion" by, say, a husband who finds his wife in bed with another man. If the wronged husband kills before a reasonable person in the same situation would have cooled off, the killing, although still unlawful, is usually reduced from murder to voluntary manslaughter. But if the husband did not act immediately and instead plotted the killing for a few weeks, he could be charged with murder because he waited beyond a reasonable cooling-off period.

Involuntary Manslaughter. Unlike murder and voluntary manslaughter, involuntary manslaughter ordinarily is an *unintentional* killing. The death results from the suspect's criminal negligence, rather than any intent to kill the victim. For example, if a driver speeding down a residential street loses control of the car and runs over and kills a child playing on the sidewalk, that is involuntary manslaughter.

A drunk driver who causes an accident resulting in the death of a pedestrian or someone in another car has traditionally been held guilty of involuntary manslaughter. But some courts have held that when an intoxicated person takes control of an automobile—in effect, a dangerous weapon—he or she acts with a reckless disregard for the safety of others and can therefore be held liable for voluntary manslaughter or even second-degree murder.

Just as there is the "felony-murder" rule, there is also a "misdemeanor-manslaughter" rule: a person who accidentally kills another during the course of a misdemeanor is guilty of involuntary manslaughter. For example, if Joe punches Don in the face, and Don falls, hits his head on the sidewalk, and dies, Joe can be held liable for involuntary manslaughter.

Other Crimes

Prostitution, Pandering, and Pimping

Prostitution is engaging in sexual activities in exchange for money or property. It is illegal in most states, although a few parts of Nevada allow legalized prostitution to some extent. The prostitute is often the one prosecuted, but it is a crime for the customer as well.

"Pandering" is the procurement of a person to become a prostitute. "Pimping" is the crime of soliciting on behalf of a prostitute or deriving support from a prostitute's earnings. Suppose, for example, Lance approaches a young runaway and offers her a place to stay and half of everything she makes if she will have sex with the people he finds for her. Lance finds several men who will pay for sex with the girl. The men pay Lance, the girl has sex with them, and Lance gives the girl half the money. Lance is guilty of pandering, since he procured the girl to become a prostitute. Lance is also guilty of pimping, not only because he derived support from the girls' earnings, but also because he solicited the men to have sex with her.

Bigamy, Incest, and Adultery

"Bigamy" is the crime of being married to more than one person at a single time. "Incest" is marriage to, or having sex with, a close relative: a parent, child, uncle or aunt, nephew or niece, grandchild or grandparent, great-grandchild or great-grandparent, and, in some states, a first cousin, stepparent or stepchild, father- or mother-in-law, or son- or daughter-in-law. "Adultery" occurs when a married person has sexual intercourse with a person other than his or her spouse. Although it was a fairly major crime at one time, adultery is not a crime in many states today, and even where it is still on the books, it is rarely enforced.

Loitering and Vagrancy

"Loitering" and "vagrancy" are the "crimes" of sitting or standing around in a public place with apparently nowhere to go. Statutes prohibiting loitering or vagrancy are often struck down as unconstitutional for being too vague or because they prohibit lawful conduct as well as illegal conduct.

Disturbing the Peace and Malicious Mischief

You disturb the peace when you do something that unreasonably disturbs the public peace and order, such as getting into a brawl in public or setting off firecrackers in the early hours of the morning. "Malicious mischief" is the defacement of property, such as spray-painting the side of a building or throwing a rock through a store window.

Perjury

A person commits perjury when he or she knowingly gives false testimony while under oath. Lying at a trial is perjury, as is lying at a deposition or other proceeding when the witness is under oath. The lie must concern a material matter; there is no perjury if it involves a trivial matter or something unrelated to the issue at hand. "Subornation of perjury" is the procuring of someone to commit perjury for you. Paying someone $500 to lie and establish an alibi for you, for instance, is subornation of perjury. (And the witness who lies on the stand is guilty of perjury.)

Defenses to Criminal Charges

If you have done something that ordinarily constitutes a crime, is there any way out? Yes, if you can prove that you had a valid legal excuse or justification—a "defense"—for your actions. Here are the major defenses that make otherwise criminal conduct lawful.

Consent of the Victim

Is an act that would otherwise be a crime still a crime if the victim consents to it? That depends on the crime involved. It's not rape if the "victim" is of age and freely and voluntarily consents to have sex with the alleged "rapist." (If the victim is under age, her consent is ineffective, and the man is guilty of statutory rape.) Neither is it larceny if the person voluntarily parts with or abandons his or her property. But the victim's consent is never a defense to more serious crimes, such as murder or mayhem. Consent is also not a defense to crimes against the general public, such as prostitution or selling drugs. The fact that a prostitute and her customer consent to have sexual relations or that a person wants to buy the illegal drugs is no defense. Two men who agree to fight can still be guilty of a public brawl or disturbing the peace.

You Were Defending Yourself

It is frequently asserted in cases of murder, manslaughter, and assault and battery that a person was acting to protect himself or herself from being hurt. This is the defense of "self-defense": you are entitled to use reasonable force to protect yourself when it reasonably appears that you are in danger of immediate harm from someone else. Suppose that one night you are walking down a dimly lit street in a neighborhood known for robberies, muggings, and rapes. As you pass a bush, a man lunges out at you. Thinking he is trying to attack you, you begin kicking and beating him. If the man was in fact trying to rob or assault you, no one would question your right to defend yourself. But suppose it turns out that the man works for the water company and was making some emergency repairs. As he emerged from the bush, he tripped over a branch and fell in your direction. Will your claim of self-defense hold up in this situation, even though you weren't actually in danger? Yes. In this case, your actions were probably justified, since it reasonably appeared that the man was trying to attack you. You are therefore not guilty of an assault and battery.

Your right to defend yourself includes the right to use "deadly force" in appropriate situations. Deadly force is force that is likely to result in the death of or serious injury to a person—using guns, knives, heavy pipes or branches, even moving cars, for example. You can use deadly force to defend yourself only when you are in immediate danger of death or serious injury, and deadly force is reasonably necessary to protect yourself. You can't shoot someone to protect yourself from, say, a slap in the face. If you do, and the person dies, you are guilty of voluntary manslaughter, maybe even murder. On the other hand, shooting someone who is attacking you with a knife or tire iron is probably justified.

In a number of states, you must try to back away ("retreat") before using deadly force to stop your attacker, unless you are in your home at the time or you cannot retreat safely. If someone is threatening you with a knife, for example, you ordinarily must try to walk away. But you don't have to if it's apparent that the person will still attack you.

Many people mistakenly believe that they have almost a license to kill anyone who breaks into their home. Indeed, some even think that if you shoot an intruder who is outside your home, then drag him or her into your hallway, your acts will not be questioned. But before you can legally use deadly force against the intruder, he or she must reasonably appear to pose a threat of imminent danger to the lives and safety of you and your family. For example, suppose that Benny breaks into the Miller house in the middle of the night while the Millers are sleeping. Mr. Miller wakes up, hears some noise in the dining room, takes his revolver from his nightstand drawer, and goes to investigate. When he turns on the light in the dining room, he finds Benny with a bag full of silverware. Benny drops the bag, puts his hand up, and says, "Please don't shoot." Mr. Miller shoots anyway, hitting Benny in the leg. Mr. Miller is guilty of assault with a deadly weapon, since there was no reason to fire: Benny had surrendered and did not pose any apparent danger when Mr. Miller shot him.

You Were Defending Someone Else

Not only do you have the right to protect yourself from criminal assaults; you have the right to protect others as well. Originally, you could only take advantage of the "defense of others" rule when defending a member of your own family. Today you can step in and defend anyone—even a stranger—who is being attacked. You can use deadly force to protect someone else, but under the same conditions that apply when you are using it to protect yourself: the person must be in immediate danger of serious harm, and deadly force is reasonably necessary to prevent it.

Suppose you come upon a fight between Tom and Randy. Tom is clearly pummeling Randy, so you step in and hit Tom. When everything finally settles down, you learn that Randy was trying to rob Tom, and when you arrived on the scene, Tom had just managed to turn the tables: you rescued the assailant, not the victim. If criminal charges are filed against you, can you raise the defense of others, even though you mistakenly believed that you were protecting the victim? In some states, you are guilty of an assault and battery on Tom because mistakes don't count in this situation. You have the right to defend the person only to the extent he or she has the right to protect himself or herself; you "step in the shoes" of the person you are protecting. In this situation, Randy had no right to protect himself, since he was the one who started the fight. You therefore had no right to protect Randy either. In other states, however, you are not guilty of a crime if, when you arrived on the scene, it reasonably appeared that Tom was the aggressor and Randy the victim.

You Were Defending Your Property

You have the right to use force to defend your property in appropriate situations. For instance, if you see someone trying to break into your car, you can use reasonable force to prevent it. Before using any type of force to defend your property, you ordinarily must first warn the other person to stop and leave, unless doing so would put you in danger.

Can you use deadly force to protect your property? Generally not. If it comes down to a choice between, say, a car stereo and a human life, human life always prevails. Even if, for instance, a twice-convicted felon is trying to steal or destroy a priceless painting, you can't shoot the felon to protect the painting. About the only time you can use deadly force to protect any property is when you are protecting your house, but only if you are home at the time and deadly force is reasonably necessary under the circumstances. In this situation, you really are protecting yourself and the safety of your family as much as you are protecting the house. You can't, however, aim a shotgun at the front door and rig it to go off if the door is opened when you're not home.

Suppose you hear a noise and see someone running down the street with your toolbox. You give chase, tackle the culprit, and retrieve your toolbox. Is that within the bounds of defending your property? Yes. You were in "fresh pursuit" of your property and can use reasonable force to get it back. But if, for example, you find out two days later who stole your toolbox, and you go to that person's house, barge in without permission, and retrieve your toolbox, you would be guilty of breaking and entering. If you strike the person, you would be guilty of assault and battery. The best way to handle a situation like this is to ask the person to return your toolbox and leave if he or she refuses. Then call the police and report that you located your stolen toolbox.

Prevention of Crime

Police officers generally are entitled to use reasonable force—including deadly force, when necessary—to prevent a crime or to apprehend or prevent the escape of a person who has committed a felony or a misdemeanor involving a breach of the peace. Can the police shoot a fleeing suspect? That depends on whether the person poses a threat of harm to the community. If the person is suspected of killing several people and is fleeing with a gun, there could be sufficient reason to believe that the community is threatened. But if the crime is less serious, and the suspect has no gun and doesn't appear to be a danger to the community, the police generally cannot use deadly force to stop him or her.

As a private citizen, you can use reasonable force to prevent a felony that is attempted in your presence, even though you yourself are not endangered by it. But if you are mistaken and use force to apprehend someone who has not committed or attempted a crime, you can be held liable for the death of or injuries to the "felon."

Insanity

Insanity is a valid, though often maligned, defense to a criminal charge. The defense of insanity is relatively unsuccessful, but widespread press coverage of a few celebrated trials involving pleas of insanity (as in the case of John F. Hinckley, Jr.'s attempt on the life of President Reagan) has led many people to question whether we shouldn't abolish it completely.

Insanity is a legal term, not a psychiatric one. Indeed, psychiatry and psychology purposely avoid using the word *insane*. The closest psychiatric equivalent of *insane* is "psychotic," which basically refers to a loss of touch with reality.

Most states use one of two tests of insanity. Under one standard, you are insane if, because of a "diseased condition" of your mind, you are unable to understand the nature of your act (in other words, you didn't know what you were doing) or, if you knew what you were doing, you lacked the mental capacity to distinguish right from wrong. This is known as the "M'Naughten Rule" and is the oldest test of insanity used today. The other test of insanity in common use: you are insane and therefore not criminally responsible if, because of a mental disease or defect, you lacked "substantial capacity" to appreciate the criminality of your conduct or to conform your conduct to the requirements of the law. This test is less rigid than the M'Naughten Rule.

The question of insanity as a defense involves your state of mind at the time you committed the alleged crime. You could be sane before the act and sane afterward, but if you were insane when committing the crime, insanity (in this case "temporary insanity") would be a valid defense.

Unlike insanity, the plea of "diminished capacity" is not a complete defense to a crime but rather a means of reducing an offense to a less serious charge. If a person kills another but is not sufficiently mentally disturbed to be judged insane, for example, the jury may convict him or her of voluntary manslaughter rather than first-degree murder. The diminished-capacity defense was a focus of national attention in the murder trial of Dan White, charged with the 1978 killings of the mayor of San Francisco, George Moscone, and Harvey Milk, a city supervisor. White raised the infamous "Twinkie" defense—that when depressed, he would binge on junk food, and the sugar content affected him—and he was convicted of manslaughter when many people felt he should have been convicted of murder. This case contributed to a public outcry that caused many states to pass laws banning the defense of diminished capacity.

You Were Intoxicated

Voluntary intoxication is generally no defense to a crime, but may reduce the charge in a few cases where a specific intent was required. For instance, a man charged with first-degree murder may be convicted of a lesser degree by proving that he was so drunk that he was incapable of premeditating the killing.

Suppose at a party, somebody drops a powerful drug in your drink without your knowledge. Or you've been told that the punch you're drinking is nonalcoholic, when in truth it is spiked. The next morning, you wake up in jail wondering where you are and why. You soon learn that you went on a criminal rampage the night before. Can you be held guilty for your actions the night before? Not if you were so drunk or high on drugs that you didn't know what you were doing, because in this case, your intoxication was involuntary. But you can use involuntary intoxication as a defense only if you weren't sober enough to realize what you were doing and could not control your actions.

You Were Acting under Threats or Coercion

You are not normally liable for crimes you commit while acting under physical duress or coercion. If Jim takes your son hostage, for example, and tells you that he will kill the boy unless you steal a car for him, you can avoid criminal responsibility for auto theft even if you comply with Jim's demand. It is Jim who would be guilty of auto theft, just as if he had done the act himself. Duress or coercion does not, however, apply in cases of murder or manslaughter—for example, someone puts a gun to your head and orders you to kill someone else. If you do, you will be held criminally responsible.

The Police Entrapped You

Entrapment is a valid defense to certain crimes, such as solicitation for prostitution and selling drugs. But it is not a defense to crimes involving physical injury or property damage, such as murder, rape, arson, or robbery. Entrapment occurs when the police talk the defendant into committing a crime that he or she was not otherwise predisposed to commit. In other words, the police put the thought into the defendant's mind.

Entrapment is often asserted when a person is charged with soliciting an undercover police officer for prostitution. At issue is whether the defendant approached the undercover officer and offered money in exchange for sexual services, or whether the officer approached the defendant and offered to engage in sex for a certain price. In short, whose idea was it, the customer's or the police officer's? If the latter, the defendant is not guilty of solicitation.

Entrapment is frequently raised as an issue when the police set up an operation to catch suspected drug dealers. Entrapment is a valid defense only if you can prove that before the undercover agent approached you, you were not inclined to deal in drugs.

Domestic Authority

Parents and schoolteachers are generally entitled to use reasonable force to discipline their children or pupils, without being criminally liable for assault or battery. If, however, the punishment is excessive, and the child is injured, the privilege is lost and the person is liable for assault and battery. The use of deadly force to discipline a child is never permitted, and if deadly force is used, and a child dies from it, the person can be guilty of manslaughter or even murder.

Children

Under the common law rules that some states still apply, a child under the age of seven is legally incapable of committing a crime. Children between the ages of seven and fourteen are presumed incapable of committing a crime. A child can be convicted of a crime, however, if the evidence shows that the child was sufficiently mature to understand what he or she was doing.

Other Defenses

A person who has already been tried and convicted or acquitted of a particular crime cannot be tried a second time for the same crime. If the state tries to prosecute a second time, the defendant can assert the defense of "double jeopardy" (see discussion below). Another procedural defense is that the "statute of limitations"—the time that the prosecution has for filing criminal charges—has expired, and it is now too late to prosecute. Most crimes have a time limitation on how long after the crime charges can be filed. For instance, there may be a ten-year limitation in filing a criminal complaint for burglary. If ten years pass without the charges being filed, they generally can no longer be filed. One major exception is murder, however; there is no limit on when murder charges can be filed. If, say, the crime is solved fifty years later or the killer confesses, he or she can still be prosecuted.

THE CRIMINAL JUSTICE SYSTEM

The criminal justice system sets the rules that the police, the district attorney (or other prosecutor), and the courts must abide by before you are even arrested until the time when the sentence is carried out. At the heart of the whole system of American criminal justice are the Fifth and Fourteenth amendments to the Constitution, which mandate that no one shall be deprived "of life, liberty, or property, without due process of law." Due process means that before you can be fined, imprisoned, executed, or otherwise punished for a crime, the government must respect your constitutional rights—specifically, the right not to incriminate yourself; freedom from unlawful searches; the right to retain an attorney or have one appointed for you free of charge if you can't afford one; the right to confront and cross-examine your accusers;

and the right to have your case heard before a fair and impartial jury. When you are denied any of these and other constitutional rights, you are deprived of due process of the law, and your conviction cannot stand.

The criminal justice system is the least stable of all the areas of law. It is in a continuous state of change. Since the early 1980s, for instance, the United States Supreme Court has shifted noticeably from protecting the rights of the individual accused of a crime to expanding the powers of the police, in the interests of public safety. Proponents of this shift contend that the judicial system has long been too lenient with criminals and feel that it is about time the courts did something to crack down on crime. On the other hand, some have criticized this trend on the basis that the Constitution is designed to protect the individual from arbitrary and abusive government intrusion. The government (and therefore society) can protect its own interests much better than the individual can protect his or her own, and because of this, the rights of the individual should be paramount.

The pendulum will continue to swing back and forth as long as the Constitution endures, since the interests of the individual and those of society as a whole will always be competing with each other. Sometimes the individual will prevail; other times the government will win.

When Can the Police Stop, Question, and Frisk You?

Suppose you're walking down the street one day, doing nothing wrong, when a police officer stops you, asks for identification, and questions you for ten minutes about your activities. Can the officer do this? Only if he or she has an "articulable and reasonable suspicion that criminal activity is afoot." In other words, the officer must have some basis for thinking that you might be committing or about to commit a crime, or have already committed one. A police officer cannot stop and question you on a whim or simply to harass you.

In determining whether you might be up to something illegal, the officer can base his or her assessment of the situation on experience and the surrounding circumstances. For example, suppose that early one morning you're on your way home from a camping trip. The pickup truck you're driving has a camper shell, and the truck is weighted down with all of your gear. Although you're not speeding or breaking any other traffic laws, a police car with two officers pulls you over to the side of the road. The officers ask for your driver's license and vehicle registration, then ask where you're coming from, where you're headed, and what you've been up to. After you answer their questions, the officers inform you that the road you're on is frequently used by drug smugglers, who drive overloaded pickup trucks with camper shells. The officers then tell you you're free to go. Did this brief stop violate your rights? Probably not. The officers had a reasonable suspicion for stopping you based on their experience and on the fact that your vehicle fit the method of operation of drug smugglers. The officers only stopped you for as long as necessary to confirm or deny their suspicions, and they did not harass, abuse, or threaten you.

When you are stopped for questioning, can the police officer pat you down ("frisk" you)? Yes, but only for weapons, and then only if the officer has a reasonable belief that you are carrying a weapon. Suppose, for example, that Paula, a police officer, suspects that Denny may be intoxicated or under the influence of drugs, and she goes over to investigate. Paula asks Denny for identification and asks some routine questions. There is no odor of alcohol or marijuana, or any other evidence of drugs. Although Denny doesn't appear to have a gun on him and is not threatening Paula in any manner, Paula decides to frisk him anyway, hoping to find some drugs on him. During the frisk, Paula finds a small metal case in Denny's shirt pocket, opens it, and finds several amphetamines in it. This would most likely be considered an unlawful search because Paula had no reason to suspect that Denny might have a weapon on him. And even if she did, she could not look inside the small case, since it couldn't conceal a weapon.

Your Right to Be Free from Unreasonable Searches

The Fourth Amendment to the United States Constitution protects citizens against *unreasonable* searches and seizures. Except as discussed below, the police normally must obtain a search warrant before searching you, your house (or apartment), or your car. To get a search warrant, the police apply to a judge (or magistrate). The judge will issue a warrant only if the police present sufficient testimony and affidavits to establish probable cause that contraband (drugs, for example, or stolen property or illegal firearms) or evidence of a crime (the murder weapon, for instance, or the rope used to bind a kidnap victim) will be found on the person or premises to be searched. The warrant must carefully describe the person or premises in question, as well as the type of evidence sought.

During the search, the police must stay within the scope of the warrant, which is determined by the object they are looking for. Something that is small and easily concealed justifies a more intensive search than a large object. For example, if the warrant is for drugs or a handgun, the police can open drawers, go through cupboards, take air vents off to look in ventilation shafts, and so forth, because drugs or a handgun can be hidden almost anywhere. But if the search warrant is for a stolen 25-inch color television set, the police would not be justified in going through drawers and other places too small to conceal the television.

When Can the Police Search You without a Warrant?

Here are the major situations in which the police can make a search without first obtaining a warrant:

If You Consent to the Search. A warrant is not required if you voluntarily consent to the search. But even when you permit a search, the police must stay within the bounds of your consent and must also search only those areas where the object could physically be concealed. For instance, if you're suspected of stealing a car, the police could only look for it in, say, your garage; they're not going to find it in a dresser drawer or in the attic.

Suppose you change your mind after giving the police consent to the search and ask the police to leave. Do the police have to stop the search? Yes. You can revoke your consent at any time, and the police normally must leave and obtain a warrant before they can search any further. But if by that time they have already found something incriminating that gives them probable cause to arrest you (see discussion below), they can do so on the basis of that evidence.

Can a landlord give the police permission to search a tenant's apartment? Usually not. A landlord does not have the authority to permit a search of a tenant's apartment; only the tenant does. Suppose your roommate tells the police that it's okay to search the apartment—including your bedroom and everything in it— and the police find some drugs in your dresser drawer. Is that search lawful? No. Your roommate could consent to a search of his or her private area or to areas used by both of you, such as the kitchen and living room, but not to the areas that you use exclusively, such as your bedroom.

Suppose the police want to search a child's room. If the parents consent to it, will that stop the child from claiming that the search was illegal? No. Children as well as adults have the right to be free from unreasonable searches. The parents can permit the police to search areas of the child's room where the parents themselves are permitted to go. But if, say, the child has a trunk that he or she keeps locked and has the only key to, then only the child can give the police the permission to open it without a warrant.

When an Object Is in Plain View. The police do not need a search warrant if the object is in "plain view." If a gun or packet of cocaine is lying uncovered on the seat of a car parked on a public street, for instance, and a police officer walks by and sees it, no warrant is necessary, since anybody passing by could have seen it. Suppose, though, that the car is parked inside your garage, and the officer (without your consent) opens the garage door and sees the object on the car seat. Is the object then in plain view? No. The plain view rule applies only when the police officer has the right to be where he or she is at the time the officer sees the object. Since the officer doesn't have the right to go inside your garage without your consent or a warrant, the objects on the car seat are not in plain view.

The plain view doctrine also applies to searches conducted pursuant to a warrant. If, for example, the police have a warrant to search a house for weapons and in the process find some drugs, weapons, or spoils from a burglary on the floor, the evidence can be used in court to convict the defendant.

When You Are Arrested. When you are lawfully arrested, you can be searched without your consent. If you are arrested but not taken into custody, the police can search you for weapons and to prevent you from destroying any evidence. Should you be taken into custody, the police can conduct a full search of you, as well as the immediate area around you in case you hid something when the police arrived. At the police station or the jail, you may be strip-searched if there's a possibility that you may be concealing drugs, weapons, contraband, or evidence on your body. Usually a police officer of your own sex must do the search or at least be in the room observing it.

When You Are in a Car, Truck, or Motor Home. If the police have probable cause to believe that contraband or evidence of a crime is in your car, truck, motor home, or other vehicle, a search warrant usually is not required. Why not? Because you could easily flee the scene before the police could get back with a warrant. Of course, a police officer can't single your car out for no reason and search it. There must be sufficient justification to conduct the search in the first place, or it is illegal.

Suppose you're stopped for speeding. The police officer asks you to get out of the car, then searches it thoroughly, including the glove compartment and trunk. The search reveals an open bottle of whiskey under your coat on the back seat. The officer then cites you not only for speeding, but also for having an open container of alcohol in the passenger compartment. (Not all states have open-container laws.) Whether this search was legal depends on whether the officer had any reason to suspect that there might be alcohol in the car. If you had alcohol on your breath, the search might have been justified. But if you didn't, the search would probably be unjustified. The mere fact that you are stopped for speeding or many other traffic infractions does not ordinarily justify a search of the car's interior.

When Can the Police Enter and Search a House?

The police almost always need a warrant to enter and search your house. (A mobile home that is fixed to the ground is considered a "house," since, unlike a motor home, it cannot readily be moved.) One time the police do not need a search warrant to enter a house is when they are in hot pursuit of a dangerous suspect, and there is reason to believe that the suspect is inside the house. Once inside, the police can search anyone who could be a threat to them. If, while lawfully inside the house, the police spot anything in plain view, it is admissible as evidence in court.

Consider the following example: Responding to a call reporting an armed robbery at a liquor store, the police arrive in time to see a man fleeing from the store with a gun in one hand and a paper sack in the other. The suspect gets into a car and takes off, with the police right behind. The suspect stops in front of a house and runs inside, followed by the police. When they enter the house, the police officers see several guns and some drugs on the coffee table. The suspect is found hiding in the upstairs bathroom and gives himself up without incident. He is searched, and the police find a gun and some cocaine on him. In this case, the entry into the house is justified, because the police were in hot pursuit of an armed robber. The search of the suspect was justified, since it took place in connection with a lawful arrest (see discussion below). Because the police had a right to enter the house, the guns and drugs on the coffee table were in plain view and could therefore be used as evidence at the trial. Suppose, though, that there were no guns or drugs on the coffee table, but an officer rifled through the suspect's dresser drawers and found the incriminating items there. Could the guns and drugs found in the dresser be used against the suspect? No. Since they were not in plain view, a warrant would have been necessary to search for them.

Another time the police can lawfully enter a house without a warrant is when they have reason to believe that a crime victim inside needs immediate aid. In this situation, the police can also search the house to see if there are other victims or if a suspect is still on the premises. Evidence that is in plain view of the officers would be admissible in court, but the police would have to obtain a warrant to conduct a more exhaustive search.

When the police obtain a warrant to search a home, ordinarily they must knock first and announce who they are and why they are there. The police usually can't just barge in unannounced, even if they have a warrant. But if they aren't let inside within a reasonable time, they can then force their way in. And the police need not knock and announce themselves if the people inside would likely destroy the evidence. If the search warrant is for drugs, for instance, the police do not have to announce themselves and wait outside while the drugs are flushed down the toilet. The police also need not "knock and announce" when doing so would put them in danger of being shot or otherwise seriously hurt by the people inside.

Can the Police Tap Your Phone or Bug Your House?

Using electronic and other devices to listen in on a private conversation is considered a "search." Federal law prohibits the police from listening in on or tape recording a telephone conversation without a warrant unless one party to the conversation consents. Some states, however, require that *all* parties to the telephone conversation be informed of and consent to the eavesdropping if no warrant has been obtained.

In fact, unless the police have the consent of one party, they cannot use electronic eavesdropping equipment to listen in on *any* private conversation without a search warrant. But a warrant is not required if the police—not using any surveillance equipment—are in, say, a public park or movie theater and overhear a loud conversation.

The Exclusionary Rule

Suppose the police illegally search you (or your house or car) and discover incriminating evidence that implicates you in a crime. Can you prohibit the district attorney from using that evidence against you at trial? Yes. Evidence found in an illegal search cannot be used against you in court. This is the so-called exclusionary rule. And not only is that evidence itself not admissible in court; neither is any other evidence discovered as a result of that evidence. This is known as the "fruit of the poisonous tree" doctrine. Since the original evidence was unlawfully obtained, the other evidence bears the "taint" of that illegality. For example, the police illegally search Nancy's car and find a shotgun and a bloodstained blanket in the trunk. They show this to Nancy, who immediately confesses to having shot and killed her boyfriend. Not only are the gun and blanket inadmissible at Nancy's trial, but so is her confession.

Why do we have the exclusionary rule? Suppose for a moment that the exclusionary rule doesn't exist. The police break into your house without a warrant, go through everything, and find evidence of a crime—say, some burglar's tools and stolen property, drugs, an illegal weapon, or obscene material. The police have violated your constitutional rights. But without the exclusionary rule, what recourse do you have? You can sue the police in civil court, but a jury probably won't award you very much, if anything at all. The result is that you will essentially be deprived of your constitutional right against unreasonable searches. What the exclusionary rule does is provide a simple and effective method of deterring the police from violating your rights: it prevents the illegally obtained evidence from being used against you in court. It also serves as an incentive to prevent the police from indiscriminately searching persons for no reason at all.

Suppose you suspect your neighbor of committing the recent rash of burglaries in your area. One day while he is out, you break into his house and find items stolen from neighborhood houses. Does the exclusionary rule prevent the prosecution from using this evidence at the trial? No. The exclusionary rule applies only to evidence obtained through an unlawful search conducted by or at the direction of the police, not to illegal searches that are completely the idea and doing of a private citizen. This is because the Fourth Amendment protects only against unlawful government actions, not actions of private individuals. (If you did break in, though, you would be guilty of a crime and also subject to a civil lawsuit.)

The exclusionary rule is the most strongly criticized of all "legal technicalities." A common misconception is that many criminals are freed because the police did not conduct a search with absolute propriety. The truth is that only a minute percentage of defendants who raise this objection are successful with it. A study by the General Accounting Office of the United States suggests that fewer than one-half of 1 percent of all serious federal crimes are dismissed for this reason.

Until recently, there were no exceptions to the exclusionary rule. If there were any faults with the search at all, the evidence would have to be excluded from trial. For example, if a search warrant incorrectly listed the address as 123 Main Street, rather than 125 Main Street, the warrant would have to be corrected before the police could lawfully search 125 Main Street. If the police did not get the warrant changed and searched 125 Main Street, all of the evidence obtained during the search would be inadmissible in court.

The one exception now recognized by the Supreme Court is that when the police are acting in "good faith" on a warrant that turns out to be defective, the evidence is admissible if the defect was not apparent on the face of the warrant. For instance, if the judge issued the warrant based on a faulty affidavit—one grounded in hearsay, perhaps, rather than the witness's own firsthand knowledge—and the police did not know that anything was wrong with the warrant, the evidence obtained in the search would be admissible.

Your Rights When Arrested

Under what circumstances can the police arrest you? Anytime there is "probable cause" to believe that you are committing or have committed a crime. The police have probable cause when there are enough facts to lead a reasonable person to conclude that you are committing or have committed a crime. This is a considerably higher standard than the mere "suspicion" an officer needs in order to stop you briefly to investigate possible criminal activity.

Can a police officer make an arrest without a warrant? Sometimes. The officer doesn't need a warrant to arrest you if you commit a crime in his or her presence, for instance. A warrant also isn't necessary if the officer has probable cause to believe that you committed a felony, even though it was not committed in his or her presence. Otherwise, the officer generally needs a warrant to make an arrest.

Your Miranda *Rights*

After you are arrested, the police must advise you of your *Miranda* rights before they can question you. But in a mere "stop and frisk" situation (discussed earlier), the police do not have to advise you of your rights before questioning. If the police are conducting a routine investigation, for instance, and asking a number of people what they know about the crime, each person need not be advised of his or her *Miranda* rights before questioning.

What are the *Miranda* rights? In the 1966 case of *Miranda v. Arizona*, the Supreme Court ruled that an incriminating statement obtained during a "custodial interrogation"—one in which you are not free to leave anytime you want—is not admissible in court unless, before the police question you, they advise you of certain fundamental rights: that you have the right to remain silent; that anything you say can be used against you in court; that you have the right to have an attorney present during questioning; and that if you want to have an attorney represent you but cannot afford one, one will be provided for you without cost.

After the police read you your *Miranda* rights, they will ask whether you understand those rights. If you reply that you do, you will be asked whether, having your rights in mind, you wish to talk to the police at that time, without a lawyer. If you agree to talk, you have waived your *Miranda* rights, and any confession or incriminating statement you make can be used against you in court. To ensure that there is no dispute about whether the police have read you your *Miranda* rights, some police departments will have you sign a card that contains the *Miranda* rights and states that they were read to you and that you understand them.

Contrary to what you are accustomed to seeing on television, the police do not have to read you your *Miranda* rights at the moment you are arrested. They only have to inform you of your rights before they question you. Often the arresting officers will not ask a suspect any questions and will leave that task to the detectives back at the station. Since the arresting officers aren't asking any questions, they don't need to advise the suspect of his or her rights. Suppose the arresting officers don't read you your rights and don't ask any questions, but on the way to the station, you blurt out that you are sorry you committed the crime. In this instance, the remark can be used against you at the trial; the police weren't questioning you, so they didn't have to inform you of your rights.

Are there any situations in which the police don't have to

read you your *Miranda* rights before questioning you? Yes. The police can question you briefly upon their arrival, and without advising you of your rights, if there is an immediate threat to public safety. Suppose the police are called to a murder site. When they arrive, they find the victim lying on the porch, dead of a gunshot wound. A crowd is gathering on the lawn in front of the house. Witnesses point out the man who apparently killed the victim. The police approach the suspect and, before advising him of his *Miranda* rights, ask him where the gun is. The suspect replies that he threw it in the bushes in front of the house. The police search the bushes and recover the gun, which is later proved to be the murder weapon. The suspect's statement that he threw the gun in the bushes is admissible in court, even though he was not advised of his *Miranda* rights. In this case, public safety was threatened by the fact that a loaded gun may have been lying around, so the police were justified in trying to find out where it was as soon as possible.

What to Do If You Are Arrested

What should you do if you are ever arrested? The first thing is to stay calm and to obey all of the police officer's instructions—even if you feel that you have done nothing wrong and that the arrest is unlawful. You don't need to actually have committed a crime in order to be arrested; the officer needs only to have probable cause to arrest you. And the penalty for resisting arrest can be much more serious than that for the charge on which you were originally arrested. A more practical reason for cooperating with the police's instructions is that by resisting arrest, you run the risk of being seriously hurt or killed by the police officer. The place to challenge the officer's decision to arrest you is in court, not on a street corner or in a dark alley.

After you have been arrested, volunteer nothing. The only information you should give is your personal information: name, address, telephone number, and the like. You have the right to remain silent, so use it. If the police read you your *Miranda* rights and then start questioning you, insist on speaking to a lawyer before answering anything. Your right to have a lawyer present during questioning is your best protection when you are arrested, so take advantage of it. If you can't afford a lawyer, tell the police, and request that one be appointed for you immediately. Until you've talked to a lawyer, refuse all attempts by the police to ask "just a few routine questions."

Don't be persuaded into making a confession in return for the police officer's promise to do everything he or she can for you. Only the district attorney can make deals. Also, don't talk to your cell mates or anyone else about the specifics of the incident. Nothing in the law prohibits the district attorney from calling your cell mates to the witness stand to testify that you admitted committing the crime.

What Happens after Your Arrest

Booking

After you are arrested and taken into custody, you are transported to the police station, where you are "booked." Booking consists of logging your name and the reason for your arrest in the record book and taking your picture ("mug shot") and fingerprints. If you will be held in jail for any length of time, your personal belongings are taken from you, and you are given a receipt for them. Read the receipt carefully before signing it to make sure everything is listed. You will have the opportunity to make at least one telephone call, which should be to your lawyer if you have one, and if not, to the person you can most count on to help you—your spouse, parents, or closest friend, for instance.

What happens next depends on how serious your crime is. If the crime is minor, you may be given the chance to post bail (see discussion below), and the police will release you on your promise to appear in court on a certain day and at a certain time for your arraignment (see discussion below). If your crime is more serious, you will be held in jail until you are arraigned.

Arraignment

At your arraignment, which takes place in court, the judge will inform you of the charges against you and ask you how you plead: guilty or not guilty. You can also enter a plea of nolo contendere, or no contest, which means you're not going to fight the charges. A plea of no contest has the same general effect as pleading guilty, except that it applies only to that case. It can't, for instance, be used against you in a civil case for injuries another person suffered as a result of your criminal conduct. Suppose you're charged with battery. If you plead guilty (or the jury finds you guilty after a trial), your plea of guilty can be used against you if the victim sues you in civil court for his or her injuries. But if you plead no contest, it can't be used against you in the civil case.

At the arraignment, the judge will also inform you of some rights, including the right to have a lawyer represent you and be appointed for you if you can't afford one (and if you aren't already represented by one). The judge will also set the amount of bail if it hasn't been set already. If bail was set earlier, but you feel it is too high, you can ask the judge to reduce it at this time or to release you on your own recognizance (see discussion below).

How soon after your arrest you are arraigned depends on where and when you were arrested. If you were arrested in a small town on a Friday night, you might not be arraigned until Monday. But if you're arrested in a major city, you could be arraigned the night of your arrest. In any event, you must be arraigned promptly, usually no more than 48 or 72 hours after your arrest if you're not released on bail.

What happens if you plead guilty at your arraignment? If the crime is minor, the judge may impose your sentence—perhaps a $100 fine or a couple days in jail—on the spot. Otherwise, the judge will set a date for your sentencing and send your file to the probation department. There, a probation officer will review the case, your criminal record, and your current situation and make a recommendation to the judge regarding appropriate punishment.

Bail

"Bail" is the money you post with the court to ensure that you will show up at the arraignment and all other proceedings and not "disappear" until your case is resolved. You will get your money back at the end of trial, unless you "jump," or "skip," bail—in other words, not show up in court as you were required. In that case, you will forfeit the bail, and a warrant for your arrest is issued. (After your arrest on this warrant, you will be required to post a new bond—at a considerably higher amount than the original bond, since you're a proven bad risk.)

The amount of bail must be reasonable in light of the crime committed, your previous criminal record, your roots in the area— how long you've lived or worked there—and the chances that you will skip bail or commit another crime while out on bail. Bail of $500,000 for a simple assault case in which the defendant has no previous record and has lived in the area all of his or her life is clearly unreasonable. But when murder is charged, a very high amount of bail is justified. In fact, some suspected murderers are held without bail.

In lieu of bail, the judge may release you on your "own recognizance" ("O.R."). All that is required in this case is your promise to appear in court at a later date. Ordinarily, you will be released on your own recognizance only when the crime is not serious, when you have no previous criminal record, and when you have lived in the area for a substantial length of time.

Although traditionally bail could be posted only in cash, many states now let you use a bank card, such as Visa or MasterCard. Bail bond services—which abound near jails, open

24 hours a day, 365 days a year—will post your bail for a certain fee, such as 10 percent of the full amount. If, for example, your bail is set at $2,500, the bond service may charge $250 to post the bond. (You don't get this $250 back even if you attend all proceedings as required.) What happens if you don't show up for your arraignment, trial, or other proceeding? The bond service has to pay $2,500 to the court. It then goes looking for you (or the person who guaranteed the bond) for full reimbursement.

How You Are Formally Charged with a Crime

If you're accused of a misdemeanor, you are formally charged with the crime by a criminal complaint signed by the arresting officer if he or she saw you commit the crime and, if not, by the victim (the "complaining witness"). The complaint is reviewed by the district attorney's office, and if they feel it is justified, they will file it with the court.

If you're suspected of a felony, you must be charged either by a judge after a preliminary hearing or by an indictment issued by a grand jury. The purpose of each procedure is the same: to determine whether there is sufficient cause for charging you with a crime.

A preliminary hearing is held before a judge (or magistrate), who decides whether there is enough evidence to hold ("bind") you over for trial. At the preliminary hearing, you can have a lawyer represent you, and your lawyer can cross-examine the witnesses called by the district attorney. The judge will order you to stand trial only if the evidence shows that it is probable that you committed a crime. (This is a lower standard than the "beyond a reasonable doubt" test needed to convict you of the crime.)

In a grand jury proceeding, the district attorney presents a document called an "indictment," or "bill of indictment," to the grand jury, a panel of residents (usually numbering 12 to 24) selected from the local community. The grand jury has the power to subpoena witnesses to appear before it and can consider just about any type of evidence it wants, including evidence that may not be admissible at your trial. If, after considering all of the evidence presented to it, a majority of the grand jury finds that there is probable cause to believe that you have committed a crime, the foreman will approve and sign the indictment as "a true bill." The grand jury indictment can come before or after an arrest. More often than not, however, the grand jury investigates the case after the suspect's arrest. (In federal cases, the opposite is true: usually the grand jury issues an indictment; then the person is arrested.)

Grand jury proceedings are an anomaly, in that they are one of the few aspects of the criminal justice system that take place in private, behind closed doors, beyond the scrutiny of the public and the press. This is justified on the grounds that the grand jury is merely an investigative body trying to determine whether there is a basis for charging a person with a particular crime. And because the grand jury is merely investigating the possibility of a crime, it does not have to advise you of your *Miranda* rights before questioning you—even if you are under investigation—nor do you have the right to have your lawyer present, cross-examine witnesses, or even present evidence in your own defense. The one right you do retain is the Fifth Amendment right not to incriminate yourself. Frequently, a person under investigation by the grand jury will invoke this right and refuse to answer the grand jury's questions.

The grand jury system has been criticized for being a tool of the district attorney rather than an independent body that gives each side an equally fair chance. In many cases, the district attorney runs the whole show, deciding whom to investigate and what evidence to present to the grand jury and what evidence to withhold. Because of this, many states have abolished or limited the role of the grand jury in favor of the preliminary examination. (In fact, England, which created the grand jury system, has abolished it completely for these very reasons.)

Plea Bargaining

Sometime after your arrest, the district attorney may be willing to "plea bargain." Plea bargaining is an agreement between the prosecution and the defendant in which the defendant agrees to plead guilty to a crime, in exchange either for the prosecution dropping a more serious charge or for a less than maximum sentence. For example, when a person is arrested for the first time for drunk driving, in some states the prosecution may drop that charge if the person pleads guilty to a lesser charge of reckless driving. Or the prosecution may give a defendant the opportunity to plead guilty to second-degree murder in lieu of prosecuting him for first-degree murder. As another example, an armed robber may agree to plead guilty upon the assurance that the prosecutor will recommend to the judge that the jail sentence be five years instead of the maximum sentence of, say, ten years' imprisonment.

A typical condition of a plea bargain is that the defendant will accept it only if the judge agrees to impose the sentence recommended by the district attorney. In most cases, the judge will approve the suggested sentence. But when the crime is serious or the defendant has a long criminal record, the judge will review the district attorney's recommendation more carefully.

Plea bargaining, though one of the most maligned practices of our criminal judicial system, is a necessary evil. Why does plea bargaining exist? The answer is simple: It keeps our judicial system from being handcuffed. Without an incentive for pleading guilty, many more defendants would ask for trials, inundating our already pressed courts. Our court system would quickly collapse if every defendant wanted a trial. To accommodate all of these trials, we would need thousands more courthouses, tens of thousands more judges and prosecuting attorneys, hundreds of thousands more courtroom staff members, and millions more citizens for jury duty. The cost and logistics would be enormous. Plea bargaining allows the criminal justice system and everyone involved to operate at a manageable pace.

Your Rights at the Trial

When you are charged with a crime, you have the right to a speedy and public trial. A state statute may require your trial to start within a certain time (say, 30 or 45 days) after your arraignment. If your trial doesn't begin within the requisite time, you can ask the judge to dismiss the charges against you. Often a criminal defendant will agree to waive the right to have a trial within the specified time, since his or her lawyer usually needs more time to prepare the case for trial. Many criminal trials don't start until four months to a year after the defendant's arraignment.

You are entitled to be tried by a jury, unless you are charged with only a petty offense—one for which the maximum penalty is imprisonment for six months or less. Petty offenses are usually decided by a judge. Traditionally, criminal cases have been heard by twelve jurors, all of whom must agree for a conviction. A number of states now permit six or eight jurors to hear the case, particularly for less serious offenses.

The American system of criminal justice presumes that a defendant is innocent until proven guilty. The prosecutor has the burden of proving that the defendant is guilty, and must do so "beyond a reasonable doubt." This is a higher standard than that used in civil trials, where the plaintiff need only prove his or her case by a preponderance of the evidence, a "probability" that the defendant did what he or she is accused of.

You have the right to be confronted by and to cross-examine your accusers, and to subpoena witnesses in order to compel their attendance at the trial. Before the trial, you have the right to discover what evidence the district attorney plans to present, so that you can prepare a defense accordingly. If you feel that any of the evidence the district attorney plans to use at the trial resulted from an illegal search or from the failure of the police to advise you of your *Miranda* rights before questioning you, you can file a "motion to suppress" that evidence. If the judge agrees with you and grants your motion, the district attorney will be barred from presenting that evidence to the jury at the trial.

What can you do if there is a threat that the news coverage of your case will be so widespread that it will be difficult to find a jury who has not heard or read about the incident and formed certain opinions based on news reports? You can ask the judge to close the pretrial proceedings to the public and to issue an order prohibiting the principals from talking to the media—a "gag order." If you still can't get a fair trial because of prejudicial pretrial publicity, then the case must either be transferred to another county (a "change in venue") where there has been less publicity, or be put on hold until the effects of the adverse publicity dissipate. And if there is the prospect of heavy media coverage during the trial, the jury may be sequestered for the duration of the trial to prevent the press from influencing deliberations.

The structure of a criminal trial is basically the same as that of a civil one (see chapter 17). First, a jury is chosen. The prosecution then makes its opening statement, followed by the opening remarks of the defendant's attorney. The prosecution presents its case in chief, calling witnesses (whom the defendant's lawyer can cross-examine) and offering evidence; the defense then presents its witnesses. (Occasionally, the defendant's attorney will not present any evidence but will rely completely upon the prosecution's failure to convince the jury or upon his or her own cross-examination of the prosecution's witnesses to exonerate the defendant.) Closing arguments are made by the prosecution and then the defendant's attorney. The judge instructs the jury on the applicable law, and the jury retires to the jury room for deliberations. If the jury reaches a verdict (it must be unanimous), the verdict is read in court by the judge's clerk. If the jury is hopelessly deadlocked and unable to agree upon a verdict, the judge will declare a mistrial, and the district attorney must evaluate the case to see whether the chance of winning a conviction might be better at a second trial before a different jury.

If you are acquitted, you cannot be tried a second time for the same crime. To do so would violate your constitutional guarantee against "double jeopardy." There are, however, times when you can be tried twice for the same crime. Suppose, for example, at your first trial the jury convicts you. You appeal your case and win a reversal; the district attorney can then prosecute you again. You can also be tried twice if the jury can't agree on a verdict (a "hung jury") or if the judge declares a mistrial because of, say, the misconduct of your attorney.

Juvenile Court

Minors accused of crimes are usually tried in juvenile court rather than the traditional criminal court. If a youth is charged with a serious crime or has a significant history of previous offenses, however, the district attorney may ask the judge to allow the child to be prosecuted in regular court as an adult. An important distinction between juvenile court and regular court lies in the focus each has: regular court concentrates on punishment, while juvenile court emphasizes education and rehabilitation to keep the minor from getting further caught up in the criminal cycle. Punishment does, of course, still play a major role in the juvenile court system.

Juvenile court is less formal than its adult counterpart, but the accused minor is still entitled to all of the major constitutional protections, such as the right not to incriminate oneself, the right to be represented by an attorney, and the right to confront and cross-examine his or her accusers. As in regular court, the prosecution must prove beyond a reasonable doubt that the youth did what he or she is accused of doing. The only major right that a minor does not have in juvenile court is the right to have the case tried by a jury. The judge alone listens to the evidence and decides whether the minor is guilty or innocent. A minor who is found guilty of committing the alleged crime is declared a "juvenile delinquent," and the judge then determines what action would be appropriate. The youth may be sent to a reform school or another public institution, placed in a foster home, or returned to his or her parents and placed on probation.

After the Verdict

Overturning the Verdict

What can you do if you feel the jury wrongly convicted you because of some impropriety before or during the trial? Your lawyer can ask the judge who presided over the case to disregard ("set aside") the jury's verdict and declare you innocent. Failing that, your lawyer can appeal your case to a higher court and ask it to reverse the verdict and give you a new trial. But you should note that the alleged impropriety must be important enough that it could have affected the jury's decision (a "prejudicial error"). If the jury's result clearly would have been the same even if the impropriety never happened, the appellate court will not reverse your conviction.

Here are the main reasons a conviction can be overturned:

• The judge allowed the prosecution to present evidence that was obtained in violation of the defendant's constitutional rights— if, for instance, the defendant wasn't advised of his or her *Miranda* rights before police questioning and the defendant confessed, but the trial judge still permitted the district attorney to use the confession against him or her.

• The judge admitted evidence that should not have been admitted. For example, in criminal cases, the defendant's previous arrest and conviction record normally cannot be presented at the trial for fear the jury will convict the defendant on the basis of that record rather than on the facts of the case it is deciding. So if, for instance, the judge allowed the prosecution to show that the defendant in a robbery trial had previously been convicted of assault and battery and drunk driving, this could be grounds for reversing the conviction.

• The prosecution did not adequately inform the defendant of what evidence it would be presenting at the trial, so the defendant could not properly prepare a defense against it.

• The judge made a mistake when instructing the jury on the law to apply to the case. For instance, in a burglary case, the judge might have neglected to instruct the jury that the defendant must have had the intent to commit a felony inside the house *before* he or she entered it.

• The prosecution did not prove its case beyond a reasonable doubt or engaged in unfair tactics or made prejudicial remarks that affected the defendant's case.

• After the trial, the defendant (or defendant's attorney) found new evidence that was unavailable at the time of the trial. For instance, the person who really committed the crime confessed after the defendant had been convicted, or the defendant finally located the witness who could establish his or her alibi.

Suppose that after the defendant is convicted by a jury and sentenced to prison, the victim states that he or she made the whole thing up, no crime happened, and an innocent person was sent to jail for a crime that was never committed. Will the defendant be released from prison because the victim has recanted his or her testimony? Generally not. The judicial system views recantation with considerable suspicion. If the evidence was strong enough for a jury to convict the defendant, there is usually some basis for believing that the defendant committed the crime in question. Cases that are completely fabricated from the beginning are usually discovered by the police during the investigation of the case or by the district attorney's office during its preparation. And a victim may recant his or her testimony for many reasons that have nothing to do with the defendant's guilt. For instance, the victim may feel that the defendant has served enough time in jail, or friends of the defendant may threaten the victim with harm if he or she doesn't recant.

Sentencing, Punishment, and Probation

After a defendant pleads guilty to the crime or the jury finds the defendant guilty, the judge will impose the defendant's punishment, or "sentence." Ordinarily, it consists of time in jail, payment of a fine, or both. Sometimes the judge will order a defendant to make restitution to the victim—return stolen property, for instance, or pay the victim what it takes to repair any damaged property.

Can a person convicted of stealing a car be put to death for that crime? Can a person who simply punched someone be sentenced to 50 years in jail? No. In both examples, the punishment would clearly be excessive for the crime and would violate the constitutional safeguard against cruel and unusual punishment. When is punishment cruel and unusual? The basic test is whether the punishment is so disproportionate to the crime that it shocks the conscience and offends fundamental notions of human dignity. Punishment that is barbaric—for instance, cutting off a pickpocket's hands—also violates the guarantee against cruel and unusual punishment.

At one time in this country, capital punishment was an accepted and frequently imposed sentence. Many criminals were put to death for crimes that today are not considered serious enough to justify the death penalty—cattle rustling, for instance. During a later period, the death penalty was absolutely prohibited. But beginning in the mid-1970s, the United States Supreme Court reinstated the death penalty for some murders. Advocates of the death penalty contend that it deters criminals from committing serious crimes. But capital punishment has never been conclusively demonstrated to be a deterrent to crime.

As part of the sentence, the defendant may be put on "probation" for a length of time. Probation gives the defendant freedom with some restrictions. If the criminal violates any terms of the probation, the judge can terminate the probation and order the criminal punished according to the terms of the original sentence. For instance, suppose the judge sentences the defendant to six months in jail but suspends that sentence—which means the defendant doesn't go to jail—and places the defendant on two years' probation. If the defendant violates the terms of the probation, the judge can then order the defendant imprisoned for six months as per the original sentence. There are two main reasons for probation: to help rehabilitate the criminal and to prevent our prisons from becoming overcrowded.

Parole and Clemency

A criminal sentenced to prison may be granted a "parole" before serving out the whole term of his or her prison sentence. A parole is essentially the same as probation; the difference lies in when each occurs. Probation is granted at the time of sentencing, while parole is granted after the person has served time in prison. Like probation, parole serves two objectives: to help rehabilitate the convict by reintegrating him or her into society, and to prevent prison overcrowding. Parole has another objective as well: it gives prison inmates an incentive for good behavior in prison, since the better their conduct, the earlier they can be released. A parolee who violates the terms of his or her parole can be returned to prison to finish out the original sentence.

A state governor (in the case of a state crime) or the president of the United States (if the offense is a federal one) can alter a convict's sentence by granting "clemency" when there is clearly an injustice. The governor (or the president) can give clemency in any case, but in reality clemency is rarely granted.

Clemency usually means a pardon, a commutation of sentence, or a reprieve. A pardon normally declares a person innocent, ends his or her punishment, and erases the conviction from the person's record. A commutation of sentence reduces the punishment—to time already spent in prison, for example—but it doesn't change the fact that the person is guilty of the crime.

A reprieve (or "respite") is a temporary suspension of punishment. For example, when a criminal on death row gets a reprieve from the governor, this means only that his or her execution is postponed. If a court or the governor does not reduce the sentence to, say, life imprisonment (a commutation), the defendant can still be put to death when the reprieve ends.

19

FINDING THE RIGHT LAWYER

WHEN CAN YOU BE YOUR OWN LAWYER? Anytime you want. You can represent yourself in court in any type of case, from a minor traffic ticket to a divorce action to a murder case. Many times, however, it's not advisable to be your own lawyer, and at those times you'll want to be represented by a competent lawyer. Generally, you should never be your own lawyer in court, except in small claims court or traffic court (and then only if you're not facing punishment more serious than a small fine).

Finding a good lawyer when you need one can be a hard and aggravating task if you don't know where to look. With a little effort in the right direction, you can find a lawyer who is an honest, hard-working professional sincerely interested in protecting your interests. This chapter will give you practical advice on finding the right lawyer for you—and at a reasonable cost. It will also help you recognize when you need a lawyer and will discuss lawyers' fees and what to do if a problem arises between you and your lawyer. One bit of preliminary advice: when you need a lawyer's help, get it immediately. The earlier you get legal assistance, the better. A lawyer might be able to keep a difficult situation from snowballing out of control, and save you money in the process.

Although England has separate classes of lawyers—"barristers," who can try cases in court, and "solicitors," who advise clients and prepare cases for barristers—we make no such distinction in the United States. "Lawyer," "attorney," "attorney-at-law," and "counselor" all mean the same thing.

When Do You Need a Lawyer?

Do you need a lawyer every time one of your legal rights is threatened? No. There are everyday legal situations that people handle quite well without a lawyer. (For those times, a review of the applicable material in this book will help you understand your rights and will give you the edge in dealing with the other person.) But other times you just can't do without one. How do you tell when you need a lawyer?

First, look at what's at stake. If you're talking about a jacket ruined by the dry cleaners or a small dent to your car's fender, then by all means take care of it yourself. It may cost you more than it's worth to talk to a lawyer about the situation. But when you're dealing with something more serious—a real estate dispute, for instance; severe injuries or extensive damage; or time in jail—you would be ill-advised to attempt to handle it yourself. Throughout this book, there are suggestions about when you can attempt things on your own and when you need a lawyer. Here is a good rule of thumb to follow: In civil disputes, you can usually try to get by without a lawyer if the amount involved is less than or near the small claims court limit in your state (see chapter 15). With the help of this book, you may be able to settle the dispute in many situations just by coming to an agreement with the other party; if you can't, this book will assist you if you decide to take your case to small claims court. But if you encounter any unexpected problems, it may be advisable for you to talk to a lawyer. In criminal matters, you need a lawyer if more than a small fine is involved or if a conviction will result in jail time or a permanent bad mark on your record—something that could affect, say, your chances of future employment.

If the problem is borderline—maybe a lawyer is needed but maybe you can handle it on your own—one thing you can do is read the chapters in this book that apply to your situation and then see whether you can work the problem out with the other person (or his or her lawyer) by sitting down and discussing it rationally. If the other person isn't receptive to your settlement efforts, then you have several options—among them, contacting a lawyer, filing in small claims court if appropriate, or simply forgetting the whole thing. You may achieve a speedier resolution by a willingness to compromise, even if you feel you're totally in the right.

. When a dispute arises, you may be contacted by the other person's lawyer or insurance company; they may try to negotiate a quick settlement and have you sign a document releasing the other person from all further liability. The lawyer or insurance adjuster may even tell you that you don't need a lawyer, that a lawyer won't get you any more money and will keep as much as half of the settlement as his or her fee. Keep in mind that these lawyers and insurance adjusters are trained negotiators and are trying to get the best deal for their clients. Their objective is to settle the claim as quickly and as cheaply as possible. They are not looking out for your best interests. Only your attorney will do that. Unless the money or damage involved is relatively minor, it is usually advisable to hire a lawyer as soon as you are contacted by an insurance adjuster or learn that the other person has hired a lawyer.

What Type of Lawyer Is Best for You?

When you need a lawyer, the trick is finding the lawyer who is right for your problem. The right lawyer for your situation may not be the most expensive, the best known, or even the best in the particular field. Why spend $5,000 to get the top lawyer in town when a lawyer just out of law school can do the same thing just as well for $750? Then again, why save a few hundred (or thousand) dollars by getting a less experienced lawyer when you need as good a lawyer as you can get?

You don't need to go to the city's best lawyer in estate planning if all you want is a simple will drawn up. Nor do you need the top divorce lawyer in town if your divorce doesn't involve a lot of money or property, and child custody and visitation rights pose no great problem. But if you're charged with murder, you want the best defense lawyer you can afford. Or if you're paralyzed in an accident, you need a lawyer with experience in that type of injury, not a whiplash expert.

Will a general practitioner do, or do you need a specialist in the field? A "general practitioner" is a lawyer who practices many areas of law, rather than concentrating in one field—the legal profession's "family doctor." (Although many lawyers call themselves general practitioners, there are few true general practitioners these days. You'll find that most general practitioners limit their practices to four or five areas of law, such as wills, probate and estate planning, divorces, personal injury, defense of drunk drivers, and routine business matters.) A specialist is a lawyer who concentrates on one area of the law, such as divorce, workers' compensation, or personal injury. There are even specialists within a specialty: lawyers who handle only murder trials or medical malpractice cases, for example.

What qualifies a lawyer as a specialist? Years of experience in the area of specialty. Unlike medicine, the legal profession does not have an extensive specialty licensing or certification program. Many states do have programs by which a lawyer can become a certified specialist, but these programs cover only a few fields—typically family law, criminal law, workers' compensation, and taxation. And you get no assurance that a certified specialist is any better than or even as good as a specialist who is not certified. The ability, experience, and reputation of the lawyer are what count, not whether he or she is certified as a specialist.

Whether or not you need a specialist depends on the nature and complexity of your legal question. For routine matters, a general practitioner is fine. But for more complex problems, a specialist may be necessary. A good general practitioner will recognize his or her limitations and will either consult with or refer you to a specialist when appropriate.

Is it better to hire a big law firm (with, say, twenty-five to a hundred lawyers) than a small one (with two to ten lawyers, for instance)? Is it better to have a small firm represent you than an attorney who practices alone (a "sole practitioner")? The answers depend on your problem and on how much you can afford. You'll usually get more personal attention from a small law firm or a sole practitioner than you will from a big firm. In a big firm, you're likely to get shuffled from one lawyer to another for different problems, while with a small firm you'll generally be represented by the same lawyer. Depending on their experience and areas of practice, small firms and solo practitioners are often better for routine legal matters, while larger firms can handle more complex matters—at a price, of course. Larger firms tend to charge more than small firms, and specialists usually cost more than general practitioners. If you hire a large law firm or a specialist to do some routine legal work for you—drawing up a simple will, for instance—you may have to pay as much as two or three times over what a sole general practitioner would charge for the same thing.

Should you hire a lawyer with offices downtown, or will a lawyer near your home do? The downtown lawyer will probably charge more, if only because rent downtown is generally more expensive than in outlying areas. On the other hand, a downtown lawyer may be closer to the court. Because lawyers charge for "travel time"—the time it takes to get from the office to the court and back again—it may cost you less in the long run to pay the higher hourly rates of the downtown lawyer if your case will involve many court appearances by the lawyer. But if your legal problem involves little or no time in court, a lawyer closer to home may be able to do the job for less money.

Where to Look

After determining the type of lawyer you need, you have to find one who fits the bill. The usual way to start is to ask relatives and friends if they can suggest a lawyer for your situation. If, for instance, a friend recommends a particular lawyer, ask whether your friend has ever consulted the lawyer, and if so, for what reason. Was he or she pleased with the quality of the work, and was the final charge close to the fee initially quoted by the lawyer? Did the lawyer return your friend's phone calls promptly and keep him or her informed of the status of the case? Did the lawyer take the time to explain things in plain English? What were the lawyer's shortcomings? Would your friend go back to the lawyer?

A referral may not mean much if the person's legal problem was considerably less complex than yours, or if it concerned a totally different problem. If your friend recommends the lawyer who handled his or her divorce, for instance, but your problem involves a dispute with a home-remodeling company, the lawyer might not be qualified to handle your type of case. But if your friend vouches for the lawyer's integrity, consider arranging an interview with that lawyer. If nothing else, the lawyer may be able to refer you to a lawyer competent to handle your problem.

If your problem is not related to your job, ask your employer who his or her attorney is. Large companies may have an in-house lawyer who can refer you to an outside lawyer (you may even be able to wangle some free advice out of the in-house lawyer). Unions can often give members referrals to good lawyers.

Another way to get a referral to a lawyer is by looking in the Yellow Pages, under the heading "Attorney Referral Service." Most referral services use only lawyers who subscribe to it. Often they are younger lawyers who need the business. You may have no better assurance of getting a good lawyer through a referral service than by opening the telephone directory to the "Attorneys" listing, closing your eyes, and putting your finger anywhere on the page. Although it costs you nothing to call the lawyer referral service and get the name of a lawyer, the lawyer may charge you for the initial interview. This fee, if any, should be quoted to you by the referral service.

Lawyers are now permitted to advertise, but outside of the Yellow Pages, relatively few lawyers take advantage of this opportunity. Large cities tend to have a few lawyers who saturate the late-night movies or daytime game shows with commercial after commercial. Should you pick a lawyer based on a television commercial? There's no reason not to—although neither is there any reason why you should. You get no assurance that the lawyer who advertises is better or worse than any other lawyer.

A number of "legal clinics" have sprung up throughout the nation. Some are single clinics; others are part of a statewide or nationwide chain. These clinics generally offer routine legal services, often at lower prices than you might find in a regular law office. But as with lawyers who advertise extensively (which some legal clinics also do), these clinics survive on volume, and many make exhaustive use of paralegals to cut down on the lawyers' time. You may have less direct contact with the lawyer than if you went to a regular firm. As a caution—don't blindly assume that you're going to be charged less at a legal clinic. Get an estimate from both a solo practitioner or a small firm and the legal clinic and compare the two prices—and the services—before making a choice.

What if you can't afford a lawyer but need one now? That depends on the nature of your problem. If you've been injured in an accident, the lawyer usually takes his or her fee out of your settlement or award when you get paid, so your inability to pay now doesn't make a difference. But if your situation involves paying a flat fee or hourly charge (for instance, to defend you for drunk driving or to represent you in a divorce action), you have several options.

If you're charged with a crime and can't afford a lawyer, you are entitled to have one appointed for you at state expense. You usually must accept the lawyer appointed for you; you don't get to pick and choose from the public defender's staff. If your request to have a lawyer appointed for you is turned down because your income and assets are above the limits, you will have to provide your own lawyer. Many lawyers accept credit cards for payment of their services, and others will let you make a down payment and pay the balance in monthly installments. To ensure that you make the payments, the lawyer may ask you to pledge something as collateral, such as your car or house.

If your legal problem is civil in nature, such as a will, a divorce, or a landlord-tenant dispute, you may qualify to be represented by a Legal Aid society, which provides law services to the poor at little or no cost. You can get the number for your local Legal Aid office by calling your county's bar association or by looking in the phone book. Many law schools also provide legal assistance programs to the public at no charge. Contact the law school for more information. If your problem involves a violation of your civil rights, try the American Civil Liberties Union (ACLU) or the National Association for the Advancement of Colored People (NAACP).

Your Initial Consultation with the Lawyer

Before you make the first appointment with the lawyer, find out how much it's going to cost. Many lawyers do not charge for the initial consultation (usually 20 to 30 minutes long); others charge a relatively small fee, such as $20.

Bring all the documentation you have concerning your situation to the interview. If a written contract is involved, take it along. Medical bills, estimates, pictures of the accident scene, and any correspondence between you and the other person (or his or her insurance company or lawyer) should also be given to your lawyer.

At the interview, be open and honest with the lawyer. The advice given and strategy planned by your lawyer are determined by the facts of the situation. Don't lie or embellish. If you don't remember something, tell the lawyer so. If something might hurt your case, don't hide it. Be up front with it. It may not be as damaging as you think. And even if it is, your lawyer can often minimize the damage if he or she knows about it first. Everything you say to the lawyer is protected by the "lawyer-client privilege"—it is all confidential between the two of you. Telling your lawyer that you're going to commit a crime is the one exception. But if you confess to a crime you've already committed, that is protected by the lawyer-client privilege.

Ask the lawyer what experience he or she has in handling your type of problem. What areas of law make up the bulk of the lawyer's practice, and what area is the lawyer most experienced in? Does the lawyer routinely send clients copies of all correspondence and legal documents involving their cases? Will the lawyer give you regular status reports informing you of what is being done with your case? Does the lawyer send regular itemized bills showing all charges, and will you get a full accounting of all money and expenses at the end of your case? Will the lawyer listen to your suggestions on how the case should be handled? As important as anything else—will the lawyer take the time to explain things to you, and in plain English?

At this first consultation, the question of fees (see discussion below) needs to be addressed openly and frankly. Don't authorize a lawyer to begin work unless you know what it's going to cost.

At the end of the interview, the lawyer will make an initial evaluation of your situation and decide whether to represent you. (Sometimes the lawyer will want to do some preliminary investigating or research before determining whether to take your case.) Some of the lawyer's considerations: how much time your case will take, whether it is within the lawyer's fields of competence, the likelihood of success, the size of the fees involved, and whether the lawyer has a conflict of interest (if, for instance, the other person is a friend of the lawyer). The lawyer may refer you to someone else. If the lawyer feels you don't have a case, you should have your case evaluated by another lawyer before deciding not to pursue it—in other words, get a legal "second opinion."

Lawyers' Fees

A lawyer may bill you for legal work in a number of ways: a flat fee for the whole job, an hourly rate, or a percentage of the money the lawyer recovers or saves for you (a "contingency fee"). Sometimes a lawyer will charge a client an hourly rate or a flat fee, plus a percentage of the amount recovered for the client. For example, if you hire a lawyer to collect a $10,000 debt, the lawyer may charge a flat fee of $1,000, plus 15 percent of everything recovered above that.

The amount a lawyer charges you depends on a number of factors, not the least of which are the nature and complexity of your problem and the lawyer's ability. The more serious and difficult your situation, or the higher the stakes, the more the lawyer is going to charge. Likewise, the more qualified and experienced the lawyer, the higher his or her fee is likely to be. If it's an emergency situation requiring fast action, the lawyer will probably charge more than if the matter could be taken care of in the normal course of events. If your situation involves a novel or unsettled area of the law, then the lawyer will have to spend more time researching the issue than if the law were already well established, and will charge you accordingly.

How negotiable are the lawyer's fees? In one sense, not very. If a lawyer typically charges $100 an hour, it's doubtful that he or she will agree to work for you for $80 an hour, unless perhaps the lawyer can make it up in volume. But in another sense, attorneys' fees are very negotiable: you can probably find another lawyer who will charge only $80 an hour. That lawyer may be a little less experienced, but if your problem isn't too complex, he or she should be able to do just as good a job as an older, more experienced lawyer.

Always get the complete terms of your fee agreement in writing, and make sure the written agreement is signed by the lawyer. Unless an emergency precludes it, never give the lawyer authorization to go ahead and start working on your case until you have looked over the fee agreement. Make sure you understand everything; if you don't, ask the lawyer to explain it to you. Because fee disputes are one of the main reasons for a client's disappointment with a lawyer (see discussion below), have the lawyer spell everything out in writing before you hand over a check or the authority to represent you.

One thing to remember about lawyers' fees is that time is a lawyer's stock in trade. Expect to be charged for any of the lawyer's time you take up, whether it's in person, over the telephone, or writing a letter.

Hourly Rate

Hourly rates for lawyers generally range anywhere from a low of about $65 an hour to $300 or more ($100 to $150 are the most frequent), depending on the ability, experience, and reputation of the lawyer, and the task to be done.

Before hiring a lawyer to work for you on an hourly basis, get a written estimate from him or her as to the cost of the work, including the lawyer's hourly rate, how many hours will probably be needed, and how much money will be spent on such things as court costs, filing fees, deposition expenses, travel expenses, and investigation.

Flat Fees

For certain types of routine legal work, the lawyer may charge you a single flat fee. A simple will, for instance, may cost you $75; a divorce with no children involved may cost $400; and defense of a first-time charge of drunk driving may cost $250.

Before agreeing to have legal work done for a flat fee, first find out just how "flat" that fee is. Does it include "costs and

expenses" (see discussion below)? It usually doesn't, so your "flat"
fee may be increased by $100 or more. Before you authorize the
lawyer to start the work for you, have him or her itemize—in
writing—*all* costs, expenses, and other charges in addition to the
lawyer's fee.

Retainer Fees

A retainer fee is money you pay when you hire, or "retain,"
a lawyer. There are several types of retainer fees. One is a yearly
fee paid by a client (usually a large corporation or wealthy individual) to ensure that the lawyer will be there if and when the
client needs legal advice. The average person doesn't keep a
lawyer on retainer from year to year. If you've found a good
family lawyer, you will generally enjoy the same benefits as if the
lawyer were on retainer. Another type of retainer is actually a
flat fee: the lawyer estimates how much time he or she will have
to spend on your problem and calls this a retainer.

The type of retainer you're most likely to encounter is one
that is really a down payment for legal services. If you hire a
lawyer to represent you in a divorce case, for example, the lawyer
might ask for a $250 retainer up front. This retainer is credited
toward the legal services the lawyer performs for you. So if the
entire cost for the divorce is $400, you will owe the lawyer $150.

Contingent Fees

In some types of cases—especially personal injury cases—
the lawyer who represents the injured person takes a percentage
of the money the client receives from either an out-of-court settlement or a verdict. This is a "contingent fee," the contingency
being that the lawyer must win the case for you before he or she
gets anything. The amount the lawyer receives generally ranges
from 25 percent to 40 percent—33.33 percent is used the most—
depending on the nature and difficulty of the case and the expertise of the lawyer. A contingent fee of 50 percent is generally
too high but may be proper when there are several lengthy ap-

peals, or if an extraordinary amount of preparation is needed to bring the case to trial.

Less frequent is the contingent-fee agreement in which the lawyer gets a percentage of the money he or she saves you. For example, suppose you're sued for $50,000. The lawyer agrees to defend you for 25 percent of what he or she saves you. If the jury returns a verdict against you for $25,000, the lawyer has saved you $25,000 and gets a quarter of that ($6,250).

Some contingent-fee contracts provide that the size of the fee the lawyer receives depends on when the case is resolved. For example, the agreement may provide that if the case is settled out of court before the lawyer files a complaint, the lawyer gets 20 percent of the settlement; if the case is settled one year after the complaint is filed, the lawyer gets 25 percent; and after that, the lawyer receives 33.33 percent of the recovery.

Suppose a jury awards you $30,000, but the defendant declares bankruptcy, and you only collect $15,000. The contingent-fee agreement provides for your lawyer to receive one-third of the money. Is the lawyer's share figured on the jury's award or on the money the defendant actually paid? It's figured on the money actually paid; the lawyer would get one-third of the $15,000, rather than one-third of the $30,000.

Contingent-fee agreements are not appropriate in all cases. In fact, overall they are probably more the exception than the rule. For instance, the lawyer who probates a deceased person's will cannot ask for a contingent fee, since there is really no contingency to achieve (and fees in probate cases are usually set by law or by the judge). Criminal cases are handled on an hourly or flat fee basis. Contingent fees are not permitted in most divorce cases. A lawyer can't, for example, promise to charge you only if he or she manages to get you custody of your child.

Statutory Limits on Fees

At one time, lawyers who had been in practice for a while wanted to protect their fees from being undercut by their less-established competitors and pushed for the enactment of minimum fee schedules. They argued that minimum charges were needed to preserve the integrity of the legal profession and that this would encourage lawyers to give competent advice and spend a fair amount of time on each case. The American Bar Association was all in favor of this proposal: "The establishment of suggested or recommended fee schedules by bar associations is a thoroughly laudable activity. The evils of fee cutting ought to be apparent to all members of the Bar." But the only "evil" was that established members of the bar might lose some business to less established members who charged less for the same work. In 1975, the United States Supreme Court held that minimum fee schedules were illegal because they violated the Sherman Antitrust Act.

Today many states have laws that restrict the *maximum* fee a lawyer can charge in certain cases. For example, in personal injury suits against the United States government, a federal statute limits the lawyer for the injured party to no more than 25 percent of the settlement or award. The fee an attorney can charge for probating a will is set by statute in some states. Many states now have limits on the fee the plaintiff's lawyer can receive in medical malpractice cases (see chapter 9).

Some states impose limits on the amount of a lawyer's contingent fee in any type of personal injury case. New Jersey, for example, prohibits an attorney from charging more than the following:

50 percent of the first $1,000 recovered;
40 percent of the next $2,000;
33½ percent of the next $47,000;
20 percent of the next $50,000; and
10 percent of anything over $100,000.

Using the New Jersey contingent-fee schedule, a lawyer who recovers $150,000 for his or her client can charge no more than $32,045 as a legal fee—about 21.5 percent overall.

Costs and Expenses

In addition to the lawyer's fees, there may be a number of related costs and expenses that you will have to pay. For instance, if the lawyer files a lawsuit on your behalf, the court's filing fee must be paid, and it costs to have someone serve the defendant with the summons and complaint (see chapter 17). There are other expenses as well, including the cost to investigate the case, deposition charges, often travel expenses, and perhaps the cost of having an expert or two evaluate the case.

Regardless of the type of fee arrangement you have with your lawyer (hourly, flat, contingent, or a combination), you are usually responsible for the costs and expenses in addition to the lawyer's fee. This should be spelled out in the written fee agreement your lawyer gives you at the outset. Make sure that the agreement calls for the lawyer to submit an itemized list of costs and expenses you are being charged for, and proof of the expenses if you request it.

Let's say you're injured in an accident. You want to sue the person who injured you, but you don't have the money for the court's filing fee or for other expenses. Can your lawyer pay those for you? Yes. A lawyer can usually advance money on behalf of the client to pay the costs necessary to litigate a case.

Now let's say that your lawyer spends $1,250 to prosecute your case, but you lose the case. Do you have to reimburse your lawyer though he or she told you at the outset that there would be no fee if you lost your case? Yes. Although you don't owe the lawyer anything for legal services, you are still responsible for all expenses advanced by the lawyer on your behalf—but only to the extent that those expenses are reasonable. For example, the lawyer can't bill you for the expenses of a three-day trip out of town if the business could have just as easily been transacted over the phone or through the mails. Or if the trip was necessary—to interview a witness, for instance—but should have taken only, say, an afternoon, the lawyer can ask you to reimburse him or her for only one night's lodging, not three.

Let's say that your case is settled for $50,000, and the contingent fee agreement calls for your lawyer to get a third of that. Your lawyer advanced $3,500 in costs and expenses for you. Is your lawyer's fee based on the full $50,000, or on $46,500 (the settlement amount minus the costs and expenses)? That depends on what the contingent fee agreement states. Most of the time, the lawyer's fee is based on the full settlement, and the costs and expenses are deducted from your share. So the settlement would break down like this:

AMOUNT OF SETTLEMENT	$50,000
Lawyer's 33.33 percent	$16,665
Plus Costs and Expenses	$ 3,500
NET TO LAWYER	$20,165
NET TO CLIENT	$29,835

Now let's look at the difference if the costs and expenses are deducted from the award before the lawyer's fee is calculated.

AMOUNT OF SETTLEMENT	$50,000
Less Costs and Expenses	$ 3,500
Net Award	$46,500
Lawyer's 33.33 percent	$15,500
Plus Costs and Expenses	$ 3,500
NET TO LAWYER	$19,000
NET TO CLIENT	$31,000

You receive $29,835 when the costs and expenses are deducted from your share alone, and $31,000 when they are deducted from the entire award. The higher the costs and expenses, the larger this discrepancy.

Before signing a contingent-fee agreement, read it carefully to determine how expenses are deducted. Ask the lawyer to explain it in simple terms if you don't understand it. And if the agreement calls for the costs and expenses to be deducted from your share, try to negotiate for them to be deducted from the gross settlement or award before the lawyer takes his or her fee.

Loans to Clients for Living Expenses

Suppose you've been injured in an automobile accident that was the other driver's fault, and you can't work for a long time. Or suppose an investment company defrauded you out of your retirement savings, the interest from which provided your main source of income. You file a lawsuit, but in the meantime you can't even afford the bare necessities of life. Can your lawyer lend you money for things such as food, clothing, and shelter until the case is resolved? In most states, no; a lawyer can advance money on behalf of the client only for the costs and expenses of litigation, not for living expenses.

A client who can't pay for the basic necessities of life may be under considerable pressure to settle his or her case quickly—often for an amount that is clearly inadequate for the injuries. This was noted by the Supreme Court of Louisiana, which observed: "If an impoverished person is unable to secure subsistence from some source during disability, he may be deprived of the only effective means by which he can wait out the necessary delays that result from litigation to enforce his cause of action. He may, for reasons of economic necessity and physical need, be forced to settle his claim for an inadequate amount." A few states therefore permit attorneys to lend their clients money for minimal living expenses in some cases, so the clients won't be forced into fast but unfair settlements.

Problems with Your Lawyer

A client's unhappiness with his or her lawyer can cover a wide range of grievances—everything from the lawyer's failure to return phone calls as quickly as the client would like to the lawyer's getting a fat settlement check for the client, then forging the client's name to it and leaving the country with the money. When a problem comes up between you and your lawyer, you should usually first discuss it candidly with him or her. (If it's a serious matter, such as your lawyer absconding with your settlement check, call the district attorney's office immediately.) Perhaps it is nothing more than a minor misunderstanding, and an explanation from the lawyer will ease your fears. Or the lawyer may have put your file aside during a busy period, and a word or two from you will prompt him or her to be more diligent with it in the future.

One thing you must realize is that your lawyer is, after all, in business. There are other clients to talk to, other court hearings to attend, other briefs or wills to prepare, and so on. But if you feel your lawyer is remiss in preparing your case or advising you of progress, call or write your lawyer, and say that you are beginning to worry. If this doesn't solve the problem, then more drastic action (see discussion below) is called for.

When the dispute involves the amount of money you owe the lawyer or how your fee agreement should be interpreted, and you can't work things out with your lawyer, send your lawyer a letter stating the nature of the dispute and requesting to have the dispute arbitrated. Many states have a voluntary informal—and often free—arbitration system that gives you a way to resolve fee disputes quickly. The dispute is usually heard by another lawyer in his or her office, and you and your lawyer each explain your positions. The arbitrator's decision generally is not final. If you don't like it, you can have the issue decided in court.

Some problems arise through business dealings between the lawyer and client outside the lawyer-client relationship. For instance, a lawyer and client might invest money together in real estate or another business venture, which then goes sour. Is it proper for a lawyer to have such business dealings with clients? There is nothing unethical in it per se. But a lawyer must deal with the client in the utmost good faith, much more so than when the lawyer is dealing with someone who is not a client. And a lawyer must never use his or her knowledge of the client's situation to take advantage of the client. For instance, suppose Mary is close to filing bankruptcy. Her lawyer tells her that she can avoid bankruptcy by selling her car and using that money to pay off her bills. The lawyer then offers to buy Mary's car (worth $12,000) for $6,000—the amount Mary needs to get out of her financial problem—and Mary, desperate, agrees. This would be unethical for the lawyer, since the price the lawyer is paying for the car is clearly far too low. But the transaction would probably be fine if the lawyer paid the fair market price for the car.

What are your options if the lawyer doesn't adequately reassure you after a frank discussion of the problem—or refuses to discuss the problem at all? You can fire the lawyer and hire a new one; if the lawyer has done something unethical, you can report him or her to the state bar; if you suspect the attorney of fraud, theft, or another crime, you can contact the district attorney; or, when appropriate, you can sue the lawyer for malpractice. Each of these is considered below.

Firing Your Lawyer

Just as you have the right to change doctors at any time (see chapter 9), so, too, can you fire your lawyer with or without a reason. But, as when you leave your doctor, you are still responsible for all outstanding fees owed to the lawyer.

Suppose you have a contingent-fee arrangement with your lawyer by which he or she gets one-third of the recovery. You take your case to a new lawyer before it is over, who also takes the case on a contingent-fee basis, also for one-third. When your case finally ends, and you receive some money, do you have to pay each lawyer a third, so you end up with only a third of the proceeds? Generally not; your first lawyer is entitled only to a reasonable amount of the fee for the work done for you up to the time you discharge him or her. This amount is based on the lawyer's standard hourly fee, the number of hours the lawyer put in on your case, and how much that work helped your case.

Contacting the State Bar Association or District Attorney

If you suspect your lawyer of unethical or illegal conduct, and the lawyer will not give you a straight answer or adequate explanation for his or her actions, you should call the state bar (if the number isn't in your telephone book, call your county bar association for it) to see how and where to file a complaint. For instance, if you think the lawyer is misusing or stealing your funds, and, despite your request, the lawyer does not provide you with an itemized statement and proof (receipts, canceled checks, and the like) showing how the money was spent, contact the state bar. Another time to contact the state bar is when an attorney is incompetent or shows a clear lack of diligence in your case—if, for instance, the lawyer doesn't prepare your case properly, shows up for a court hearing drunk and unable to represent you properly, or doesn't take the time to research the law. You should also contact the district attorney's office if you feel the lawyer may be committing fraud, theft, or any other crime.

Suing Your Lawyer for Malpractice

When you suffer damages because of a lawyer's suspected incompetence or unethical doings, think about contacting another lawyer to see if you have grounds for a legal malpractice suit against your first lawyer. Like doctors (see chapter 9), lawyers must use sufficient care and diligence in representing and advising their clients. If a lawyer is negligent, he or she is liable to the client for the damages the client suffers because of the lawyer's carelessness. An obvious example of legal malpractice would be if an attorney failed to file a complaint on time, so it was barred by the statute of limitations (see chapter 17). (But to win your legal malpractice suit against your first lawyer, you would have to prove that you probably would have won the case if it had been filed on time.) Deliberately misusing a client's funds is also grounds for a malpractice suit against the lawyer—if, for instance, the lawyer settled your case without your permission, forged your name on the settlement check from the defendant, cashed it, and kept it, all the while telling you no progress was being made on your case.

How difficult is it to find a lawyer willing to sue another lawyer for malpractice? Not very. Many lawyers who handle personal injury cases will represent clients in lawsuits against lawyers for malpractice. Some lawyers even specialize in suing other lawyers for professional negligence.

LAWS, THE COURTS, AND YOU

MOST OF THIS BOOK has concentrated on handling specific situations involving you and the law. This chapter takes a different approach and provides an overview of the whole legal system and how it affects you in a broader sense. How do laws regulate our daily lives? What are laws, and where do they come from? How are the court systems organized? What is your role in the judicial system, especially when you are called for jury duty? Reading this chapter certainly isn't critical to understanding your rights as we've discussed them throughout this book. But like the last piece that completes a puzzle, the following material brings everything together to give you the whole picture.

Laws

How Laws Affect Our Daily Lives

What are laws, and why are they so important to us? Laws are the rules of society by which we all must live and abide. Laws both restrict and protect us. They tell us what we can and can't do to others and what others can and can't do to us. Our daily conduct is regulated three ways: by contracts, by criminal law, and by civil law.

When you make a contract (see chapter 13), you voluntarily agree to do something that you are not otherwise obligated to do. For instance, let's say you buy a new car, put 10 percent down, and finance the rest through a bank. The loan agreement between you and the bank is a contract that requires you to do something you otherwise wouldn't have to do—make payments according to the terms of the agreement. The loan agreement will require you to do other things as well, such as keeping the car adequately insured. It will also prohibit you from doing certain things—selling the car without the bank's permission, for instance. All of these restrictions on your conduct are imposed by the contract you made.

Now let's say that you've had too much to drink and get behind the wheel of your car. A police officer sees your car weaving from side to side and pulls you over. You flunk the field sobriety test; the police officer arrests you for drunk driving and takes you back to the station, where you are given a breath test. The results of the test show that your blood alcohol level is over the legal limit. You are prosecuted for drunk driving, convicted, and punished accordingly. Nothing in the contract with the bank specifically forbade you from driving while drunk. But the criminal law makes it illegal for you to do so.

Finally, let's say one of your tires goes flat. Your friend Jim offers to help you change it. You place a jack under the bumper and raise the car, but while Jim is taking the tire off, the car slips off the jack because you didn't follow the instructions, and Jim is injured. Nothing in your contract covers this, and it's not a crime not to follow the instructions. Still, a reasonably careful person would read and follow the instructions—which is exactly what the law of torts (see chapter 8), a branch of civil law, requires you to do. Since you didn't, you must pay Jim for the injuries he has suffered because of your negligence.

Contract law, criminal law, and civil law frequently overlap. For instance, let's say Janice gets a loan to buy a car but doesn't obtain insurance as required by the financing agreement and her state's law. Her failure to do so is both a breach of contract (the financing agreement) and a criminal violation. Or suppose that Dan drives while drunk and causes an accident. He is guilty of the crime of driving under the influence and is also civilly liable to the people in the other car for their injuries.

Sources of American Law

Where does the law come from? Here are the main sources of law in the United States:

- The United States Constitution

- Federal statutes and regulations

- State constitutions

- State statutes and regulations

- County and city ordinances

- The common law

The Constitution. The prime source of law in the United States is the Constitution and its amendments. Most of our fundamental individual rights are found there: the right to free expression or freedom of religion, the right to bear arms, the right to a fair trial, and the guarantee of due process of the law, for instance. No law is valid and enforceable if it is contrary to the provisions of the federal Constitution. Each state also has its own constitution, patterned generally after the federal one. But the federal and state constitutions are only the starting points for our laws. Most of our laws are found elsewhere—in statutes, local ordinances, and the common law, for example.

Statutes. "Statutes" are laws passed by Congress or state legislative bodies. Statutes enacted by Congress are found in the United States Codes; individual states have their own code books (or "books of statutes") for state laws. A statute becomes the law if the legislative body that passed it had the power to do so and followed the correct parliamentary procedures, and if the statute does not violate any constitutional guarantees. How long does a statute remain on the books? Unless the statute by its own terms ends on a given date, it lasts until the legislative body that enacted it revokes it or until a judge rules that it is unconstitutional. A judge cannot change or revoke a statute; only the legislature can do that. A judge can, however, interpret a statute when the parties to a lawsuit dispute its meaning. In interpreting a statute, the judge will look at the legislative history of the law to determine the legislature's intent in passing the law. This review can include reading the legislative debates recorded in the *Congressional Record* (or the state equivalent).

Regulations. A government, whether the United States government or your state government, creates various administrative agencies to implement the laws its legislature passes. Each agency is usually given the power to make regulations to achieve its goals. These regulations, if it is within the agency's power to make them, have the effect of law. For example, an air quality management district may pass regulations concerning permissible emission standards for factories. A factory that doesn't comply with those regulations can be fined or even shut down.

Local Ordinances. Laws passed by counties and cities are "ordinances." They are similar to statutes passed by Congress or state legislatures, but their effect extends only to the county's or city's border, as the case may be. Zoning laws are the most familiar example of local ordinances.

The Common Law. The final type of law is that made by judges—"common law." The common law system originated in

England around the beginning of the twelfth century. The judge decided a dispute based on the acceptable social customs of the time. If there wasn't a custom, the judge used wisdom and common sense to make a ruling that was fair and just. Once made, the ruling became the law for all similar disputes—a "precedent" (see discussion below). All states except Louisiana adopted the English common law and have expanded on it to one extent or another. (Louisiana, for historical reasons, has an exhaustive "civil code" system—only the legislature, through the code, can give or take away rights, not the judge. The judge is limited to interpreting the code. If the code doesn't cover a dispute, the party who claims to have been wronged can't recover damages.) In these states, if no law addresses a situation, the judge can make law as appropriate to permit the wronged person to recover damages. This is called "case law," because it is the law of the case— that is, the particular lawsuit. Case law is the American equivalent of English common law.

The Role of Precedents in the Law

You've probably heard of the law's reverence for "precedents," the principle of following the law as declared in a previous case. Under the doctrine of stare decisis (literally, "to follow decisions"), if a dispute involves a legal question that has earlier been decided in court in another case, the judge simply follows the rule previously laid down. Why this emphasis on precedents? Because it gives stability and continuity to the law. If the law were changing every day on the same point, we would never know what to do. One day, something might be prohibited; the next day, it might be allowed; then the following day, it could be prohibited again. Because the law adheres to precedents, we have an idea of what is expected of us from day to day.

But if judges unwaveringly followed earlier decisions, they would simply be enshrining the laws of earlier times. The eminent United States Supreme Court jurist Oliver Wendell Holmes, Jr., once remarked of precedents: "It is revolting to have no better reason for a rule of law than it is as laid down in the time of Henry IV. It is still more revolting if the grounds upon which it was laid down have vanished long since, and the rule simply persists from blind imitation of the past." Because laws must change with the times, precedents are not ironclad, and judges need not always follow outdated laws. But even when a law is clearly out of date and sorely in need of change, there are still some limitations on a judge's ability to change it. As noted earlier, a judge can't revoke or limit a law passed by the legislature (a statute) unless it is unconstitutional. Judge-made law (common law or case law) can be changed more easily, but there are still restrictions. A judge of a lower court (see discussion below) is bound to follow an earlier ruling of a higher court, even if that ruling was made over 100 years ago and is clearly out of step with modern times. For instance, a superior or district court judge cannot overturn a previous decision of an appellate court, nor can an appellate court change a law made by a supreme court.

Since it is the highest court in the land, only the United States Supreme Court can change a law that it makes. How often does the Supreme Court reverse itself? Not very often. And when it does, the reversal usually involves a practice that the Supreme Court upheld during the first century of this country's existence but that should now be banned because of the changes in society. Consider this example: At one time, the Supreme Court ruled that it was constitutional for a school district to provide separate schools for blacks and other minorities, so long as the schools afforded an "equal" education. But in the 1954 case of *Brown v. Board of Education*, the Supreme Court held that racial segregation in public elementary schools was unconstitutional, because it violated the Fourteenth Amendment guarantee of equal protection under the law. Declaring that "separate educational facilities are inherently unequal," the Supreme Court reversed a string of previous decisions permitting separate treatment of minorities.

Are There Too Many Laws?

To get an idea of how many laws there are, just visit any law library. There you will find several floors filled with rows upon rows of bookcases bursting at the seams with books on the law. Some people claim that we have far more laws than we need and are being "lawed" or regulated to death. Things would be much simpler, they say, if only we had the same number of laws that we had, say, a hundred years ago.

How valid are these complaints? It is true that we have many more laws than ever before. And every day new laws are being added. But the number of laws simply reflects how complex society has become. The more advanced the society, the more rules there will be to regulate conduct. That is the nature of the beast. Technological breakthroughs have led to many laws and regulations that have contributed to a safer society, particularly in the area of consumer protection. Other laws are necessary to protect interests that didn't exist 50 years ago. For instance, before computers were invented, we didn't need laws regarding computer piracy. Likewise, until the videocassette recorder came along, there weren't many questions about taping television programs or copying movies for private or public use. So as long as society continues to grow in new directions, the law will grow with it to cover our rights and obligations in new situations.

Where to Find the Law

When you have a problem and want to find out what the law is on the issue, where can you look? Your nearby public library contains some law books: city and county ordinances, for instance, and probably a set of the state's codes as well. A public county law library is located in or near the main courthouse in the county. Law libraries are also found in law schools. Both a general public library and a law library usually have some self-help books written for the layperson.

How practical is it for you, a nonlawyer, to research the law effectively? Realistically speaking, outside of finding your local ordinances and the like, not very practical at all. Finding the law that applies to your case can be an arduous task. Law students receive in-depth instruction on how to use a law library, and it still takes them several months before they are able to use the law library efficiently and effectively. You certainly can't expect to find your way around a law library in only an hour or two. There's much more to it than just knowing which section contains which books. And even if you manage to figure out where the different types of legal books are and can find the law applicable to your situation, you'll ordinarily have a tough time making heads or tails out of the information. Legal decisions and law books are written in legalese, an obscure language all its own, with myriad citations and references that seem designed to confound a layperson. It's like reading the schematic drawings and technical information for a sophisticated computer: once you have the drawings and specifications, you're not going to make much sense of them if you don't have an engineering background.

How the Courts Are Structured

There are two separate judicial systems in America—the federal system (which includes a separate system of military justice) and the state systems. Some legal matters are handled only in federal courts, because the Constitution gives Congress the exclusive power to regulate certain areas. Bankruptcy and copyright and patent infringements are examples of cases that can be brought solely in the federal court system. Other matters are handled only in state courts: divorces and probates, for instance, and most personal injury cases. Occasionally the two systems overlap, giving you the choice of which court system to sue in.

The Federal Court System

The federal court system consists of three levels (see Figure 20.1). The lowest level is composed of the United States District

Courts, Bankruptcy Courts, Tax Court, the Court of Claims, and the Court of International Trade (formerly Customs Court). It is in these courts that cases are actually tried. Which court a particular case is filed in depends on the nature of the dispute. Most cases in federal court are filed in a United States District Court. The other courts handle specific types of cases. If you want to file for bankruptcy, you must file in Bankruptcy Court. Disputes involving federal taxes are handled in the Tax Court. Certain types of cases against the United States come under the jurisdiction of the Court of Claims, while disputes involving customs tariffs are decided by the Court of International Trade.

If you are not satisfied with the results of the trial, you have the right to appeal your case to a higher court. In the federal court system, the second level of courts consists of the intermediate appellate courts: the United States Circuit Courts of Appeal and the Court of Customs and Patent Appeals. A panel of judges (usually at least three) will review the transcript of your trial, the evidence presented there, and the legal briefs filed by your attorney and your opponent's attorney. Unlike a trial, an appeal does not involve the presentation of witnesses or evidence in court; if something is not in the trial record, the appellate judges will not consider it. The parties' lawyers usually have the option of making an oral presentation to the panel of appellate judges, which is usually limited to 30 minutes for each side.

Suppose you lose your case in the District Court, and the Circuit Court of Appeal upholds ("affirms") the lower court's decision. What is your next step? You can ask the United States Supreme Court to hear your appeal. Most of the time, however, unlike the intermediate appellate courts, which *must* consider your appeal, the Supreme Court does not have to hear your appeal. It has the power, or discretion, to decide which cases it hears. Your attorney must ask the Supreme Court for permission to appeal the case to it by filing a petition for certiorari. The United States Supreme Court receives tens of thousands of these petitions each year and approves only a very small percentage. The Supreme Court ordinarily accepts only cases that will affect

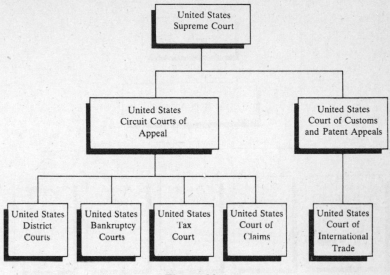

Figure 20.1

Federal Court System

many more people than just the parties to the dispute. (In an attempt to reduce the Supreme Court's workload, a Temporary Emergency Court of Appeals was recently created to act as a buffer between the federal Circuit Courts of Appeals and the Supreme Court.)

The United States Supreme Court has the final say on most legal matters. If the Supreme Court rules that a particular law passed by Congress violates the Constitution, for instance, Congress cannot pass another bill stating that the Supreme Court's decision is wrong, and the law is constitutional. Once the Supreme Court declares a law unconstitutional, there are only two ways to change that decision: by amending the Constitution (a long and difficult process, which has been successful only twenty-six times since the Constitution was written in 1787), or by a later decision of the Supreme Court declaring the law constitutional (in other words, by the Supreme Court reversing its earlier de-

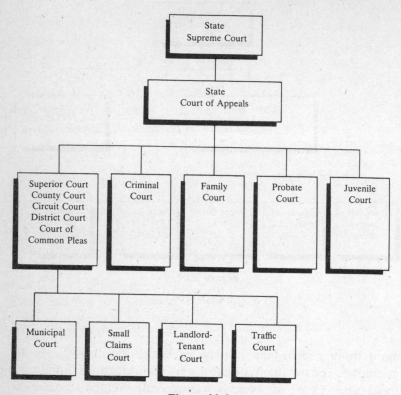

Figure 20.2

State Court System

cision). Sometimes the Congress can rewrite the bill and remove the unconstitutional portions.

Congress has the power to determine the number of judges on the Supreme Court, but since 1869 the number has remained steady at nine. To become a Supreme Court justice, the person must be appointed by the president, with the advice and consent of the Senate. The Constitution provides that all federal judges "shall hold their Offices during good Behaviour." Once confirmed, a justice can only be removed by impeachment for and conviction of treason, bribery, or other serious crimes.

The Military Justice System

The federal judicial system also includes a special system to deal with military offenses committed by servicemen and servicewomen. These offenses are spelled out in the Uniform Code of Military Justice. Many of the offenses involve acts that are detrimental to the military, such as falling asleep or being drunk during guard duty, refusing to obey orders, assaulting a superior officer, desertion, and "acts against good order and discipline." Offenses that are crimes under state law (robbery, murder, rape, and assault and battery, for example) usually can be tried in civilian courts as well.

When a person in the military is charged with an offense under the Uniform Code of Military Justice, a court-martial is ordered by the commanding officer. (Unlike a civilian court, a court-martial is temporary and lasts only as long as it takes to dispose of the case; the court-martial is then dissolved.) The accused is offered a military lawyer to defend him or her, but can choose instead to hire a civilian lawyer at his or her own expense. The jury in a court-martial is composed of military officers; if the accused is an enlisted man or woman, he or she has the right to ask for enlisted persons on the jury.

A person who feels that he or she has been wrongly convicted can appeal the decision of the court-martial. The first appeal is to the accused person's commanding officer. The next appeal is to the Military Court of Review (if the offense is serious) or to the Judge Advocate General. After that, the accused can appeal the case to the United States Court of Military Appeals. The final appeal is directed to the president of the United States, not the Supreme Court.

State Court Systems

Most states have a tripartite court system similar to the federal system: the lowest level of courts, where cases are tried; a second level consisting of the intermediate appellate courts; and the third level made up of a supreme court (see Figure 20.2).

Alaska, Nebraska, and Rhode Island, though, have only two levels of courts—the trial courts and a supreme court. There is also some disparity among the states regarding the names of the courts. For example, in New York, the "Supreme Court" is the equivalent of a superior court or district court in other states. The intermediate appellate court in New York is the "Supreme Court, Appellate Division," and its highest court is the "Court of Appeals."

In many states, the lowest level of courts—the trial courts—actually comprises two levels of courts. One level (called superior court, county court, circuit court, district court, or court of common pleas) handles more serious matters, such as felonies and civil cases involving more than, say, $15,000. Frequently, there are courts designed for specific controversies, such as criminal court, family court (to handle divorces, adoptions, and paternity disputes, for example), probate court (or surrogate court), and juvenile court. The other level (municipal court) handles smaller problems, such as misdemeanors, and civil cases under $15,000. Some courts on this level may handle specific problems, such as small claims court, landlord-tenant court, and traffic court.

As in the federal system, in a state court system you can appeal your case to a higher court if you disagree with the trial results. And like the U.S. Supreme Court, a state supreme court is generally free to hear only those appeals it wants to hear. The number of justices on the state supreme court varies from state to state, from a low of five to a high of nine. The length of service for supreme court justices also varies, from six years to life, depending on the state. In some states, the government appoints judges to the supreme court, subject to confirmation by the legislature or a commission on judicial appointments. In other states, the voters elect the justices.

When It's Your Turn to Be a Juror

Trial by jury is the cornerstone of American justice. Evidence is presented to an impartial jury, who look objectively at all the facts and make a decision. When the jury system began in England, only persons familiar with the dispute—in other words, witnesses—could be jurors for the case. The jurors would listen to the parties, then make a decision based on their own knowledge. This practice was abolished in the fifteenth century amid growing complaints that juries were biased (many jurors were family, friends, and neighbors of the parties), bribed, or intimidated. The rule was changed so that only persons who had no knowledge of the dispute and could therefore reach an impartial decision were qualified as jurors.

If you're over 18, sooner or later you're likely to be summoned for jury duty. When you receive the notice summoning you for jury duty, the first question you'll probably have is, "How can I get out of it?" Be advised that it's not nearly as easy to get excused from jury duty as it once was. So many people were being exempted that there weren't enough people left to fill the jury pool adequately. Because of that, most courts have cracked down on letting people out of jury duty. Generally, you are excused only if you are physically disabled (if you're blind, for example, or deaf), if you are seriously ill (although if it's only a short-term illness, such as the flu, your obligation will just be postponed for a month or two), or if your business would shut down without you there. To get excused, you'll have to call the clerk—the number should be on the summons—or go to the clerk's office at the courthouse before the date when you're supposed to show up for jury duty. What happens if you simply ignore the summons? If you don't call the clerk or appear on the appointed date and don't have a good reason (if, for instance, you were in the hospital or out of state the entire time), you could be found in contempt of court and fined or even jailed.

The first morning of jury duty, report to the room listed on the summons. You will receive an orientation—it may be a booklet or a speech by a judge—and you will then be directed to the jurors' lounge to wait. At some point, a panel of you and some other members of the jury pool—perhaps 20 or more—will be sent to a courtroom. You and 11 other members of the panel will be directed to the "jury box," the area of the courtroom where the jurors sit during the trial. The lawyers for both sides will question you to determine if they want you to decide the case. It is important that you answer the lawyers' questions honestly and frankly. If you are excused, you will be sent back to the jurors' lounge to wait for your next call. Unless you're chosen to sit on a jury, your obligation for jury duty is usually over in one or two weeks. In many areas, after the first day of jury duty, if you haven't been picked for a jury, many courts let you call in the night before to see if you'll have to show up the next day. If you are required to go to the courthouse every day, take along a good book or the daily paper to read, since you'll probably be doing a lot of sitting around and waiting.

If you are selected for the jury, you stay in the jury box while the other jurors are picked. Once all twelve jurors are chosen, the trial begins (see chapter 17). Pay attention during the trial. Keep in mind the fact that the fates of at least two people are in your hands. Listen carefully to what each witness says. Also look closely at how the witness acts on the stand; a witness's body language often reveals more than his or her words.

A jury trial is an adversarial contest—one person against another, much like a boxing match. The courtroom is the ring, the judge the referee. The parties' lawyers do the actual fighting, bobbing and weaving their way through the trial with strategy, objections to evidence, and the like, delivering punches with witnesses' testimony and incriminating evidence. Sometimes one lawyer delivers a knockout blow, and the judge throws the case out of court. Most of the time, though, the case goes to the jury, who, like the ringside judges in a boxing match, vote for the winner. Unlike the boxing judges, however, who make their decisions independently of one another, the jurors discuss the case among themselves before reaching a verdict.

How long does the average trial last? Most trials take less than a week. Some are over in half a day, and many take only two or three days. When a trial is expected to last longer than a week or two, the judge will usually ask prospective jurors whether they have any commitments or problems that prevent them from serving on the jury for an extended period of time.

Do you get paid for the time you spend on jury duty? Yes, but not very much—usually only $5 to $20 a day. And if you miss work because of jury duty, your employer doesn't have to make up the difference unless your employment contract or a collective bargaining agreement requires it.

Let's say that while you're sitting as a juror in a case, a question comes to your mind that neither lawyer has thought to ask the witness. Can you raise your hand and ask the question yourself? No. Generally, you must leave the questioning to the lawyers and the judge. (Quite often you'll find your question is answered, if not by this witness, then by a later one.) When jurors are permitted to ask questions, the normal procedure is for the juror to put the question in writing and give it to the bailiff to hand to the judge, who will then ask it if he or she thinks it is relevant.

Suppose that you're sitting as a juror on a case, and in the hall during a lunch break, you run into an attorney for one of the parties. The attorney recognizes you and asks how you think the trial is going. What should you do? Politely tell the attorney that you can't talk about the case, leave, and immediately report the encounter to the judge or bailiff. During a trial, it is important that jurors do not discuss the case with anyone, especially the parties to the case, their lawyers, and witnesses. If you feel that anyone involved with the case is trying to influence your decision, you should report it to the judge right away.

The vote you cast in the jury room should be your own, not one your fellow jurors want you to cast. Don't feel pressured to change your vote because you are the lone holdout. You should evaluate the positions of the other jurors and listen to their reasoning—just as they should give you the courtesy of listening to you and thoughtfully considering your points. Be as conscientious as possible in making sure that your vote is the correct one before casting it; you wouldn't expect any less from someone who was entrusted with the duty of deciding your fate.

Index